The Contested Commons

The Contested Commons

Conversations between Economists and Anthropologists

Edited by

Pranab Bardhan and Isha Ray

Blackwell
Publishing

BLACKWELL PUBLISHING
350 Main Street, Malden, MA 02148-5020, USA
9600 Garsington Road, Oxford OX4 2DQ, UK
550 Swanston Street, Carlton, Victoria 3053, Australia

First published 2008 by Blackwell Publishing Ltd

1   2008

Library of Congress Cataloging-in-Publication Data

The contested commons : conversations between economists and anthropologists / edited by Pranab Bardhan and Isha Ray.
     p. cm.
  Includes bibliographical references and index.
   ISBN 978-1-4051-5716-2 (hardcover : alk. paper)   1. Commons.   2. Natural resources, Communal.   3. Communication in international relations.   4. Economic anthropology.   5. Developing countries $x Economic conditions.   I. Bardhan, Pranab K.   II. Ray, Isha.

  HD1286.C66 2007
  333.2—dc22

                  2007033295

A catalogue record for this title is available from the British Library.

Set in 10/12pt Times
by Graphicraft Limited, Hong Kong
Printed and bound in Singapore
by C.O.S. Printers Pte Ltd

The publisher's policy is to use permanent paper from mills that operate a sustainable forestry policy, and which has been manufactured from pulp processed using acid-free and elementary chlorine-free practices. Furthermore, the publisher ensures that the text paper and cover board used have met acceptable environmental accreditation standards.

For further information on
Blackwell Publishing, visit our website:
www.blackwellpublishing.com

Contents

Commentaries

Contributors

Arun Agrawal, University of Michigan, Ann Arbor

Arjun Appadurai, The New School, New York

Pranab Bardhan, University of California, Berkeley

Kaushik Basu, Cornell University, New York

Amita Baviskar, Institute of Economic Growth, New Delhi

Kanchan Chopra, Institute of Economic Growth, New Delhi

Cecile Jackson, Institute of Development Studies, Brighton

Ravi Kanbur, Cornell University, New York

Sharachchandra Lélé, Center for International Studies in Environment and Development, Bangalore

David Mosse, University of London

Pranab Mukhopadhyay, University of Goa, Panaji

Jean-Philippe Platteau, University of Namur

Vijayendra Rao, The World Bank, Washington, DC

Vyjayanthi Rao, The New School, New York

Isha Ray, University of California, Berkeley

Annelise Riles, Cornell University, New York

Nirmal Sengupta, Indira Gandhi Institute of Development Studies, Mumbai, and Madras Institute of Development Studies, Chennai

Rajiv Sethi, Columbia University, New York

E. Somanathan, Indian Statistical Institute, New Delhi

A. Vaidyanathan, Madras Institute of Development Studies, Chennai

Erik Olin Wright, University of Wisconsin, Madison

Preface

This volume was inspired by a workshop entitled "Conversations between Economists and Anthropologists II," held in Goa, India, in August 2003. The title was borrowed from an older workshop, which was followed by a book of the same name, edited by Pranab Bardhan and published in 1989 by Oxford University Press. Several of the participants at "Conversations II" were subsequently invited to write chapters for this volume, and others who in retrospect should have been at that workshop – but alas were not – graciously agreed to write original chapters or commentaries for it. We present *The Contested Commons* as a continuation of the methodological conversations started in the 1980s, and since then enriched by cross-disciplinary conferences, working papers, and edited books. Several of the more recent efforts have been discussed in the introductory chapter, where we also lay out a guide to the chapters contained in this volume.

We gratefully acknowledge the Ford Foundation, New Delhi office, for its financial support in hosting the 2003 workshop that ultimately made this volume possible. We are of course grateful to the Goa participants for the compelling and always generous conversations that animated our workshop and that convinced us that a book was in the making. We especially thank David Szanton, our co-convener for "Conversations II," for his sustained efforts at seeing the workshop to fruition as well as his insightful comments on our Introduction to this book.

Some of the chapters of *The Contested Commons* have appeared earlier, in their current or modified forms, as journal articles. We thank the University of Chicago Press, Wiley-Blackwell and Annual Reviews for permission to reprint these works. Laura Stearns of Wiley-Blackwell was very helpful in seeing the book through from its original chapter drafts to the finished version. We thank Anita Milman for her excellent work in preparing the index to this volume. Finally, we would like to acknowledge the numerous colleagues, students, and friends with whom the ideas presented in this volume were discussed and commented on over the past four years. The intellectual commons of which the editors and contributing authors are a part is a flourishing and vigorously contested one, for which we are collectively most grateful.

Pranab Bardhan
Isha Ray
Berkeley, May 2007

Acknowledgments

Pranab Bardhan and Isha Ray (chapter 1)

We would like to thank Vijayendra Rao, David Szanton, and Jeffrey Williams for helpful discussion and comments.

Arun Agrawal (chapter 3)

This chapter is a revised version of a paper commissioned by the National Academy of Sciences for their volume *The Drama of the Commons*. A shorter version of the paper appeared in *World Development* under the title "Common property institutions and sustainable governance of resources" and in the *Annual Review of Anthropology* as "Sustainable governance of common-pool resources: context, methods, and politics." I would like to thank Ashwini Chhatre, John Galaty, Geoffrey Garrett, Clark Gibson, Donald Moore, Elinor Ostrom, Amy Poteete, Paul Stern, and Oran Young, among others, for their engagement with the paper and careful comments. I also want to acknowledge acute questions and suggestions from members of the audience when I presented earlier drafts of the paper at Indiana University, McGill University, and the International Association for the Study of Common Property.

Isha Ray (chapter 4)

I thank David Szanton, Jeffrey Williams, Kristi Hansen, Seemin Qayum, and Amita Baviskar for helpful discussions and comments on this chapter.

David Mosse (chapter 5)

This chapter is based on research undertaken with the support of the UK Economic and Social Research Council and the Ford Foundation, New Delhi. I am grateful to M. Sivan for research assistance. The chapter was written while I held a visiting research fellowship at the World Bank in Washington, DC. Thanks to John Harriss, Biju Rao, Isha Ray, Esha Shah, and Michael Woolcock for engagement and support. I am grateful to participants at seminars in Washington, DC, and Norwich, UK, and to John Strauss and anonymous referees for comments on an earlier draft.

Rajiv Sethi and E. Somanathan (chapter 7)

We are grateful to the editors, two anonymous referees at *Economic Development and Cultural Change*, Kaushik Basu, Kanchan Chopra, and participants of the workshop Conversations between Economists and Anthropologists II, Goa, 2003, for helpful comments on earlier versions of this chapter circulated under a different title.

Pranab Mukhopadhyay (chapter 8)

Earlier versions of this chapter were presented at the workshop Conversations between Economists and Anthropologists II, Goa, 2003, and at the conference on Environmental History of Asia, New Delhi, 2002. Research support for this chapter is acknowledged to the South Asian Network for Development and Environmental Economics, Kathmandu. The author would like to acknowledge the comments of Kaushik Basu, Kanchan Chopra, Rohan D'Souza, Celine Dutilly-Diane, Jose Furtado, S. Iyengar, A. de Janvry, Sunita Narain, D. Rangnekar, Isha Ray, A. Sequiera, E. Somanathan, Teotonio de Souza, and A. Vaidyanathan. I am grateful to the Centre for the Study of Globalisation and Regionalisation, Warwick University, for a visiting fellowship which allowed me to complete this chapter.

Vijayendra Rao (chapter 10)

Please address correspondence to vrao@worldbank.org. I am indebted to Rukun Advani, Arjun Appadurai, Pranab Bardhan, Kaushik Basu, Scott Guggenheim, David Mosse, Menno Pradan, Isha Ray, Sita Reddy, Mike Walton, participants in the Goa conference (2003) on Conversations between Economists and Anthropologists, and my DECRG colleagues for extremely helpful suggestions. The opinions expressed in this chapter are solely those of the author and in no way represent the views of the World Bank, its executive directors, or member countries.

Sarachchandra Lélé (chapter 11)

This is a substantially revised version of a paper presented at the workshop Conversations between Economists and Anthropologists II, Goa, 2003. The chapter has benefited significantly from discussions in the workshop, for which I am grateful to the organizers and participants. Special thanks to Richard Norgaard, Esha Shah, and an anonymous referee for their insightful comments, and to Esha for supplying me with a set of readings on interdisciplinarity that I found invaluable.

Cecile Jackson (chapter 12)

The author would like to thank two anonymous referees for comments on an earlier draft: *Development and Change*, 37 (3): 525–47 (2006).

1: Economists, Anthropologists, and the Contested Commons

Pranab Bardhan and Isha Ray

Interdisciplinary work in the social sciences is always challenging, because while the research themes are often similar, the intellectual histories, the questions that are considered salient, the field research methods, and the ways in which theories are applied to empirical observations vary widely from discipline to discipline. As a result economists, political scientists, sociologists, anthropologists, and geographers often fail to make their analyses and even their assumptions comprehensible to the others. In this volume we present a selection of chapters on common-pool resources primarily from two disciplines – economics and anthropology[1] – to illustrate these differences and to explore the possibilities of bridging some of them. Economics and anthropology are often seen as extremes along the social science continuum, therefore interdisciplinary work accommodating the two has been especially challenging.

Our goal in this introductory chapter is not to resolve the methodological, epistemological and normative divides between economics and anthropology. Rather, we believe that understanding what is important to the other discipline, and seeing the differences in the light of that understanding, is critical for interdisciplinary scholarship. We argue that for economists and anthropologists alike, a critical re-examination of the foundational assumptions of each discipline, and an explicit appreciation of the theoretical and methodological implications of those assumptions, are important steps towards respectful conversation. We hope that this introduction will help to reduce the oft-heard complaints from anthropologists that economists are "often in error but seldom in doubt";[2] and from economists that anthropologists spend forever in the field but never bring back any properly tested hypotheses.

---

[1] When we say "anthropology," we mean social and cultural anthropology.

[2] This quote has been attributed to the physicist Lev Landau; he was apparently denigrating cosmologists.

Recent Cross-disciplinary Conversations

In 1985 the Social Science Research Council, with the support of the Ford Foundation, facilitated an innovative workshop in Bangalore, India, that brought together economists and anthropologists to discuss and compare their analytical methods. The workshop – "Conversations between Economists and Anthropologists" – focused on diverse approaches to the measurement of economic change in rural India. Key themes included data collection through large n surveys versus intensive village-level studies, and the inability of macro-surveys (favored in economics) in capturing "dynamics, processes and relations" (the domain of anthropology). That first econ-anthro dialogue exposed both "unsuspected areas of potential agreement" and "legitimate rock-bottom differences"[3] and, twenty years down the road, remains an insightful guide to interdisciplinary field research methods.

The period since the millennium has seen a revival of workshops, seminars, papers, and books focused on crossing the boundaries between economics, anthropology and sociology. In March 2001, the *Qualitative versus Quantitative* (or "*Q2*") theme was discussed in a workshop convened at Cornell University by Ravi Kanbur.[4] Particular attention was paid to how (and if) borrowing from "quant" methods could make "qual" methods more generalizable and comparable, and to how "qual" could explicate relationships between variables and so introduce context into "quant" research. In 2002, the journal *World Development* published a series of papers on development economics and the "other" social sciences,[5] in which John Harriss, Cecile Jackson, and Howard White critiqued the too-powerful role of economics in development circles, and made the case that sociology, anthropology and politics should be equal players in development policy. The dominant impressions from many of the *Q2* and the *World Development* papers are that (1) cross-disciplinary work on social problems is critical and (2) the onus is mostly on the economists to change.

The two latest additions to cross-boundary conversations between economists and anthropologists are *Culture and Public Action*, in which economists and anthropologists discuss the role of culture in furthering, and even defining, the goals of development (Rao and Walton 2004); and *Foundations of Human Sociality*, in which economists and anthropologists present new findings about human social behavior from a series of experimental games in so-called traditional cultures around the world (Henrich et al. 2004). In the opening essay of *Culture and Public Action*, the editors recognize the contributions of cultural anthropologists such as Mary Douglas and Arjun Appadurai who have already been in conversation with economists, and of economists such as Amartya Sen whose work has engaged that of philosophers as well as anthropologists. The contributors to *Foundations of Human Sociality* use ethnographic methods to test the standard predictions of

---

[3]   The quotations in this paragraph are from the Introduction in Pranab Bardhan (ed.), *Conversations between Economists and Anthropologists: Methodological Issues in Measuring Economic Change in Rural India*; p. 6 (Oxford University Press, 1989). This book contains many of the papers presented at the Bangalore workshop.
[4]   The papers from the conference and more recent work on similar themes can be read at www.q-squared.ca.
[5]   *World Development*, 30 (3): 2002. The introductory essay is by Ravi Kanbur: "Economics, social science and development."

bargaining and allocation games in traditional cultural settings. The results showed huge variances among these societies, mostly not in line with the predictions of standard economic theory.

It would be premature to suggest that key conclusions have emerged from these conversations on how economists and anthropologists can most fruitfully collaborate with each other. On the one hand, economics has steadily modified its standard behavioral premises about, for instance, common-pool resources and natural resource management based on the results of anthropological case studies. Anthropology, too, can claim a distinguished tradition of engagement with the economic concepts of bargaining, markets and self-interest (Polanyi 1954; Geertz 1978). On the other hand, economists and anthropologists are still divided on their views of human agency, on what constitutes data,[6] on how to interpret their respondent's words, and on what counts as an adequate explanation. It could be argued that differences along these dimensions divide but also in some way define the disciplines. As Appadurai wrote in the first *Conversations*: "At bottom, in my opinion, are not issues about sampling size, respondent error . . . though these are important issues . . . The deeper issue is *epistemological*" (Appadurai 1989: 276, italics in the original).

The selection of chapters in this volume represents another such contribution to this ongoing conversation.[7] This particular endeavor is focused on methodological and epistemological approaches to the analysis of local common-pool resources – a topic that touches upon economic security, ecological sustainability, identity formation, and participatory decision-making, particularly in the developing world.

Why the Local Commons?

There are four reasons for choosing the local commons as an anchor for this conversation. First, the pressures of population growth, migration, uneven market integration, social inequality, and competing claims on the same resource have gradually degraded much of the natural resource base upon which millions of poor people depend (such as forests, fisheries, grazing lands, and irrigation water). Therefore the sustainable and equitable management of such resources remains a central problem for the field of development and environment.

Second, both economists and anthropologists have long records of research on what has been called "*the question of the commons*" (McCay and Acheson 1987). For many years after the publication of Garret Hardin's *The Tragedy of the Commons* (1968) and

---

[6]   Lélé (ch. 11) and Rao and Appadurai (ch. 9) in this volume do point out that economists and anthropologists both have more expansive views on the nature of "data" than they did in the 1980s.

[7]   Several of the chapters in this collection (Agrawal, Rao/Appadurai, Baviskar, Lélé, Mukhopadhay, V. Rao. Ray, Sengupta, Sethi/Somanathan, and Vaidyanathan) are substantially re-worked versions of papers presented at a workshop – "Conversations between Economists and Anthropologists II" – held in Goa, India, in August 2003. Whenever the chapters mention "Conversations II," this is the workshop being referred to. We take this opportunity to thank the Ford Foundation for its generous support of the workshop. We also thank all the participants, many of whose comments and questions have found their ways into this introduction. In addition to those named above, the participants included Pranab Bardhan, Kaushik Basu, Kanchan Chopra, John Harriss, N. S. Jodha, Ajith Menon, Esha Shah, Alito Siqueira, and David Szanton (co-organizer of "Conversations II").

Mancur Olson's *The Logic of Collective Action* (1965), the working assumption among economists and political scientists was that self-interested individuals, without external coercion, would not act collectively to provide common goods or to protect common resources. Yet throughout this period and subsequent decades, socio-anthropological evidence came in, suggesting that poor countries were strewn with examples of what certainly looked like collective protection and collective use of local common resources.[8] It was shown, theoretically and empirically, that norms of cooperation and trust could emerge and be sustained in local communities with a history of repeated and interlocking interactions (Wade 1988; Ostrom 1990; Seabright 1993). A rich literature on social movements developed, arguing that, in their struggles to protect their common resources, groups developed a sense of identity and collectivity (Guha 1989; Escobar and Alvarez 1992). In response to these observations, and also to experiments in social psychology and economics, new theories of cooperation and non-cooperation emerged. Mainstream economic theory today has changed considerably in response to anthropological work on the commons (though there has perhaps been less trade in the other direction).

Third, there has been a resurgence of interest in local collective action and participatory development – and the common-pool resource literature is the source of much of the theorizing on, and the optimism in, such collective action and participation. The enthusiasm over "participation" unites segments of the political right, who believe that market failures can be overcome by rational individuals acting together under enabling incentive structures; and of the political left, who have grown disenchanted with the centralized state as the primary provider of development needs. New work in anthropology has now critically re-examined the case for local control of the commons, or of participatory development for that matter, and has revealed the political limits and dangers of "localism" (Gadgil and Guha 1993; Li 1996; Mohan and Stokke 2000).

Finally, we hear widely expressed concerns about local common resources being eroded everywhere; or urbanization, privatization and globalization as inevitably undermining the commons; or community management as at best a romanticization of communities and at worst a cover for within-group exploitation. But these relentless narratives of decline and degradation of traditional common-pool resources conceal the emergence of new common resources and new avenues for local collective action. In the USA, for example, the increasing numbers of neighborhood watch groups and community gardens can be seen as a bid to reclaim the local commons. In developing countries, community-based drinking water sources such as harvested rainwater (Agarwal and Narain 1997), and common sanitation facilities in crowded peri-urban areas (Hogrewe et al. 1993), are proliferating. Agro-forestry experiments and research aimed at sustainable village-based livelihoods are seriously examining the interaction between ecology and community. Who claims these resources, how are they appropriated, how are they maintained and how are they seen by different groups or users within the community? These questions are very much alive in economics as well as in anthropology, and so the commons are very much with us.

---

[8]   See e.g. E. Ostrom (1990), *Governing the Commons*; and J.-M. Baland and J.-P. Platteau (1996), *Halting Degradation of the Commons: Is There a Role for Rural Communities?*

Economics versus Anthropology?

The chapters in this volume illustrate the wide variation in approaches to the commons, and to research itself, both across and within economics and anthropology. They do not cover all the active strands of research in economics and anthropology, but collectively provide a broad sampling of methodological approaches to the local commons in both fields.[9] In discussing the methods that distinguish these two disciplines, the chapters in this collection make generalizations about mainstream economics and anthropology that may gloss over debates and differences *within* each field. We do, of course, recognize that both disciplines are moving targets for which all broad-brush statements are ultimately inappropriate.

One way to contextualize these chapters is through thinking about key dichotomies that distinguish mainstream economics from mainstream cultural and social anthropology. The chapters as a group – some explicitly and others implicitly – illustrate the persistent legacies of these dichotomies. We do not present these as defining the fields, rather they are presented as emblematic of them. Explicitly methodological differences between economics and anthropology include quantitative versus qualitative (referring to the nature of data and their analysis), aggregative versus particular (referring to how the data are used to illuminate social situations), and positivist versus reflexive (referring to the role of the researcher towards the data or the subjects of study). However, as many analysts have concluded, the social sciences are most often split along epistemological lines such as: How do economists and anthropologists view individual agency and social choice? What do economists and anthropologists seek to explain? What, indeed, are the characteristics of a good – or even adequate – explanation? These are foundational questions for any social science, and we address them via the dichotomies of autonomy versus embeddedness, outcomes versus processes and parsimony versus complexity.

Autonomy versus embeddedness

The debate over whether individuals are best understood as autonomous agents within the constraints of social structures, or as products of the structures that bound their agency, is an old – some might say sterile – one. "Men make their own history," wrote Marx, "but they do not make it just as they please; they do not make it under circumstances chosen by themselves" (Marx 1852).[10] Who could disagree? What largely separates economists from anthropologists, then, is the question of what is a meaningful construct

9 Two important strands of research that we have not engaged with are evolutionary anthropology and experimental economics. Evolutionary anthropologists use game theoretic and other mathematical models to explain the emergence of culture, cooperation, and norms in human and primate societies (e.g. Boyd and Richerson 1994). Experimental economists test key hypotheses in laboratory, and occasionally in real-world, conditions, to shed light on the validity and relevance of these hypotheses under different conditions. Recent experimental games show how wealth inequalities affect the governance of common resources (Cardenas 2003), and how field results differ from earlier laboratory games (Heinrich et al. 2004).
10 While Marx was referring to what economists somewhat crudely would call a constrained optimization equilibrium, the historian François Furet would suggest multiple equilibria and unintended consequences in saying, "Men make history but do not know which one."

of agency given what we want to explain. Three particularly contentious constructs in economics are methodological individualism, optimizing behavior, and exogenous preferences.

For (non-Marxist) economists, the individual is the unit of analysis and his or her thoughtful ("rational") choices under a set of constraints are what must be explained. Agency and autonomy reside in the individual. Societal characteristics reflect the aggregated result of individual characteristics – a point of view known as methodological individualism. Methodological individualism as an analytical concept comes in several versions (Bhargava 1993; Basu 2000: 253–4), the most constraining of which have been critiqued from within economics itself (Arrow 1994). Contrary to some perceptions, methodological individualism does not imply that all social characteristics are reducible to individual characteristics – many norms and practices can emerge as the unintended consequences of thousands of uncoordinated decisions (Schelling 1978; Sugden 1989). But economics is fundamentally a social science that explains social phenomena, such as cooperation or trade, in terms of individual choices and motives.

In most economic analyses, individuals are self-regarding – they try to do the best they can for themselves given the constraints of their economic endowments, their information sets and their tastes and preferences. Adam Smith called this trait "the desire of bettering our condition," and claimed that "the greater part of men propose and wish to better their condition" by "an augmentation of fortune" (Smith 1776: 362–3). This behavioral assumption was subsequently reduced to "utility maximization" (where utility could, but need not, consist only of one's own welfare). In recent years economists have recognized that a person could exhibit reciprocal rather than self-regarding behavior, and be selfish to those who were selfish to him but generous to those who were generous to him (Rabin 1993; Charness and Rabin 2002). Nevertheless, the default assumption in much of microeconomics is that people are exclusively self-regarding. As Sethi and Somanathan explain in their chapter (7), economists worry that frequent deviations from this assumption could open the doors to an "anything goes" mentality and *ad hoc* explanations.

Finally, tastes and preferences in economic analysis are exogenously given and stable. Why some members of a village community have cooperative as opposed to non-cooperative propensities is not a question within the domain of mainstream economics. Methodological individualism, utility maximization and exogenous preferences together create what might be called a thin theory of human action (Taylor 1988) but it is this thinness that gives microeconomic models their precision, parsimony and predictive power. It enables the researcher to ask under what rules and incentives a group of self-regarding individuals would cooperate to govern the commons (Bardhan 1995), and whether or not specific asymmetries would prevent cooperation from emerging (Ostrom and Gardner 1993; Ray and Williams 2002). Much economic analysis on the commons consists of being precise about the conditions under which cooperation would emerge and be sustained, with the understanding that the temptation to defect or free ride is always present.

With few exceptions, social and cultural anthropologists find these three characteristics unsatisfactory as a comprehensive account of human agency. In particular, the notion of exogenous preferences, formed and held at the individual level, has been widely critiqued. Bourdieu famously argued that preferences reflect the inner workings of culture and power in a society, that preferences are formed just as much by the desire for social differentiation as by the inherent properties of the preferred object (Bourdieu 1979). In a similar vein, Appadurai has critiqued survey research methods that treat the household as an autonomous choice-making unit – he argues that reciprocal relationships between households are central to the choices made by their individual members (Appadurai 1989: 254). More recently, Klamer has made the case that many social values and preferences are formed through dialogue, negotiation, and learning – far from being stable they are constantly being reassessed (Klamer 2004). For most meaningful interactions, then, the individual as the locus of "given" preferences, is not a recognizable object of anthropological inquiry.

The critique of exogenous preferences is one aspect of the broader discomfort with the economist's individual agent. Individuals do have agency, say anthropologists, but they are situated, embedded beings rather than autonomous beings who view life as a series of constrained optimization problems. Autonomy in a social vacuum is not meaningful; rather, as Lélé writes, individual selves are "inherently part of social and political relationships" (ch. 11, this volume). This ontological position implies that the central puzzle of common property analysis may not be why individuals cooperate to provide or protect a resource. Why they would not cooperate to protect a critical resource is just as much in need of explanation (e.g. Wright, commentary 2, this volume). Why free-riding should be one's first instinct is also open to question (e.g. Basu, commentary 1, this volume). But if autonomy is indeed embedded, what is it embedded in?

The operationalization of "embeddedness" has a rich tradition in anthropology. Polanyi (1954) argued that individuals are characterized by relationships of reciprocity rather than utility-maximizing motives, and that this was particularly the case for pre-capitalist economies. Even ostensibly market interactions were embedded in, and inseparable from, larger moral and political commitments. Bourdieu (1977; 1990) bounded agency and strategy within *habitus* – the practices, the principles, and the rules that gave individuals a sense of belonging in society. Geertz (1963) and Scott (1976) framed peasant societies in South-east Asia as moral economies rather than utilitarian economies. In a moral economy, individuals act not to advance their own well-being, but to make sure that resources and risks are pooled so that everyone has a place in the system. These moral economy analyses, while classics in the field of anthropology, have since been critiqued from within the discipline as being naïve about how power permeates the social fabric. These critics argue that what appears to be a moral economy could be a manifestation of asymmetric power or hegemonic control. Embeddedness in reciprocity is in fact embeddedness in unequal relations and multiple notions of identity and interest (Hart 1997). Even the idea of "community" in community-based management is a gross simplification in the light of multiple and overlapping intra-group heterogeneities (Li 2002).

Of embeddedness in values, commitments, power and norms, the one intrinsically collective concept that has gained real traction in economics is that of norms. By definition, and unlike preferences, norms cannot be held at the individual level. Basu (2000) makes a strong argument that economists should build norms explicitly into their models, lest they embed them unconsciously instead. He divides norms that are useful for economic analysis into three categories: rationality-limiting, preference-changing, and equilibrium-selecting (Basu 2000: 72–3). A rationality-limiting norm restricts a person from doing things, such as stealing her neighbor's newspaper, whether or not such an action would increase her utility. Preference-changing norms are those that become internalized into the utility function – the norms become preferences or cause too much guilt or shame if they are violated (see Elster 1989; Rao, ch. 2, this volume). Equilibrium-selecting norms help people to choose from amongst multiple equilibria, such as driving on the right side of the road in the USA but on the left hand side when in the UK. Most of the economic literature is on this third type of norm, which may or may not benefit everyone or even anyone, but once such norms take hold no one individual has an incentive to deviate from them.[11]

How norms emerge and why they persist are two different questions. Mainstream economic analysis, true to its methodologically individualist roots, explains the emergence of norms as the aggregate (and frequently unintentional) effect of many intentional but individual decisions. For instance, Sugden (1989) shows that cooperative norms in the use of driftwood can emerge, "spontaneously" and without explicit coordination, within the users' group. Once norms have emerged, however, they often persist because it is at least in some individuals' interest to sustain them, or in no one's interest to diverge from them. In other models, norms of restraint in resource use evolve and are stable if at least some members in the community are willing to punish rule-violators, even if sanctioning imposes material costs on the punishers (Sethi and Somanathan 1996). In short, norms, once the domain of anthropology, are now firmly on the economist's agenda.

Platteau's chapter (2) argues that norms and beliefs can act as a bridge, making the efforts of both disciplines complementary. In a break from mainstream game theory, Platteau argues that norms, histories and the expectations these generate, rather than actual gains and losses from cooperation, could determine whether or not cooperation occurs.[12] One of his examples concerns the migrant fishermen of Kayar, Senegal, who fished alongside native fishermen for part of the year. A commission was in place to ensure and monitor fishing quotas, but the migrants perceived the authorities to be useless (i.e. negative expectations took hold). Follow-up studies showed that fish catches had successfully been curtailed and that fish prices were significantly higher as a result. Yet interviews with the fishermen showed that the natives believed that the quotas had been successful while the migrants believed otherwise. Therefore, they violated the rules in order to pre-empt the (expected) behavior of the native fishermen. In Platteau's words, "effective cooperation can be established only if the appropriate beliefs and expectations have come to prevail. There is no reason to believe that such beliefs and expectations spontaneously arise when there is a need for collective efforts."

Anthropologists view common resources such as land or water as cultural systems with material as well as symbolic value (Bourdieu 1977; Mosse: ch. 5, this volume). They would thus want to go beyond explaining how norms and histories govern or undermine cooperation. The remarkable influence of Michel Foucault in contemporary anthropology has, in fact, led anthropologists to view cooperation-sustaining norms with a critical eye. Foucault argued that governance consists of certain arts and practices such

---

[11]   It should be noted that all three norm categories are considered constraints in economics – they are exogenous to the individual and they restrict her feasibility set. Norms as "givens" will work for social scientists with structuralist leanings, but not for others. If norms are seen as dynamic, then cooperation over resources and resistance to changing property regimes would also produce, rather than merely be shaped by, commitments and norms (Giddens 1993).

[12]   A similar point was illustrated theoretically by Fernandez and Rodrik (1991), who showed that if some agents were uncertain about whether they would gain or lose from cooperation, they would not cooperate. This is so even if, *ex post*, the non-cooperators would in fact have been gainers.

as measurement, observation and education, through which individuals become disciplined and governable subjects (Foucault 1991). The wide acceptance of these disciplinary forces circulates through society at large in the mutual enforcement of norms and of legitimate political and cultural discourses. Looking at economists' models of repeated games on the local commons and the enforcement of cooperation through "shared" norms, anthropologists would certainly ask not only how these norms emerged, but how their emergence reveals the dynamics of power working through everyday practices, and how the norms enforce the *status quo* – in short, how norms ensure the "normality" of the ostensibly free individual.

This point goes directly to the challenge raised by Agrawal's chapter – he sharply critiques the "sovereign selves" and "apolitical institutions" that underpin common-pool resource studies. Agrawal (ch. 3) argues that the nature of the embedded individual evolves with changes in her natural and social environment, and with her own responses to these changes over time. He says that methodological critiques and attempts to improve causal explanations by improving upon traditional social science methods are not enough to advance research on the commons. Nor is it enough, in the wake of Foucault, to analyze the power hierarchies that "embed" the individual purely as constraints on agency. Rather, the challenge – following the work of poststructural scholars and critical theorists – is to understand how individuals come to see themselves in relation to their environments, and how norms and power both constrain and enable. Agrawal's point is that "practices make persons." It is this shaping of identity through practices of cooperation, co-option or resistance around the local commons that remains central to the commonality invoked by these commons. There is little room for the economist's autonomous agent in this framework.

If interactions within local communities are not to be conceptualized as the aggregate effect of individual interests, but as the living out of shared understandings of what is just, of what is normal and of who has the power to do what, then these shared understandings are themselves a sort of common resource. Rao's chapter (11) in this collection focuses not on the physical commons, but on shared constructs such as identity formation and nationalism, which he calls *symbolic public goods*. Like traditional public goods these are non-rivalrous in consumption, and excludability within the group is difficult. Comparing post-independence India and Indonesia, Rao says that Javanese ideology holds that social interaction is "collective, consensual and cooperative." This was parlayed into the notion that, to be a good Indonesian, one should contribute labor and cash for development projects. Thus nationalism as a symbolic public good was constructed, deploying "traditional" beliefs that made the individual subservient to the community, in order to promote decentralization and efficiency in public services. Post-Independence India emphasized central planning to promote growth and development. Public goods such as schools, roads, and clinics were almost entirely centrally funded – and became symbols of the state largesse rather than of ownership by the community. As a result, they represented opportunities for corruption and patronage, and resulted in the inefficient delivery of public services. Rao concludes that paying attention to the symbolic commons illustrate how, in India and Indonesia, nationalism played a material role in local governance and community action.

In defense of the economist's autonomous self-regarding agent, Krugman writes, "*homo economicus* is a highly implausible caricature, but a highly productive one, and no useful alternative has yet been found" (Krugman 1995: 78). Our contention is that the portrayal of persons as rational creatures with individually held choices and preferences, or as relational creatures with multiple allegiances and overlapping identities, stems from deep differences in worldview. This difference is reflected in the questions, methods and explanations of commons scholarship in economics and anthropology. The thin concept of agency that economists use would generally be inadequate for the layered explanations of anthropology, and the concept of embedded agency that anthropologists use would rarely be sharp enough to predict model outcomes in economics.[13]

Outcomes versus processes

"Economics is mainly about outcomes; anthropology is mainly about processes." So begins Michael Lipton's review of *Conversations I* (Bardhan 1989) in the journal *World Development*, 1992. Lipton goes on to acknowledge that models reach their outcomes through processes such as making choices, bargaining etc. But these are modeled processes – economists do not conduct empirical investigations of processes themselves. Anthropologists, in contrast, while interested in e.g. the economic outcomes of social relationships, are most concerned with "the structure and function of the relationships themselves" and with the processes of exchange or the exercise of power that they generate. Appadurai's essay in *Conversations I* also argued that facts about village life, such as the rights to local commons, were "relational and not merely distributional" (Appadurai 1989: 268). The implication was that empirical research in economics samples outcomes (such as the distribution of water from a common watercourse), and does not usually sample, and so may gloss over, processes (such as how relationships between rule-maker and rule-breaker in water distribution are shaped).

The outcome–process distinction is difficult to define with precision, and is not always congruent with the economics–anthropology divide. Nevertheless, it seems to be understood by economists as a point of departure between their discipline and the other social sciences. In an interview with Arjo Klamer, when questioned about the "realism" of macroeconomic models, Robert Lucas says, "A lot of our theorizing is about outcomes and is very weak on the process" (Klamer 1988: 47). And in the introduction to the more recent *Foundations of Human Sociality*, the authors say that the goal of experimental economics is to change economic theory so that "the processes determining outcomes matter as well as the outcomes themselves" (Henrich et al. 2004: 2). Anthropologists, of course, have always claimed that economists are overly-focused on predicting outcomes at the expense of a processual understanding of social life, and of the diversity and negotiations that characterize institutions. Even economists have expressed concerns with theories of the commons that under-emphasize processes and transitions (Sengupta, commentary 3, this volume).

Outcomes in economic analysis have two characteristics – they serve as predictions, thus allowing economists to serve as policy advisers, and (when possible) they describe equilibrium points in the economy. Many anthropologists acknowledge that prediction is

---

[13]   Here is the definition of "agency" from the *Dictionary of Anthropology*, edited by Thomas Barfield, 1997. Agency is "the capacity of human beings to affect their own life chances and those of others and to play a role in the formation of social realities in which they participate. It is less a force of individual action than a dimension of the institutions and relations that human beings form such as social class, hegemonizing ideologies and bureaucracies that deprive them of agency."

valuable in thinking about social change, and that the sharp predictions of economics make it more influential in policy circles than the "softer" social sciences. But they are concerned that economists' assumptions and models are too simple to be socially useful, or that prediction of a phenomenon under a given set of constraints is too readily conflated with justification of an existing institutional set-up (see Bardhan 1989: 238). Moreover, not all feasible outcomes are known to be so from the start, and therefore cannot be predicted – economics does not handle well those problem-solving interactions where ends and means co-evolve, and outcomes are discovered in the process (Wright, commentary 2, this volume).

Whether prediction is or is not an explanation, and whether understanding the process is as important as predicting the outcome, are both questions that relate to the nature and purpose of explanation in the social sciences. What makes for a good explanation is too big a question to address here.[14] We concentrate instead on causal explanations, in which we identify the initial conditions and the mechanisms that caused the explained event to occur, or at least made it highly likely to occur. Causal explanations are important in economics and in anthropology, though some anthropological modes of explanation such as symbolic interactionism or discourse analysis are non-causal in nature.

Causal explanations draw upon repeated empirical observations of the event and its supposed cause, as well as upon theories of the underlying mechanisms or structures that supposedly produce the explained event. Both inductive and theoretical reasoning are common to economics and anthropology, but the preferred modes of explanation in the two fields stem from their respective foci on outcomes and processes. In economic theorizing, the causal arrow from cause C to event E is usually clearly specified. It is explicitly built into the model specification, and the model (at least in theory) stands or falls or wobbles on the basis of the accuracy of its predictions. Game theoretic work on the commons falls into this category (e.g. Weissing and Ostrom 1991; Ostrom and Gardner 1994). Attributing causation in a regression analysis is a more complex matter – real data naturally create real problems. The causal arrows are not specified in statistical models, they have to be inferred from the strength and significance of the correlation between the dependent variable and the relevant independent variables. The potential problem with such "explanations" are that correlation on its own, however strong, cannot pass for causation. Because of the complexity of real-world data (and because of most researchers' reliance on secondary data), the most common problems econometricians struggle with are sample selection (is the sample random or was there self-selection?); reverse causality (does X cause Y or Y cause X?); and omitted variable bias (is the inference of "X causes Y" spurious because there is a third omitted variable that varies systematically with both X and Y?). In recent years economists' attempts at deciphering causal process in hypothesis testing have become much more rigorous, particularly through creative use of instrumental variables and random evaluations of interventions.

One of the most important explanatory modes in social and cultural anthropology is the case study method.[15] Case studies are well-equipped to, and often do, investigate causal

---

[14]   A good introductory text is Little (1991).

[15]   The term "case study" could imply that the case in question belongs to a family of cases with similar or generalizable characteristics. Anthropologists who view their work as explaining what is particular or unique about a situation would therefore reject the "case" terminology.

processes directly. An anthropologist's case study could include a small number of cases, compare two cases, or even conduct within-case analysis of a single case of interest (Ragin 1987). Some political scientists use what George (1979) calls "process-tracing" which focuses on an analysis of sequential processes in a causal chain within a single case (and not on correlations across cases). On the one hand, as most anthropologists recognize, the few-cases method restricts the researcher's ability to generalize beyond his or her study site.[16] On the other hand, anthropologists generally have a better insight into the wellsprings of human behavior, since they often live with the respondents, observe their practices and participate in some fashion in their daily lives. When the contributors to *Foundations* discovered that their respondents routinely undermined the predictions of bargaining theory, they were able to ask them explicitly about their motives. It was thus discovered that the way that specific games were played mirrored everyday interactions among the players (Henrich et al. 2004). In addition, where many alternative causal paths lead to the same outcome (sometimes called the "equifinality" problem), the processual case study method may be better equipped to handle these. We note, however, that case studies are also prone to errors of sample selection, reverse causality and omitted variable bias, though these problems are not always addressed (or even acknowledged) in the studies.[17]

While anthropologists are thus better at telling us *how* a variable mattered to the outcome, economists are often better at measuring *how much* it mattered. One creative way in which to combine the strengths of economics and anthropology is "participatory econometrics" (Rao 2002). This approach includes participatory appraisals (by the researched), focus group discussions, participant observation (by the researcher) and large-n structured surveys in the design of which the respondents participate. Labor- and skill-intensive, participatory econometrics is likely to yield better insights into causal processes than traditional econometric methods, and yet be more generalizable than traditional case study methods.

The contribution by Ray in this volume (ch. 4) is also focused on how to combine the strengths of the two disciplines. The author asks if and how (1) the inferences of economic models can better be interpreted through anthropology-inspired questions about structure and process, and (2) the research of anthropologists can be informed by outcomes or correlations from economic models. The argument in this chapter is that an explanation of any model outcome is invariably about process and structure. Therefore without a processual and place-based understanding of cooperative outcomes, new institutions for cooperation cannot be fostered. In addition, anthropologists pay attention to what has been said as well as to what remains unsaid. In that spirit, one must ask if models that abstract from caste or influence or self-respect implicitly suggest that these factors are less important, and that village-level cooperation can take place largely on the basis of economic and ecological factors. Finally, anthropologists are critical of economic models for their simplicity and excessive faith in quantifiable outcomes. But every now and then economic models surprise with counter-intuitive results or non-obvious correlations, and such

---

[16]   Agrawal (ch. 2, this volume) argues that the reliance on the case study method has hindered the systematic attribution of causation in the commons literature.

[17]   Of course, the problems of inference in both the quantitative and qualitative traditions arise from "social scientists" use of observational data rather than controlled experiments, therefore rival hypotheses are always difficult to eliminate.

results should be an invitation to anthropologists as well as economists to investigate social processes that were hitherto not anticipated.

One of the strengths of anthropologists' concern with process, and the detailed analysis that the case study method requires, is the ability to explain how power operates within a society, and the multiple ways in which it manifests itself. Economists are also interested in understanding power relations, and in how structure and authority permit dysfunctional institutions to persist. Much work on the effect of inequality on cooperation on the commons has been done by economists.[18] But economists usually model power asymmetries as a standing condition, operationalize them as measurable inequalities, and then work through their consequences for the relevant economic agents. This leads them to overemphasize the material benefits and costs of asymmetry, and to underemphasize the symbolic and disciplining dimensions of power, where power and authority are regularly articulated through commons institutions.

Anthropologists, drawing on social theory as well as field observations, have brought a much richer understanding of power to the literature on common-pool resources. First, power is not just the ability to make someone do something that is not in the doer's interest – which is what economics can analyze (e.g. Basu 1986). As mentioned, power has symbolic as well as material dimensions, which have to be revealed in the course of observation and analysis (Li 2002; Mosse: ch. 5, this volume). Second, an understanding of power is incomplete without a grasp of the resistance that oppression can generate, and the history of common resource struggles is replete with such resistance. From struggles to retain the right to use common forest resources in Indonesia (Peluso 1992), to the protests to stop the displacement of tribal people from their traditional lands along the Narmada River (Baviskar 1995), to the mass squattings and land take-overs of the landless in Brazil (Wright and Wolford 2003), the exercise of power has generated collective actions that can only be understood as dynamic *movements and processes*. Not as predictable outcomes, not as rules of management, and certainly not as equilibria.

The chapter (5) by David Mosse shows how collective action over tank irrigation in Tamil Nadu, India, is as much an issue of allocating water as it is of maintaining or resisting social power. The author's (earlier) study of irrigation started with traditional institutional-economic questions such as, why did farmers in some villages cooperate to manage scarce resources, while in others, crucial resources were neglected. At first blush, institutional-economic explanations in terms of risk and individual incentives made sense to him. But his deeper probing into the processes of exercising power showed that the economic models overlooked the structures of caste authority and the cultural construction of irrigation systems. Mosse concluded that anthropological research did not explain outcomes any better than institutional-economics research. But how those outcomes were produced, and the historical processes involved, were crucial to the understanding of what people actually *did* in practice. For example, his analysis revealed that local common resources, contrary to the premises of economic models, were not managed to maximize economic utility, but to minimize social conflict and to enhance the prestige of existing leadership.

Third, power is, at its most subtle, the ability to frame social policy and the terms of discussion such that the powerless may not even recognize their powerlessness, or if they

---

[18]   See e.g. papers from the *MacArthur Research Network on Inequality and Economic Performance*: http://globetrotter.berkeley.edu/macarthur/inequality/.

do, they cannot develop the language to articulate it (Lukes 1974). In this way, and without crude coercion, people at all levels can be disciplined into becoming governable subjects (Foucault 1980; 1991). The ascendance of critical social theory and post-structuralism has brought the language and framing of particular issues into the core of current anthropology. Their starting point is not "the objective truth" but rather the multiple and co-existing interpretations of social and environmental problems. In this framework, "truths are statements within socially produced discourses rather than objective "facts" about reality" (Peet and Watts 1996: 13). A true statement is one that has been discursively validated, not a subject-invariant property of the data (Kanbur and Shaffer 2005).[19] The ways in which different groups and individuals represent concepts[20] such as "protection of the commons," and the politics of such representations, can thus be dissected to reveal the everyday workings of power. How (only) some environmental problems such as soil degradation or acid rain come to be seen as problems, and how these "problems" are framed for policy purposes, are important research questions from this standpoint (e.g. Hajer 1995; Leach and Mearns 1996).

Anthropological research in the wake of critical theory undermines the "naturalness" of familiar categories by revealing how all such categories and regimes are socially constructed, and by so doing, undermines the regimes of power that naturalize these categories. By rejecting the "community" or the "local" as pre-existing starting points, for example, Gupta and Ferguson (1997) argue that the researcher is free to explore the feelings, power dynamics and processes that go into "the construction of space as place and locality in the first instance" (p. 67). The policy and the political implications of accepting or of interrogating these categories are sharply different. Many economists, at least those who are reflexive about their discipline, would probably agree that "the way a question is framed reveals the kind of accommodation being reached" (Dasgupta 2002), but framings and discourse as instruments of social control are far from central to economic analysis. In her chapter (6), Baviskar claims that power imbalances and inequalities are key to the shaping of individual and collective choices. "Adding a dash of 'culture' and a pinch of 'power' to the [economist's] recipe for understanding collective action around the commons" does not go far. Rather, an anthropological approach would transform the questions that are considered meaningful for analysis. Questioning the bases of institutionally produced knowledge, she argues that there is utility in not playing a prescriptive role or confining one's inquiry to the problem as defined by ongoing policies around the commons. Including the political process by which we come to concur on the *definition* of the problem reveals unexamined assumptions that shape the commons debates. In short, the dominant institutional-economic conception of the commons creates "knowledge" that occludes other, equally valid, ways of understanding why the commons matter and why collective action matters. To seek knowledge is simultaneously to seek or validate a power structure,[21] and prominent social institutions perpetuate their power by socializing subjects to internalize the limits of what is permissible and desirable.

---

[19]   Note that participation and argument are critical to the production of truth by this criterion, because this is the only way to come to an understanding of intersubjective meanings.

[20]   In anthropological writings, these questions are often phrased in a somewhat disembodied or agent-less manner: *"How does this issue get represented? How does it get used? How does discourse get reproduced?"*

[21]   But here is an economist's objection to this position: "An epistemic methodology that sees the pursuit of knowledge as entirely congruent with the search for power is a great deal more cunning than wise" (Sen 2005).

Finally, power is also understood to permeate the interaction between the anthropologist and her respondents, and their subsequent portrayal in the research. Anthropology as a discipline has a history of being concerned with non-Western non-capitalist economies, with a mission to explore the particular and the unique, and to translate other "lifeworlds" into social scientific discourse. There was time when this mission was not especially progressive, let alone emancipatory – rather, it served to cement colonial stereotypes or exoticize other cultures (see e.g. Asad 1991). Today, however, the role of the anthropologist in research is conceived in a more complex way than that of the economist. For example, an empirical economist adopts the role of a neutral observer when in the field, gathering (intersubjectively-observable) data about his subject while remaining at all times a dispassionate outsider. Analyzing conflict or cooperation on the commons, economists might impose pre-conceived categories on the respondents' answers or seek subject-invariant interpretations of these. But an increasing number of anthropologists are not willing to admit the possibility of a scientifically neutral position. The attention to the formation of the subject at the intersection of power and knowledge have made them conscious of the power asymmetries implicit in conducting surveys and interviews, which then purport to "represent" their respondents to the wider world. Thus these researchers may see themselves as empathetic rather than neutral observers, or interpreters of speech and action "from the inside," or even as partners in their respondents' aspirations and struggles (Blaikie 2000: 52). Such uses of power can only be uncovered through process analysis, and as of now they are squarely in the anthropologists' corner.

Parsimony versus complexity

We have just shown that the explication of the multiple ways in which power works through commons institutions is a strong suit for anthropology. Though power imbalances are indeed pervasive, power does not play a central role in all social explanation. Many economic models allow social structures and cultural norms to emerge from millions of disaggregated decisions, with no explicit role for power in the emergence. Each individual choice may be reasonable but together the choices may create an inefficient, unjust or a downright awful society. Dasgupta argues that this feature is an achievement of modern economics, "because it does not rely on postulating predatory governments, or thieving aristocracies, or grasping landlords. This is not to deny their existence, but *you don't need* an intellectual apparatus to conclude that a defenseless person will be robbed if there is an armed robber bent on robbing her" (Dasgupta 2002; italics added). In a similar spirit, discussing von Thünen's pioneering work on agricultural land use, Krugman shows that a complex theory of power and history *was not needed* to explain how land was allocated in the von Thünen model – the assumption of self-interested behavior and strategic interaction was sufficient to allow the spatial pattern of land use to emerge (Krugman 1995: 75). The point that we do not need a particular assumption to explain a particular outcome is an expression of the principle of parsimony, also known as that of Occam's razor.[22] If there are two theories with equal explanatory power, we should choose the one with

---

[22]   Named for William of Occam (also spelled Ockham), born in the village of Ockham in Surrey, ca. 1285 – an influential philosopher and theologian.

the fewer assumptions. If, however, the simpler theory can no longer explain the facts, it should be abandoned. This has been a guiding principle for model-building in the physical sciences.

It may not, however, be reasonable to assume that simplicity provides an insight into a particular society, which is a historically evolved system, with layers of change and modification building upon what was already there before it. This is the argument against parsimony that Francis Crick makes with respect to biology, "While Occam's Razor is a useful tool in the physical sciences, it can be a very dangerous implement in biology. It is . . . rash to use simplicity and elegance as a guide in biological research" (Crick 1988: 138). So why has parsimony been embraced by economics, which is not, after all, a physical science?

The first and most obvious reason is that economics looks for patterns in economic life that, while not universal, are widely generalizable. If, despite differences in culture, norms and values, a similar-enough set of behaviors can be observed in many places and over time, then a small set of simple assumptions should be sufficient to explain them. The most critical element of parsimony in economic theory has been the assumption of the self-regarding choice-making individual – usually but not always simplified to a utility-maximizing agent. This one assumption, allied in modern economics to strategic inter-action, has given economics its theoretical generalizability and practical policy relevance. This assumption is under attack from experimental and behavioral economists, but even here they look for systematic departures from the canonical model so that, for example, other-regarding behavior can be formalized and used for suitable generalizations.

The chapter by Sethi and Somanathan (7) in this volume is a good example of a par-simonious theory of collective action on the commons. It explicitly lays out the assump-tions of the model and how these depart from prior models, and makes predictions about cooperative equilibria and when these will occur. The chapter starts with a classic question: What makes cooperation on the commons more likely? One way to produce cooperation in traditional models of self-interested behavior is to make resource extraction a repeated game where the future matters. However, the authors point out, infinitely many equilibria with different degrees of resource exploitation are supported by these models. Prediction becomes impossible with an embarrassment of equilibria. Now the authors introduce their own model, which has two new assumptions. The first is a stringent form of bounded rationality. The second is that individuals are not simply selfish – they are reciprocal. From these and a few other simple assumptions, the model predicts that cooperation is more likely when communication is cheap; public-good provision is productive; effective punish-ment opportunities are available at low cost, and group size is large (*ceteris paribus*).

We can contrast this parsimonious and generalizable approach with that of Mukhopadhay's contribution (ch. 8, this volume). Mukhopadhyay, too, starts with a classic question: What explains the transition from a commons tenurial system to private property? The chapter begins with the explanatory factors made famous by Demsetz (1967) – technological advance, access to markets and the market value of the resource. However, through a historical analysis of the redistribution and privatization of community lands in Goa, India, the author shows that none of these factors, nor an underlying drive for efficiency or equity, accounted for the transition. Rather, rural governance structures in the pre- and post-colonial periods, and in particular the post-Independence change to electoral democracy, appeared to be the most important reasons. The democratically elected

Goa government, under pressure to seek votes, used land ownership as a way to buy them. While the institutions of rural governance (rather than efficiency, equity or sustainability) were responsible for the privatization of the Goan commons, such context-specific analyses cannot readily be transported to other contexts with other histories.

The second and possibly less obvious reason for parsimony in economic theory is the modeler's aesthetic sense. Parsimonious theories that explain many observations with few assumptions have come to be regarded as elegant in model-building.[23] The conventional argument in the social sciences, including in economics, is that empirical tests are the final judges of whether a theory or hypothesis is a good one. Of course, the conditions under which the hypothesis holds – the *ceteris paribus* condition – should be as precisely specified as possible, so the tests conducted are relevant ones. However, there are disagreements among economists about how to test particular theories, about whether in a particular case the *ceteris paribus* condition was (approximately) met, about model specification, and so on. All the social sciences have running debates about what the data show, and as a result, more than in the natural sciences, several competing and conflicting theories and hypotheses co-exist within each discipline. In these circumstances, despite official agreement on the importance of empirically informed theorizing in economics, if there appear to be trade-offs between elegance and relevance, parsimony is likely to be the guiding principle (Klamer 1988: 245).

Parsimonious explanations are not particularly favored in anthropology. There are two important and related reasons for this – the role of the anthropologist in her research and the methodological philosophies of major schools of anthropology. We have discussed above the role of the researcher relative to the researched, so we concentrate here on the second issue. The epistemological position of major schools of anthropology is not to focus just on the seen and heard, but to look for hidden meanings, to listen for the unspoken, to interpret culture from the insider's perspective – in short to "make strange the familiar." The traditional concern of anthropology with the particular and the unique has also made the genealogical approach of Foucault (1980; 1997) especially influential in this discipline. The genealogical approach argues that societies change through a series of power struggles and that there is no overarching or predictable trajectory to this unfolding. There are no universalizable evolutionary laws, no "grand theory" of change as such. The methodological consequence of this framework is that the role of the social scientist is to reveal the *contingent* course that has shaped a society, and through this method, to contest notions of necessary orders and structures.[24] It is particularly important, in this framework, to investigate the political processes that go into everyday understandings of everyday concepts, such as "the commons" or "the community." This is a very different project from that of economics – if anything, the project is to complicate rather than simplify, question the unquestioned, and be wary of neat and tidy "parsimonious" explanations.

---

[23]   However, Blaug reminds us that what is considered simplicity or parsimony in a theory is itself conditioned on the perspective of scientists at any given time. The elegance of Newton's theory of gravity, much appreciated in the nineteenth century, apparently eluded Newton's seventeenth-century contemporaries (Blaug 1992: 24).

[24]   In contrast, we may note that while sociologists do consider Foucault to be a key social thinker, the structuralist roots of the discipline have made him far less central to sociology than to anthropology.

Rao and Appadurai (ch. 9) present the commons as an analytical and political, rather than a physical, category. The "best methods for understanding the social, cultural and collective implications of the commons might also turn out to be eclectic and diverse," they write – thus staking out a role for complexity rather than parsimony in analysis. First, as landscapes change (through state intervention, urbanization, and globalization) the units of analysis also change. We cannot decide how to act on the commons without understanding what led to the definition of "commons" in our analysis. Second, the effects of measurement and information design should be part of the analysis. New and cross-disciplinary practices of measurement change the locus of the commons and allow communities to confront policies that threaten their interests. Finally, values and meanings are also transformed. In some cases the physical resource may remain unchanged but its significance may change; in other cases the resource may undergo physical changes and yet retain continuity in its symbolic value. The authors show how difficult it is to characterize societies in flux where everything seems to be up for negotiation.

The difference between a parsimonious and a complicating approach has had enormous consequences for the role of economics and anthropology in policy circles. In formulating causal explanations, the parsimony principle leads economists to insulate the effect of one variable, controlling for others, so that they can measure its direct effect. Anthropologists throw into the analysis a much larger set of factors to capture the essential multi-dimensionality of action – without telling us what the effect of each factor by itself will be. A cause may never be attributable to one factor, the symbolic and the material may be considered inseparable in judging effect. The economists' approach is needed if we want to use the research results to guide policy advice. We would want to know about the impact of a particular policy that largely has an impact on one variable (e.g. property rights). We could legitimately argue that too much inseparability and too much multi-dimensionality would make policy advice impossible, and could lead to an accumulation of possibly relevant factors, without providing clues about how to sort the accumulated evidence.

Most anthropologists acknowledge that policy advice requires simplifying assumptions and generalizable conclusions, and detailed analyses of complex situations are not conducive to either.[25] But they could legitimately point out that the attempt to isolate the effects of single causal factors has frequently been too simplistic and has had unintended consequences when applied as policy. Policies are implemented in unequal social, cultural and economic structures and these inequalities and their impacts are more complex and more interrelated than policy analysts realize (Rao and Walton 2004: 360), or even want to know. Simplification for the sake of policy could lead to new ways of social control (Li 2002). A focus on rule-making in sharing water could overlook the point that rules are not followed as such, rather, they show how public behavior should be represented (Mosse: ch. 5, this volme). And parsimonious explanations of central tendencies could lead to the further marginalization of the already marginal, particularly in terms of

---

[25]   Anthropologists do, however, have some unresolved problems with the generalization question. For example, we have found anthropological studies where generalization much beyond the study site has implicitly occurred, without acknowledgment of this practice. In addition, critics from within anthropology have pointed out that interviews and context-based conclusions have a generalizing effect on the reader – even if the author disavows the goal of generalization (see e.g. d'Andrade 1995).

learning about omitted variables. As Rao (2002) argues, much can be learned from having "tea with an outlier."

One final point. The anthropologists' concern with process and structure is related to their tendency to complicate, but the two need not go together. For example, many political scientists are concerned with complex political processes such as voting behavior, and with difficult-to-define variables such as democracy or nationalism or patriotism (Brady 2004: 62). Nevertheless, the tendency in mainstream political science is to simplify these processes into e.g. their measurable constituent parts, or to operationalize complex variables such that they can be proxied or incorporated into a scale or index (King et al. 1994). Naturally all these proxies and operationalizations are contested within political science – but the project, we would argue, remains one of the simplification of complexity. This is by and large not the case with cultural and social anthropology today.

Disciplines and Interdisciplinarity

We have so far considered those dichotomies across economics and anthropology that relate to their basic concepts, methods of data collection and analysis and embedded assumptions. Several contributors to this collection have been explicitly bridging – Platteau embellishes traditional game-theoretic approaches with historical analysis to emphasize the role of norms and expectations in economics as well as anthropology; Ray seeks to explain why trade is so difficult in this era of disciplinary specialization, but also explores the mutual advantages of methodological exchange; Agrawal shows the difficulty of establishing causality through traditional case-based analyses, and argues that both economics and anthropology can gain from a deeper exploration of subject-formation with respect to the natural resource base; and Rao takes the commons beyond physical resources to symbolic resources such as collective identity and nationalism, and shows how these cultural commons materially affect the path of economic development.

This collection also includes six short notes or "commentaries" by social scientists who have worked on cross-boundary and other methodological problems. These commentaries represent the views of their writers on important aspects of interdisciplinary exchange. Ravi Kanbur and Annalise Riles – an economist and an anthropologist respectively – present a conversation in which they explain to one another what the commons problem is, and on the strengths and weaknesses of each discipline with respect to the commons "problem." Erik Wright discusses the implications of the broad palette of actions and motives in sociology versus the narrower economists' model in which self-interested motivations are privileged. Kaushik Basu critiques the economist's insistence on incentive compatibility in collective action, arguing that successful economies are ones where individuals are more prone to work in society's interest even when that may clash with their self-interests. Nirmal Sengupta acknowledges the advances made by game theoretic approaches to the commons, but suggests that we have to go beyond game theory to understand how the commons can adapt to market penetration and how to theorize the processes of such transitions. A. Vaidyanathan suggests that greater effort in linking the social with the natural-physical sciences, or a "systems approach" will lead to new and important insights on sustainable use of CPRs. Kanchan Chopra shows that when interdisciplinary teams work together with an explicit focus on policy, disciplinary differences tend to narrow and converge towards a more consensual framework.

In addition to dominant methods and assumptions, all the disciplines harbor dominant (though not monolithic) normative views on what is important in the world, and therefore (in our case) on what the goal of common-pool resource management should be. It is easy to observe that, in different chapters by different researchers, efficiency in resource use, or sustainability of the resource or equality of access to the resource is considered *good*. These normative concerns are a result not only of the internal characteristics of the diverse disciplines, but also of their historical development and of the way in which the societies within which they developed came to view them and to use them (Jasanoff 2002; Fourcade-Gourinchas 2001). In what ways do moral and ideological positions, whether explicitly acknowledged or held by default, either enable or disable the project of interdisciplinarity?

The chapter (11) by Lélé considers the normative and societal divisions within the social sciences and across the natural science – social science categories. He argues that whereas methodological differences and even epistemological differences are acknowledged and (occasionally) seriously discussed, normative differences and differences stemming from the attitudes of society at large to the disciplines are rarely acknowledged. For example, when disciplines (or sub-disciplines) study the same phenomenon but differ in their explanatory models, how do we know which is the superior explanation? In the case of complex socio-environmental phenomena, it is not easy to reach clear conclusions from the empirical evidence, and therefore allegiance to one's school and its ideologies may become the most important goal. Lélé provocatively suggests that if subject matters and therefore knowledge bases differ, as amongst the natural sciences, interdisciplinarity is easier to achieve. But if the subject matter is in effect the same, with all the social sciences trying to explain human behavior, differences in theory, method and normative values become more central and therefore more difficult to reconcile.

While the fields of welfare economics and social choice theory in economics deal with normative issues, much of economics takes values and social goals as given or defined by political and social authorities. Anthropologists, in contrast, are more engaged in debates about the moral and political goals of their research, and about how (and if) a researcher's moral vision or political position should find voice in his or her research output. In a well-known debate between Roy d'Andrade and Nancy Scheper-Hughes, d'Andrade protested that postmodernist influences and the blurring of the positive with the normative had made anthropology into a moral project rather than an empirically based science (d'Andrade 1995). Scheper-Hughes, rejecting the very possibility of morally neutral research, argued the case for an explicitly political, reflexive and emancipatory anthropology (Scheper-Hughes 1995).

The feminist critique within mainstream anthropology has also argued that the social construction of gender and the values motivating research are crucial subjects for interrogation. Especially from the 1990s on, feminist scholars have explicitly acknowledged the values, situated-ness[26] and partial perspectives of the researchers themselves. Jackson's contribution to this volume (ch. 12) suggests that this more reflexive and value-based approach to research could be important across the social sciences, especially in

---

[26]   We borrow this term from Haraway (1991).

development studies. Feminist methods, as the author says, have always gone beyond the qualitative versus quantitative divide. Feminists identify with those who have struggled and are disadvantaged, and their research reflects that *positionality*, but this does not mean that it is any more "biased" than traditional, supposedly value-neutral, research. Rather Jackson's position is that epistemologies that explicitly draw on feminist reflexivity, feminist objectivity and the politics of "voice and choice" can serve as a bridge between disciplines in the social sciences. The author concludes that commonality of motives and shared values of social justice, rather than commonality of methods, could be powerful (though at present rather neglected) incentives for interdisciplinarity.

Conclusion

In this chapter we have argued that one of the key barriers to interdisciplinary work between economists and anthropologists is differences in epistemology – in what the two disciplines consider important to explain, and how they evaluate the criteria for a good explanation. It is an introduction to a collection of chapters and commentaries on economics, anthropology, and the question of the commons, that illustrate some of these differences, and that suggest both the potential and the pitfalls of trying to bridge these epistemological gaps.

Our goal in this chapter was not somehow to *resolve* the methodological, epistemological and normative divides between mainstream economics and anthropology. Rather, we were motivated by the belief that understanding what is important to the other discipline, and seeing the differences in light of that understanding, is important for interdisciplinary work and for respectful conversation. We have highlighted three dichotomies that are emblematic of some of these differences: autonomy versus embeddedness, outcomes versus processes and parsimony versus complexity. We also touched upon the role of normative concerns – be they shared or not, and acknowledged or not – in the development of disciplinary modes of explanation. We hope our discussion leads at least some economists and anthropologists critically to examine the assumptions and modes of analysis that may sometimes go unquestioned within their disciplines. In the words of Bertrand Russell: "In all affairs it's a healthy thing now and then to hang a question mark on the things you have long taken for granted."

References

Agarwal, Anil and Sunita Narain. 1997. *Dying Wisdom: Rise, Fall and Potential of India's Traditional Water Harvesting Systems*. New Delhi: Centre for Science and Environment.

Appadurai, Arjun. 1989. "Small-scale techniques and large-scale objectives." In Pranab Bardhan (ed.), 1989: 250–82.

Arrow, Kenneth J. 1994. "Methodological individualism and social knowledge." *American Economic Review*, 84: 1–9.

Asad, Talal. 1991. "Afterword: from the history of colonial anthropology to the anthropology of western hegemony." In George W. Stocking (ed.), *Colonial Situations: Essays on the Contextualization of Ethnographic Knowledge*. Madison: University of Wisconsin Press.

Baland, Jean-Marie and Jean-Philippe Platteau. 1996. *Halting Degradation of the Commons: Is There a Role for Rural Communities?* Oxford: Clarendon Press.

Bardhan, Pranab (ed.). 1989. *Conversations between Economists and Anthropologists: Methodological Issues in Measuring Economic Change in Rural India*. New Delhi: Oxford University Press.

Bardhan, Pranab. 1995. "Rational fools in a poor hydraulic economy." In K. Basu, P. Pattanaik, and K. Suzumura (eds), *Choice, Welfare and Development: A Festschrift in Honour of Amartya K. Sen*. Oxford: Clarendon Press.

Basu, Kaushik. 1986. "One kind of power." *Oxford Economic Papers*, 38: 259–82.

Basu, Kaushik. 2000. *Prelude to Political Economy: A Study of the Social and Political Foundations of Economics*. Oxford and New York: Oxford University Press.

Baviskar, Amita. 1995. *In the Belly of the River: Tribal Conflicts over Development in the Narmada Valley*. Delhi and New York: Oxford University Press.

Bhargava, Rajeev. 1993. *Individualism in Social Science: Forms and Limits of Methodology*. Oxford: Oxford University Press.

Blaikie, Norman. 2000. *Designing Social Research*. Malden: Blackwell.

Blaug, Mark. 1992. *The Methodology of Economics*. Cambridge: Cambridge University Press.

Bourdieu, Pierre. 1977. *Outline of a Theory of Practice*. Cambridge: Cambridge University Press.

Bourdieu, Pierre. 1979. *Distinctions: A Social Critique of the Judgment of Taste*. London: Routledge.

Bourdieu, Pierre. 1990. *The Logic of Practice*. Stanford: Stanford University Press.

Boyd, Robert and Peter Richerson. 1994. "The evolution of norms: an anthropological view." *Journal of Institutional and Theoretical Economics*, 151: 269–85.

Brady, Henry. 2004. "Doing good and doing better." In Henry Brady and David Collier (eds), *Rethinking Social Inquiry: Diverse Tools, Shared Standards*. Lanham: Rowman & Littlefield, 53–68.

Cardenas, Juan-Camilo. 2003. "Real wealth and experimental cooperation: experiments in the field lab." *Journal of Development Economics*, 70: 263–89.

Chambers, Robert. 2001. "Qualitative approaches: self criticism and what can be gained from quantitative approaches." In Ravi Kanbur (ed.), *Qual-Quant: Qualitative and Quantitative Poverty Appraisal: Complementarities, Tensions and the Way Forward* (www.q-squared.ca).

Charness, Gary and Matthew Rabin. 2002. "Understanding social preferences with simple tests." *Quarterly Journal of Economics*, 117: 817–69.

Crick, Francis. 1988. *What Mad Pursuit: A Personal View of Scientific Discovery*. New York: Basic Books.

D'Andrade, Roy. 1995. "Moral models in anthropology." *Current Anthropology*, 36: 399–408.

Dasgupta, Partha. 2002. "Modern economics and its critics." In Uskali Mäki (ed.), *Fact and Fiction in Economics: Models, Realism and Social Construction*. Cambridge: Cambridge University Press.

Escobar, Arturo and Sonia Alvarez. 1992. *The Making of Social Movements in Latin America: Identity, Strategy, and Democracy*. Boulder: Westview Press.

Elster, Jon. 1989. *The Cement of Society: A Study of Social Order*. New York: Cambridge University Press.

Fernandez, R. and Dani Rodrik. 1991. "Resistance to reform: status quo bias in the presence of individual specific uncertainty." *American Economic Review*, 81: 1146–55.

Foucault, Michel. 1980. *Power/Knowledge: Selected Interviews and Other Writings, 1972–1977*. Edited and translated by Colin Gordon. Sussex: Harvester.

Foucault, Michel. 1991. "Governmentality." In G. Burchell, C. Gordon, and P. Miller (eds), *The Foucault Effect: Studies in Governmentality*. London: Harvester Wheatsheaf.

Foucault, Michel. 1997. *The Essential Works of Michel Foucault, 1954–1984*. Edited by Paul Rabinow. New York: New Press, distributed by W. W. Norton.

Fourcade-Gourinchas, Marion. 2001. "Politics, institutional structures and the rise of economics: a comparative study." *Theory and Society*, 30: 397–447.

Gadgil, Madhav and Ramachandra Guha. 1993. *This Fissured Land: An Ecological History of India*. Berkeley: University of California Press.

Geertz, Clifford. 1963. *Agricultural Involution: The Process of Ecological Change in Indonesia*. Berkeley: University of California Press.

Geertz, Clifford. 1978. "The bazaar economy: information and search in peasant marketing." *American Economic Review*, 68: 28–32.

George, Alexander L. 1979. "The causal nexus between cognitive beliefs and decision-making behavior." In I. S. Falkowski (ed.), *Psychological Models in International Politics*. Boulder: Westview, 95–124.

Guha, Ramachandra. 1989. *The Unquiet Woods: Ecological Change and Peasant Resistance in the Himalaya*. New Delhi: Oxford University Press.

Gupta, Akhil and James Ferguson. 1997. "Beyond culture: space, identity and the politics of difference." In Akhil Gupta and James Ferguson (eds), *Culture, Power, Place: Exploration in Critical Anthropology*. Durham, NC: Duke University Press.

Hajer, Maarten. 1995. *The Politics of Environmental Discourse: Ecological Modernization and the Policy Process*. Oxford: Clarendon.

Haraway, Donna. 1991. "Situated knowledges: the science question in feminism and the privilege of partial perspective." In *Simians, Cyborgs, and Women: The Reinvention of Nature*. New York: Routledge.

Hardin, Garrett. 1968. "The tragedy of the commons." *Science*, 162: 1243–8.

Hart, Gillian. 1997. "From rotten wives to good mothers: household models and the limits of economism." *IDS Bulletin*, 28: 14–25.

Henrich, Joseph, Robert Boyd, Samuel Bowles, Colin Camerer, Ernst Fehr, and Herbert Gintis (eds). 2004. *Foundations of Human Sociality*. Oxford: Oxford University Press.

Hogrewe, William, Steven Joyce, and Eduardo Perez. 1993. "The unique challenges of improving peri-urban sanitation." WASH Technical Report 86. Washington: US Agency for International Development.

Jasanoff, Sheila. 2002. "Reading between the lines: the disciplines and the environment." In S. Lélé, G. Kadekodi, and B. Agrawal (eds), *Interdisciplinarity in Environmental Research: Concepts, Barriers and Possibilities*. New Delhi: Indian Society for Ecological Economics.

Kanbur, Ravi. 2002. "Economics, social science and development." *World Development*, 30: 477–86.

Kanbur, Ravi and Paul Shaffer. 2005. "Epistemology, normative theory and poverty analysis," Q-Squared Working Paper 2 (www.q-squared.ca).

King, Gary, Robert Keohane, and Sidney Verba. 1994. *Designing Social Inquiry: Scientific Inference in Qualitative Research*. Princeton: Princeton University Press.

Klamer, Arjo. 1988. *Conversations with Economists*. Totowa: Rowman and Allanheld.

Klamer, Arjo. 2004. "Cultural goods are good for more than their economic value." In Rao and Walton (eds): 138–62.

Krugman, Paul. 1995. *Development, Geography and Economic Theory*. Cambridge, MA: MIT Press.

Leach, Melissa and Robin Mearns (eds). 1996. *The Lie of the Land: Challenging Received Wisdom on the African Environment*. Oxford: James Currey.

Li, Tania M. 1996. "Images of community: discourse and strategy in property relations." *Development and Change*, 27: 501–27.

Li, Tania M. 2002. "Engaging simplifications: community-based resource management, market processes and state agendas in upland Southeast Asia." *World Development*, 30: 265–83.

Lipton, Michael. 1992. "Economics and anthropology: grounding models in relationships." *World Development*, 20: 1541–6.

Little, Daniel. 1991. *Varieties of Social Explanation: An Introduction to the Philosophy of Social Science*. Boulder: Westview Press.

Lukes, Steven. 1974. *Power: A Radical View*. London: Macmillan.

Marx, Karl. 1981 [1852]. *The Eighteenth Brumaire of Louis Bonaparte*. New York: International Publishers.

McCay, Bonnie J. and James M. Acheson (eds). 1987. *The Question of the Commons: The Culture and Ecology of Communal Resources*. Tucson: University of Arizona Press.

Mohan, Giles and Kristian Stokke. 2000. "Participatory development and empowerment: the dangers of localism." *Third World Quarterly*, 21: 247–68.

Mosse, David. 1997. "The symbolic making of a common property resource: history, ecology and locality in a tank-irrigated landscape in South India." *Development and Change*, 28: 467–504.

Olson, Mancur. 1965. *The Logic of Collective Action*. Cambridge: Harvard University Press.

Ostrom, Elinor. 1990. *Governing the Commons: The Evolution of Institutions for Collective Action*. Cambridge: Cambridge University Press.

Ostrom, Elinor and Roy Gardner. 1993. "Coping with asymmetries in the commons: self-governing irrigation systems can work." *Journal of Economic Perspectives*, 7: 93–112.

Ostrom, Elinor, Roy Gardner, and James Walker. 1994. *Rules, Games and Common-pool Resources*. Ann Arbor: University of Michigan Press.

Peet, Richard and Michael Watts. 1996. *Liberation Ecologies: Environment, Development, Social Movements*. New York: Routledge.

Peluso, Nancy. 1992. *Rich Forests, Poor People: Resource Control and Resistance in Java*. Berkeley: University of California Press.

Polanyi, Karl. 1954. *The Great Transformation*. Boston: Beacon.

Rabin, Matthew. 1993. "Incorporating fairness into game theory and economics." *American Economic Review*, 83: 1281–1302.

Ragin, Charles. 1987. *The Comparative Method: Moving beyond Qualitative and Quantitative Strategies*. Berkeley: University of California Press.

Rao, Vijayendra. 2002. "Experiments in participatory econometrics." *Economic and Political Weekly*, May 18.

Rao, Vijayendra and Michael Walton (eds). 2004. *Culture and Public Action*. Stanford: Stanford Social Sciences.

Ray, Isha and Jeffrey Williams. 2002. "Locational asymmetry and the potential for cooperation on a canal." *Journal of Development Economics*, 67: 129–55.

Schelling, Thomas. 1978. *Micromotives and Macrobehavior*. New York: Norton.

Scheper-Hughes, Nancy. 1995. "The primacy of the ethical: propositions for a militant anthropology." *Current Anthropology*, 36: 409–20.

Scott, James. 1976. *The Moral Economy of the Peasant*. New Haven: Yale University Press.

Seabright, Paul. 1993. "Managing local commons: theoretical issues in incentive design." *Journal of Economic Perspectives*, 7: 113–34.

Sen, Amartya. 2005. *The Argumentative Indian: Writings on Indian History, Culture and Interests*. New Delhi: Penguin Viking.

Sethi, Rajiv and E. Somanathan. 1996. "The evolution of social norms in common property use." *American Economic Review*, 86: 766–88.

Smith, Adam. 1776. *An Inquiry into the Nature and Causes of the Wealth of Nations*. London: printed for W. Strahan and T. Cadell.

Sugden, Robert. 1989. "Spontaneous order." *Journal of Economic Perspectives*, 3: 85–97.

Taylor, Michael. 1988. "Rationality and revolutionary collective action." In M. Taylor (ed.), *Rationality and Revolution*. Cambridge: Cambridge University Press.

Wade, Robert. 1988. *Village Republics*, Cambridge: Cambridge University Press.

Weissing, Fritz and Elinor Ostrom. 1991. "Irrigation institutions and the games irrigators play: rule enforcement without guards." In R. Selten (ed.), *Game Equilibrium Models II: Methods, Morals and Markets*. Berlin: Springer-Verlag.

Wright, Angus and Wendy Wolford. 2003. *To Inherit the Earth: The Landless Movement and the Struggle for a New Brazil*. Oakland: Food First Books.

2: Managing the Commons

The Role of Social Norms and Beliefs

Jean-Philippe Platteau

During the last decades, social scientists, including economists, have devoted a lot of effort to the study of village commons. Such convergence of interests raises the fascinating issue of the potential complementarity that exists between various social sciences, particularly between economics, on the one hand, and sociology and anthropology, on the other hand. This chapter precisely aims at addressing the above issue by arguing that norms and beliefs are a privileged bridge that both sorts of disciplines can use to make their efforts complementary. As a matter of fact, the use of game theory to understand human interactions has led economists to view behavior as strategically determined and, therefore, to reckon the critical role of beliefs and expectations of individual actors. In so far as beliefs, values, and norms have always been a central preoccupation of sociologists, a clear domain emerges where economists and sociologists can usefully join hands. This is especially true in the field of management of common property resources (CPRs) where the ability of users to cooperate and to collective organize is critical.

The first section starts by elaborating on this point by drawing attention to two possible ways of envisaging cooperation in managing the commons. The first approach emphasizes strictly decentralized decisions by individual resource users and the role of reputation-based governance mechanisms. As for the second approach, it assumes that a collective authority exists to ensure proper regulation of the use of the commons. The critical role of beliefs and expectations is brought to light for both approaches.

The next section describes two cases where the wrong kind of expectations and beliefs prevented resource users from achieving efficiency in the commons. The contexts of the two examples differ in the sense that decentralized governance mechanisms are dominant in the first study area, that of Teelin Bay (Ireland), while regulatory mechanisms prevail in the second study area, that of Kayar (Senegal). In both cases, the antecedents of these beliefs could be traced back in a rather precise manner. The existence of counterfactuals for which cooperation could be established provide convenient reference points from which to assess the impact of norms and beliefs, as well as the path-dependent manner in which they came to prevail.

By contrast, attention is then drawn to Japan, where management of village commons has generally been quite successful. Here, beliefs and expectations have prevailed that are conducive to cooperation in the commons. Two contrasted explanations of the Japanese success are highlighted. The first explanation emphasizes the crucial role of inborn norms and values, while the second one stresses the need to view such norms and values as largely circumstantial, in the sense of beliefs historically produced by particular events. Note that the empirical material used for the earlier discussions is extracted both from studies in which the author has been personally involved and from researches conducted by several social scientists. The chapter has a concluding section.

The Role of Beliefs and Expectations: Lessons from Economic Theory

The reference case of open-access, decentralized anarchy: the Tragedy of the Commons

Let us consider a standard "tragedy of the commons." We know from economic theory that in a situation of open access resource users harvest the resource inefficiently, implying that the rate of harvesting of the resource flows exceeds the level that maximizes the social surplus. In fact, the rent attached to the resource is entirely dissipated at the open access equilibrium. In a situation of unregulated common property – in which membership is fixed yet no rules prevail to govern the use of the commons – the rent is partially dissipated. And if membership rules exist but the number of rightsholders is very large, the equilibrium level of harvesting under the unregulated common property becomes similar to that achieved at the open access equilibrium: rent is reduced to zero. In such a setting, the choice of each user regarding his or her own level of extraction of the resource flows depends on the level chosen by the other users, thereby determining a framework of strategic interactions among the users.

To illustrate the main result of the tragedy of the commons, a simpler, two-agent game format is often employed. The game used is the familiar prisoner's dilemma whose pay-offs can be represented by the matrix (table 2.1).

In a one-period framework, there are two actions available to the two players: cooperate (denoted by C) and non-cooperate or free ride on the effort of the other player (denoted by NC). Cooperation here means that an agent agrees to limit his or her extraction level so as to allow a socially efficient use of the resource (ideally, each agent sticks to a level equal to half the efficient level). Non-cooperation therefore means that the limiting level is somehow exceeded. The payoffs associated with the (NC, NC) outcome are $d > 0$ for each player, and d is smaller than the payoff accruing to each player when they both cooperate, that is, c. Yet, d is larger than the payoff earned by the player (the "sucker"

Table 2.1   The tragedy of the commons

		Agent 2	
		C	NC
Agent 1	C	c, c	s, v
	NC	v, s	d, d

or exploited player) who restricts himself or herself while the other player free rides, that is, payoff s. Finally, the payoff obtained in the opposite situation of a player exploiting the other user, called v, is greater than c, and, a fortiori, than d and s. We therefore have the following ordering of the payoff values: $v > c > d > s$.

With such a payoff structure, there is a unique, so-called Nash equilibrium, and this is the socially dominated (NC, NC) outcome. In other words, interacting in a completely decentralized manner leads the resource users into the trap of the inefficient situation. In fact, they are themselves responsible for the emergence of this regrettable outcome. Two motives actually drive them to choose the wrong action. First, there is the fear of being exploited by the other user that drives them to protect themselves so as to avoid the worst payoff, s, by playing NC. Second, there is the lust for maximum profit that induces a player to free ride on the other's effort whenever that action can yield greater benefits than going along with him or her. To sum up, each player has a dominant strategy (unlike what obtains under a more accurate description of the commons' problem), which is always to play NC, and this is what drives the socially inferior outcome to be established.

Decentralized mechanisms of CPR governance: the role of reputation

How can resource users be deterred from choosing the wrong action, so that they can contribute to making the efficient equilibrium emerge? Two solutions are available. The first solution is suggested by a fundamental result of repeated game theory: if, instead of being played once, the above game could be played for an infinitely long period, or for an indeterminate period of time, cooperation could be achieved by the threat of future non-cooperation (Abreu 1988). In other words, resource users can be disciplined into limiting their extraction efforts if acting otherwise would spark off punishment in the form of some form of social ostracism at the hands of the other players. Such a solution obviously embodies a reputation mechanism that is carried out within the community of resource users, and whereby people refuse to cooperate with known free riders (Kandori 1992).

How can such a decentralized ostracization mechanism be set to work in a community of resource users? One apparent method is that of "linked games," which are grounded in the "embedded" nature of many village societies (Aoki 2001: ch. 2). In this setting, two games are being simultaneously played, an economic game of resource use and a social exchange game. It is assumed that players cannot be easily excluded from access to the village-level resource, say, because it is difficult to see how, acting in a purely decentralized manner, users could displace someone among them. As a result, free riding in the former game can only be punished in the latter game. In the social exchange game of the community, which is played repeatedly, each family can contribute to the production of social goods with some costs, and enjoy the benefit from the consumption of social goods (e.g., regular invitations to social events). At the beginning of each stage game, any family can be excluded from participating in the production and consumption of social goods by other families, if it has not cooperated in the economic game of resource use. It is assumed that there exists a saturation point in the productivity of social goods, otherwise the community would incur some loss by ostracizing a member.

In these conditions, it can then be shown that the threat of the conditional social ostracism is credible and cooperation among a minimum number of families in the linked (economic) game can become an equilibrium outcome even if there is a strong incentive for free riding in the stand-alone economic game. That happens if the benefit from free riding in the latter game is smaller than the present-value sum of the sacrifice of future benefits arising from ostracism. To sum up, strategies that are not an equilibrium (and are not self-enforceable) in an isolated (economic) domain can become profitable strategies for agents, when that domain is "embedded" in a community social exchange domain.

Note carefully that, to be an effective mechanism of punishment of deviance in the economic game, participation in the social exchange game needs not involve tangible benefits. Thus, the social good produced and consumed in the social exchange game can be thought of as social consideration or prestige, while exclusion from that game means incurring public humiliation and opprobrium. For example, based on observations among the *Mossi*, the dominant ethnic group in Burkina Faso, Jean Badini writes:

> Activated by social rebuke and the accompanying public humiliation, the feeling of shame appears as the most formidable weapon in the service of the traditional *Moose* pedagogy (the *moaga*). Above the individuals, indeed, this feeling asserts the supremacy of social judgment and constitutes a powerful regulating mechanism to which everybody submits . . . Since a person can exist only through collective opinion, it is collective opinion that rates people and rare are those who are willing to incur the risk to defy it. The point is that its verdict is merciless and without appeal. (Badini, 1994: 146–7, my translation; see also Foster 1965: 303–5; Ndiaye 1998: 183)

Likewise, water-access rules in the lagoon fishery of Bahia, Brazil, are essentially enforced through a decentralized mechanism based on an ethical code of honor and social respect. In the words of John Cordell and Margaret McKean (1986):

> It is impossible to fish for long in a given community without receiving and showing *respeito*. People honor each other's claims because of *respeito*, which is created, bestowed, and reaffirmed through sometimes trivial and sometimes substantial acts of benevolence bordering on self-sacrifice . . . Failure to cooperate in these practices can be much more devastating for a fisherman than would be breaking a government law. *Respeito* is a cognitive reference point to the community conscience. It influences how fishermen evaluate each other's actions on and off the fishing grounds. It is a yardstick for measuring the justice of individual acts, especially in conflicts. Collective social pressure to conform to the ethics of fishing is reflected in the *ôlho do povo* (watchfulness of the community's eye, or sense of justice), reminiscent of the forceful moral and ethical standard in Palauan fishing, "words of the lagoon." Reputations rise and fall in terms of the *ôlho do povo*. The *ôlho do povo* determines whether territorial competition in fishing is deliberate or accidental, and whether it is antagonistic enough to require counteraction. (Cordell and McKean 1986: 94, 98)

It is important to emphasize that the availability of a good social communications network is not a sufficient condition to achieve a stigmatization equilibrium. Also needed are shared and self-sustaining beliefs about the punishment that is meted out by a community of people connected through the information network whenever the standard of conduct is violated, in this case social estrangement or exclusion of free riders. Masao Aoki (2001: 49) calls a "community norm" such a standard of cooperative behavior that is supported by the shared beliefs of collective punishment of shirking (see also Basu 2000: 87–88; Greif 1994; 2002).

By its very definition, a social norm is thus a self-supported belief among many other possible ones. This consequence is to be related to a major result of repeated game theory known as the "folk theorem": when a game, such as the prisoner's dilemma, is repeated infinitely, there actually exist "a profusion of equilibria," and the socially efficient outcome is one of them. For the latter, cooperative equilibrium to be established, the right kind of self-supported beliefs about expected punishment must have come to prevail. In the words of Kreps, "a good way to interpret the folk theorem, when the players can engage in explicit pre-play negotiation, is that it shows how repetition can greatly expand the set of self-enforcing agreements to which the players might come" (Kreps 1990: 512). In particular, by allowing individuals to reveal and signal their intended plans of action and to learn about each others' intentions, human interactions in small-scale settings may help them converge on the cooperative equilibrium (Baland and Platteau 1996: 77).

Regulatory mechanisms of CPR governance: the role of local authorities and procedures

In the absence of cooperation-supporting beliefs – such as a commonly shared culture of social opprobrium and shaming – or, more realistically, whenever the governance mechanisms resulting from such beliefs work only imperfectly, an external enforcement mechanism is needed to ensure that rules of good conduct are properly followed. An enforcement mechanism of this sort typically involves the establishment of a village-level authority structure that is put in charge of laying down rules, as well as monitor and sanction violations by resource users.

Thus, in the aforementioned instance of Bahia's fishery, reputation effects (enhancement or loss of reputation) are not always sufficient to grind rule-breaking to a halt. When they are not, external sanctions are resorted to that involve more directly coercive measures (such as when an entire network of captains decides to deny territorial use rights to a troublemaker by sabotaging his equipment, boobytrapping net-casting spaces, engaging in deliberate net crossing, etc.) aimed at forcing renegade fishermen to mend their ways or leave the community (Cordell and McKean 1986: 98). Moreover, when serious rifts occur between different families or factions within the same community, certain individuals (usually retired fishing captains) are called upon to serve both as mediators and as "role models" since they "epitomize *respeito* in all they do." The conflict-resolution mechanism works in the following way:

> Mediators must be able to comprehend and soothe social relationships that have fluctuated and festered over a long period of time . . . To promote reconciliation, the mediator must invoke respeito, the cooperative ethic, as it is reflected in the *ôlho do povo*, and bring it to bear on individual consciences. Thus, the way out of a dispute is not to fix blame and then to punish the wrongdoer, but to negotiate reunion (by appealing to the sense of justice) and to restore equality. A simple face-saving gesture by either one of the parties will suffice for openers. This involves humbling oneself and showing that one no longer wishes to carry a grudge. If successful, this strategy will lead to an exchange of favors or kindness . . . Through an exchange of just such small favors and concessions, fishermen are frequently able to come to terms, reestablish *respeito*, renew cooperative relations, and reaffirm the value of honor and deference in avoiding water space challenges. (Cordell and McKean 1986: 99–100)

It bears emphasis that beliefs and expectations are also important when the use of local CPRs is governed by regulatory bodies and external sanction procedures rather than by

Table 2.2   Overcoming the tragedy of the commons through an external enforcement mechanism: the case of multiple equilibria

		Agent 2	
		C	NC
Agent 1	C	c, c	$s, v - F$
	NC	$v - F, s$	d, d

informal reputation-based mechanisms. Indeed, an authority structure can be effective only if it has earned a high enough degree of legitimacy in the eyes of the villagers. It is legitimate when the resource users have enough confidence that the rules are fair and impartially enforced. To see the implications of this point more clearly, we proceed in two steps. In the initial step, it is assumed that the regulatory body instituted by the resource users performs the three following duties. First, it decides the (maximum) amount of extracting effort that everyone is allowed to undertake, and this is done with a view to achieving efficient use of the resource. Second, it inspects the behavior of all the users so as to detect possible violations of the quota rule. And, finally, it threatens to impose a fine that is large enough to deter users from breaking the quota rule. Denoting the amount of the fine chosen by F, the latter condition implies that $F > v - c$, where the right-hand side term indicates the gain from free riding on the other player's cooperative behavior.

To complete the description of the new game thus obtained, it is assumed that the authority punishes every violating user, but only as long as some users follow the quotas. In other words, it ceases to operate if everyone fails to cooperate. The game that obtains has the structure of a coordination game and its two-agent version is presented in table 2.2. There are two Nash equilibria in this new game, (C, C) and (NC, NC), with the former one Pareto-dominating the latter. Whether the Pareto-efficient equilibrium is chosen or not depends on the expectations of the players. It is only if a player is confident enough that the other player will cooperate that he or she will feel inclined to also cooperate. Otherwise, a player prefers to cause the collective regulation to unravel for fear of being exploited by the other player.

Algebraically, if we denote by p the belief of a player that the other player will cooperate (it is a probability comprised between zero and one), and by $(1 - p)$ the opposite belief that the other player will defect or free ride, it is easy to show that a player will decide to follow the rule if:[1]

$$p > p^* = \frac{d - s}{(c + d) - (v + s) + F},\tag{2.1}$$

where both the numerator and the denominator of the RHS of the inequality (2.1) are positive by assumption. Indeed, $d > s$, and the denominator can be rewritten as $(c - v + F) + (d - s)$, where the positive sign of $(c - v + F)$ follows from our assumption that $F > v - c$.

---

[1]   Indeed, a player will choose to cooperate if the expected payoff from cooperating exceeds that from free riding, that is, if: $pc + (1 - p)s > p(v - F) + (1 - p)d$, which implies that: $p(c - s - v + d + F) > (d - s)$.

Moreover, it is now evident that the RHS of (2.1) is also smaller than one. Simple exercises in comparative static allows us to show that, as expected, the probability p decreases in F, c, and s, while it increases in v and d.[2] The implication is that the greater the amount of the fine, or the greater the benefit from universal cooperation or, else, the greater the payoff obtained in following the rule in the presence of defection by the other player, s, the smaller the probability p needs to be to induce the player to follow the rule. On the contrary, the belief that the other will cooperate needs to be stronger if the benefit from free riding on the other's cooperative effort, or the benefit from universal free riding, is larger.

The existence of two equilibria in the above game arises because the penalty for opportunistic breach stops being imposed once the breach is generalized. This is a natural assumption to make if members of the regulatory body (the so-called rule enforcers) are themselves users of the resource, possibly rotated from one period to another. As a matter of fact, they then participate in another choice situation in which they have to decide whether to impose the fine or not. By sanctioning a breach of the quota, they derive a material benefit, since they contribute to marginally reduce the amount of the externality imposed by the violator upon the other resource users, including themselves. In addition, they receive a psychic reward if they attach value to the righteous fulfillment of their moral duty as rule enforcers. If these benefits exceed the cost that punishment entails for the rule enforcer, the latter will always choose to carry out the punishment threat and impose the fine F whenever a breach is detected.[3] In the event of generalized violations, however, the cost of punishing violators may be so high, and/or the perceived benefit so low, that sanctioning is no more profitable for rule enforcers. Even moral considerations may stop coming into play if everybody cheats or free rides.

If it is alternatively assumed that rule enforcers are unflinchingly clinging to their duty (the psychic reward is very large), whatever the circumstances – say because they belong to the traditional elite and conceive their role of rule enforcers as constitutive of their leadership status – the payoff structure of the game is transformed in such a way that the Pareto-superior outcome becomes a unique equilibrium rather than a mere possibility (see table 2.3). For this to happen, the amount of the fine must exceed the benefit from violating the quota when the other player does it. Formally, $F > d - s$. Combining with the first condition, we have that $F > Max \{v - c, d - s\}$. When the fine is thus appropriately fixed, the role of expectations and beliefs vanishes, since the players have a dominant strategy, which is to obey the rule laid down by the village authority.

The crucial assumption allowing for the optimistic result obtained in table 2.3 is the existence of an impartial third party enforcement mechanism. If the regulatory body is biased and resource users know it, the result may just be reversed: there exists a unique equilibrium which corresponds to the socially inferior outcome. One way to see this is as follows (see Platteau and Strzalecki 2004). The user group is decomposed into two

---

[2] While the results are straightforward for c, v, and F, they obtain for d and s because of our assumption that $(c - v + F) > O$. Indeed, $sign[\delta p/\delta d] = sign[c - v + F]$, while $sign[\delta p/\delta s] = sign[-(c - v + F)]$.

[3] There are several additional assumptions involved in the simplified case discussed here. Thus, the proceeds from the collection of the fines accrue to the community of resource users, and not to the members of the regulatory body. Moreover, enforcing good behavior on the part of the latter is costless. In other words, we assume away possible rule violations by rule enforcers.

Table 2.3   Overcoming the tragedy of the commons through an external enforcement mechanism: the case of a unique equilibrium

		Agent 2	
		C	NC
Agent 1	C	c, c	$s, v - F$
	NC	$v - F, s$	$d - F, d - F$

subgroups characterized by different identities – for example, because they belong to two different ethnic entities – and the regulatory body is dominated by one of these two groups, say group A. Members of this body are susceptible to external pressure on the part of resource users from their own group.

More precisely, a user from group A caught violating the rule can more easily persuade the authority to condone his or her failing than a user from group B could. Indeed, if those who dominate the authority have strong identity affiliations, they will incur a psychic cost, when punishing a fellow villager. If this cost, henceforth called identity cost, is large enough, the authority becomes biased and stops penalizing members from group A, punishing only those of group B who cannot influence the rule enforcers.

Therefore, if feelings of group identity dominate benefits from sanctioning rule violations, including the sense of duty, so that leniency is shown to users belonging to a particular group, the game that obtains is no more the coordination game with two equilibria described in table 2.2, but the one-sided prisoner's dilemma depicted in table 2.4. In this game, members of group B are required to pay the fine F if caught exceeding their quota, while members of group A stand unpunished and can therefore keep their "exploitative" payoff v, if caught in the same situation. In such a setting, generalized free riding is unavoidable: the non-cooperative outcome is the only Nash equilibrium. Knowing that they will not be punished in the event of rule violations, users from group A break the rule and, knowing that much, users from group B also choose to exceed their quotas lest they should be exploited by members of the favored group.

If we assume that the fine F is imposed on users of group B in all circumstances, including in situations of generalized free riding, that is, if the regulatory authority does not collapse in such extreme conditions, we obtain the game presented in table 2.5. In that game, there is again a unique Nash equilibrium, but it is not the same as that obtained in table 2.4: here, users from group B follow the rule (so as to avoid paying the fine), whereas those from group A systematically break it. Because situations of this kind are probably

Table 2.4   Failing to overcome the tragedy of the commons due to a biased enforcement mechanism

		Group B	
		C	NC
Group A	C	c, c	$s, v - F$
	NC	v, s	d, d

Table 2.5   Failing to overcome the tragedy of
the commons due to a biased enforcement
mechanism

		Group B	
		C	NC
Group A	C	c, c	$s, v - F$
	NC	v, s	$d, d - F$

not sustainable, the assumptions in which the game presented in table 2.5 is grounded do
not seem to be very realistic.

Let us embark upon the final step of our analytical journey by relaxing the simplified
assumptions made above regarding the informational structure of the games considered.
We assume now that members of the favored group, group A, know the magnitude of
the identity cost faced by the officers in charge of the regulatory authority, while members of the discriminated group, group B, ignore it. As a result, the latter only have a subjective assessment of the cost for a rule enforcer to sanction a fellow user from group A.

In fact, knowledge about the level of identity cost within the village authority is equivalent to knowledge as to whether the game that is being played is the one presented in
table 2.2 or the one presented in table 2.4. To capture this idea formally, let $\{Hi, Lo\}$ be
the type space of users from group A, where Hi corresponds to the case of a high identity cost (sufficiently large to exceed the benefit from sanctioning a fellow resource user
from group A), and Lo corresponds to the case of a low identity cost (sufficiently low
not to exceed that benefit). Our hypothesis states that users from the favored group know
their type with certainty, but users from the discriminated group attach probability π to
Lo and $1 - \pi$ to Hi.

We will show that there are two possible Bayesian Nash equilibria of this game. First,
if the strategy of users from group B is to break the rules (play NC), then the best response
of users from group A is also to break the rules, regardless of their type. For users from
group B to play NC is a best response to this (pooling) strategy of users from group A,
so that the two strategies constitute a Bayesian Nash equilibrium, which is clearly non-
cooperative. Second, if the strategy of users from group B is to follow the rules (play C),
the best response of those from group A is to play C if they are Lo and to play NC if
they are Hi. Playing C is the best response of users from group B to this (separating)
strategy if and only if it yields a higher expected payoff than playing NC, that is when:

$$\pi > \pi^* = \frac{d - s}{(c + d) - (v + s) + F} \tag{2.2}$$

Hence these two strategies form a Bayesian Nash equilibrium only if members of the
discriminated group are optimistic enough to believe that the authority will be not biased
$(\pi > \pi^*)$. This situation corresponds to the cooperative equilibrium of the game considered. Note that the expression in (2.2) is identical to the expression in (2.1), and it can
be interpreted in the same manner. For example, the larger the amount of the fine, the
lower should be the expectation of group B members that rule enforcers are impartial to
induce them to follow the rule rather than break it.

Collective Action Failure in the Commons: Two Examples

To illustrate the potentially crucial role of beliefs and expectations in driving or avoiding inefficient use of village commons, two different examples are described below. The empirical material in these two examples is especially interesting because it contains a sort of counterfactual that can be used to guide the interpretation of the failures observed. Expectations and beliefs of resource users follow a dichotomized pattern, according to location in the first story, and to community group in the second one. Whereas in the first story the community of resource users is homogeneous, it is heterogeneous in the second story in the sense defined in the latter part of the preceding section. It is purely coincidental that, in the two cases, the CPR at stake is a fishery.

Location-specific expectations: the case of Teelin Bay, Ireland

The following account is based on a research conducted by Lawrence Taylor (1987) in Teelin Bay (Ireland), where the estuarine salmon fishermen use a rotation system of access to the most valuable fishing spots.[4] Apparently, only exceptional and slight violations of the underlying code of conduct are observed. The fact of the matter is that, according to Taylor, abidance of the rules of the salmon rotation system within the restricted space of the local community "is perceived as merely the 'natural' expression of local behavior" and rests "only on the egalitarian ethos of communal reciprocity, which is, in turn, understood as natural" (Taylor 1987: 299, 302). Few would or did try to violate these rules and, when a violation takes place, it is striking that collective punishment does not seem to be resorted to. The reason is that the opprobrium of informal social control follows any act of deviance, under the form of "an enormous amount of pointed whispering gossip in pub and household," and this is apparently sufficient to deter deviants from cheating again. The egalitarian ethos of the community is thus preserved since no one "is perceived as having the authority to directly reprimand or punish the offender" (pp. 299, 303).

Here is, therefore, an ideal context where cooperation appears so "natural" to the local fishermen that no formal sanction system exists to enforce it: norms of cooperative behavior are well established and reputation effects are quite sufficient to deter free riding. One would thus have expected that, when a priest came to the village in 1973 to convince its inhabitants to extend cooperation to the whole Glen River, he would have met with a positive response. In actual fact, things turned out quite differently: not only was the opposite reaction observed but Teeliners even displayed an attitude of resolute resistance to the priest's project!

A plausible reason for this resistance is the fact that the realization of the project required the collective purchase by the community of the fishing rights currently owned by a non-profit organization based in Dublin (known as Gael-Linn). Yet, Taylor dismisses such an explanation on various grounds that are not worth reviewing here. Much more interesting is his case that the main reason for the fishermen's paradoxical unwillingness to extend their cooperative habits in a new portion of the Glen River is their lack of a tradition of cooperation in this part of their customary fishing grounds.

---

[4]   A summary account of this research has also been presented in Baland and Platteau (1996: ch. 12).

More precisely, riverine salmon fisheries have long been a privately or institutionally owned and managed resource. In post-medieval times, landlords claimed such fisheries as adjoined their estates and they did not open them to the peasantry: "locals might be employed to tend the landlord's weir or crew his net-boats, but unauthorized fishing was theft" (Taylor 1987: 295). From this time onwards, there developed a tradition of poaching: "there were even a few individuals who would venture out at night and stretch a net across the entire width of the narrowest part of the river" (p. 295). Over time, these poaching practices came to be regarded by local fishermen as a sort of sport run at the expense of the landlord vis-a-vis whom latent hostile feelings were thereby manifested. When the government took over the ownership of the concerned portion of the river, the local cultural significance of poaching as an expression of hostility and opposition to outside authority persisted. In Taylor's words:

> Poaching, however, was also a valued tradition. Just as the landlord's role was to police his holdings, the tenant's role was to poach. Old men spoke with undisguised relish about the good old days, when close watch over the waters made poaching a true challenge. Otherwise law-abiding men would wink and smile at their own reminiscences of successful expeditions and even of capture and confinement. Today, small fines and the lack of effective enforcement seem to have made poaching a somewhat less challenging sport, but sport it remains. Evidently the fact that the landlords are gone and the Irish government or Gael-Linn's bailiffs are now the regulators makes little difference in the local perception of the "sides"; it is still locals versus outside authorities. (Taylor 1987: 300)

Given the above culturally rooted perception, Teelin fishermen have no trust in one another's readiness to put an end to poaching practices. "The problem, as they see it, is that poaching, as long as it does not violate local rights of access as defined in the rotation system, is a 'natural' local characteristic. No one could imagine giving it up" (Taylor 1987: 300–1).

Taylor's story of Teelin fishermen is instructive because it shows how tradition or historical precedents can shape expectations and beliefs and, thereby, determine the environment in which human interactions in a commons take place. In a portion of the water space which has long been open to locals, a long tradition of cooperation regarding access to fishing sites has imparted a kind of "naturalness" to the cooperative behavior displayed by the fishermen. In this portion, optimistic expectations regarding others' behavior are entertained and confirmed over time by successful experiences. On the contrary, where there has been a long tradition of inveterate poaching for historical reasons, the minimum trust does not exist among the same fishermen to get a concerted action started. There, self-sustaining pessimistic expectations prevail that have the effect of preventing the emergence of a convention of cooperation by analogy with what obtains in the other resource domain of the community space.

Teelin fishermen willingly concede that it would be better if everyone would stop poaching in that water area. None the less, and revealingly, the only realistic way in which they consider feasible to establish cooperation consists of involving an external authority able to impose punishment on poachers in an unyielding manner. Perhaps the most interesting lesson from the story told by Taylor is thus that, precisely because they are self-sustained (they constitute norms), beliefs and expectations are not easily reversed or changed. In terms of economic theory, it is hard to shift from one Nash equilibrium to another in a game where there are multiple equilibria.

Moreover, the establishment of a local authority generated by the resource users themselves and endowed with the power to punish rule violations does not appear to be an easy approach either. Indeed, expectations continue to exert their influence and, if the authority is formed by the users, it may be reticent to sanction poaching in everyday practice. Users would not expect the authority to enforce the rule and that latter would confirm their beliefs by showing leniency in actual cases of rule breaking. In such circumstances, resorting to an external enforcement mechanism to initiate a new convention based on newly formed expectations and beliefs appears as the only realistic solution.

Community-specific expectations: the case of Kayar, Senegal

Basic facts

Fishermen operating from the port of Kayar, along the so-called Petite Côte in Senegal, all belong to the same ethnic group of Wolof-speaking people. However, they differ in an important way according to whether they are native fishermen who have been born in Kayar, or temporary migrant fishermen originating from the northern city of Saint-Louis. Migration results from the fact that the fishing zone of Saint-Louis (Guet Ndar) is not sheltered from the strong winds of the Atlantic Ocean and is therefore accessible only during a limited part of the year. The distinction between native and migrant fishermen would not have mattered and would not have undermined the local collective action potential had there not been a corresponding differentiation in the realm of technology that caused serious conflict between these two communities in the past. It is telling that, in another fishing location, Soumbedioune close to the capital city of Dakar, where the same two groups do coexist, and where such a conflict did not erupt for technology-related reasons, inter-community tensions do not prevail.

Whereas in the example of Teelin Bay decentralized behavior based on reputation effects provided us with a theoretical guide, games embedding a potentially biased authority in charge of enforcing rules on the local commons will serve as our theoretical reference point in the following discussion of a problematic collective action in Kayar. The story of this partial failure is told below in several steps and lessons from the standpoint of the role of beliefs and expectations are drawn in the course of the discussion. The empirical material used is taken from a more comprehensive study the results of which have been reported in Gaspart and Platteau (2002), Platteau and Gaspart (2007) and Platteau and Strzalecki (2004).

The original conflict opposed bottom-set net operators with fishermen using lines and purse seines. It has the form of a tragedy of the commons to the extent that the latter category of fishermen perceived the operation of bottom set nets in their waters as the cause of declining catches and increased gear accidents (due to entanglement of seines and lines with bottom set nets). Note that, while bottom-set nets are gill nets specially designed to catch fish on the bottom of the sea,[5] purse seines are nets characterized by the use of a purse line at the bottom of the net which allows the net to be closed like a purse and to thus retain the fish caught. The conflict was exacerbated by the fact that all the bottom-set net operators belong to the same social group of migrant fishermen from Saint-Louis.

---

[5]   Gill nets are a type of gear designed to gill, entangle, or enmesh the fish. They may be used to catch fish on the surface, in mid-water, or on the bottom. In the final case, they are called bottom-set nets.

The reverse is not true since there are members of both groups among line and purse seine fishermen. In addition, bottom-set net operators happen to be completely specialized in the use of this gear, as a result of which their livelihood entirely depends on the incomes thus earned during the period of their migration in Kayar.

Further complicating the problem was the existence of two different conceptions of sea tenure between native and migrant fishermen. As a matter of fact, the latter have a long tradition of mobility along the West African coast and, as a consequence of deep-rooted migration habits, they tend to consider the sea as an open access resource that does not belong to any community in particular. People from Kayar have an almost opposite conception of sea tenure: "being originally an agricultural community with lands located not far from the sea, they are inclined to view the adjacent water space as their own territory, much in the same way as they see their agricultural lands" (Platteau and Strzalecki 2004).

In such a context, it is perhaps not surprising that tension rapidly built up between the two communities. The situation soon got out of control as acts of physical violence multiplied and several death casualties occurred in the course of the year 1985. Public authorities decided to intervene to prevent further damage and, in February 1986, the government of Senegal set up a special commission charged with the task of defining and monitoring an exclusive fishing zone, marked by buoys, in which bottom-set nets were prohibited from operating. Unfortunately, owing to imperfect monitoring of the contentious water area by the authorities, such measures did not prove sufficient to reduce conflicts significantly, as illegal encroachments upon the exclusive zone remained quite frequent. Furthermore, fishermen who consider that their rights have been infringed tend to punish the alleged culprits without informing the special commission created by the government (typically, bottom-set nets are seized and re-sold by resident fishermen without the intervention of the commission), thereby creating "a suspicious atmosphere where reference to justice easily conceals unavowable motives and obscure settlements of private accounts" (Gaspart and Platteau 2002: 81). Later efforts to correct the situation by local fishermen's leaders from the two communities did produce some results, but these remained below expectations.

The above conflict was all the more nasty as all migrant fishermen started to identify themselves with the cause of the bottom-set net operators, whether they actually operated that technique or not. A rift was thus created between the two communities that would not have happened if the inter-community differentiation was not paralleled by (partial) technological polarization. In the early 1990s, however, a special opportunity arose for mending that rift. Indeed, all fishermen of Kayar became involved in a collective struggle against a common enemy, namely the fish merchants. Such a struggle was motivated by the fishermen's determination to encroach upon the market power wielded by the fish merchants so as to raise producer prices for the fish landed on the beach.

After a series of events and experiments that are described elsewhere (Platteau and Gaspart forthcoming), fishermen decided to opt for effort-limiting schemes, first applied to purse seines in the form of effort quotas (1992), and later extended to line fishing canoes in the form of output quotas (1994). The price and quantity data available enabled us to show that there was a genuine potential for increasing producer prices through collective action – for a number of important species of fish, price elasticities with respect to output were significantly different from zero in the early 1990s (see Gaspart and Platteau 2002: 103) – yet did not allow us to measure the actual impact of the fishermen's cartel on producer

Table 2.6   Proportions of fishermen with a positive assessment of effort regulation, according to migrant/native status and to geographic location (%)

	Kayar	*Soumbedioune*
Native fishermen	80	76
Migrant fishermen from Saint-Louis	44	70

Source: Platteau and Strzalecki 2004

prices. However, a household survey specifically designed to elicit information about the way fishermen themselves assess the effects of effort regulation did produce some interesting results.

Two such results deserve to be emphasized in the context of the present chapter. To begin with, a significant proportion of fishermen believe that there is a high incidence of rule violations (Gaspart and Platteau 2002: 83–4). This proportion is much larger among line fishermen (56 percent) than among purse seine fishermen (25 percent), a predictable outcome given the fact that it is much easier to monitor fishing trips (in the case of purse seines) than to detect opportunistic breaches of output quotas (in the case of line canoes).

Second, when asked to express their opinions about the effectiveness of the schemes implemented in Kayar (that is, about whether catch limitations succeeded in causing producer prices to rise), fishermen turned out to differ in their assessment depending upon the group, native residents or migrants, to which they belong. More precisely, while as many as 80 percent of the native fishermen professed an optimistic belief regarding the usefulness of their collective efforts to limit landings, only 44 percent of the migrant fishermen from Saint-Louis did so. In addition, it is striking that such a pattern of dichotomized beliefs did not obtain for the other fishing location, Soumbedioune, where the proportion of optimistic fishermen does not significantly vary between the two groups and where it comes remarkably close to the one observed among the native fishermen of Kayar.[6] These findings are depicted in table 2.6.

The dichotomized pattern of expectations highlighted in table 2.6 for Kayar could just reflect a spurious relationship resulting from some exogenous characteristics of a group that bear upon the more or less optimistic opinions expressed by the members of that group. For instance, it could be the case that many migrant fishermen handle lines and are thus subject to quota limitations that are notoriously difficult to monitor (see supra), hence their rather negative assessment of collective endeavors to limit fishing effort. Such possibilities have, however, been duly checked by resorting to the econometric technique. What comes out is that, even allowing for a number of other possible influences, the migrant fishermen of Kayar have a significantly more pessimistic assessment of the economic effects of effort regulation than the native fishermen. This central result proves to be quite robust

---

[6]   Note that, in Soumbedioune, no effort-limiting scheme has been attempted to this date, yet there is lingering discussion about the possibility of emulating the fishermen of Kayar. The proximity of the Dakar market and the interconnectedness between many close fishing ports are likely to make a cartel much more difficult to achieve, though.

to alternative specifications of the regression equation (see Platteau and Strzalecki 2004, for details).

Discussion

The above-reported findings support the view that something specific to Kayar must account for the pessimism of the migrant fishermen residing there during part of the year. Since the severe inter-community tensions that erupted in Kayar following the operation of bottom-set nets in disputed waters did not occur in Soumbedioune where such nets have never been in use, local history of conflict appears to have played a determining role in shaping subsequent expectations about collective initiatives. The implication of this interpretation is that the pessimistic beliefs which we recorded were already prevailing at the start of these schemes, and were not posterior beliefs that were updated in the course of the regulation experience itself.

There are two reasons why we think that these beliefs prevailed initially. First, perceptions of rule breaking do not differ between native and migrant fishermen of Kayar: about the same proportion of people in each category believe that rule violations are frequent. This means that the information used by both categories of fishermen for updating their initial beliefs is the same. If migrant fishermen updated their beliefs in a pessimistic direction as a result of their observing repeated violations of the quotas, native fishermen should have done the same, and they did not. Therefore, the fact that the posterior beliefs are more pessimistic for migrants than for native fishermen implies that their prior beliefs were also more pessimistic. Second, distrust on the part of the migrant fishermen is not confined to attempts to limit fishing effort, but also extends to other cases of cooperation with local fishermen (see Platteau and Strzalecki 2004, for more details and a more elaborate argument).

It can thus be concluded that pessimistic expectations of Kayar's migrant fishermen have been decisively shaped by the legacy of inter-community resentment born of a severe conflict affecting a subgroup of these fishermen (the bottom-set net operators). Identity or community feelings ensured that the victimization experienced by this subgroup spread throughout the entire population of migrant fishermen residing in the area. The migrants' pessimistic beliefs were reflected in serious doubts about the impartiality of the fishing committees in charge of enforcing the quota rules. Indeed, a frequent complaint heard from the migrant fishermen is their perception that these committees are dominated by native fishermen who tend to act in the interests of their own communal group. In terms of equation (2.2), their belief π is lower than the threshold value π^*, with the consequence that they prefer to break rules. In other words, given their historically rooted prejudices, they choose not to cooperate in order to preempt the expected behavior of the native fishermen.[7]

---

[7]   The question could be asked as to why the Kayar's native fishermen continue to hold positive expectations in spite of frequent breaches of quota rules. A plausible explanation is that "their positive judgment has been made in the light of the immediate beneficial effect of collective organization, namely the ending of the most glaring collusive practices of the fish merchants acting as agents on behalf of export companies. If this is the correct interpretation, it is not effort regulation per se that produced benefits for the fishermen, but a collective struggle aimed at compelling fishmerchants to abandon their most blatant trade malpractices under the pressure of a showdown. Awareness of the low enforcement performances of the output-limiting schemes did not, then, really affect the assessment of the whole collective endeavor by native fishermen" (Platteau and Strzalecki 2004).

What we have learned from the above story is that, through the formation of pessimistic expectations, bad reminiscences of painful past events created a trauma that undermined cooperation in subsequent games. In such circumstances, it is essential that a proper external enforcement mechanism is devised and put into place so that the victimized party can be reassured about the expected behavior of the other agents. This is precisely the condition that was lacking in the case of Kayar, in spite of good intentions on the part of native fishermen and the local elite: by overestimating the merits of a voluntarist approach, the local elite underplayed the negative effect of past trauma and the consequent need for institutional arrangements able to reduce deep-rooted prejudices and create new, positive expectations.

Two Contrasted Views of the Japanese Success in Managing the Village Commons

In matters concerning the management of village CPRs, the case of Japan is especially instructive in the present context. Indeed, in this country all sorts of collective actions and regulatory endeavors have a long history which gets reflected in well-entrenched norms of cooperation and institutions, including "literally thousands of highly codified sets of regulations for the conservation of forests and the use of all commons" (McKean 1986: 549). Many authors have also stressed the remarkable continuity of traditional resource management practices in Japanese villages. In the words of Margaret McKean:

> the [Japanese] villagers themselves invented the regulations, enforced them, and meted out punishments, indicating that it is not necessary for regulation of the commons to be imposed coercively or from the outside. This, along with the fact that villagers could change their own rules through a process of consultation and consensus that was democratic in form if not always in fact, almost certainly increased the legitimacy of the regulations. Although the Tokugawa social order was very oppressive toward individuals whom it classified as "deviant," the village itself was largely self-regulating in this regard, and did not require intervention by an autocratic state to protect the commons. (McKean 1986: 571)

In the following, two contrasted views of the Japanese success story are presented: a "cultural" view according to which Japanese villages enjoy the benefit of cooperative habits ingrained in the national culture; and an "institutional" view that emphasizes the specific historical circumstances that caused the emergence of such habits and the accompanying expectations and beliefs.

A "cultural" explanation of Japanese success

A proponent of the first view is Ruddle (1987). He points out that values of harmony, and community or group orientation, had long been in existence in Japanese society, and were actually reinforced "during the long feudal era, when Confucian values [imported from China] and a national ideology put down deep roots in a Japan that was firmly closed to outside influences" (Ruddle 1987: 3; see also Ishikawa 1975: 464–6; Morishima 1982: ch. 1). Even after the second world war when traditional values based on the key notions of loyalty and self-sacrifice came under severe attack at the national level, collective unity for the attainment of group goals remained predominant at local levels, particularly at the level of village communities. Here, indeed, "the concept of harmony and conflict avoidance remain idealized norms," and the group or community continues to be "a constant source of emotional and other support": "Coupled with group orientation is the abhorrence of isolation and the extreme psychological trauma suffered by members pushed out of their group as a consequence of persistent anti-social behavior" (Ruddle 1987: 3–5).

Ruddle willingly admits that there has been a clear tendency to exaggerate the social harmony and collective unity virtues of Japanese society, especially among Japanese social scientists. Conflicts have always been present in the core of Japanese societal life, including village life. Nonetheless, it is fair to say that, compared to many other societies in the world, harmony and related qualities have been a major force in Japanese society at least up until very recent times (p. 4). Note that the above-sketched "cultural" view falls in line with Ruth Benedict's contrasting picture of Japanese and American cultures. Unlike the American people, the Japanese fear competition and the individuous comparisons that it entails. They are moved by a deep-rooted sense of honour and a desire to avoid anxiety and shame feelings. Such motives determine their predisposition toward cooperation (Benedict 1946: ch. 8).

The author's own research experience with Japan points up the danger involved in this sort of broad generalizations. In a study devoted to income-pooling practices in the Toyama Bay's fishery, Jean-Philippe Platteau and Erika Seki (2001; 2007) came to a much more nuanced conclusion when attempting to understand the reasons why the members of one fishery cooperative (in Shinminato) succeeded in pooling their incomes while members of the other one failed in the same effort. As a matter of fact, captains from both cooperatives repeatedly stressed the pervasive incidence of inter-individual comparisons of performances among them. Yet, while captains from the successful income-pooling boats tended to stress the positive effects for cooperation of intra-group competition for rank, those from the unsuccessful income-pooling boats had the opposite attitude of emphasizing the negative impact of such competition. In the words of the authors: "For the former, interindividual comparisons act as an incentive to work hard and manage assets cautiously while for the latter, on the contrary, such comparisons arouse anxiety, stress, and tensions that ultimately undermine effort, lower morale, and destroy trust" (Platteau and Seki 2001: 386).

The central lessons from Platteau and Seki's study are the following. First, in both cooperative associations fishermen's initial expectations with regard to the prospects of income-pooling were equally optimistic. As a result, both groups experimented with pooling. Second, initial heterogeneity in individual abilities and skills proved to be a decisive factor for the subsequent confirmation or undermining of the initial expectations, as well as for the strengthening or the erosion of cooperative practices. In the failing group, too wide a gap in initial performance differentials tended to discourage participants from pursuing the pooling experience whereas a reasonable gap in the successful group had the opposite effect of fostering mutual cooperation. Clearly, therefore, cooperation does not depend only on favorable initial predispositions toward it. To be sustainable, objective conditions must also make it profitable for all the participants involved.

It is true that pooling incomes is an extremely requiring form of cooperation and there are few instances in which it is actually observed across the whole world. The record of Japanese rural communities in terms of communal management of local-level resources remains quite impressive. This said, the conclusions of Platteau and Seki's study, as well as those from other studies pointing in the same direction (see, e.g., Hayami and Kikuchi 1981), suggest that a broad "cultural" explanation is surely too simple to account for Japan's impressive record. The alternative, "institutional" explanation presented below precisely avoids the pitfall of attaching too much weight to ingrained cultural factors.

An "institutional" explanation of Japanese success

According to this alternative view, a decisive event in Japanese history occurred around the middle of the sixteenth century when an advanced form of feudalism replaced the hereditary manorial system under Oda Nobunaga (Morishima 1982: 41–4). On that occasion, indeed, "the warriors had been removed from the countryside to the castle town in order to eliminate the danger to the lord of armed retainers directly in control of land and subjects" (Smith 1959: 202). In this way, an administrative and government system emerged which made possible "an extraordinary economy of force and officialdom" and was essentially based on the competence and reliability of local government. The only official between the village and the castle town was the district magistrate who usually had no military force at his command "except a handful of armed men for guard duty"; he was charged with governing thousands of peasant families on behalf of the lord, which implied collecting taxes, administering justice, maintaining public order, etc. In fact, these burdensome tasks were delegated to village communities because no alternative solution was available once the lord's armed retainers were requested to reside with him in the castle town. This forced such communities to become autonomous from the direct control of the samurai class, to assume new responsibilities and to settle almost all local affairs and problems on their own. In the words of T. C. Smith:

> Nowhere, for instance, did the lord undertake to levy taxes on individual peasants; rather, he laid taxes on villages as units, leaving each to allocate and collect its own, and to make up any deficit that might occur in the payments of individual families. This was but one of many administrative functions performed by villages in all parts of the country. Villages maintained their own roads and irrigation works, policed their territories, administered common land and irrigation rights; validated legal transactions among members, mediated disputes, and passed sentence and imposed punishment in petty criminal cases; enforced the lord's law and their own, stood responsible as a whole for a crime by any of their members, borrowed money, made contracts, sued and were sued. Aside from transmitting the lord's instructions to the villages, the magistrate normally did little more than help assess villages for taxes and receive their payments and hear the more serious civil and criminal cases they referred to him. (Smith 1959: 202–3)

A major effect of the removal of the samurai from the countryside just before the starting of the Tokugawa period was thus to grant an extraordinary measure of political autonomy to the village communities. In the same process, there emerged an egalitarian structure of the village. These circumstances forced but also enabled rural communities to self-organize with a view to solving pressing problems arising at the local level (such as the organization of irrigation, or the regulation of access to, and use of, village pastures and forests), as well as at the interface between this local level and the central political power (e.g., payment of taxes).

In particular, the construction, maintenance, and use of the local (gravity) irrigation system was entrusted to the autonomous control of the village community. Despite technological non-excludability of free riders, there was the credible threat of ostracizing the opportunistic family through the practice known as *mura hachibu*, literally meaning 80 percent separation from the village. Other village families could thus refuse to co-operate with a free rider by denying him mutual aid when necessary and excluding him from participation in social events such as ritualistic village parties and seasonal festivals. According to Masao Aoki (2001: 46), "this threat was effective in eliciting a high degree of cooperative effort" without the intervention of an external enforcement mechanism.

Such a situation is in stark contrast with the contemporaneous situation in the Korean Peninsula. There, indeed, the Yi Dynasty dispatched local administrators on a rotational basis to the lowest administrative units and made them responsible for tax collection. These administrators had themselves family backgrounds as wealthier landholders, and com-petition for the available official posts was extremely stiff in spite of the strict require-ments of the function (mandarinate examination). The social barrier between this class of landholding bureaucrats (known as the *yangban*) and other classes "made it rather dif-ficult for encompassing norms to spontaneously emerge and support the development of the local public goods as we observed in contemporaneous Japan. Their capacities to sanction others in a different social class are simply asymmetric . . . and the threat of ostracism could not serve as a disciplinary device" (Aoki 2001: 56). Interestingly, how-ever, around the *yangban* residential area, clusters of commoners gradually developed as satellites and, in each of these clusters, there evolved cooperative associations for vari-ous purposes, including rotating-and-saving associations, mutual aid and irrigation groups. In the 1930s, it was found that the most effective irrigation systems "evolved in the area where the traditional irrigation associations had been active since the late Yi Dynasty, whereas the irrigation associations founded according to the legal stipulations of the colonial government and including new Japanese landlords had only a limited success" (p. 57).

To sum up, even when badly needed, cooperation may fail to arise if the social and political structure at village level is not conducive to collective efforts. In particular, a very differentiated structure (such as prevailed in the seventeenth- and eighteenth-century Korean Peninsula) is likely to hinder the emergence of the sort of beliefs and norms that can best support effective governance mechanisms at local level.

Conclusion

Whether governance of the village commons is ensured through decentralized mechanisms, such as stigmatization or ostracism, or through external enforcement mechanisms involv-ing authority structures and regulatory procedures, effective cooperation can be established only if the appropriate beliefs and expectations have come to prevail. There is no reason to believe that such beliefs and expectations spontaneously arise when there is a need for collective efforts. Several case studies reviewed in this chapter have shown that collect-ive action may succeed or fail depending on the specific historical antecedents of the community concerned. It is actually through expectations that past historical events may influence cooperation prospects in a positive or a negative direction. Previous conflicts may persistently obstruct collective endeavor when they are kept lively in the collective memory through rituals and tales. On the other hand, if bad antecedents do not exist, collective action and the required cooperation-supporting beliefs may endogenously and gradually develop over time, but only provided that the prevailing social and political structure is not too differentiated.

When deep inequalities exist, it is true that local public goods can be produced under the strong leadership of the village elite using its authority to mobilize the labor of the subject classes. Inequality is even an advantage when considering the difficult problem of initiating collective action and setting up the appropriate regulatory bodies (Baland and Platteau 1998; 1999; 2001). Ample historical evidence, however, illustrates that more or less forced participation of small people in collective endeavors at village level may easily prompt them to run away from their community as soon as better opportunities arise in surrounding areas. In other words, "cooperative" equilibria based on power asymmetries are inherently unstable and, owing to that important weakness, they may be costly to maintain.

References

Abreu, D., 1988, "On the Theory of Infinitely Repeated Games with Discounting," *Econometrica*, vol. 56, no. 2, pp. 383–96.

Aoki, M., 2001, *Toward a Comparative Institutional Analysis*, Cambridge, MA, and London: MIT Press.

Badini, A., 1994, *Naître et grandir chez les Moosé traditionnels*, Paris and Ouagadougou: Sépia–ADDB.

Baland, J. M. and J. P. Platteau, 1996, *Halting Degradation of Natural Resources: Is There a Role for Rural Communities?*, Oxford: Clarendon Press.

Baland, J. M. and J. P. Platteau, 1998, "Wealth Inequality and Efficiency in the Commons. Part II: The Regulated Case," *Oxford Economic Papers*, vol. 50, no. 1, pp. 1–22.

Baland, J. M. and J. P. Platteau, 1999, "The Ambiguous Impact of Inequality on Local Resource Management," *World Development*, vol. 27, no. 5, pp. 773–88.

Baland, J. M. and J. P. Platteau, 2001, "Institutions and the Efficient Management of Environmental Resources," in G. Mähler and J. Vincent (eds), *Handbook of Environmental Economics*, Amsterdam: North-Holland, ch. 4, pp. 127–90.

Basu, K., 2000, *Prelude to Political Economy: A Study of the Social and Political Foundations of Economics*, Oxford: Oxford University Press.

Benedict, R., 1946, *The Chrysanthemum and the Sword: Patterns of Japanese Culture*, Boston: Houghton Mifflin.

Cordell, J. C. and M. A. McKean, 1986, "Sea Tenure in Bahia, Brazil," in National Research Council, *Proceedings of the Conference on Common Property Resource Management*, Washington, DC: National Academy Press, pp. 85–112.

Foster, G., 1965, "Peasant Society and the Image of Limited Good," *American Anthropologist*, vol. 67, pp. 293–314.

Gaspart, F. and J. P. Platteau, 2002, "Collective Action for Local-level Effort Regulation: An Assessment of Recent Experiences in Senegalese Small-scale Fisheries," in J. Heyer, F. Stewart, and R. Thorp (eds), *Group Behaviour and Development: Is the Market Destroying Cooperation?* Oxford: Oxford University Press, pp. 75–103.

Gaspart, F. and E. Seki, 2002, "Cooperation, Status Seeking and Competitive Behavior: Theory and Evidence," *Journal of Economic Behavior and Organization*, vol. 51, no. 1, pp. 51–77.

Greif, A., 1994, "Cultural Beliefs and the Organization of Society: A Historical and Theoretical Reflection on Collectivist and Individualist Societies," *Journal of Political Economy*, vol. 102, no. 5, pp. 912–50.

Greif, A., 2002, *Genoa and the Maghribi Traders: Historical and Comparative Institutional Analysis*, Cambridge: Cambridge University Press.

Hayami, Y. and M. Kikuchi, 1981, *Asian Village Economy at the Crossroads*, Tokyo: University of Tokyo Press and Baltimore: Johns Hopkins University Press.

Ishikawa, S., 1975, "Peasant Families and the Agrarian Community in the Process of Economic Development," in L. Reynolds (ed.), *Agriculture in Development Theory*, New Haven and London: Yale University Press, pp. 451–96.

Kandori, M., 1992, "Social Norms and Community Enforcement," *Review of Economic Studies*, vol. 59, pp. 63–80.

Kreps, D. M., 1990, *A Course in Microeconomic Theory*, New York: Harvester Wheatsheaf.

McKean, M. A., 1986, "Management of Traditional Common Lands (Iriaichi) in Japan," in National Research Council, *Proceedings of the Conference on Common Property Resource Management*, Washington, DC: National Academy Press, pp. 533–89.

Morishima, M., 1982, *Why Has Japan "Succeeded"? Western Technology and the Japanese Ethos*, Cambridge: Cambridge University Press.

Ndiaye, M., 1998, *Les Moodu Moodu ou l'éthos du développement au Sénégal*, Dakar: Presses Universitaires de Dakar.

Platteau, J. P. and E. Seki, 2001, "Community Arrangements to Overcome Market Failures: Pooling Groups in Japanese Fisheries," in M. Aoki and Y. Hayami (eds), *Communities and Markets in Economic Development*, Oxford: Oxford University Press, pp. 344–402.

Platteau, J. P. and T. Stzralecki, 2004, "Collective Action, Heterogeneous Loyalties, and Path Dependence: Micro-Evidence from Senegal," *Journal of African Economies*, vol. 13, no. 3, pp. 417–45.

Platteau, J. P., and F. Gaspart, 2007, "Heterogeneity and Collective Action for Effort Regulation," in J. M. Baland, P. Bardhan, and S. Bowles (eds), *Inequality, Cooperation, and Environmental Sustainability*, Princeton: Princeton University Press, pp. 159–204.

Platteau, J. P. and E. Seki, 2007, "Heterogeneity, Social Esteem and Feasibility of Collective Action," *Journal of Development Economics*, vol. 83, no. 2, pp. 302–35.

Ruddle, K., 1987, "Administration and Conflict Management in Japanese Coastal Fisheries," *FAO Fisheries Technical Paper* 273, Rome: FAO.

Smith, T. C., 1959, *The Agrarian Origins of Modern Japan*, Stanford, CA: Stanford University Press.

Taylor, L., 1987, " 'The River Would Run Red with Blood:' Community and Common Property in an Irish Fishing Settlement," in B. J. McCay and J. M. Acheson (eds), *The Question of the Commons: The Culture and Ecology of Communal Resources*, Tucson, AZ: University of Arizona Press, pp. 290–306.

3: Sustainable Governance of Common-pool Resources

Context, Method, and Politics

Arun Agrawal

Introduction

The literature on common-pool resources and common property has grown swiftly since the 1980s: as a result of pervasive concerns about environmental degradation, and the relative ineffectiveness of state management, and market-oriented policies. This chapter presents a critical assessment of the field. After discussing briefly the major findings and accomplishments of the scholarship on the commons, I follow with two distinct strategies of critique. The first strategy accepts and uses concepts fundamental to writings on the commons. These concepts include the idea of a sovereign, self-governing self and systems of property that stand above politics. The first set of criticisms demonstrates that scholars of commons have discovered far more variables of analysis that are they tend to favor. I go on to identify some possible ways to address the problem of "too many variables." Unlike other fields of social inquiry beset with similar problems – such as comparative politics – scholars of commons have readily available alternative methods and approaches with which to address the problem.

The second line of critique proceeds differently. It asks how analyses of common property might change, and what they need to consider, if they loosen assumptions about sovereign selves and apolitical property rights institutions. I suggest that loosening these assumptions is likely to help the scholarship on the commons be more faithful to the reality of commons governance, and also open new and fruitful lines of inquiry from which different fields in the social sciences can learn. I conclude this chapter with an emphasis on the need to (1) attend more carefully to processes of subject formation by attending more deeply to historical change, and (2) investigate common property arrangements with much more insistent attention to the politics and power dynamics that accompany every effort to craft institutions.

Findings and Accomplishments of the Commons Literature

The major concern of writings on common property is to show that variations in forms of property rights make a difference to resource management outcomes. Such variations affect outcomes by shaping incentives of users and managers. An allied preoccupation of commons scholars has been to demonstrate that markets or private property arrangements, and public ownership or state management do not exhaust the range of plausible institutional mechanisms to govern natural resource use. The alternative that commons theorists have identified – community and common ownership and management – is rooted in the practices of millions of households around the world. At the same time, it resonates with theoretical puzzles that concern scholars of social movements and revolutions, voting and other forms of political participation, collusion, and cheating, formation of institutions and their maintenance, cooperation, and conflict. In all these situations, participants attempt to solve collective action problems. By focusing on the conditions under which users of renewable resources cooperate to achieve efficient management (or fail to do so) the literature on common property has created the grounds on which its findings can resonate with broader concerns in the social sciences.

In investigating the impact of different institutional structures on resource management, commons theorists have also shown the importance of both formal and informal institutions as an influence on human behavior. They have drawn and built upon the works of other property rights theorists and institutionalists (Bates 1989; Knight 1992; Libecap 1990; North 1990), but have produced additional evidence on the role of informal norms in influencing human actions. Because they conceptualize institutions deliberately in an abstract manner, as sets of enforceable rules that facilitate and constrain human action, their conclusions about property rights, a subset of institutions, possess significant generalizability. For commons theorists, property rights institutions are best seen as sets of rules that define access, use, exclusion, management, monitoring, sanctioning, and arbitration behavior of users with respect to specific resources (Schlager and Ostrom 1992). At the same time as such rules are significant in governing patterns of use, they are also the principal mechanisms through which policies regarding resource management work (Alchian and Demsetz 1973; Furubotn and Pejovich 1974). It is not surprising therefore that the findings of common property theorists have found direct application in government policy choices.

Many scholars of the commons have also come to emphasize the political nature of institutions. Institutions come into being as consequences of human action, and allow specific individuals and groups to reap advantages from altered social circumstances rather than allowing societies as a whole to capture efficiency gains. In this connection, the work of new institutionalists such as Knight (1992) and Bates (1981; 1989) is especially important. Earlier property rights theorists had used a functionalist evolutionary logic to suggest that inefficient institutions are eliminated over time and efficient institutions survive (Alchian 1950; Demsetz 1967). But now commons theorists have come to emphasize the fact that institutions change mainly as a result of attempts by specific social actors, and therefore institutional change is likely to occur only when relevant political actors perceive gains from institutional change. The emergence of new institutions thus is a highly political affair as also is their impact (Gibson 1999; Peluso 1992). Whether new institutions that emerge will also be efficient for a society depends on the extent to which the interests of groups attempting institutional change intersect or overlap with those of the larger collective.

In their empirical research, scholars of commons have focused primarily on producing case studies of successful community management of coastal fisheries, forests, pastures, irrigation, and groundwater (Ascher 1995; Bromley 1992; McCay and Acheson 1987; Peters 1994; Tang 1992). Their work, in conjunction with other writings on participation, indigenous knowledge, and political ecology, has encouraged resource comanagement programs by governments. Comanagement programs assign local communities some share in control over and benefits from renewable resources (Agrawal and Ribot 1999; FAO 1999). Many of them delegate only very limited authority and often communities gain only a limited share. But the altered policy environment constitutes a substantial change over the colonial and immediate postcolonial environment when states saw themselves as best suited to resource control and management. The increase in the stakes of communities has meant a resurgence of interest in community and communal management, and contributed to the growth of what might be called "The New Commons."

The extensive theoretical and empirical research of commons scholars pays due attention to individuals as decision-makers, and to the circumstances in which decisions are made. A number of writings have undertaken important theoretical development to focus on the commons dilemmas that confront communities of users (Cheung 1970; Dasgupta and Heal 1979; Oakerson 1992; Ostrom 1990; Runge 1984). These writings have helped clarify the nature of resources that are used jointly, how technological or institutional aspects of use can influence resource characteristics, and how the structure of the situations in which resources are utilized affects use and management decisions and use patterns.

Indeed, it is the institutional nature of the analysis conducted by common property theorists that makes their work so valuable in recent discussions of decentralization of environmental management. Around the world, more than sixty countries have now begun to involve local communities and lower level decision-making units in protecting and managing the environment (FAO 1999). These new policy trends are based on the recognition that the fiscal capacity of the state to undertake coercive conservation is limited and that communities can often manage their resources better than either private actors negotiating through market-based exchanges. In many cases, communities are seen also to be characterized by high levels of social capital that permits them to undertake collective tasks far more efficiently in comparison to state bureaucracies, and do so far more equitably than market-based solutions. Indeed, recent work on common property has begun to draw upon the vast literature on social capital (Putnam 1993). Several scholars have begun to examine the extent to which common property institutions are based upon stocks of social capital and whether and how they enhance the networks through which social capital is generated (Katz 2000; Muldavin 2000; Robbins 2000).

Critique from Within

A review of three studies

Although scholars of commons have demonstrated that variations in property arrangements matter and that community-based, common-property institutions can guide sustainable resource use, there is widespread disagreement among them on what accounts for successful and sustainable resource use. One significant reason for divergent conclusions is that most empirical studies of commons follow the case study method. The multiplicity of research designs, sampling techniques, and data collection methods means that there are few compelling analyses that systematically test findings, compare postulated causal connections across contexts, or carefully specify the contextual and historical factors relevant to success.

These rather bold claims can be illustrated by a comparison of three of the most careful studies of the commons to appear since the mid-1980s. The works by Robert Wade (1994), Elinor Ostrom (1990), and Jean-Marie Baland and Jean-Philippe Platteau (1996) are path-breaking book-length analyses of local, community-based efforts to manage and govern common-pool resources. They are carefully comparative, theoretically informed, and in contrast to single case-oriented research, use a relatively large sample of cases to analyze the validity of theoretical insights. Each presents a summary set of conditions critical to sustainability of commons institutions. Together, their conclusions form a viable starting point to analyze the findings of the common property literature.

The three authors differ in their methods and research design. Wade (1994) relies primarily on original data from 31 south Indian villages in a single district. His sample is not representative of irrigation institutions in the region, but at least we can presume that the data collection in each case is consistent. Ostrom (1990) uses detailed case studies that other scholars generated. The independent production of the research she samples means that all her cases may not have consistently collected data. But she examines each case using the same set of independent and dependent variables. Baland and Platteau (1996) motivate their empirical discussion by a wide-ranging review of the economic literature on property rights, and the inability of this literature to generate unambiguous conclusions about whether private property is superior to regulated common property. To test the validity of their conclusions, they use information from several different sets of cases. In an important sense, therefore, the "model specification" is incomplete in each test they conduct (King et al. 1994).

Wade's analysis of commonly managed irrigation systems examines when it is that corporate institutions arise in these villages and what accounts for their success in resolving commons dilemmas. He (1994: 215–16) argues for the importance of 14 conditions in facilitating successful management of the commons. According to him, effective rules of restraint on access and use are unlikely to last when there are many users, when the boundaries of the common-pool resource are unclear, when users live in groups scattered over a large area, and when detection of rule-breakers is difficult, and so on (see also Ostrom 1986; Ostrom et al. 1994: 319). Wade lists his conclusions in greater detail by classifying different variables under the headings of resources, technology, user group, noticeability, relationship between resources and user group, and relationship between users and the state.

Some of Wade's facilitating conditions parallel findings from other comparative work with which he may have been in conversation. Consider Ostrom's (1990) design principles, based on her investigation of fourteen cases. A design principle for Ostrom is not part of a blueprint, but "an essential element or condition that helps to account for the success of these institutions in sustaining the CPRs and gaining the compliance of generation after generation of appropriators to the rules in use" (1990: 90). Like Wade, Ostrom also emphasizes small group size, well-defined boundaries on resources and user groups, and ease of monitoring and enforcement. So, in common with Wade, most of the principles are generalizations about local rule systems and institutional relationships. Nine of her principles are present in a significant manner in all the robust commons institutions she analyzes, and the tenth covers cases that are more complex, such as federated systems.

Baland and Platteau (1996), in their comprehensive and synthesizing review of a large number of studies on the commons, begin with an examination of competing theoretical claims by scholars of property regimes. Carefully comparing features of common property with private property, they suggest that *"regulated common property and private property are equivalent from the standpoint of the efficiency of resource use"* (p. 175, emphasis in original). Note that their result is a formalization of Coase's (1960) insight that property rights are irrelevant in the absence of transactions costs and with full information. Their review of empirical studies of the commons leads them to emphasize small size of a user group, a location close to the resource, homogeneity among group members, effective enforcement mechanisms, leadership, and past experiences of cooperation as some of the factors significant to achieve cooperation to manage resources (1996: 343–5).

The brief review above of three landmark works makes evident some of the patterns in their conclusions. They each argue that members of small local groups can design institutional arrangements to help manage resources sustainably. They go further and identify a small set of conditions that are positively related to local self-management of resources. Finally, they use theoretical insights to defend and explain the empirical regularities they find.

The regularities in successful management that they discover pertain to one of four sets of variables: (1) characteristics of resources, (2) nature of groups that depend on resources, (3) particulars of institutional regimes through which resources are managed, and (4) the nature of the relationship between a group and external forces and authorities such as markets, states, and technology. Characteristics of resources can include, for example, such features as well-defined boundaries of the resource, riskiness and unpredictability of resource flows, and mobility of the resource. Characteristics of groups, among other aspects, concern size, levels of wealth and income, different types of heterogeneity, power relations among subgroups, and past experience. Particulars of institutional regimes have an enormous range of possibilities (Ostrom 2005), but some of the critical identified aspects of institutional arrangements concern monitoring, sanctions, adjudication, and accountability. Finally, a number of characteristics pertain to the relationships of the locally situated groups, resource systems, and institutional arrangements with the external environment in the form of demographic changes, technology, markets, and different levels of governance. Table 3.1 summarizes, and lists under these four basic categories, the different conditions that the three authors under consideration have identified as significant (initials in parentheses following each condition indicate which of the three authors considers that condition important).

Locating missing variables

The analysis of the information in the table reveals significant gaps in the collective conclusions of these three authors. They pay relatively little attention to features of resources that affect sustainable governance; they also attend only cursorily to the social, political-institutional, and physical environment in which commons are situated. It is necessary to turn to other studies of commons that investigate these factors more carefully to gain a

Table 3.1   Synthesis of facilitating conditions identified by Wade, Ostrom, and Baland and Platteau

1   *Resource system characteristics*

   (a) Small size (RW)
   (b) Well defined boundaries (RW, EO)

2   *Group characteristics*

   (a) Small size (RW, B&P)
   (b) Clearly defined boundaries (RW, EO)
   (c) Shared norms (B&P)
   (d) Past successful experiences – social capital (RW, B&P)
   (e) Appropriate leadership – young, familiar with changing external environments, connected to local traditional elite (B&P)
   (f) Interdependence among group members (RW, B&P)
   (g) Heterogeneity of endowments, homogeneity of identities and interests (B&P)

(1 and 2) *Relationship between resource system characteristics and group characteristics*

   (a) Overlap between user group residential location and resource location (RW, B&P)
   (b) High levels of dependence by group members on resource system (RW)
   (c) Fairness in allocation of benefits from common resources (B&P)

3   *Institutional arrangements*

   (a) Rules are simple and easy to understand (B&P)
   (b) Locally devised access and management rules (RW, EO, B&P)
   (c) Ease in enforcement of rules (RW, EO, B&P)
   (d) Graduated sanctions (RW, EO)
   (e) Availability of low-cost adjudication (EO)
   (f) Accountability of monitors and other officials to users (EO, B&P)

(1 and 3) *Relationship between resource system and institutional arrangements*

   (a) Match restrictions on harvests to regeneration of resources (RW, EO)

4   *External environment*

   (a) Technology: low-cost exclusion technology (RW)
   (b) State:
      (i)   Central governments should not undermine local authority (RW, EO)
      (ii) Supportive external sanctioning institutions (B&P)
      (iii) Appropriate levels of external aid to compensate local users for conservation activities (B&P)
      (iv) Nested levels of appropriation, provision, enforcement, and governance (EO)

more intimate understanding of the contexts within which property rights produce their effects on resource conditions.

The limited attention to resource characteristics is unfortunate. For many resources that can be considered examples of a type of commons, differences in characteristics play a critical role in whether institutional arrangements will be effective in promoting efficient utilization, or how the flow of benefits or harms from the resource will be allocated. Think about wildlife. Its extensive movements and unpredictability of such movement can render it ill suited to local management alone (Naughton-Treves and Sanderson 1995). The broad spatial impact of greenhouse gases or ozone depleting chemicals presents similar dilemmas for managers of commons because of mobility, volatility, and unpredictability in the flow of harms. The unpredictable and volatile distribution of rainfall in many semi-arid regions may mean that pastoral grazing grounds are better managed as open access resources than as commons or privately held assets.

In a carefully argued paper on resource characteristics, Blomquist et al. (1994) focus on two physical features of resource systems: stationarity and storage. Stationarity refers to whether a resource is mobile and storage concerns the extent to which it is possible to "collect and hold resources" (p. 309). After examining the impact of these two physical characteristics of resources on externalities, Blomquist et al. conclude that these factors have an impact on management because of their relationship to information. Greater mobility of resources and difficulties of storage make management more difficult for users because of problems associated with reliability and costs of information. Naughton-Treves and Sanderson (1995) also note that unpredictability adversely affects the ability of users to allocate available resources or undertake activities that augment supply.

Wade's, Ostrom's, and Baland and Platteau's relative inattention to external social, political-institutional, and physical environment can be illustrated with reference to three important forces that shape the contexts in which common property institutions function: demographic change, market penetration, and state policies. None of the three authors considers demographic issues carefully in their analysis of commons institutions and resources. Nor do they place much emphasis on market-related demands that may make local pressures on resources seem relatively trivial. Similarly, state policies that often shape whether commons will emerge and survive receive some attention in these three works, but the impact of central governments on local resource management systems is so extensive that it needs far more careful analysis. Indeed, an enormous literature focuses on questions of forces related to demographic, market, and governance issues, and asserts their importance.

Writings on the role of population in resource management have a long history and an impressive theoretical pedigree (Ehrlich 1968; Malthus 1960). Many conclude that population growth leads rather straightforwardly to environmental degradation (Low and Heinen 1993; Pimental et al. 1994). A smaller but vocal group of scholars suggests the impact is far more limited, and may even be positive (Tiffen et al. 1994; Leach and Mearns 1996). The story is similar where markets are concerned, except that the terms of the debate are less polarized and there is wider agreement that increasing integration with markets usually has an adverse impact on the management of common-pool resources (Colchester 1994; Young 1994). Analogous to market articulation is the question of technological means available to exploit the commons. Sudden emergence of new technological innovations that transform the cost–benefit ratios of harvesting products from commons are likely to affect the sustainability of institutions.

The arrival of markets and new technologies, and the changes they might prompt in existing resource management regimes, is not a bloodless or innocent process (Oates 1999). New demand pressures create varying incentives about the products to be harvested, technologies of harvest, and rates of harvest. In many cases, as new market actors gain access to a particular common-pool resource, they seek alliances with state actors to defend the primacy of their claims (Azhar 1993). State officials can themselves become involved in the privatization of commons (Sivaramakrishnan 1999; Skaria 1999).

As the ultimate guarantor or property rights arrangements the role of the state and overarching governance structures is central to the functioning of common property institutions. Although the three authors are more attentive to the potential role of central governments than they are to the role of population and market pressures, the nature of local–state relations requires more careful exploration. Although a number of scholars have begun to focus on resource management-related laws and national policies (Lynch and Talbott 1995; Repetto and Gillis 1988; Ribot 2003), systematic examinations and clear understandings of variations in state–locality relationships are still missing.

One reason scholars of commons have focused relatively little on external factors like markets, technology, states, and population pressures lies simply in the nature of their intellectual enterprise. In trying to demonstrate the importance of local groups, institutions and resource-system related factors, they have tended to ignore how the local is created in conjunction with the external and constituted in relation to its context. The almost exclusive focus upon the local has made the work on common property vulnerable to the same criticisms that apply to the work of those anthropologists who saw their field sites as miniature worlds in themselves, changing only in response to political or economic influences from outside.

My argument in favor of attention to markets, demography, and the state addresses the nature and importance of contextual factors only to a partial degree. Clearly, the context of any study comprises far more than just markets, demographic changes, and encompassing governance arrangements. Context can be defined as the encompassing variables that remain constant for a given study, but not across studies. Precisely because the historical, spatial, social, or political context of a given study likely remains constant for all analytical purposes in a given study, it becomes possible to ignore it. But in any real world situation, the state of contextual variables affects the impact of variables being studied explicitly.

In addition to underlining the importance of the context, it is worth pointing out that even where the locality itself is concerned, and even where some important features of groups that manage commons are concerned, there are important gaps in our understanding. Take three aspects of groups as an illustration: size, heterogeneity, and poverty.

According to an enormous literature on the commons and collective action, sparked in part by Olson's seminal work (1965), smaller groups are more likely to engage in successful collective action. But other scholars (Hardin 1982) remark on the ambiguities in Olson's argument and suggested that the relationship between group size and collective action is not very straightforward. Marwell and Oliver (1993: 38) claim, "a significant body of empirical research . . . finds that the size of a group is positively related to its level of collective action." Agrawal and Goyal (2001), use two analytical features of common-pool resources – imperfect exclusion and lumpiness of third party monitoring – to hypothesize a curvilinear relationship between group size and successful collection action, and to test this hypothesis. The current state of knowledge is perhaps best summarized by Ostrom (1997), who says that the impact of group size on collective action is usually mediated by many other variables. These variables include the production technology of the collective good, its degree of excludability, jointness of supply, and the level of heterogeneity in the group (Hardin 1982: 44–9).

Cumulation of knowledge into a consistent and empirically supported theory has proved even more difficult in relation to group heterogeneity. It can fairly be argued that most resources are managed by groups divided along multiple axes, among them ethnicity, gender, religion, wealth, and caste. Especially significant are gender-related differences within groups because of the often critical role women play in the gathering and harvesting of products from common-pool resources. But other forms of heterogeneity within groups can be equally pernicious, and at any rate, can have multiple and contradictory effects on the possibilities of collective action. Empirical evidence on the matter is still highly ambiguous (Baland and Platteau 1999; Quiggin 1993). Thus even in groups that have high levels of heterogeneities of interest, it may be possible to ensure collective action if some subgroups can coercively enforce conservationist institutions (Jodha 1986; Peluso 1993; but see also Bardhan and Dayton-Johnson 2002 and Libecap 1990). On the other hand, the role of intra-group heterogeneities on distribution may be more amenable to definition. Significant research on the effects of development projects and also on commons suggests that better-off group members are often likely to gain a larger share of benefits from a resource (Agrawal 2001).

Another critical locality related factor on which much research has been carried out without a consensus is the impact of poverty on common-pool resources. Whether poverty leads to a greater reliance on the commons (Jodha 1986) and their degradation, or do increasing levels of wealth, at least initially, lead to greater use of commons by users, is a question on whose answer the shape of many commons-related policies would hinge. But to an important degree, government interventions in this arena are based on limited information and even less reliable analysis.

Whether group size, group heterogeneity, and poverty have a positive, negative, or neutral relationship to sustainability of commons institutions seems subject to a range of other contextual and mediating factors, not all of which are clearly understood. Elster suggests about the study of local justice, that "it is a very messy business, and that it may be impossible to identify a set of necessary and sufficient conditions that constitute a theory of local justice" (1992: 14). His diagnosis for local justice may be equally applicable to the study of commons, as also his prescription: instead of making a choice between theory and description, focusing on identifying mechanisms or "identifiable causal patterns" (p. 16). Commenting on a similar tendency in political analysis, Ostrom argues that, "political systems are complexly organized, and that we will rarely be able to state that one variable is always positively or negatively related to a dependent variable" (1998: 16).

Table 3.2 constitutes an effort to supplement the set of variables presented in table 3.1. The additional factors presented in the table are the ones that are not followed by the name of a particular author. Although the factors in table 3.2 are among those that many scholars of commons would consider most important for achieving institutional sustainability on the commons, they do not form an exhaustive set. Nor is it likely that an undisputed exhaustive set of variables can ever be created.

Some of the factors in table 3.2 are also important to the emergence of commons institutions. It may be evident that there is an overlap between conditions that facilitate emergence and those that facilitate continued successful functioning of institutions. This

Table 3.2 Critical enabling conditions for sustainability on the commons

1 *Resource system characteristics*

    (a) Small size (RW)
    (b) Well defined boundaries (RW, EO)
    (c) Low levels of mobility
    (d) Possibilities of storage of benefits from the resource
    (e) Predictability

2 *Group characteristics*

    (a) Small size (RW, B&P)
    (b) Clearly defined boundaries (RW, EO)
    (c) Shared norms (B&P)
    (d) Past successful experiences – social capital (RW, B&P)
    (e) Appropriate leadership – young, familiar with changing external environments, connected to local traditional elite (B&P)
    (f) Interdependence among group members (RW, B&P)
    (g) Heterogeneity of endowments, homogeneity of identities and interests (B&P)
    (h) Low levels of poverty

(1 and 2) *Relationship between resource system characteristics and group characteristics*

    (a) Overlap between user group residential location and resource location (RW, B&P)
    (b) High levels of dependence by group members on resource system (RW)
    (c) Fairness in allocation of benefits from common resources (B&P)
    (d) Low levels of user demand
    (e) Gradual change in levels of demand

3 *Institutional arrangements*

    (a) Rules are simple and easy to understand (B&P)
    (b) Locally devised access and management rules (RW, EO, B&P)
    (c) Ease in enforcement of rules (RW, EO, B&P)
    (d) Graduated sanctions (RW, EO)
    (e) Availability of low-cost adjudication (EO)
    (f) Accountability of monitors and other officials to users (EO, B&P)

(1 and 3) *Relationship between resource system and institutional arrangements*

    (a) Match restrictions on harvests to regeneration of resources (RW, EO)

4 *External environment*

    (a) Technology
        (i) Low-cost exclusion technology (RW)
        (ii) Time for adaptation to new technologies related to the commons
    (b) Low levels of articulation with external markets
    (c) Gradual change in articulation with external markets
    (d) State:
        (i) Central governments should not undermine local authority (RW, EO)
        (ii) Supportive external sanctioning institutions (B&P)
        (iii) Appropriate levels of external aid to compensate local users for conservation activities (B&P)
        (iv) Nested levels of appropriation, provision, enforcement, and governance (EO)

overlap points to the close and complex relationship between origins and continued existence without any suggestion that the two can be stated as an identical set.

Addressing problems of method

The list of factors in table 3.2 raises some important methodological obstacles. One important problem stems from the fact that most of the conditions cited in table 3.2 are expected to pertain to all common-pool resources and institutions, rather than being related to or dependent on some aspect of the situation. Consider the first two conditions in table 3.2 under the broad class of resource system characteristics: small size, and well defined boundaries. According to Wade, relatively small sized resource systems are likely to be managed better under common property arrangements, and according to both Ostrom and Wade, resources that have well defined boundaries are likely better managed as common property. But it is in principle possible, and perhaps more defensible, to think of the effects of resource size or boundary definition as dependent on the state of one or more other variables.

For example, well-defined boundaries of resources may promote sustainable use when flows of benefits are predictable and groups relying on them stationary. But when there are large variations in benefit flows, and/or the group relying on the resource is mobile, then fuzzy resource boundaries may better accommodate variations in group needs and resource flows. A large body of research on pastoralists makes this point especially clearly (Fratkin 1997). This example also brings home the importance of context.

As another example, consider the question of fairness in allocation of benefits from the commons. Typically, intuition as well as much of the scholarship on the commons suggests that fairer allocation of benefits is likely to lead to more sustainable institutional arrangements. But in a social context characterized by hierarchical social and political organization, institutional arrangements specifying asymmetric distribution of benefits may be more sustainable even if they are entirely unfair. The caste system and racial inequalities constitute two familiar examples of such hierarchical social arrangements.

But the most significant problems of method are a consequence of the sheer number of conditions that seem relevant to the successful management of common-pool resources. Wade, Ostrom, and Baland and Platteau jointly identify 36 important conditions. If one eliminates the common conditions across these 3 studies, 24 different conditions still remain (as in table 3.1). It is difficult to eliminate *a priori* any of the conditions they consider important. Indeed, the above discussion of their conclusions suggests that the 24 factors they have identified do not by any means exhaust the full set of conditions relevant to sustainable common-pool resource management. Once we take into account additional important factors identified in the vast literature on the local governance of common-pool resources, it is reasonable to suppose that the total number of factors that affect successful management of commons may be somewhere between 30 and 40 (table 3.2 lists a total of 33 factors). At present, we do not have any reliable way to assess the degree of correlation among these factors, or their relative contribution to successful institutional governance even within a given context, let alone across contexts.

Further, since the effects of some variables may depend on the state of other variables, careful analyses of sustainability on the commons need to incorporate interaction effects among variables. As soon as we concede the possibility that somewhere between 30 to 40 variables affect the management of common-pool resources, and that some of these variables may have important interaction effects, we confront tremendous analytical problems.

When a large number of causal variables potentially affects outcomes, the absence of careful research design that controls for factors that are not the subject of investigation makes it almost impossible to be sure that the observed differences in outcomes are indeed a result of hypothesized causes. If commons researchers do not explicitly take into account the relevant variables that affect success, then the number of selected cases must be (much) larger than the number of variables. But no studies of common-pool resources develop their research design by explicitly taking into account the different variables considered critical to successful management as specified in table 3.2. In an important sense, then, many of the existing works on the management of common-pool resources, especially those conducted as case studies or those that base their conclusions on a very small number of cases, suffer from the problem that they do not specify carefully or explicitly the causal model they are testing. In the absence of such specification, qualitative studies of the commons are potentially subject to significant problems of method. Two of the most important of these problems are those stemming from "omitted variable bias," and the problem of endogeneity (King et al. 1994: 168–82, 185–95). These biases resulting from deficiencies of method have the potential to produce an emphasis on irrelevant causal factors, inattention to relevant factors, and the generation of spurious correlations.

The large number of variables potentially affecting the sustainability of institutions that govern common resources, thus, has important theoretical implications for future research. The most important implication is perhaps for research design. Because the requirements of a random or representative selection of cases are typically very hard to satisfy where common-pool resources are concerned (even when the universe of cases is narrowed geographically), purposive sampling easily becomes the theoretically defensible strategy for selecting cases whether the objective is statistical analysis or structured comparative case analysis. In purposive sampling, the selected cases will be chosen for the variation they represent on theoretically significant causal variables. This strategy can be defended both because it is easier to implement than an effort to select a representative random sample, and because it requires explicit consideration of theoretically relevant variables (Bennett and George 2005).

The large number of variables also has implications for data analysis. One of the strategies that scholars on the commons may need to follow is to reduce the number of closely related variables by constructing indices that combine them. Thus for example, several of the factors listed under "institutional arrangements" in table 3.2 may be sufficiently correlated to permit the creation of an index of "enforcement strength." Especially suitable for such an index may be, "graduated sanctions," "ease in enforcement of rules," and "availability of low cost adjudication." Such indices may also be formed out of variables that are listed under different headings in that table. Thus, an indicator of stress on existing institutions might be revealed by bringing together such factors as "gradual change in levels of demand," "low levels of articulation with external markets," and "gradual change in articulation with external markets."

There is no general theory of purposive sampling apart from the commonsensical consideration that selected cases should represent variation on theoretically significant causal factors. Therefore two factors are likely to be critical in research design: awareness of the variables that are theoretically relevant, and deep knowledge of the case(s) to be researched so that theoretically relevant variables can be operationalized. For example, when constructing a research design where the variables of interest has to do with mechanisms of monitoring and sanctioning, it would be important for the researcher to be aware of the different forms of monitoring that groups can use. The presence or absence of a guard may only be indicative of the presence or absence of third party monitoring, and may reveal nothing about whether the group being studied has monitoring. Other forms of monitoring would include mutual monitoring and rotational monitoring, where households in a group jointly share the tasks related to monitoring and enforcement.

The information presented in table 3.2, organized under four major categories, can therefore be useful in the creation of a research design, and case selection for comparative studies or data collection for statistical studies. Given a particular context, the information in table 3.2 can help in the selection of the variables that need closest attention in the selection of cases. For example, if the cases to be selected lie in the same ecological zone and represent the same resource type, then variables related to resource characteristics may not be very important for case selection. The obvious trade-off for this reduction in the number of variables is that the research is likely to have limited generalizability. Overall, the problems of contingent and multiple causation make it necessary that even those researchers of the commons who use statistical data postulate causal relationships among the critical theoretical variables they have identified, explain why the variables they do not examine are likely not important for their work, and only then test the causal links they have postulated among their variables.

A two-pronged approach to advance the research program related to institutional solutions to commons dilemmas, then seems advisable. On the one hand, scholars of commons need to deploy theoretically motivated comparative case analyses to identify the most important causal mechanisms and narrow the range of relevant theoretical variables and their interactions. On the other hand commons scholars also need to conduct large-N studies to identify the strength of causal relations (White and Runge 1994; McCarthy et al. 2003). Only then would it be possible to advance our understanding of how institutional sustainability can be achieved on the commons.

Beyond Apolitical Institutions and Sovereign Subjects

The arguments and criticisms advanced in the previous section do not question the two basic assumptions that most studies of the commons take for granted: autonomous, decision-making selves, and configurations of institutional arrangements (property rights) within which such selves make decisions to maximize their benefits. Thus, much of the discussion summarizing the literature on the commons focused on the factors that promote more sustainable governance of resources without calling into question the desirability of sustainability or the potentially fraught nature of attempts to sustain resources, the meaning of institutions as they intersect with conceptions of rights and interests, and the extent to which individuals are autonomous decision-making subjects. Recent developments in social theory, especially contributions by scholars of resistance and subalternity provide some reasonable grounds to think about other social aspirations and values that compete with sustainability – among them equity and political engagement. But insights from poststructuralist writings also make it possible to raise doubts about the extent to which institutions and identities premised on utility maximization are appropriate in the context of the governance of the commons. These new avenues promise exciting opportunities for exploration.

Resistance and subalternity

Perhaps the most important set of questions to which theorists of commons can attend better concern the extent to which intra-group politics and issues of power and resistance shape resource use and management strategies, and the ways in which the use of common-pool resources undermines or exacerbates other socio-political and economic inequalities. In the preoccupation to show that common property arrangements can lead to sustainable resource governance outcomes, scholars of commons may have ignored the possibility that all successful enforcement institutions are also coercive, and that the burden of coercion tends to fall unequally on those who are less powerful. Indeed, if institutions are the product of conscious decisions of specific individuals and groups, as many commons theorists argue, then it may also be reasonable to suppose that institutional choices by powerful groups deliberately aim to disadvantage marginal and less powerful groups. The other side of the coin of institutional sustainability then may be unequal allocation of benefits from commonly managed resources: not as a by-product, but as a common consequence.

If existing institutions are the expression of past political alignments, attention to current political relationships within communities can help produce a better understanding of how existing institutions are contested, and what future institutions may look like. Institutional arrangements for allocating resources are best viewed as an expression of an idealized status quo. Actual human behavior, even in the context of well-enforced institutional rules, is unlikely to conform precisely to institutional contours. Perfect enforcement is far too costly ever to be achieved in the context of resources that are valuable, and over which different users and social groups compete. When resources devoted to enforcement of institutional rules are limited, resource use patterns are far more likely to diverge from what rules specify. Attention to power and micro-politics within communities is therefore critical in understanding how resources are used and managed (Gibson 1999; Moore 1998; 1999). The point is not just to try to understand politics as its effects on resource use and governance are mediated through the prism of institutions. Rather, it is also to try to understand how political relationships imbue resource use even without being mediated by institutional arrangements.

Greater attention to the dynamics of resistance and domination is likely to help explicate better the relationship between property and politics. But the investigation of the nature of power and resistance also possesses significant inherent theoretical and practical merit as subaltern scholars and writers on everyday protest have argued (Guha and Spivak 1988; Scott 1985). Attention to strategies followed by subaltern actors in relation to resource use is necessary to understand how attempts at control and regulation are always challenged by those who are subjected to control. Issues of agency, the mutually productive relationship between domination and resistance, and the creation of institutional arrangements can be understood only with greater attention to micropolitics. Such a shift in focus can also help address the criticism that scholars of common property have, for the most part, ignored how rural residents can shape attempts by outside agents such as the state or aid agencies to intervene in their lives and modify existing patterns of resource use.

An analogous critique of commons scholarship also aims at their interest in sustainable management of resources. It is suggested by some observers of commons theorists (Goldman 1997) that by not examining the internally differentiated nature of communities, commons scholars assume that members of these communities are similarly receptive to ideas about more efficient resource management, progress and modernization. But the processes of development and modernization, and attempts to make the use and management of commons more efficient may well tie into state-centered efforts to intervene in local affairs. By focusing on how common resources can be more efficiently managed, scholars of commons become enmeshed in the same logic of greater productivity that advocates of privatization discuss (Goldman 1997). This critique of the commons borrows extensively from Foucault's arguments about biopower and biopolitics (1990), effectively deployed by such authors as Mitchell (1991) to critique colonization and modernization in Egypt, by Escobar (1995) to question development, and by Ferguson (1994) to investigate development projects initiated by agencies like the World Bank.

A greater focus on how power works within communities and in the governance of common-pool resources can help strengthen greatly the force of writings on commons property. On the one hand, such a shift in focus would facilitate a better understanding of how power and status are related to access and use of resources; on the other, it would complement the near-exclusive focus of common property theorists on institutions and rules.

Indeed, a number of observers of the literature on the commons, especially those with an interest in political ecology and local environmental politics, have pointed to the political dynamics and struggles common in settings that witness efforts to introduce new property regimes over resources (Moore 2005; Peters 1994; Robbins 2004). In some ways, then, it is important to ask how a closer engagement with politics can help make scholarship on the commons more pertinent to the concerns of those who depend on the commons, at the same time as it promotes further cross-disciplinary conversations.

Ultimately, power is not just what planning and management attempt to exclude. Rather, power and politics imbue the process of management thoroughly and unavoidably. Management is not just about providing technical solutions to objective problems of development and environmental conservation. It may be important to consider that these problems and their solutions may themselves be part of a political process. Without attention to the politics that generates underdevelopment and environmental degradation as universal problems, it may be impossible to address poverty, underdevelopment, and environmental degradation effectively.

In this sense, a greater concern with politics and power would prompt scholars of commons to a more critical engagement with the policy processes that are creating new commons around the world, often in the guise of institutional structures that are supposed to make commonly held resources more accessible to marginal and disadvantaged groups. But as an emerging literature on environmental policy decentralization is beginning to show, efforts at decentralization are more effective in the claims and counter-claims they generate than in producing changes in social relations around resources or the processes through which access to resources is shaped. One important lesson from these studies is that the creation of institutional structures resembling common property arrangements may be as vulnerable to manipulation by the elite and the capturing of resource-related benefits by small groups of powerful individuals as has often been the case with private ownership or government-owned resources.

Politicized institutions, emerging subjects

Perhaps the most neglected aspects of resource use and management in the commons literature is the changing relationship between the environment and the human beings who use environmental resources. Indeed, this is perhaps a common failing on much of the social research that places human beings at the core of its concerns: it fails to consider how humans change from one time period to another in response to an immense range of forces, and how persons differ from one context to another. The effort to understand the connections between institutions and identities, practices and preferences, sociality and subjectivities was central to the late nineteenth- and early twentieth-century social-scientific writings of Marx, Weber, and Durkheim (Rose 1999). But it has received far less attention in the past few decades than is its due. In our discipline-bound social-scientific enterprise, economists and many political scientists have placed their faith in a dehistoricized model of rational man that is insensitive to contextual differences. The writings of historians and anthropologists may profit by comparison, but it can be said that much of the work on subjectivity in these latter disciplines is insufficiently sensitive to variations in self-formation as such variations are shaped by power and politicized institutions. And perhaps it is not out of place to note that theories of agency and the relationship between agency and structure are generally inadequate as lenses through which to understand the making of subjects, tied as they are to an ontological view of power as constraint.

The relevance of all this to the scholarship on the commons is simply that in investigating how changes in institutional arrangements may also be linked to changes in identities and subjectivities, scholars of commons may be able to contribute to some of the central puzzles in the social sciences, not just help address a problem that is basic to resource management and governance. In this context, it is important to point out that if commons scholars consider politics only through the prism of institutions, and human actions only as subject to power (and therefore institutions) as constraints, they will fail to attend to deep changes and variations in human subjectivities in relation to the environment.

Instead, it is useful to understand that institutional strategies to govern forests – to allocate, to monitor, to sanction, to enforce, to adjudicate – do not simply constrain the actions of already existing sovereign subjects. They also change subjects. Nor is it the case that people's responses to new forms of regulatory strategies are exhausted by the continuum between resistance and conformity. Instead, these strategies and their effects on flows of power shape human subjects, their interests, and their agency. As individuals confront problems of scarcity and gain a stake in addressing these problems through their everyday practices embedded in institutions, they do not remain unaffected by what they do: practices make persons. By focusing on these strategies as the means through which individuals become different kinds of subjects, it may be possible to specify the micromechanisms at work in the reconfiguration of environment-related subjectivities. Explanations of why and when people respond in particular and differentiated ways to new strategies of institutionalized power requires attention to their structural locations and the extent to which they are already privileged, or marginalized by new strategies of power. To insist on variations in how subject positions change is also to insist on the evident fact that the effects of new forms of institutions are neither totalizing nor permanent (Agrawal 2005). One reason there have been so few studies of the relationship between changes in subjectivities and shifts in institutional regulation is the limited historical scope of most studies of the commons. Diachronic examination of common property arrangements together with studies of human understandings and subject positions related to the environment have the potential to transform how governance of common property is understood.

Ultimately, the success of institutional changes in prompting better use and governance of environmental resources may depend crucially on changes in human subjectivities. Attempts to change how people act, when such attempts are based solely on coercive threats in hierarchical organizations, are either formidably expensive or evidently impractical (Holmstrom 1982). Commons scholars need to focus more clearly and more directly on this underinvestigated relationship between institutions and identities as a fascinating new avenue of inquiry, one that will help build new bridges to scholarship in the social sciences and the humanities.

Conclusion

In reviewing the literature on the commons through an interdisciplinary vantage point, this chapter has deployed two different strategies. Using the assumptions that are basic to most research on the commons, it pointed to some problems of methods that bedevil studies of common property. Because scholars of commons have identified literally scores of factors that are important to successful governance of common-pool resources, their favored strategy of analysis and investigation is a poor means through which to generate further advances in understanding how institutions shape resource conditions and changes in resource conditions. Instead, the chapter points toward more appropriate statistical analytical procedures that may help lead to a better and more thorough understanding of the role of institutions in promoting or undermining sustainable resource governance.

More significantly, the chapter identifies two arenas of analysis in which the scholarship on common property has been relatively deficient. In attending to the relationship between resource condition/change and institutional arrangements, and trying to show that common property arrangements have often been key to sustainable resource governance, scholars of the commons have downplayed the extent to which institutions that lead to sustainable resource management may also produce unequal allocation of resources, or match highly inequitable social arrangements. Greater attention to the ways in which political asymmetries shape resource governance and allocation will likely lead the scholarship on the commons toward more critical engagements with policies claiming to decentralize power and resources, but also toward arguments that are more attentive to individuals and groups that are politically and economically marginalized.

At the same time, scholars working on the commons can contribute significantly to the relationship between environmental institutions and social identities by examining how variations and changes in institutional arrangements, often through state policies, relate to variations and changes in identities and subjectivities. For such an orientation to become an effective element in the scholarship on the commons, it will be necessary to conduct diachronic rather than single time-period studies of institutional change and its diverse social impacts.

References

Agrawal, A. 2001. State formation in community spaces: the forest councils of Kumaon. *Journal of Asian Studies*. 60(1): 1–32.

Agrawal, A. 2005. *Environmentality: Technologies of Government and the Making of Subjects*. Durham, NC: Duke University Press.

Agrawal, A. and Goyal, S. 2001. Group size and collective action: third party monitoring in common-pool resources. *Comparative Political Studies*. 34(1): 63–93.

Agrawal, A. and Ribot, J. C. 1999. Accountability in decentralization: a framework with South Asian and West African cases. *Journal of Developing Areas*. 33(summer): 473–502.

Alchian, A. 1950. Uncertainty, evolution and economic theory. *Journal of Political Economics*. 58(3): 211–21.

Alchian, A. and Demsetz, H. 1973. The property rights paradigm. *Journal of Economic History*. 33: 16–27.

Ascher, W. 1995. *Communities and Sustainable Forestry in Developing Countries*. San Francisco: ICS Press.

Azhar, R. 1993. Commons, regulation, and rent-seeking behavior: the dilemma of Pakistan's *Guzara* forests. *Economic Development and Cultural Change*. 42(1): 115–28.

Baland, J. M. and Platteau, J. P. 1996. *Halting Degradation of Natural Resources: Is There a Role for Rural Communities?* Oxford: Clarendon.

Baland, J. M. and Platteau, J. P. 1999. The ambiguous impact of inequality on local resource management. *World Development*. 27: 773–88.

Bardhan, P. and Dayton-Johnson, J. 2002. Unequal irrigators: heterogeneity and commons management in large-scale multivariate research. In E. Ostrom, T. Dietz, N. Dolšak, P. C. Stern, S. Stonich, and E. U. Weber (eds), pp. 87–112, Washington: National Academy Press.

Bates, R. H. 1981. *Markets and States in Tropical Africa: The Political Basis of Agricultural Policies*. Berkeley: University of California Press.

Bates, R. H. 1989. *Beyond the Miracle of the Market: The Political Economy of Agrarian Development in Kenya*. Cambridge: Cambridge University Press.

Bennett, A. and George, A. 2005. *Case Studies and Theory Development in the Social Sciences*. Cambridge, MA: MIT Press.

Blomquist, W., Schlager, E., Tang, S.Y., and Ostrom, E. 1994. Regularities from the field and possible explanations. In Ostrom, Gardner, and Walker (eds), pp. 301–16.

Bromley, D. (ed.) 1992. *Making the Commons Work: Theory, Practice and Policy*. San Francisco: ICS Press.

Cheung, S. N. S. 1970. The structure of a contract and the theory of non-exclusive resource. *Journal of Law and Economics*. 13: 49–70.

Coase, R. 1960. The problem of social cost. *Journal of Law and Economics*. 3: 1–44.

Colchester, M. 1994. Sustaining the forests: the community-based approach in south and south-east Asia. *Development Change*. 25(1): 69–100.

Dasgupta, P. and Heal, G. 1979. *Economic Theory and Exhaustible Resources*. Cambridge: Cambridge University Press.

Demsetz, H. 1967. Towards a theory of property rights. *American Economic Review*. 57(2): 347–59.

Ehrlich, P. 1968. *The Population Bomb*. New York: Ballantine.

Elster, J. 1992. *Local Justice: How Institutions Allocate Scarce Goods and Necessary Burdens*. New York: Russell Sage Foundation.

Escobar, A. 1995. *Encountering Development: The Making and Unmaking of the Third World*. Princeton, NJ: Princeton University Press.

Ferguson, J. 1994. *The Anti-politics Machine: "Development," Depoliticization, and Bureaucratic Power in Lesotho*. Minneapolis: University of Minnesota Press.

Food and Agriculture Organization. 1999. Status and progress in the implementation of national forest programmes: outcomes of an FAO worldwide survey. Mimeo. Rome: FAO.

Foucault, M. 1990. *The History of Sexuality: An Introduction*, vol. 1. New York: Vintage.

Fratkin, E. 1997. Pastoralism: government and development issues. *Annual Review of Anthropology*. 26: 235–61.

Furubotn, E. and Pejovich, S. (eds) 1974. *The Economics of Property Rights*. Cambridge, MA: Ballinger Publishing.

Gibson, C. C. 1999. *Politicians and Poachers: The Political Economy of Wildlife Policy in Africa*. Cambridge: Cambridge University Press.

Goldman, M. 1997. "Customs in common:" the epistemic world of the commons scholars. *Theory and Society*. 26(1): 1–37.

Guha, R. and Spivak, G. C. (eds) 1988. *Selected Subaltern Studies*. Delhi: Oxford University Press.

Hardin, R. 1982. *Collective Action*. Baltimore: Johns Hopkins University Press.

Holmstrom, B. 1982. Moral hazard in teams. *Bell Journal of Economics*. 13(2): 324–40.

Jodha, N. S. 1986. Common property resources and rural poor in dry regions of India. *Economic and Political Weekly*. 21(27): 1169–82.

Katz, E. G. 2000. Social capital and natural capital: a comparative analysis of land tenure and natural resource management in Guatemala. *Land Economics*. 76(1): 114–32.

King, G., Keohane, R., and Verba, S. 1994. *Designing Social Inquiry: Scientific Inference in Qualitative Research*. Princeton: Princeton University Press.

Knight, J. 1992. *Institutions and Social Conflict*. New York: Cambridge University Press.

Leach, M. and Mearns, R. (eds) 1996. *The Lie of the Land: Challenging Received Wisdom on the African Environment*. Oxford, UK, and Portsmouth, NH: James Currey and Heinemann.

Li, T. M. 1996. Images of community: discourse and strategy in property relations. *Development Change*. 27(3): 501–27.

Libecap, G. 1990. *Contracting for Property Rights*. New York: Cambridge University Press.

Low, B. and Heinen, J. 1993. Population, resources and environment: implications of human behavioral ecology for conservation. *Population and Environment*. 15(1): 7–41.

Lynch, O. J. and Talbott, K. 1995. *Balancing Acts: Community-based Forest Management and National Law in Asia and the Pacific*. Washington: WRI.

McCarthy, N., Dutilly-Diané, C., and Drabo, B. 2003. Cooperation, collective action and natural resources management in Burkina Faso: a methodological note. CAPRi Working Paper 27. Washington, DC: CAPRi.

McCay, B. J. and Acheson, J. (eds) 1987. *The Question of the Commons: The Culture and Ecology of Communal Resources*. Tucson: University of Arizona Press.

Malthus, T. 1960. *On Population* (First Essay on Population, 1798, and Second Essay on Population, 1803). New York: Random House.

Marwell, G. and Oliver, P. 1993. *The Critical Mass in Collective Action: A Micro-social Theory*. Cambridge: Cambridge University Press.

Mitchell, T. 1991. *Colonizing Egypt*. Berkeley: University of California Press.

Moore, D. S. 1998. Subaltern struggles and the politics of place: remapping resistance in Zimbabwe's eastern highlands. *Cultural Anthropology*. 13(3): 344–81.

Moore, D. S. 1999. The crucible of cultural politics: reworking "development" in Zimbabwe's eastern highlands. *American Ethnologist*. 26(3): 654–89.

Moore, D. S. 2005. *Suffering for Territory*. Durham, NC: Duke University Press.

Muldavin, J. 2000. The paradoxes of environmental policy and resource management in reformera China. *Economic Geography*. 76(3): 244–71.

Naughton-Teves, L. and Sanderson, S. 1995. Property, politics and wildlife conservation. *World Development*. 23(8): 1265–76.

North, D. 1990. *Institutions, Institutional Change and Economic Performance*. Cambridge: Cambridge University Press.

Oakerson, R. 1992. Analyzing the commons: a framework. In Bromley (ed.), pp. 41–59.

Oates, J. F. 1999. *Myth and Reality in the Rain Forest: How Conservation Strategies Are Failing in West Africa*. Berkeley, CA: University of California Press.

Olson, M. 1965. *The Logic of Collective Action*. Cambridge, MA: Harvard University Press.

Ostrom, E. 1986. An agenda for the study of institutions. *Public Choice*. 48: 3–25.

Ostrom, E. 1990. *Governing the Commons: The Evolution of Institutions for Collective Action.* Cambridge: Cambridge University Press.

Ostrom, E. 1997. Self-governance of common-pool resources. W97-2, Workshop in Political Theory and Policy Analysis, Indiana University, Bloomington.

Ostrom, E. 1998. A behavioral approach to the rational choice theory of collective action. *American Political Science Review.* 92(1): 1–22.

Ostrom, E. 2005. *Understanding Institutional Diversity.* Princeton: Princeton University Press.

Ostrom, E., Gardner, R., and Walker, J. 1994. *Rules, Games and Common-pool Resources.* Michigan: University of Michigan Press.

Peluso, N. L. 1992. *Rich Forests, Poor People: Resource Control and Resistance in Java.* Berkeley: University of California Press.

Peluso, N. L. 1993. Coercing conservation: the politics of state resource control. *Global Environmental Change.* 3(2): 199–217.

Peters, P. 1994. *Dividing the Commons: Politics, Policy and Culture in Botswana.* Charlottesville: University of Virginia Press.

Pimental, D., Harman, R., Pacenza, M., Pecarsky, J., and Pimental, M. 1994. Natural resources and an optimal human population. *Population and Environment.* 15(5): 347–69.

Putnam, R. 1993. *Making Democracy Work: Civic Traditions in Modern Italy.* Princeton: Princeton University Press.

Quiggin, J. 1993. Common property, equality, and development. *World Development.* 21: 1123–38.

Repetto, R. and Gillis, M. (eds) 1988. *Public Policies and the Misuse of Forest Resources.* Cambridge: Cambridge University Press.

Ribot, Jesse. 2003. Democratic decentralization of natural resources: institutional choice and discretionary power transfers in sub-Saharan Africa. *Public Administration and Development.* 23(1): 53–65.

Robbins, P. 2000. The rotten institution: corruption in natural resource management. *Political Geography.* 19(4): 423–43.

Robbins, P. 2004. *Political Ecology: A Critical Introduction.* Oxford: Blackwell.

Rose, N. 1999. *Powers of Freedom: Reframing Political Thought.* Cambridge: Cambridge University Press.

Runge, C. F. 1984. Institutions and the free rider: the assurance problem in collective action. *Journal of Politics.* 46: 154–81.

Schlager, E. and Ostrom, E. 1992. Property rights regimes and natural resources: a conceptual analysis. *Land Economics.* 68(3): 249–62.

Scott, J. C. 1985. *Weapons of the Weak: Everyday Forms of Peasant Resistance.* New Haven: Yale University Press.

Sivaramakrishnan, K. 1999. *Modern Forests: Statemaking and Environmental Change in Colonial Eastern India.* Stanford: Stanford University Press.

Skaria, A. 1999. *Hybrid Histories: Forests, Frontiers, and Wildness in Western India.* New Delhi: Oxford University Press.

Tang, S. Y. 1992. *Institutions and Collective Action: Self-governance in Irrigation.* San Francisco: ICS Press.

Tiffen, M., Mortimore, M., and Gichuki, F. 1994. *More People, Less Erosion: Environmental Recovery in Kenya.* Chichester: John Wiley.

Wade, R. 1994. *Village Republics: Economic Conditions for Collective Action in South India.* Oakland: ICS Press.

White, T. A. and Runge, C. F. 1994. Common property and collective action: lessons from cooperative watershed management in Haiti. *Economic Development and Cultural Change.* 43(1): 1–41.

Young, K. R. 1994. Roads and the environmental degradation of tropical montane forests. *Conservation Biology.* 8(4): 972–6.

4: Cooperative Conversations

Outcomes and Processes in Economics and Anthropology

Isha Ray

Conversations between Economists and Anthropologists

[*The scene is a crowded coffee house and an economist and anthropologist are sharing the same table. This did not happen by design, but the café is full and there is no choice but to share tables. The economist and the anthropologist are not talking. The economist is reading a short paper on how evolutionary game theory, given four assumptions, can explain how norms of cooperation spontaneously arise in communities throughout the world. The anthropologist is reading a long paper on the micro-politics of resistance to the hegemonic alliance of the state and multinationals in a struggle for control over local forests in a part of Asia that the economist has never heard of. It isn't clear why one of them suddenly breaks his silence.*]

A: You see why we never talk? You're a physicist in disguise who wants to come up with three theories that explain 90 percent of human behavior. And what is the reality? You have 90 theories that explain maybe 3 percent of human behavior. But that doesn't deter you. You produce your "findings" with carefully chosen axioms and then run to the World Bank to tell them what to tell poor people to do. Or you run some regressions on data you never even collected and you produce "significant" correlations whose significance is – what, exactly? You make these predictions, and it's OK if they don't come true because you can easily produce others. Worst of all, no one can understand your mathematical gymnastics. You pay lip service to values and culture but, underneath, the individual you're most comfortable with is a utility-maximizing rat that *no one* would want to have coffee with.

E: You talking to me? You take a random sample of the people here, right now, and you ask them what an economist does. They will hazard a not unintelligent guess. You ask these same good people what an anthropologist does. They won't have a clue. So who are you to accuse me of being unintelligible? [*here he grabs the other's paper*]. Look at this! You say no one understands my equations – do you think people understand what "trouble the distinctions between" means? Or "constitutes and is constitutive of" means? I model rational behavior while you meander vaguely in unknown places; I simplify the world while you complicate it still further. But I wouldn't care – I assume you are maximizing your utility this way – if you only left me alone. But no. You routinely insult me in print; I'm arrogant, I'm atomistic, I'm hegemonic. Do I carry on about you? No, I behave like a gentleman and I simply ignore you.

[*Silence once more; and this time a distinctly disgruntled one.*]

The "conversation" reported above is not uncommon, though perhaps it rarely occurs face-to-face. It isn't that economists and anthropologists never talk to one another civilly.[1] They do, but usually from different ideological, epistemological, and methodological perspectives. Many international research groups and donor organizations have both sets of professionals working for them, but they typically produce parallel research documents, with occasional references to the work of the other group. But when economists and anthropologists do come together in an open and mutually respectful dialogue, the results can be both useful and fascinating.

My entry point into the economics – anthropology conversation is the first line Lipton's book review of an earlier such conversation: "Economics is mainly about outcomes; anthropology is mainly about processes" (Lipton 1992).[2]

Lipton went on to argue that a true conversation – *sacra conversazione* – between economists and anthropologists has to come to terms with the distinction between outcome-focused research in economics and process-focused research in anthropology. Are there ways of bridging this gap, Lipton asked, and should the attempt even be made?

The division between a focus on the outcomes of social processes and a focus on the interactions, negotiations and contestations that characterize the processes themselves reflects an epistemological as much as a methodological divide. The epistemological foundations of a discipline establish the grounds of explanation and knowledge within the discipline. Overall, epistemological arguments "justify or legitimize the vision on how to formulate arguments" (Klamer 1988: 245). These tend to be overlooked in cross-disciplinary debates, with more attention being given to differences in the scales of research or the means of data collection and analysis. For example, it is often pointed out that empirical economists get their data from large-scale surveys, aiming for wide coverage, while fieldwork-oriented anthropologists work at village or community scales and collect much of their own household data (see e.g. various essays in Bardhan 1989 or Kanbur 2001). But this gap has narrowed in recent years – economists routinely conduct detailed household surveys (e.g. Deaton 1997) and studies of globalization are well entrenched in anthropology (Appadurai 2002; Gupta and Ferguson 2002). The outcome–process difference, however, has endured.[3]

---

[1]   There are, in fact, leading economists and anthropologists who have engaged seriously and constructively with the work of the other group. Examples include Geertz (1978), Sen (1999), Douglas (1992), Douglas and Isherwood (1996), Dasgupta (1993), and Appadurai (1989; 2004). But this is the road less taken.

[2]   The book review was of Bardhan (ed.), 1989, *Conversations between economists and anthropologists: methodological issues in measuring economic change in rural India*, New Delhi: Oxford University Press.

[3]   Statements such as this reflect a certain degree of generalization about economics and anthropology. These generalizations may broadly be valid but may also blur the distinctions amongst techniques and practitioners *within* each discipline.

Outcomes and Processes

Outcomes are the findings of research such as hypotheses to be tested, or the rejection or corroboration of hypotheses after testing them, or answers to "what-if" questions from manipulating model parameters and assumptions. Outcomes in economic analysis have two characteristics:

1   They serve as predictions, saying what various actors will do in response to specific changes, given the assumptions and starting conditions of the model.
2   They describe equilibrium solutions for the economy. The concept of equilibrium was borrowed from physics, and describes a state in which economic agents have no incentive to change their behavior (MIT 1999: 129).

Processes are the dynamic steps through which particular outcomes may or may not be reached, and through which social relations may be re-shaped. The outcome-process distinction, while difficult to define with precision, nevertheless seems to be understood by economists as a point of departure between their discipline and the other social sciences.[4] Anthropologists are, by and large, wary of the equilibrium-focused way of viewing the world, with its implication of harmony and satisfaction where everyone is already doing the best he or she can do. They have always claimed that economists are overly concerned with predicting outcomes at the expense of a nuanced and processual understanding of social life.

The outcome–process divide does not mean that economists are uninterested in processes, or that anthropologists think of outcomes as irrelevant. Rather, it means that research in economics is driven primarily by the need to predict outcomes while anthropology is driven by a concern with relationships, values and power dynamics. Take the case of local common-pool resources, or the "commons." Why do economists and anthropologists study the commons? For economists, the historical motivation has been the resolution of the commons dilemma – how can self-regarding individuals, with cooperative as well as conflicting interests, act collectively to protect their common resources (Runge 1984; Seabright 1993; Sethi and Somanathan: ch. 7, this volume). A second motivation is to affect public policy, to suggest the conditions under which aggregate welfare enhancing collective action can be fostered.

For most anthropologists efficient management and policy advice are not the most salient concepts. In the contemporary anthropological literature on the commons, there is less emphasis on the rules of collective management and more on collective resistance to prevent the appropriation of lands or forests (Peluso 1992; Baviskar 1995). Another, more recent, set of concerns stems from discourse analysis in general and the knowledge/power interface in particular (Foucault 1980). Anthropologists are thus sensitive not only to what has been said, but also to what has not been said, because not saying is a way of saying. Does the discourse that takes hold over allocation rules and the common good, for example, undermine or strengthen the workings of power in society? These questions

---

[4]   See e.g. the quotes from Klamer (1988) and Heinrich et al. (2004) in the introductory chapter of this volume.

have led to critical interrogation of the dominant (and often laudatory) discourse on community-based "solutions" to common property resources (Li 1996; Goldman 1997).

Economists and anthropologists may also find it difficult to borrow one another's results and insights and use them in their own work, because one group's style of reasoning may not be well understood by the other group, and the interpretation of one another's research results may be problematic. The epistemologies of anthropology have an interpretive component,[5] which posits that human societies cannot be understood through the "neutral" definitions, observations and measurements that define economics. There are no brute facts in social life; rather, it is essential to grasp the subjective meanings of social actions and categories.[6] Here the research product is a contextual understanding of not what e.g. a farmer does, but the processes that act on him and that he acts on, and the interaction of power, values, and norms within which his actions *make sense*. Thus the well-defined and, in principle, measurable senses in which an economist uses terms like "cooperation" or "local" may not be generalizable to anthropological studies. If anything these differences have become more pronounced over the last two decades, widening the gulf between economists' generalizable predictions and anthropology's "situated knowledges" (Haraway 1991).

In this chapter I argue that cross-disciplinary conversations would be made easier if economists were to consider how more attention to processes could refine their own work, and if anthropologists were to consider the avenues through which the outcomes of economic modeling could inform their own research. The challenge for economics and anthropology is to illuminate one another while struggling with their sometimes-incompatible research methods and often strikingly different research motivations.

Cooperative Conversations

Approaching this conversation will be easier if it is anchored by specific studies on common property. I choose community-managed irrigation water as the focal resource for the rest of this chapter. Through critical analysis of four papers (two economics, one institutional-anthropological and one social-anthropological) I ask:

1   Can the inferences of economic models be better interpreted through anthropology-inspired questions about structure and process?
2   Can the outcomes of economic models be more precisely stated by explicitly acknowledging what is being said as well as what is not being said?
3   Can anthropologists' research be guided by results or correlations from economic models – especially counter-intuitive or unexpected results – and thereby lead to new analyses?

---

[5]   In this chapter, by "anthropologists" I mean social and cultural anthropologists. Anthropologists subscribe to a larger range of epistemologies and theoretical frameworks than do economists. The dangers of generalizing about any discipline are therefore more acute when discussing anthropology than economics.

[6]   Weber called the goal of such research *verstehen* as opposed to *erklären* – meaning, empathetic understanding as opposed to detached explanation. While not fully embracing Weber's original sense of *verstehen* – which has run into theoretical and practical problems in research practice (Giddens 1993) – interpretive research seeks to counter the detached "neutral-observer" stance of traditional social science.

The four papers I examine in some detail are:

1   Pranab Bardhan. 2000b. "Irrigation and cooperation: An empirical analysis of co-operation on irrigation in South India." *Economic Development and Cultural Change.*
2   Isha Ray and Jeffrey Williams. 2002. "Locational asymmetry and the potential for cooperation on a canal." *Journal of Development Economics.*

These are both empirical papers, one an econometric and one a mathematical programming model.

3   Robert Wade. 1987. "The management of common property resources: finding a co-operative solution." *The World Bank Research Observer.*[7]
4   David Mosse. 1997. "The symbolic making of a common property resource: history, ecology and locality in a tank-irrigated landscape in South India." *Development and Change.*

The first of these is by a political scientist, and reaches what might be called "institutional-economic" conclusions, but is rich in anthropological and historical detail. The second is by a social anthropologist who uses Wade's work as a foil for his own. Both studies are process-oriented, but reflect different research concerns and theoretical underpinnings.

Q1: Can the inferences of economic models be better interpreted through anthropology-inspired questions about structures and processes?

Analytical models are judged on whether their outcomes have been observed in the real world, and confidence builds in the model and its assumptions if they are deemed to have good explanatory power. Occasionally, models may also be judged by whether their assumptions are grounded in the real world – as Basu (2000: 246) argues they should be – but the traditional justification for accepting a model is that "it works."[8] New models are proposed, with new assumptions, on the argument that the older models could not explain some facet of economic life. New models are also proposed if older models "explain" a bit too much – i.e. produce a plethora of equilibria, most of which are never empirically observed (see e.g. Sethi and Somanathan 1996). However, while a large number of fake equilibria is a weakness in a model, and a smaller number of more plausible equilibria is a good criterion for model selection, a unique equilibrium is not always indicative of a better model.[9]

Once a model has a stable outcome, e.g. a unique Nash equilibrium, the economist takes that outcome and works backwards to infer a plausible social process from it. However, "the basic trouble is that nature is so complex that many quite different theories can

---

[7]   The contents of this and other related papers were subsequently worked into *Village republics* (1988) – a book that has been enormously influential in the common-pool resource literature.
[8]   This may be a reasonable way to think, but it is not always justified from within the model. Analytical models are *if P then Q* type statements. Logically, that tells us nothing about inferring *P* from having observed *Q*.
[9]   Nor does a unique equilibrium have an unambiguous interpretation.

go some way to explaining the results" (Crick 1988: 141).[10] Different theories may (implicitly) have particular processes embedded in them, or any one theoretical outcome could arise from any one of several processes. Some models have causal arrows explicitly specified, while others, such as the standard *mxn* game matrices, are quite spare. If this is so, then working back from an outcome can provide at best a partial guide to the process that gave rise to it, and at worst it is of no help at all. What, for instance, are the implications of cooperation if the conditions under which it is stable are as likely to be sustained by coercion as by consensus? Surely it matters for social policy if "resource conservation" is achieved voluntarily or through coercion by the state (Peluso 1993), for example. What indeed is the meaning of such cooperation for the cooperating parties? Here is where looking with an anthropological eye at the processes that lead to specific model inferences would help to interpret those inferences, and to consider alternative explanations for ostensibly the same outcomes.

Econometric models also have to contend with multiple explanations of their (unique) correlational outcomes. Take the example of Bardhan (2000) – a regression analysis of a stratified sample of 480 farmers in 48 randomly selected irrigated villages of Tamil Nadu, India. In this chapter, the author conducts a correlational analysis of the conditions that are conducive to cooperation on small-scale irrigation systems. He defines three dependent variables as indicators of cooperation – the maintenance and condition of distributaries and field channels, the number of water-related conflicts within each of the sampled villages, and the frequency with which the agreed-upon water allocation rules are violated. He defines several independent variables – such as the number of water users per system, extent of economic inequality, degree of caste homogeneity, and whether the water allocation and cost-sharing rules were devised jointly by the farmers or by the village elite. The primary data collection method was the structured survey. The idea was to regress the independent variables against the indicators of cooperation to gauge the positive or negative nature of the relationships. For instance, is the number of users positively or negatively correlated with the frequency of rule violations? Is caste homogeneity positively or negatively correlated with water conflicts? And so on.

To illustrate how a model such as this one can have unambiguous and plausible outcomes that are consistent with more than one processual-structural explanation, I focus on two very interesting results. Both relate to the degree to which the elite crafted – or were perceived to have crafted – the rules of water allocation. First, the author finds that the maintenance of field channels is negatively and significantly correlated with the degree of elite rule-making.[11] This finding is accompanied by a footnoted observation that farmers were more likely to say positive things about a system where the rules were perceived to have been democratically crafted. The outcome is clear, but the implication of this outcome is unclear. Perhaps there is no "real" negative relationship between channel maintenance and the rule of elites, but the negative relationship is one of perception?

---

[10] Crick – who approved of modeling, but only cautiously so – was one of the most insightful of writers on the relationship between theoretical and empirical work. In the piece quoted from, he was discussing the problem of theory and modeling in biology as opposed to the physical sciences. His argument rests on the relative complexity of biological processes and their outcomes. The social world is, of course, at least as complex, with theories being at best broad generalizations with many exceptions.

[11] "Significant" here means statistically significant, it does not imply economic or otherwise substantive significance (see McCloskey and Ziliak 1996).

That is, the responses reflected a generalized negative attitude towards elite control and a positive attitude towards participatory decision-making. That is plausible. Or perhaps the correlation was real, and the negative sign is to be explained by the average farmer's feeling of lack of ownership of the system? However, thinking about anthropological studies – many of which show that rules of community-based cooperation are regularly crafted by elites, and often for the benefit of the same elites – we can consider an alternative explanation of this outcome.

The districts of Tamil Nadu where this study was conducted have a number of open- as well as bore-wells, and, as elsewhere, the better-off farmers are more likely to have wells than the poorer farmers. Throughout the Deccan Plateau, shallow wells are recharged by tank and canal seepage, and since water in a private well is completely under the control of a farmer, its marginal value can be very high (Ray and Williams 1999). In poorly maintained field channels the water flow is sluggish rather than fast, so a higher proportion of that flow will seep into the ground (Chow 1959). If the elite did in fact craft the rules of cooperation, and also owned a disproportionate number of the wells, it is perfectly possible that the rules were made to emphasize water allocation shares and conflict resolution, but were deliberately less particular about channel maintenance. What is more, an economic calculation might show that some of these poorly-maintained elite-ruled channel systems are agriculturally more productive than some in which field channels are in good repair and the water allocation more equitable.

The interpretation offered in Bardhan (2000a) as well as the hypothetical one in this chapter are compatible with the regression outcome, but they do not describe the same society and would not lead to the same policy recommendations. If the negative correlation is one of perception, then other than to facilitate better communication within water users' associations, there is no obvious policy intervention. If the negative correlation is real and stems from the lack of democratic decision-making, then the state, or more likely, a civil society group, could perhaps foster more participatory processes. But if the elite deliberately keep channels poorly maintained so their wells can benefit disproportionately from canal seepage, then polite policy changes are not likely to be effective – the more powerful farmers may actively resist system "improvements."

Second, the author finds that there is perfect (negative) correlation between reports of rule violations and the perception of elites making the rules. What processes could have given rise to this outcome? One possible explanation – and that suggested in the chapter – is that the elite are more likely to break rules in general, because they can get away with it. However, when they *make* the rules they are not as likely to break them. This is believable. But why do they not break them? Is it because, having made the rules themselves the elite are normatively more committed to them? Maybe so.[12] Or perhaps the rules are crafted according to elite convenience in the first place, and generally enforced by arguing that it's good for everyone to comply with the "community" rules (see Bourdieu 1977). In this case the law-abiding elite would not need to break the rules. Or

---

[12]   In my fieldwork in Maharashtra, I did observe this tendency. The irrigation cooperative I studied had a strong elite influence. One of the three largest farmers, who had campaigned for cooperative as opposed to state control, told me that he had given up on illegal irrigation. He had supported an irrigation cooperative, he could not now ignore the rules. "It looks bad." I saw this on the Gediz Canal in western Turkey, too. There the allocation rules were enforced by the influential farmers, who did not always benefit from the enforcement, but enjoyed the additional status given to them as enforcers. They too hardly ever broke the rules.

perhaps different *de facto* even if not *de jure* rules are in place for the elite than for the rest – and at least some respondents in the elite-ruled villages simply internalized this difference and reflected it back in their responses. In this case, perfect rule compliance would also be reported. Or perhaps ordinary farmers are more afraid to break elite-crafted rules – thus significantly lowering the incidence of rule violation in such villages. (We do not know from the reported results which individuals are violating the rules in which particular village.) These contexts and therefore the explanations of the "same" outcome are entirely different. Indeed there is no *a priori* reason to assume causal homogeneity across the villages at all – inferring causation from cross-sectional data tends to force the researcher into a single explanation of each outcome, which may not be justified (Collier, Seawright, and Munck 2004).

My argument in this section has been that an explanation of any model outcome is invariably about process and structure. Working back from an equilibrium solution or from a statistical correlation is helpful in understanding central tendencies, and in eliminating processes that are incompatible with the model outcome. But it is of limited help in deciding which processes are at work. For this purpose, one has to interrogate the economist's model by thinking more like an anthropologist – by carrying out "empirical investigations of processes themselves" (Lipton 1992) – so that alternative explanations can be considered.

If analyses of specific circumstances can be undertaken during the study, or after the initial findings, then one possible path would be to be to choose a small number of cases from the larger sample for what qualitative researchers call within-case causal process analysis. This is a method by which each case is treated singly and evidence internal to the case is used to evaluate competing hypotheses (Collier, Mahoney, and Seawright 2004). Despite potential selection bias problems, cases for such studies are best *not* chosen randomly.[13] Within-case analysis of a few cases with no variance on the value of the dependent variable (in this case, little rule violation) would be a better choice. The object would not be to generalize up from those detailed process analyses, but, with closer knowledge of at least some of the cases, to get a sense of alternative paths that might lead to the same outcome, and of whether the assumption of causal homogeneity in the regression model is approximately justified.

If this last step cannot be taken, it is incumbent on the economist to interpret his or her results cautiously. Intellectual merit apart, there is a practical reason for the process-oriented interrogation of economic solutions. Without a processual understanding of cooperative outcomes, how can new institutions of community-based cooperation be fostered? The question itself explicitly assumes that community-based cooperation is desirable, because it implicitly assumes that a desirable outcome – efficient and orderly water allocation – will be the result of a desirable process. But this is not necessarily so.

Q2: Can the outcomes of economic models be more precisely stated by explicitly acknowledging what is being said as well as what is not being said?

---

[13]   Self-selection in the sample is common in the case study method, and the traditional view of quantitative research is that this introduces "bias" in the resulting analysis. But the method of within-case analysis or causal-process analysis for a few select cases is not derivative of large *n* analysis methods. Small *n* samples – when chosen and used well – are not little versions of large *n* samples; they are, as Margaret Mead once called them, "another kind of sample."

In this section I take up an issue that anthropologists consider central but economists do not explicitly take into account. In every model (and explanation) there are points that are explicitly made and others that are not made. What is explicitly said and inferred form the bases of the model's policy recommendations. But, say critical anthropologists, what is being said and not being said, and being asked and not being asked, reveal whose interests the explicit recommendations are serving, and which social structures they hold up (Li 2002). They argue that the "celebration" of community-based natural resource management as a system that upholds the common good overlooks the micro-politics of local life. Mosse (1997) is critical of institutional-economic models of common property management as "sets of rules and cooperative equilibrium outcomes internally sustained by a structure of incentives." The critique is even more trenchantly expressed by Mohan and Stokke (2000). They claim that the emphasis on local participation in the development arena, and in resource management, "tend[s] to underplay both local inequalities and power relations as well as national and transnational economic and political forces."[14]

In this light, I examine the implications of Ray and Williams (2002), a mathematical programming model of canal irrigation in Maharashtra, India. The paper was about conditions under which the theft of irrigation water on canal systems – officially called "unauthorized irrigation" – could be controlled through farmer cooperation. We hypothesized that locational asymmetry on even small subsections of the canal system was a key determinant of who was likely to cooperate and who was not likely to cooperate. In a 30-farm model of a watercourse, we gave the farmers an equal propensity to steal extra water but we made the stealing opportunity a function of the farmer's location. Upstream farmers are generally better positioned to siphon off extra water when needed so our hypothesis was that they would resist a farmer-run cooperative. We assumed that each farmer was profit maximizing, and derived a model map of the watercourse showing the (endogenous) dividing line between those who would want a cooperative with enforceable rules of water allocation, and those who preferred the rule-less free for all. We tested this model empirically by interviewing 67 farmers in 2 villages where an irrigation cooperative had recently been voted into existence,[15] and compared the model map of pro-cooperative votes to the actual village-specific one. In both cases there was a clear pattern of downstream votes in favor of a farmer cooperative, and therefore against Irrigation Department (ID) control of the canal, and upstream votes against.

I now re-examine this model – with some trepidation, let me confess – in the light of what it left out. Any economist knows that a model leaves things out – otherwise it becomes intractable and yields no useful outcomes. When I wrote the code for the program, I isolated the effect of location by leaving out wealth, caste and power inequality. Our question was: with or without these heterogeneities, does location have an independent role in the farmer's attitude towards cooperation? But in the world outside the model, wealth, caste and power influences *were* present. Was our chapter then an example of a

---

[14]   While sympathetic to the need to listen to the unspoken as well as the spoken, as it were, I should point out that many model-oriented papers on irrigation do have extended discussions on locally and historically specific forms of cooperation, on the characteristics of irrigation guards and "water-turners," and on the sometimes antagonistic and sometimes tolerant attitudes of the state to local cooperation. This is true of the work of Elinor Ostrom (1990; 1994, with Gardner and Walker) and Robert Wade (1988) – two of the most influential economic-institutional scholars of irrigation.

[15]   Both villages were on the same watercourse.

model with strategic silences and omissions, which were then not explicitly acknowledged in the policy recommendation sections? I illustrate the point with three examples from my fieldwork in Maharashtra.

First, several Muslim farmers were located downstream, and the model "predicted" that they would vote for a farmer-run cooperative on the basis of their locational disadvantage. And in fact they were overwhelmingly in favor of it. But here are the words of one of the three leaders of the cooperative movement, himself a well-off Muslim farmer:

> Basically Madam everything here goes by community. I wanted this cooperative, I did not like having to take water unlawfully. I saw that it was creating conflicts, and this was bad for the whole village. So I campaigned for the cooperative. Within a few days all the Muslims had signed up for it.

Second, caste loyalties or the lack thereof also made a difference to how specific farmers voted. For example, two quite prosperous Marwari brothers in this Maratha- and Mali-dominated region – one upstream and one downstream – both voted in favor of local-level cooperation. Therefore one of these votes, that of the upstream brother, would have been incorrectly predicted by our model. Here is that troublesome farmer:[16]

> See, these people are all decent people. We have never felt that we didn't get water because we were outsiders. My own water flow was good, my groundnut yields are the best, ask anybody. But sometimes there were fights on the canal.[17] And when there is a fight, well, we just don't have the numbers. For outsiders, laws that everyone has to follow are better than not having proper laws.

Third, several of the smaller farmers had felt humiliated by the arbitrary and arrogant behavior of the ID canal inspectors (who used to allocate the water prior to the formation of the cooperative). Many of them were located at the bottom two-thirds of the watercourse, and, as predicted by our model, they had voted overwhelmingly in favor of replacing the ID with local inspectors. They said they were always facing water shortages on account of water theft and general mismanagement. But what is more:

> To the ID's man, I was not even an insect; I was dirt. He wanted to see me on my knees, begging for water, calling him *Bhausahib, Bhausahib*.[18] But why should I do it? As soon as those society people came to me I said, I don't need any explanations, you just show me where to sign my name.

My point in re-visiting this model is not that it was "wrong" in its suggested outcomes – in fact the predicted pattern of cooperation was very close to the independently verified

---

[16]   Developing and testing a model is a strange experience. When we looked at the village map of votes for and against the cooperative, we saw that this farmer – median-sized, upstream, commercially successful, and reporting no difficulty with his pre-cooperative water supply – had voted in favor of replacing the Irrigation Department with a watercourse-based cooperative. We were initially quite annoyed with him for having gone "against" our model.

[17]   He meant before the cooperative rules were instituted, and when the watercourse was run by a very lax Irrigation Department. Conflicts about whose irrigation turn it was and who was encroaching were common.

[18]   In Marathi, *respected brother*.

pattern. The model also had a plausible mechanism for why this should be so,[19] and we concluded that location was an independent predictor of farmers' attitudes towards co-operation. We also concluded from modeling the farming system, that water's "time of arrival, its delivery frequency, and the seasonal nature of the crops' water requirements, combine with the supply of labor, seepage down the channel, and the costs of stealing water, to determine the potential for cooperation in complex, and sometimes surprising, ways." This, too, still holds as a valid conclusion. But, at least in some of the prediction-compatible cases, the left-out social and political factors played a role in the success of the prediction. So too for the prediction errors – they were not always, or were not explained as being, on account of a location-driven or agriculture-driven calculus. We did not cover up these "deviations" in our chapter, but we were silent about their implications when explaining the conclusions and significance of the model.

So the question is: do models such as this one – by abstracting from caste or influence or the desire for dignity – implicitly suggest that these factors are less important, and that village-level cooperation can take place *purely* on the basis of a cost–benefit calculus, driven by economic and geographic factors? This is what sociologists and anthropologists have been critical of, from both a social-scientific as well as a political standpoint. I could defend our work by arguing that we made clear in the paper that we wanted to isolate the effect of location so we could see if location had an effect independent of caste, community or wealth. We never claimed that wealth and influence were *not* players in village-based cooperation. But I suspect that an anthropological eye on the model would look askance at such a defense – not saying, they would claim, is also a form of saying.

Economists have to acknowledge the implications of what they are abstracting from – not to undermine the usefulness of their models, and not to lose their tractability, but because of the way that their models might be interpreted in policy circles. Modeling involves real gains and real losses, and these strategic losses should be brought back into the picture when interpreting outcomes and advising policy-makers. Sometimes the losses could outweigh the gains when modeling complex systems (Krugman 1995: 79). Since simple and general policies are easier to recommend than nuanced and contextual policies, the simple and unqualified version of a model often carries the day in the policy-advice process (Chambers 2001). There are many illuminating examples of (the better) economic models cutting through the clutter to isolate the effect of one variable from that of another. But policy has to be implemented clutter and all. Thinking through the intellectual as well as political implications of what has *not* been said and *not* been asked would bring more caution, integrity and precision into the interpretation of a model's outcomes and "answers."

Q3: Can anthropologists' research be guided by results or correlations from economic models – especially counter-intuitive or unexpected results – and thereby lead to new analyses?

---

[19]   Programming models, with their key parameters calibrated to a particular context, and the functional relationships between and amongst variables explicitly modeled, tell a clearer causal story than is sometimes possible with regression models. The causal mechanisms are built into the model and do not have to be inferred.

Economists' research on common property has already learned much from the hundreds of irrigation-related case studies conducted all over the world by anthropologists and other social scientists. It is normal to find economists justifying the assumptions of their models by reference to the field insights of anthropologists (Sethi and Somanathan 1996; Ostrom, Gardner, and Walker 1994). Anthropologists are less overtly influenced by economics, and critique of economic analysis is virtually a mini-industry is some anthropological circles. In this section I argue that, critique notwithstanding, economic models and their outcomes can (and, in the commons literature, already do) usefully inform anthropological inquiry. I also suggest that every now and then models surprise with counter-intuitive results or non-obvious correlations. Such results should be an invitation to anthropology to investigate new or changing social processes that were so far not thought of, or perhaps have started to emerge but have hitherto gone unnoticed.

One of the best-known pieces of research in the common-pool literature in general and the irrigation literature in particular is Robert Wade's 1988 book, *Village Republics*. Many of its central findings (though not the rich ethnographic detail in his research) were first published in 1987, in the *World Bank Research Observer*. Wade's research is a study of canal-based cooperation in Andhra Pradesh, India – where he noticed that some villages had elaborate cooperative organizations while others did not. His question was, when will villagers cooperate to allocate their common water resources? His study is a part anthropological part economic-institutional study, with no formal model and no regressions. Its main results are:

1   There is a positive correlation between location on the canal system (implicitly the main independent variable) and the propensity of irrigators to cooperate (implicitly the dependent variable). Fewer head-end villages have cooperative institutions in place relative to tail-end villages.
2   A set of "conditions," especially high net collective benefits from cooperation coupled with high ecological and economic risks from not cooperating over scarce water lead to irrigation-based cooperation. This explains the first finding: villages at the tail end of a canal system are more water-short, and have more to gain from formal water management rules.
3   Resource-based cooperation is rational and about "getting things done." What is more, cooperation is most often organized in accordance with traditional caste authority, otherwise the social control needed to share the water could break down. Cooperation is not about opening up democratic spaces, or about the moral economy of Scott (1976) or Geertz (1963).

In 1997, David Mosse published a historical-anthropological paper in *Development and Change*, which started with the same question as Wade: when will villagers cooperate to allocate their common water resources? Mosse's ethnographic work in tank-irrigated districts of Tamil Nadu corroborated several of Wade's results, such as the finding that economic benefits and ecological risks made collective action over water more likely. But his critique of Wade, and by extension of other common property research in the economic-institutional vein, reflects three points of departure:

1   *Conclusions*: Village-based cooperation, Mosse finds, is not merely about material gains and losses as conventionally measured, but also about creating and asserting rights to

symbolic resources. Following Bourdieu, he argues that the symbolic value of the commons, such as temples, fish and water, are inseparable from their material values.

2   *Modes of explanation*: Deterministic relationships between ecological-economic conditions and cooperation, or the analytical outcomes of "what-if" questions in models of cooperative management, ignore structures and processes of power.[20] For example, the traditional dominance of upper castes in the "cooperative" villages was historically implemented through control over water and other common resources, and these groups retained the ability to bend the rules to their own purposes. Irrigation water is *ruled* rather than managed. Villages without collective action were those where irrigation water never had been part of the mode of caste control.

3   *The role of the state*: Wade finds that the official water agency of the state had no idea of the extent of cooperative management at the village level. Mosse counters that in fact the state has always been tied to these "cooperative" ventures, from the colonial era to now. Moreover, models of harmonious cooperation under "rule regimes," where the state has little or no role, are used by donors to further currently fashionable policies of decentralized management.

What does Mosse v. Wade, and in particular Mosse's outcome-process related critique, reveal about the role of economic analysis in furthering the work of anthropology? As always, we have to start with a clear understanding of the purpose of models and of how their outcomes are to be understood. A theory or a model isn't a representation of some social phenomenon – much less a comprehensive representation. It is a demonstration of the phenomenon, and of a mechanism that might uphold the phenomenon under certain well-specified conditions. Theories (and by extension) theoretical inferences are best seen as "hints to suggest possible lines of research" (Crick 1988: 138), and as a source of ideas about "where to look." Each model provides a starting point for a new step in a research program, and suggests potentially important relationships that are worth further investigation. This is the role that models have played within the discipline of economics itself. Looking at Mosse v. Wade in that light, economic-institutional models seem to have served this purpose admirably for anthropological research on the commons, and have been doing so since Hardin's "tragedy" (Hardin 1968). Empirical studies by a range of scholars, including social anthropologists, have often confirmed the key findings of economic theory on different categories of common resources (Dasgupta 1993: 287). Even when economics provides a point of departure, or a foil against which to make the case for alternative assumptions and alternative modes of explanation, this is in itself a useful contribution. Mosse himself accepts the starting point that Wade's research affords him, and goes on to argue that his work goes beyond Wade to show that irrigation is a socio-cultural and not merely an economic system (Mosse 1997: 474). But many critical anthropologists have – without quite acknowledging the debt, if we are to listen for the unspoken – decided where to look, and from where to take off, from models of collective action on the commons.

---

[20]   This criticism of determinism directly reflects the outcome-process distinction. Of course, the longer the timeframe of analysis and the larger the number and types of variables in the analysis, the more everything becomes endogenous, and the harder it is to disentangle what causes what.

Finally, models are accused (sometimes with justification) of choosing their axioms cleverly so they can yield the desired results. Anthropologists have also been critical of economic models for their alleged simplicity and excessive faith in quantifiable outcomes, many of which appear obvious to other social scientists. Of course economic models and regression analyses can produce fairly obvious outcomes, but every now and then a model will yield an inference or a "what-if" outcome that the modeler did not expect, and that is counter-intuitive. Some of these surprises can alert researchers to potential unintended consequences of specific policy interventions that are under consideration or perhaps already in place. Such results provide avenues for anthropologists as well as economists to investigate new or changing social processes that were so far not anticipated, or that may have started to emerge but have hitherto gone unnoticed.

Both Bardhan (2000a) and Ray and Williams (2002), as well as Sethi and Somanathan (ch. 7, this volume), have non-obvious or surprising results. Bardhan (2000a) indicates that the relationship between intra-village inequality and cooperation over water is not a monolithic one. Instead, there appears to be a U-shaped relationship between inequality of asset holdings and degree of cooperation over water allocation. The hypothesis that lower levels of inequality would be conducive to cooperation would have been *a priori* a plausible one. It is not obvious what causal processes are behind the U-shaped relationship suggested in the chapter (or if indeed it holds under many conditions), and the finding itself is not obvious from the model specification. Ray and Williams (2002) show that reducing water theft and encouraging cooperation and equity in water allocation among farmers may cause the landless on the watercourse to suffer. This is because equity in water sharing alters the cropping patterns and spreads out the demand for labor over the entire year, thus leading to a greater use of family labor and reduced employment opportunities for the landless. Here the causal chain is clear but would not have been predictable simply from the model's assumptions and constraints. The Sethi and Somanathan chapter models the evolution of cooperation on the commons with the assumption that (at least some) people are reciprocal rather than maximizing. Their model predicts, amongst other things, that cooperation is more likely when group size is sufficiently large. The literature on group size and cooperation is mixed, but ever since Olson (1971) the conventional wisdom has held that smaller is better. While these outcomes were not the central argument of any of the three papers, they do have consequences for governance arrangements and sometimes indicate potential trade-offs between desirable goals. Outcomes, in short, are not merely static snapshots of a dynamic reality. Change proceeds as a sequence of outcomes, and models could predict some of these before they are evident on the ground.

Unexpected model results allow researchers to see phenomena that were not seen before, and which may just be emerging. They provide an opening for further investigation for economists and anthropologists alike. For example, are these predicted phenomena actually being observed? If yes, what processes and structures explain their particular manifestations? What norms or power relations are changing or being renegotiated as a response to these emergent phenomena? If the phenomena are not observed, what did the model overlook or what variable was simplified to the extent that it has no meaning? And of course, how should these changes be interpreted, and from whose vantage point? These are questions about process and structure that anthropologists are theoretically and empirically better-equipped to explain than are economists. As such, the surprises from otherwise plausible economics models could act as an "invitation to anthropology to widen its conceptions of how human beings engage their own futures" (Appadurai 2004).

Conclusions

The premise of this chapter is that the outcomes of economic models and process-analyses of anthropology are both essential for understanding social phenomena, including those surrounding the commons. The main argument has been that an explanation of any model outcome is invariably about process and structure – the outcomes of several models are compatible with many different causal processes. Therefore without a processual understanding of cooperative outcomes, new institutions of community-based cooperation cannot be fostered in specific places. In addition, anthropologists pay equal attention to exclusions and inclusions, to the said as well as unsaid. In that spirit, one must ask if models of resource management that are silent on e.g. political influence, or the desire for dignity, implicitly suggest that these factors are less important to cooperation than economic and ecological factors. The chapter argues that policy advice has to take into account the explicit findings of a model as well as its silences.

Anthropologists are also critical of economic models for their simplicity and often obvious outcomes. But I have argued that influential models can and do provide anthropologists with useful starting points and constructs for their own research. Besides, every now and then models surprise with counter-intuitive results, especially with respect to emergent social phenomena. Such results challenge both anthropologists and economists to investigate new or changing social processes that were so far not anticipated or have gone unnoticed. For economists and anthropologists to learn from process and outcome respectively, however, it is incumbent upon economists to interpret the outcomes of their models more modestly and more accurately than many are inclined to do. This will make it easier for anthropologists to interpret economic models, to focus their critiques, and to go beyond critique to judge the potential usefulness of models for their own work.

References

Appadurai, Arjun. 1989. "Small-scale techniques and large-scale objectives." In Bardhan (ed.), 250–82.

Appadurai, Arjun. 2002. "Disjuncture and difference in the global cultural economy." In Inda, Jonathan and Renato Rosaldo (eds), *The anthropology of globalization*. Oxford: Blackwell Publishing, 46–64.

Appadurai, Arjun. 2004. "The capacity to aspire: culture and the terms of recognition." In Rao and Walton (eds), 59–84.

Baland, Jean-Marie and Jean-Philippe Platteau. 1996. *Halting degradation of the commons: is there a role for rural communities?* Oxford: Oxford University Press.

Bardhan, Pranab (ed.). 1989. *Conversations between economists and anthropologists: methodological issues in measuring economic change in rural India*. New Delhi: Oxford University Press.

Bardhan, Pranab. 2000. "Irrigation and cooperation: an empirical analysis of 48 irrigation communities in south India." *Economic Development and Cultural Change*, 48: 847–66.

Basu, Kaushik. 2000. *Prelude to political economy: a study of the social and political foundations of economics*. Oxford and New York: Oxford University Press.

Baviskar, Amita. 1995. *In the belly of the river: tribal conflicts over development in the Narmada Valley*. Delhi and New York: Oxford University Press.

Bourdieu, Pierre. 1977. *Outline of a theory of practice*. Cambridge: Cambridge University Press.

Brady, Henry and David Collier. 2004. *Rethinking social inquiry: diverse tools, shared standards*. Lanham: Rowman & Littlefield.

Chambers, Robert. 2001. "Qualitative approaches: self criticism and what can be gained from quant-itative approaches." In Kanbur (ed.), downloadable from www.q-squared.ca.

Chow, V. T. 1959. *Open channel hydraulics*. New York: McGraw-Hill.

Collier, David, James Mahoney, and Jason Seawright. 2004. "Claiming too much: warnings about selection bias." In Brady and Collier (eds), 85–102.

Collier, David, Jason Seawright, and Gerardo Munck. 2004. "The quest for standards." In Brady and Collier (eds), 21–50.

Crick, Francis. 1988. *What mad pursuit: a personal view of scientific discovery*. New York: Basic Books.

Dasgupta, Partha. 1993. *An inquiry into well-being and destitution*. Oxford: Clarendon Press.

Deaton, Angus. 1997. *The analysis of household surveys: a microeconometric approach to development policy*. Baltimore: published for the World Bank by Johns Hopkins University Press.

Douglas, Mary. 1992. *Risk and blame: essays in cultural theory*. London: Routledge.

Douglas, Mary and B. Isherwood. 1996. *The world of goods: towards an anthropology of consumption*. London: Routledge.

Foucault, Michel. 1980. *Power/knowledge: selected interviews and other writings, 1972–1977*. Edited and translated by Colin Gordon. Sussex: Harvester.

Geertz, Clifford. 1963. *Agricultural involution: the process of ecological change in Indonesia*. Berkeley: University of California Press.

Geertz, Clifford. 1978. "The bazaar economy: information and search in peasant marketing." *American Economic Review*, 68: 28–32.

Giddens, Anthony. 1993. *New rules of sociological method: a positive critique of interpretative sociologies*. Stanford: Stanford University Press.

Goldman, Michael. 1997. "Customs in common: the epistemic world of the commons scholars." *Theory and Society*, 26: 1–37.

Gupta, Akhil and James Ferguson. 2002. "Beyond culture: space, identity and the politics of difference." In Jonathan Inda and Renato Rosaldo (eds), *The anthropology of globalization*. Oxford: Blackwell Publishing, 65–80.

Haraway, Donna. 1991. "Situated knowledges: the science question in feminism and the privilege of partial perspective." In *Simians, cyborgs, and women: the reinvention of nature*. New York: Routledge, 183–201.

Hardin, Garrett. 1968. "The tragedy of the commons." *Science*, 162: 1243–8.

Henrich, Joseph, Robert Boyd, Samuel Bowles, Colin Camerer, Ernst Fehr, and Herbert Gintis (eds). 2004. *Foundations of human sociality*. Oxford: Oxford University Press.

Kanbur, Ravi. 2001. "Q-squared? A commentary on qualitative and quantitative poverty appraisal." In Kanbur (ed.).

Kanbur, Ravi (ed.). 2001. *Qual–quant: qualitative and quantitative poverty appraisal: complementarities, tensions and the way forward*. Workshop held at Cornell University, downloadable from www.q-squared.ca.

Klamer, Arjo. 1988. *Conversations with economists*. Totowa: Rowman and Allanheld.

Krugman, Paul. 1995. *Development, geography and economic theory*. Cambridge: MIT Press.

Li, Tania M. 1996. "Images of community: discourse and strategy in property relations." *Development and Change*, 27: 501–27.

Li, Tania M. 2002. "Engaging simplifications: community-based resource management, market processes and state agendas in upland Southeast Asia." *World Development*, 30: 265–83.

Lipton, Michael. 1992. "Economics and anthropology: grounding models in relationships." *World Development*, 20: 1541–6.

McCloskey, Deirdre and Stephen Ziliak. 1996. "The standard error of regression." *Journal of Economic Literature*, 34: 97–114.

MIT. 1999. *The MIT Dictionary of Modern Economics*. Edited by David Pearce. Cambridge: MIT Press.

Mohan, Giles and Kristian Stokke. 2000. "Participatory development and empowerment: the dangers of localism." *Third World Quarterly*, 21: 247–68.

Mosse, David. 1997. "The symbolic making of a common property resource: history, ecology and locality in a tank-irrigated landscape in South India." *Development and Change*, 28: 467–504.

Olson, Mancur. 1971. *The logic of collective action; public goods and the theory of groups.* New York: Schocken Books.

Ostrom, Elinor. 1990. *Governing the commons: the evolution of institutions for collective action.* Cambridge: Cambridge University Press.

Ostrom, Elinor, R. Gardner, and J. Walker. 1994. *Rules, games and common-pool resources.* Ann Arbor: University of Michigan Press.

Peluso, Nancy. 1992. *Rich forests, poor people: resource control and resistance in Java.* Berkeley: University of California Press.

Peluso, Nancy. 1993. "Coercing conservation: the politics of state resource control." In Ronnie Lipschutz and Ken Conca (eds), *The state and social power in global environmental politics.* New York: Columbia University Press, ch. 3.

Rao, Vijayendra and Michael Walton (eds). 2004. *Culture and public action.* Stanford: Stanford Social Sciences.

Ray, Isha and Jeffrey Williams. 1999. "Evaluation of price policy in the presence of water theft." *American Journal of Agricultural Economics*, 81: 928–941.

Ray, Isha and Jeffrey Williams. 2002. "Locational asymmetry and the potential for cooperation on a canal." *Journal of Development Economics*, 67: 129–55.

Runge, Carlos F. 1984. "Institutions and the free rider: the assurance problem in collective action." *Journal of Politics*, 46: 154–75.

Scott, James. 1976. *The moral economy of the peasant.* New Haven: Yale University Press.

Sen, Amartya. 1999. *Development as freedom.* New York: Knopf.

Sethi, Rajiv and E. Somanathan. 1996. "The evolution of social norms in common property use." *American Economic Review*, 86: 766–88.

Seabright, Paul. 1993. "Managing local commons: theoretical issues in incentive design." *Journal of Economic Perspectives*, 7: 113–34.

Wade, Robert. 1987. "The management of common property resources: finding a cooperative solution." *The World Bank Research Observer*, 2: 219–34.

Wade, Robert. 1988. *Village republics.* Cambridge: Cambridge University Press.

5: Collective Action, Common Property, and Social Capital in South India

An Anthropological Commentary

David Mosse

Anthropologists and economists commonly employ opposing self-stereotypes to characterize their respective perspectives: concern with relations and processes versus the distribution of outcomes, with contextual understanding versus selective explanation; constructionist versus positivist epistemologies, inductive versus deductive research designs, participant observation versus regressions on existing data sets, and imaginary worlds populated by culturally situated groups versus rational economic maximizing individuals (Appadurai 1989; Ray: ch. 4, this volume). These contrasts set the stage for conversations between anthropologists and economists. This chapter describes a research journey in terms of one such imaginary conversation. It concerns work on collective action and common-property resources that I have conducted as an anthropologist close to the frontier with economics. Almost by definition, boundaries are places where differences are expressed, sometimes exaggerated. My argument here is that the understanding and explication of disciplinary difference can be more productive than boundary crossing, blurring, or the attempt to create a unified conceptual field. To illustrate the latter point, I will consider the case of an idea of "social capital" that its proponents claim is able, at one and the same time, to describe the relational dimension of social life and to produce aggregable data that can be subject to regression analyses that isolate "the social" as a variable at macro (e.g., national) levels. Social capital, I will suggest, is a conversation stopper.

The backdrop to this discussion is the return of "community" to the policy center stage in international development. The renewed interest in decentralization, resources management transfer (RMT), and community-driven development (CDD) focuses attention again on "local-level" institutions and collective action. Of course, governmental interest in local institutions and efforts to discover, formalize, enforce, or protect "traditional" community institutions are nothing new. Almost every region of the world that experienced colonial rule had some form of "government through community" (Li 2002; see Mosse 1999), and nationalist movements and postcolonial states discovered and molded community institutions in the image of their own modes of government (Rao 2005). The same is the case with more recent neoliberal forms of governance.

Community institutions have been idealized, homogenized, and traditionalized, but they are also the object of interventions in which they are upgraded, democratized, or modernized so as to meet new demands and fit within contemporary policy objectives. Community institutions are good vehicles for development intervention because, on the one hand, they demonstrate society as "naturally" self-regulating – an important premise of neoliberal political economy – and, on the other hand, they offer opportunities for improvement (Li 2002: 2). Furthermore, by generating new demand for transparency and bureaucratic accountability, community institutions provide a means to reform local-level governance from the bottom up.

Because representations of community so readily comply with external visions or administrative exigencies, whether colonial, nationalist, or neoliberal, it is easy to project policy preoccupations into community spaces. This chapter aims to show how awkward community institutions and local social processes can be in reality, how they confound the models and modes of analysis that dominate within donor agencies such as the World Bank. This is an anthropological view. Indeed, this article is a conversation between an anthropologist and the theories of local institutions more prevalent in donor analyses: first, institutional economics, and, second, social capital.

The chapter proceeds as follows. First, I will look at some evidence on variation in levels of collective action around common-property resources management in a south Indian region and assess different modes of explanation of this variation – institutional-economic and sociohistorical). Second, I will look at the implications of the analysis of "traditional" community institutions for the promotion of collective action through RMT and CDD interventions. Third, I will consider a certain conception of "social capital" as an analytical lens through which to view, interpret, and change local-level institutions. Two caveats are in order. First, in engaging anthropologically with economic modes of thinking about social relations, I do not discount the fact that some economists themselves are now among the critics of conventional restrictive economic models of human action. The issue of coordination and collective action, in particular, has prompted new theoretical work drawing attention to public rituals generating "common knowledge" or "symbolic public goods" to explain how rational maximizing individuals solve "problems" of coordination (Chwe 2001; Rao 2005). But, as will become clear, this does not mean that economists now seek the same kind of explanations or interpretations that anthropologists seek.[1] Second, in drawing attention to the limitations of the concept of "social capital" (premised on a false sense of common ground), my attention is on the economistic treatment of "the social," not the sociological use of the metaphor of capital. Hence, I will take the World Bank development of Robert Putnam's theory as a case rather than the work of sociologists such as Pierre Bourdieu.

---

[1]   Closer to the concerns of contemporary anthropologists might be Debraj Ray's (2004: 1; Appadurai 2004) development of the notion of "aspiration," in that the starting point is the "social grounding of individual desires" rather than the economic rationality (or function) of "culture." Chwe (2001), of course, also argues that human actions are interdependent and thus social, dependent upon mutual knowledge (a social relationship). He makes a functionalist case for the sociological a priori that humans are social, that human choices and strategizing are mediated by institutions (concepts, meanings, and values) and by shared assumptions about such things as justice, fairness, and reciprocity, which are constituted in culturally and historically specific ways (Douglas 1987). But we might go on to ask, how does common knowledge encourage coordination? When does it fail to, and why? Or, as concerns me here, how can we account for the appearance or disappearance of "rational rituals"?

Variation in Collective Action in a South Indian Tank Irrigation System

In the mid-1990s, I undertook research in the southeastern Tamil plains region of India (the districts of Ramnad and Sivaganga) on the nature of collective action around water common property. The focus was an extensive and ancient tank irrigation system developed from around the sixteenth century in which tens of thousands of interconnected reservoirs capture, store, and use surface flow (see Mosse 2003). As an anthropologist-historian, I was interested in the social organization, cultural logic, and politics of water common property. I believed that water and irrigation – something fundamental to social life but long confined to the economic domain as an input in production – needed to be treated as an institutional whole in a way that confounded the dualistic separation of economic-political and religious-cultural spheres (see Appadurai 1981). My interest was in relationships and processes, but I was also concerned with outcomes and their distribution. Together with my old friend and field assistant M. Sivan, I began research in two villages with very different practices of water acquisition, distribution, rationing, maintenance, and repair, yet both having irrigation tanks that were part of highly complex systems that were largely community rather than state operated.[2]

One village, Vayalur, was strikingly cooperative. Its water management system was well adapted to scarcity. Villagers acted collectively to ensure the water supply, diverting water from rivers, negotiating with upstream villages, and clearing channels. They agreed upon season-specific rules of water allocation (an area-based rationing calibrated to degrees of shortage, with strict preservation of water for subsistence rice cultivation on "wet land"). They had a system of distribution by water specialists, or *nirppaccis*, who undertook irrigation on the basis of detailed knowledge of the needs of individual wet-land fields, thus mitigating the usual tension between head- and tail-enders. In the other, also water-scarce, village, Alapuram, by contrast, there was no collective decision-making, and there were no formal rules of water allocation and distribution, no means to ration in times of shortage, no specialist irrigators, no means to prevent the diversion of water to dry-land cash crops or the unruly use of diesel pumps and pipes that bypassed damaged sluices and emptied the tank with remarkable speed. I began to ask questions more typical of an economist, namely, why did farmers in some villages cooperate to manage scarce resources while in other villages apparently crucial productive resources were neglected? How could intervillage variation in outcomes (degrees of collective action) be explained?[3] Pursuing this question, Sivan and I began to travel further and further afield, following water flows and finding out about water-control institutions and practices in more and more tanks and villages. Eventually our semi-structured survey, carried out through interviews, observation, and repeat visits, covered 89 interconnected tanks in 79 villages, by which time we had exhausted ourselves and our worn-out TVS moped.[4]

---

[2]   Sivan was a member of one of these villages, and I had undertaken research in the locality intermittently from 1982, working in one village for nearly two years overall.

[3]   The things that I was comparing (and taking as indicators of the strength of collective action) were, inter alia, the presence (and nature) of rules to allocate water in times of scarcity, specialist water turners and channel guards, and restrictions on the use of pumps.

[4]   We had not matched our economist questions with a research budget and a team of surveyors but insisted on that individualist and idiosyncratic relationship between researcher and data that characterizes anthropological practice.

An Economic-institutional View

What was the pattern of variation, and how was it to be explained? To answer this question, I began by taking clues from research that was framed explicitly in economic terms and that offered to make sense of a broad pattern that was emerging. The tanks/villages that we had surveyed stretched across the upper and lower parts of one minor river basin (with a total of over 2,000 tanks). In particular, they crossed a fairly sharp ecological divide marked by different soil and drainage characteristics. This corresponded to a sharp distinction in the degree of collective action around water use. The 57 villages that were surveyed in the predominantly sand soil upper catchment of the river basin were "co-operative"; they possessed institutions of water control and rationing, had specialist water turners, and in other ways shared characteristics with Vayalur. However, in the 22 villages that were surveyed in the black-soil lower catchment, as in Alapuram, these institutions of water control were wholly absent (see Mosse 2003 for details).

On the face of it, the ecology of tank-irrigated cultivation was a crucial factor and prevailing institutional economic explanations of variation in degrees of collective action in terms of risk and individual incentives made perfect sense. Simply put, on porous upper-catchment red soils, rice cultivation depended entirely on water captured in tanks. There was a high premium on maintaining sophisticated systems of water control. However, farmers could manage without these on the water-retentive black soils of the lower catchment, where tanks were less critical because a more diverse cultivation pattern combined irrigated rice with rainfed cropping (of, inter alia, chillies and rice). These findings bore a striking resemblance to Robert Wade's well-known study (1987), which was similarly concerned with variation in institutions of collective action (across a catchment in Andhra Pradesh); Wade explained such variations in terms of ecologically determined factors of risk and scarcity. Our findings appeared to confirm the general proposition that collective action was shaped by a structure of payoffs arising from ecologically determined costs, benefits, and risks. In the upper-catchment area, ecological conditions are such that both the benefits from sustaining rules for cooperative water use and the costs of not cooperating (in terms of crop loss and social conflict) were high; that is, the private costs from unregulated behavior exceed the costs of cooperation. In the other (black-soil) area, the overall risks and the benefits of cooperation are low, land interests are dispersed, and cultivation practices are "individualized."[5]

This "conversation" with institutional economics had provided a fruitful line of enquiry and promised a convincing explanation for an overall pattern of variation in outcomes (i.e., collective action) and a conception of collective action in terms of incentives and sets of rules that both allowed generalizability and offered a mechanism for policy to be put into practice (Ostrom 1990; see Agrawal forthcoming). Had I been an

---

[5]   As Esha Shah (in personal communication) has pointed out, "ecologically determined scarcity" itself should be taken as shorthand for a rather more complex relationship between ecology, technology, and society. As a relationship between supply and demand, scarcity is technologically and politically, rather than ecologically, determined. "Scarcity-prone" upper-catchment villages are actually better endowed with water, being supplied with a denser network of tanks with greater storage capacity for a given area (a function of morphology) as compared to lower-catchment villages. Scarcity is generated by agricultural technology as well as wider political-economic factors that have shaped river basin development in the region.

economist, I would no doubt have wanted to refine this finding, to define the terms more precisely, to find a statistical method to isolate ecologically determined risk and scarcity, and to relate this case to a model that would be generalizable. Such a model might view cooperative institutions as the equilibrium outcome from competitive games shaped by the structure of individual incentives (costs and benefits) (Ostrom et al. 1994).[6] I might even, following Chwe (2001), try to model, game-theoretically, the processes and public rituals of "common knowledge" generation as the precondition for the successful operation of collective action rules, sanctions, or norms.

An Anthropological Perspective

As an anthropologist, however, I had other preoccupations and other points of departure, not least of which was an interest in social power. In my view, the economic models overlooked two important things associated with successful collective action around water in Vayalur and other upper-catchment villages. The first was the presence of strong structures of caste authority, and the second was the cultural construction of irrigation systems (their rules, roles, and transactions) as public institutions through which this authority was enacted. Could insights into collective action be gained by asking not about the economic (or communicative) conditions of cooperation but rather about the role of water control (including its public rituals) in expressing or reproducing relations of power and authority? My point was that the historically shaped and regionally specific institutions through which relations of power were reproduced in rural south India had to do with the control of water. And the way in which water control was institutionalized could be subject to comparative historical and ethnographic research.

Indeed, I found that, in different Tamil regions, water-use rights and rules were tied to social privilege and the rank of dominant caste and kin groups in different ways. For instance, in the northern Tamil districts, characterized historically by landholding collectives of the dominant caste (termed *mirasi* by the British), rights in tanks remained as vestiges of extensive share-based property control, still today fused with privileged rights or shares (*pankus*) in other public institutions, especially temples (see, e.g., Mosse 2003: 276ff). Then, in areas such as Pudukkottai, where resource control rested on the clan institutions of the ruling Kallar caste, rights to tank water and temple honors are articulated in the idiom of ranked lineages, or *karai*, which attach to social groups, not to land, and so cannot be sold (Dirks 1987: 210–12; Krishnan and Mohanaraja 1995: 225).[7] In the southern Tamil districts (Sivaganga and Ramnad), by contrast, village-level systems of irrigation control are shaped, not by kin or caste-based rules of allocation, but by vertical relationships of control and dependence between hereditary headmen and Dalit caste water turners and channel watchers.[8] This is a region where localized Maravar

---

[6]   Of course, as Agrawal (forthcoming) points out, the functionalist evolutionary logic of equilibrium outcomes is only one tradition among institutionalists. More recent work emphasizes the importance of political actors intervening to bring about change perceived as advantageous.

[7]   In Tamil, *karai* means clan/lineage, "a division of co-parcenary land in a village," border, and also the bund of a tank (Cologne Tamil online lexicon).

[8]   *Dalit*, a Marathi word meaning oppressed or downtrodden, is the term now most commonly used to refer to India's many subordinated and formerly "untouchable" castes.

warrior polities (*nadus*) were forged from the seventeenth century through extending and interlinking tank systems and through control over the allocation of water and ranked shares in the irrigated produce; this is an area where vestiges of Maravar caste power and warrior rule are to be found in the organization of the commons – tank and temple (Mosse 2003).

From this line of research into relationships, power, meaning, and process, it was clear that irrigation tanks are multifaceted and socially embedded public institutions. Significantly, the way in which rights and relations around tanks were ritualized so as to legitimize the local social order found a parallel in the organization of worship at village and regional temples. It became clear to me that tanks, as well as the interests and strategic behavior around them, were about more than managing water. They were sources of symbolic, as well as material, resources – that is to say, they signaled status, rank, and honor (or subordination and servitude). As containers of symbolic resources, tanks and temple festivals are about *kattupatu* – order, control, community coordination, and social integration (see Rao 2005), but such integration is always also a political act of rule at different levels (e.g., village, region), a claim to status or for political (perhaps electoral) support. To give the obvious return to Chwe's volley at Foucault, "publicity" is about power as much as coordination or "common knowledge" (Chwe 2001).[9]

There is a further important point to be made. The ranked social relations that underpinned collective action in the Tamil plains area had never been independent of wider systems of state or bureaucracy (in precolonial, colonial, or contemporary times) that legitimized local authority and the allocation of productive resources. Rights to land and water were in the gift of kings, and shares in the harvested grain involved a hierarchy of rights, from ruler to cultivator, and a redistribution of resources notionally extracted by the state, which was overseen by state functionaries and negotiated with their collaborators and kinsmen among the village elite. Local authority continues to be underpinned by informal systems that redistribute public resources (e.g., public works budgets, auctioned tank resources), giving privileged control to village elites (as contractors), who then redistribute illegal profits upward to junior officials and politicians, as well as into temples through legitimizing acts of public religious gifting (Mosse 2003; Wade 1982). In simple terms, successful collective action is embedded in wider systems of patronage and "corruption," as well as in village social hierarchies.

So, in relation to irrigation resources, if farmers are rational optimizers (and there is no suggestion that they are irrational), they have to optimize across all of the multiple social fields that constitute their lives, and the strategies and success in the game of irrigation are not only shaped by the immediate concerns of water or labor but also by strategies in other games, whether they concern acquisition of credit or inputs, maintaining status and honor, consolidating vertical links to the bureaucracy, achieving electoral success, or resisting caste dominance (Mosse 2003: 21). To understand collective action (or its absence) around irrigation, it was necessary to understand the multifaceted nature of tanks as social and cultural systems.

---

[9]   The cultural construction of power, the kind of precolonial and colonial political integration involved in this Tamil plains region, and its significance in relation to the management of the tank water commons is the subject of research published elsewhere (e.g., Mosse 2003; see also Dirks 1987).

The conception of tank institutions as equilibrium outcomes of competitive games between "appropriators" of the water commons then presented one set of problems to a historically minded anthropologist. The idea of institutions as "rules-in-use" overcoming free-rider problems (Ostrom 1990) presented another set. There were several reasons why it was impossible to understand cooperative water control in terms of the existence of effective "rules-in-use" – rules of access, apportionment, and sanctioning, among others. Despite appearances, cooperative water-use practices were not actually governed by a system of agreed-upon rules. The fact that often such rules are not followed is recognized in the literature that distinguishes "formal" from "working" rules (or rules from practical strategies; see, e.g., Hunt and Hunt 1976; Adams, Watson, and Mutiso 1997). The point is that rules are publicly expressed as official codes rather than privately followed as guides to behavior; they establish the way in which behavior is to be represented. Now, in these Tamil villages, men of influence had the symbolic capital of authority to deviate from the rule without attracting public notice or sanction (Bourdieu 1977), for example, to divert scarce water to their dry-land chilli cash crops in the name of protecting subsistence or to influence the actions of dependent water turners through threats or private incentives.[10] They could even underscore their own reputation through public displays upholding rules and enforcing sanctions on others – typically, more marginal players. Of course, some people's interests are better encoded in the rules than others to start with, although typically such privilege is concealed behind discourses that justify rights in terms of obligations, especially to the temple and village deity; that is, privileged shares in water are linked to shares of temple festival expenses. Typically, the interests of poorer, lower-caste, or tenant cultivators, and especially women, are weakly represented in formal rules regarding water and cropping priorities. Indeed, the structure of public discourse on water effectively mutes women and excludes their concerns (Mosse 2003: 201–2).

As already noted, economists also emphasize the importance of transparency and mutual knowledge to rule enforcement within successful institutions of collective action. However, in the context of power asymmetries, information does not produce rule enforcement. In these villages, many people knew a good deal about the transgressions of others. Dalit-caste water turners, for example, had detailed knowledge of rule breaking, but they did not have the capacity to make this knowledge public. Or perhaps we should say that the cost of using the information would be high. In other words, whether and which knowledge becomes "common" (in Chwe's sense) is a matter of power. Public rituals are also public fictions.

I will make one final point on rule following. Esha Shah shows convincingly that, in tank systems in Karnataka, elites ensure that unequal systems of water allocation are built into physical designs (e.g., the layout of field channels or the selective neglect of structures), such that technology itself rather than incentives or authority is also important in

---

[10]   The resort to private incentives can also be a substitute for power over *nirppaccis* (water turners). In December 1994, when we were working on a field survey in Vayalur with the help of *nirppacci* Raman, we asked why some fields appeared well watered while others were virtually dry. Raman only half joking explained that the well-watered fields belonged to wet-land farmers from neighboring villages who, unable to exert public influence over the *nirppaccis,* instead left bottles of liquor (euphemistically, "water") for them at the field's "mouth."

ensuring rule adherence and inequity (Shah 2003).[11] In short, for various reasons, in "co-operative" villages, publicly stated rules of water allocation did not govern behavior but were part of the means of articulating, legitimizing, and reproducing relations of power.

If collective action around tank irrigation was about power and caste dominance as well as scarcity and risk, what was the significance of the lack of coordination of water use in the lower-catchment black-soil villages? What did the contrast with the upper-catchment villages reveal? From an institutional economic perspective, the answer was clear: the difference between the two types of village was that self-interested farmers were rationally constrained to follow public rules in one ecology and not in the other. But, from my perspective, an equally significant observation was that, in one set of villages, power and authority tended to be articulated through public institutions – for example, irrigation systems, temples, and service roles that recollected Maravar warrior rule – while, in another set, power operated less publicly through diffuse private networks of patronage, alliance, and personal obligation, and public goods (e.g., water, fish, temple honors, public service) were not subject to ranked redistribution but instead were managed through contractual relations, independent provision, public auctions, waged labor, and the like. Now, the institutional economic account requires no further explanation. The answer to the question of why self-interested farmers cooperate is built into the cost–benefit model. But the answer to the question of why caste power does or does not articulate through public institutions of water control (and, correspondingly, of why "rational rituals" that allow coordination persist in some places and not in others) is more complicated; it has to do with ecology and history, or political economy. Let me explain.

There is evidence to suggest that, at around the end of the eighteenth century, lower-catchment black-soil villages were in fact characterized by the same caste-based public order and ritualized relations of water control around tanks as upper-catchment villages. These included low-caste service roles, rules and shares in water and grain, and associated ritual honors. Such relations were built into revenue and rule within the same decentralized state system. The historical question is, why were collective water management institutions (and their public rituals) eroded in this region while preserved in the other? Here ecological conditions are important. The black-soil areas of Ramnad and Sivaganga offered opportunities for agricultural expansion and new settlement that were not available in the upper-catchment red-soil areas. In the late eighteenth century, the population was swelled by agriculturalist castes such as Utaiyars, displaced by wars to the north, who acquired rights from Maravar rulers to clear and settle uncultivated land, where they grew dry-land crops (various kinds of millet). By the mid- to late nineteenth century, a British tax regime, together with privatized property rights and new markets, had given these cultivators unprecedented opportunities for accumulation. Economic wealth from agricultural production (especially of cash crops) was becoming more important as compared to political power exercised by Maravar headmen through the control of redistribution (i.e., the grain share-based revenue system) linked to higher levels of the kingly state.

---

[11]   Shah (2003: 23) follows Winner's ideas on "political technology" by suggesting that the task of maintaining social order is delegated to artefacts whose designs are coded in a certain fashion. She has also rightly suggested that what I have referred to as ecology should sometimes be understood as "engineered ecology" (personal communication).

In effect, social and economic change in the nineteeth century eroded the established order and its public institutions of common property, substituting privatized control over water (e.g., private tanks and sluices and private *nirappacci* servants) and land-based forms of authority. The erosion of institutions of water control in lower-catchment villages is part of a story of changing agrarian relations and systems of state that can be traced in some detail. This history and ecology has produced conditions – a contested structure of caste power, a dispersal of landed interests beyond tank wet land, intensified and diversified rainfed cropping (making demands on the tank water), complex land-tenure arrangements, or "opting out" through pump technology – that have long militated against sustaining collective action for tank water management. In lower-catchment villages, as a matter of experience and expectation, there is no cooperation, no public order, no rules, "no control," no *kattupatu.*

By contrast, in the upper-catchment villages, ecological constraints have ensured a remarkable continuity of paddy cultivation under tanks over a 200-year period. For sure, the population has increased, paddy cultivation has intensified, and irrigation commands have expanded, but the options have been limited, and benefits from new agricultural technologies or new cash crop markets have been marginal. Agricultural continuity has played a part in allowing continuity of authoritative control over wet-land rice production and redistribution, even though the way in which local authority has been integrated into wider political systems of state has changed dramatically over two centuries (see Mosse 2003). This authority has been expressed in culturally specific conceptions of rule and service in the village public domain (*ur potu*), which have, in turn, given tank resources their symbolic significance in the articulation of hierarchical social relations. *Kattupatu* (order, control, cooperation) is historical and cultural, not simply the result of an internal structure of economic incentives among communities of irrigation users. Finally, as I have explained elsewhere (Mosse 2003: 234–8), the conceptualization of contrasted "regions of collective action" has vernacular expression, too, in the distinction between *manakalanatu* (sandy-soil [*manal*] and wetland rice [*natu*]) and *karicalkkatu* (black cotton soil [*karical man*] and dry land [*katu*]), which are not only opposed ecological zones but also social types.

So What? Outcomes and Processes

At this point, however, an economist might still ask, what extra explanatory power has all this additional social and cultural information actually contributed? What is its relevance?[12] Do caste power or public ritual independently generate collective action around commons resources? Can we isolate caste relations or the symbolic power of tank systems and correlate them with collective action? These are not unreasonable questions, but they miss the point of the argument and the evidence, which is that the variables are not independent: social relations are expressed through ecological constraints, and ecological

---

[12]   As Robert Wade put it, it is like asking: what is the relevance to understanding the content of Foucault's central arguments of the true fact that he was bald (personal communication)?

constraints are expressed through social structure.[13] If you conclude that risk and scarcity provide incentives for cooperation, you can just as well say that risk and scarcity ensure that relations of power are expressed and legitimized through systems for the control of commons resources that are scarce. In other words, scarcity and risk produce collective action by sustaining hierarchical systems of control as much as through effects on the structure of individual incentives. Moreover, it is such structures of power, rather than scarcity itself, that determine how and whether Chwe's public rituals that factiliate coordination are mounted.

From the point of view of outcomes, however, my historical and anthropological research still has not explained anything extra: collective action is determined by ecological conditions of scarcity and risk. But we now know a lot more about how outcomes are produced, about the social and historical processes involved. Is this important? Does it matter that the mesoscale patterns that reveal an association between risk, scarcity, and collective action do not explain the social dynamics involved; or that the institutional economic mechanisms imputed (incentive structures bearing on individual material maximizers) invoke a type of simplified agent that does not populate south Indian villages?[14] When trying to explain broad patterns in the distribution of collective action, perhaps it does not matter, and economic models derive their power from the ability to generalize outward across a population. But when trying to generalize "downward" to practice, it matters a great deal. It is here that institutional economic models have a specific weakness and where they have been far less successful. The problem is that, because they offer general explanations, economists' models are attractive to policy-makers, and even more so because they are understood to be predictive (to describe the conditions necessary for collective action); but they are not predictive. Generalizing to practice from outcomes is precisely where problems arise and where anthropological attention to social process and complex agency is critical. To explain this, I will look at ways in which economic models fail to predict practice, first, in the context of existing community institutions, and, second, when promoting new or modified ones through resources management transfer or community-driven development.[15]

---

[13]   Indeed, most collective action variables are mediated by other interacting variables, which is what makes common properties so unyielding to economic causal modeling (Agrawal forthcoming). This is not to say that ecologically determined risk and scarcity cannot influence cooperation without strong institutions of caste power. It is true, e.g., that, in 26 percent of the upper-catchment villages studied, irrigation institutions existed and *nirppaccis* were supported in the absence of authoritative relations of Maravar caste dominance. These are smaller single-caste (Pallar, Nadar, or Konar) villages where *nirppaccis* were not hierarchically integrated Dalit service roles. However, as a matter of social and historical fact, in the majority of cases, tank management was embedded in hierarchical caste relations, as indeed was the case in lower-catchment villages in the past.

[14]   Of course, economists recognize the importance of institutions and factor them into the equations of individual rational choice. Institutions are mechanisms to coordinate decision-making, reduce uncertainty about others' actions, and build in assurances (by ensuring that the costs of breaking rules are greater than the benefits of free riding). Moreover, game-theoretical modeling has begun to take account of ethics, norms, expectations, "common knowledge," and other forms of assurance, trust, or habit that influence or sustain cooperative solutions and the institutions that these involve (Runge 1986; Seabright 1993; Chwe 2001).

[15]   Sengupta (2007) points to the inability of game theory models explaining collective action to provide guides for action in fostering new institutions and to the tendency, therefore, for programs to be designed by sociologists (i.e., where programs are "participatory" and not solely designed by engineers). As Sengupta notes: "Economists direct their energy to finding equilibrium. They have little to say about the way to the equilibrium."

Prediction and process

There are several ways in which the models arising from an institutionalist analysis of outcomes in terms of incentives, rules, or institutional arrangements are inadequate or simply wrong, and the pursuit of them would be ineffective or misguided. Correspondingly, the things about common-property systems discovered through historical-anthropological research but concealed from economic analysis turn out to be crucial to understanding practice. Let me illustrate with reference to the present case.

First, while the institutionalist literature has promoted the view that effective collective action in resource management is associated with the presence of organizations or associations providing assurances or enforcing rules (hence, their widespread promotion in CBNRM [community-based natural resource management] programs), in our upper-catchment cooperative villages, organizations were absent and resisted.[16] Here collective action did not take corporate form (*pace* Wade 1987). Only one of the 57 villages studied had any recognizable "council" or association. Second, and related, income from commons resources was rarely reinvested in them but rather was used to underpin local authority. So money earned from the sale of fish or trees, fines or fees, or other contracts was rarely managed as a common fund or invested in tank maintenance. Instead, common funds were rapidly expended for religious purposes: on temple repair, festivals, or other rituals. These common resources were not primarily managed in ways that maximized economic utility and ensured accountability but instead in ways that minimized social conflict and served to enhance the prestige and credibility of existing leadership and to secure their upward political connections (Mosse 2003: 173). However, where structures of authority were weaker, and where public institutions were attenuated by conflict or social diversity (as in many lower-catchment villages), the moral claims on such resources were weaker; here common funds were not used to support social hierarchy and were more likely to be reinvested in the irrigation system.[17] The lack of corporate organization or the absence of reinvestment of resources into the commons where scarcity is high and collective action is strong could not have been predicted by institutional economic models (quite the reverse). Rather, these features of the irrigation system arise from the sociocultural position of tanks in southern Tamil Nadu as part of a public domain to be ruled rather than a resource to be managed. This gives all tank resources – rights to water or fish shares, the use of common money, or service roles – a symbolic significance as idioms of social standing and political power; in consequence, this makes them a focus of dispute (or political strategy) out of proportion to their material value, which may be no more than a handful of fish.

Third, where water systems are embedded in authoritarian structures of caste, they will be subject to the effects of social and political changes that challenge such power and undermine the "naturalness" of caste-class privilege (Gupta 1998). Despite a remarkable

---

[16]   There was, however, a link between collective water management and public rituals, or "Rao's public symbolic good," as a feature of caste power.

[17]   Social diversity, including religious diversity – Muslims, Hindus, and Christians – or the diversity that arises from different villages using the same water source, also produces more functionally focused corporate organization, common funds, and reinvestment in the commons.

continuity of economic and political dominance in upper-caste-controlled villages, many are now subject to the dynamics of a (still-contained) politics of protest and Dalit resistance to the social subordination manifested in their ascribed roles in tank and temple. These processes have seriously disrupted water distribution in nearly half of the upper-catchment villages surveyed. Claims to symbolic resources, such as temple honors, have gone along with demands to renegotiate water rights and roles to make them less caste specific, more contractual, and better paid.[18]

The conflict over symbolic resources in "cooperative" Vayalur had a significant impact on irrigation. For three years the village tanks lacked an effective water distribution system, and in Citanaru (another upper-catchment village), when *nirpaccis* withdrew services, farmers began to assert de facto individual control over water, leaving sluices open, impounding water in their fields immediately below the tank, and using it to irrigate adjacent land. Water wastage, inequity, and serious crop losses resulted from the absence of water distributors. Here the political logic of public rituals worked against coordination and economic rationality. But it is significant that, in contrast to lower-catchment villages, the strong economic need for *nirppaccis* here often resulted in their eventual reconstitution on terms that gave greater respect to these Dalit services. Sometimes new arrangements have been put in place, although the complex and time-consuming procedures they involve (with chits and supervisory systems) demonstrate the costs of eroding authoritative caste structures. In many places across Tamil Nadu, however, water distribution systems have become moribund, renegotiated, if at all, through the mediation of external agencies committed to RMT/CDD, promoting participatory irrigation and willing to invest in water-user's associations (WUAs).[19]

Promoting collective action

I think it is fair to conclude that the application of institutional economic models without reference to the sociopolitical specifics of collective action around tank systems in Tamil Nadu would provide a very poor guide to action or to understanding for development agencies (state or NGO [nongovernmental organizations]) mandated to promote farmer-controlled irrigation organizations under currently fashionable programs of irrigation management transfer (IMT) or participatory irrigation management (PIM). I have reviewed the experience of PIM in Tamil Nadu elsewhere (Mosse 2003: 266ff), but it is worth recalling the several ways in which evidence from case studies of WUA processes in Tamil villages demonstrate the salience of ethnographic analysis.

During the 1980s and 1990s, major investments in "tank rehabilitation" were made under a European Union–funded program, within which the Centre for Water Resources (CWR) of Anna University piloted the promotion of WUAs taking engineering contracts and managing the developed irrigation systems. These interventions were monitored

---

[18]   Pallar caste *nirppaccis* have, in some villages, insisted that members of other castes also provide this service.

[19]   The "recent" collapse of water management systems (since the 1980s) as a result of social conflict is commonly reported. See CWR (1990), Janakarajan (1997), and Krishnan and Mohanaraja (1995).

carefully through the work of village-level "process documentators."[20] While development agencies assumed that they could relatively easily promote WUAs on the grounds that there were clear economic benefits to be gained from improved works and greater efficiency in tank management, village case studies show again and again how agency staff quickly found themselves amid complex village and caste conflicts because of the unanticipated public and political nature of irrigation institutions.

First, in several cases, the "traditional local institutions" (e.g., those based on the share and lineage systems mentioned earlier) upon which agency staff expected to build new organizations were subject to intense dispute, as Dalit cultivators challenged caste-based exclusion from equal rights to scarce water, or these institutions had recently been disbanded entirely. Conflicts over water rights were inseparable from other conflicts over common property, temple honors, or obligations of service. Interventions to promote new WUAs in these circumstances amplified caste and factional conflict as various players (faction leaders or caste groups) attempted to advance particular agendas by shaping the new institutions in terms of their interests.

In Nallaneri village (Chengalpattu), upper-caste Mudaliars tried to reassert caste dominance by organizing the new WUA around the old "share" system that ensured privileged access to material and symbolic resources (Mosse 2003: 276–9). In Kannangudi village (Pudukkottai), upper-caste Vellalars and Kallars ensured that the process of enrollment and recruitment of office bearers and the executive committee (EC) of the new WUA was structured by the old system of ranked rights, or *karai*, which reproduced their dominance within the new institution. In both villages, Dalits refused these ranked forms of social integration and collective action, and they bargained the terms of their participation in the new associations, winning concessions such as EC representation and office bearing, without conceding the right to bargain wages as the principal laborers for community projects. From the start, these WUAs were at the center of a local caste politics that was sharpened by broader political trends of the 1990s. The fact that these were public institutions linked to external authority and to financial, political, and symbolic resources only intensified the caste and factional conflict focused on the WUAs, which were rarely confined to water or the material resources of tanks.

These experiences are a long way from the notion of irrigation management transfer as the stabilizing of village groups around rules of resources use crafted by communities of "appropriators" bound together by the individual economic benefits of cooperative management of shared resources (Ostrom 1990). Rather, PIM implies intensified competition over resources and disputes over social position and authority. Moreover, whereas collective-action institutions arising from PIM policies are represented and theorized as spontaneous and selfsupporting, in reality they are mostly introduced and sustained by substantial external resources and authority (government, NGOs). In the short term, WUAs depend upon expensive processes of mobilization, training, and negotiation, but their long-term survival is dependent upon reforms in the wider framework of irrigation administration and its system of incentives, which continue to meet unyielding political/institutional resistance and from which a focus on community institutions presently diverts attention (see Mosse 2003: 287ff).

---

[20]   The CWR program was supported by the Ford Foundation.

Social Capital: A New Framework for Understanding Collective Action?

Despite such experiences, within development policy circles, the dominance of economic thought, models, and research is unchallenged. The presence of anthropologists may have increased in development agencies along with the new social development goals of participation, community-driven development, empowerment, and local governance, but the influence of contextual ethnographic research has not. Human behavior is still more likely to be discussed by reasoning back from econometric regressions or equilibrium models than forward from culturally grounded ethnographic description. Those whose task it has been to advance the social development agenda within large development agencies (none more so than in the World Bank) have had to find ways to theorize "the social" that is missing from conventional economists' models in terms that allow generalization, prediction, and policy relevance and that follow economics reasoning (Bebbington et al. 2004). Currently, the most influential framework within which this has been attempted is that of "social capital," which some claim allows the combination of economists' capacity to identify central trends and general patterns through regressions while retaining the anthropologists' concern with social relationships and networks (i.e., without the need for methodological individualism). Taking social capital thinking in the World Bank as a case, in the following sections, I want, first, to set out, in the briefest way, the kind of theory or framework of social capital that is used to explain, predict, and produce collective action, and, second, to examine some of the key social capital propositions regarding collective action in the light of the Tamil village evidence.

The social capital idea

The idea of social capital that has acquired ascendancy in policy circles, especially within the World Bank, and the one with which I am concerned here, derives from Robert Putnam's thesis that "networks of civic engagement" give rise to social capital, meaning "features of social organization such as networks, norms and trust that facilitate co-ordination and co-operation for mutual benefit" (Putnam 1993: 35–6). Often summarized as the norms and networks that enable collective action, social capital has become a bundle of ideas about the causes and consequences of social interaction and their outcomes such as collective action. To understand this bundle, it is important to realize that, like "community," social capital is both the raw material and a goal of development (see Robertson 1984); it is a public good to be created or protected.[21]

In the years since Putnam's *Making Democracy Work*, the concept has been complicated and differentiated, partly in response to critique, although it still evades conceptual precision.[22] Among other things, this expansion and differentiation suggests that the concept of social capital remains dependent upon, and derivative of, other forms of social

---

[21]   "Social capital is an ingredient of CDD"; "CDD aims to mobilize a stock of social capital effectively, to invest in social mobility and capacity building, and new forms of social capital": these are not uncommon comments heard at the World Bank in Washington, DC.

[22]   In response to the criticism that Putnam's formulation did not clearly separate the close ingroup ties of clan or caste from the sort of multiple weak ties he believed correlated with effective government, the distinction between social capital as "bonding" or "bridging" was introduced Narayan 2002; see also (Putnam 2000). When

analysis. In practice, however, the conceptual specification of the term has largely been linked to a highly influential body of econometric work, initially inspired by Putnam's work on the correlation between civic engagement and governance. The production of empirical evidence provided a powerful accelerator of the social capital concept, certainly in the World Bank. Using a variety of proxy indicators – membership of groups, networks, and associations; trust of neighbors or service providers – a growing number of studies in a wide range of countries related social capital to outcome variables such as income, access to credit and services, trade, political engagement, collective action, the absence of violence and crime, and project effectiveness (Narayan and Pritchett 1999; Narayan and Cassidy 2001; Grootaert and van Bastelaer 2002).[23]

These studies have bequeathed to social capital some serious methodological and conceptual difficulties,[24] which I have to pass over here in order to get to the core social capital idea relevant for the present discussion of collective action, which is that the capacity to cooperate (and overcome free-rider and coordination problems) is itself a (by-) product of social interactions (Collier 2002).[25] Social capital is the set of durable interactions

---

it was pointed out that organizational capacities identified as "social capital" are not independent of "vertical" connections across power differentials to wider institutions of the state or market (bureaucracies, political parties, banks, etc.), the notion of "linking social capital" was added (Woolcock 1999, cited in Grootaert et al. 2003). (Given that "linkage" across power often involves patronage and strong networks of dependency and oppression into which poor people are tied, one might also speak of "binding" social capital.) Since, it was obvious that some forms of social capital (e.g., nepotism, insider trading, and political favoritism) had deleterious social effects, it was necessary to distinguish "positive" from "negative" social capital (Grootaert et al. 2003: 7). Social capital should also, some argued, include "the social and political environment that shapes social structure and enables norms to develop," thus extending social capital "to the most formalised institutional relationships and structures such as government, the political regime, the rule of law, the court system, and civil and political liberties" (http://www.worldbank.org/poverty/scapital/whatsc.htm). This introduced a distinction between government social capital and civil social capital (the latter referring to interactions not directly dependent on government rules and systems or on intra-household relations – yet another type of social capital [Collier 2002]). In recent writing, World Bank staff have tried to bring this unruly differentiation and expansion of the concept to order in definitions that distinguish social capital into six components: (1) groups and networks; (2) trust, adherence norms, and solidarity (also distinguished as "structural" and "cognitive" social capital (Grootaert et al. [2003], citing Krishna and Uphoff [2002]); (3) collective action and cooperation; (4) information and communication; (5) social cohesion and inclusion; and (6) empowerment and political action (e.g., Grootaert et al. 2003). The latter component is no doubt partly intended to respond to the broad criticism that the social capital concept adopted by policy-makers provides a depoliticized and conservative view of social relations, contrasted with the use of the term by sociologists such as Bourdieu to explore the way in which culture is contested and deployed to create stratification in society (Fine 1999; Harriss 2001; Mosse 2005b).

[23] In the World Bank, considerable effort has gone into developing instruments to measure and quantify social capital (in its different forms) within larger household surveys such as the nationallevel Living Standards Measurement Survey (Grootaert et al. 2003).

[24] Perhaps most obvious is the question of whether social capital (the combination of trust, membership of associations, etc.) composes a "class of asset endowment" of a household that can be aggregated at the local, regional, or national level and whose returns on well-being can be measured and aggregated so as to influence investment decisions (e.g., by comparing returns to investment in human or physical capital [Grootaert et al. 2003: 21]). What is at issue are not only serious questions concerning the framing of social capital questionnaires, or the uncertain causal processes that might explain regressions (Harriss 2001: 91), but also an irredeemable vagueness about what constitutes a social influence on individual behavior. Durlauf (2002) suggests that this is a question that is better addressed through social psychology of descriptive histories than by econometric analysis.

[25] Social capital is the "information, trust, and norms of reciprocity inherent in . . . social networks" (Woolcock 1998: 153).

that result in coordination capacities – either spontaneously because of generated trust or through the conscious decisions of organizations that bring about interaction and generate trust – and establish rules and allocative decisions (Collier 2002: 31). However, it is not at all clear that this idea of social capital provides any explanation of the variation in levels of collective action among our Tamil villages. For it to do so, we would have to accept that villages with different degrees of effective collective action (around water) varied either in terms of trust derived from social interaction or in terms of the presence of organizations or the intensity of associational life. The first is implausible, and the second is contradicted by the evidence (see below). If conceptualization about how social capital has its effects is weak, the analysis of how social capital is caused is vaguer still. Studies designed to identify the effects of social capital on social and economic outcomes treat social capital as an independent rather than a dependent variable; that is, they do not ask how social capital comes about or what determines its creation (Grootaert et al. 2003: 24). Social capital theory has little to say on this beyond Putnam's path dependency.

Nonetheless, social capital is an important part of current strategies for decentralized resource management, community-driven development, improved governance, and other projects of the World Bank and other aid agencies. The general reasoning is that, if levels of engagement in civil society are raised (shown by improved input indicators such as membership of associations), this will lead to improved coordination (evident in the outputs of trust and collective action) and ultimately to increased levels of accountability and democracy. It is this relationship between associational life, collective action, and democracy that can also be subject to ethnographic investigation.

My point is that descriptive history suggests that the causal relationship between associational life and collective action does not, in fact, hold in the case of the tank irrigation commons we have been discussing. Strong collective action in water management (in upper-catchment villages) is not linked to vibrant associational life or the presence of organizations; nor is the absence or decline of cooperation (in the lower-catchment villages) associated with the absence of "structural" social capital in this sense. Moreover, associations do not appear to promote democratic processes so much as to be their consequence, and these same democratic processes tend to erode existing forms of collective action in commons management. This all amounts to dangerous terrain for predictive models for CDD-type interventions.

Associational life and collective action on the Tamil plains

In relation to cooperative irrigation management in the upper-catchment villages, I want to make four points. First, as explained earlier, collective action around tank irrigation is not dependent upon trust generated through interactions and associations but is founded upon relations of caste power, graded authority, personal patronage, and the redistribution of resources (as bribes and payoffs). Second, as I have already pointed out, the persistence of coordination around common-resource management here does not depend upon the existence of organizations or associations. On the contrary, organizations (regular meetings, standing funds, etc.) are avoided on account of the transaction costs and the risk of conflict they entail, and their existence usually signals the failure of authority in one way or another.[26]

---

[26]   Two out of our 79 villages' tanks were managed through fund-holding associations. Both involved large tanks irrigating the land of several villages (five in both cases) where it was impossible to enforce rules of water use through established caste authority legitimized through ritual.

Third, where coordination is embedded in relations of social rank and control, the formation of independent associations is actively suppressed. Subordinate groups within hierarchical systems are often fearful of forming associations to promote their interests. When, for example, the Dalits of Kannangudi village (mentioned above) were eventually persuaded by an NGO to form a men's association and a women's association, they considered it expedient to invite a man and a woman from the dominant Kallar caste to take the positions of the societies' presidents, "with the aim of giving honor to the upper caste people."[27] Local history shows that, in many Tamil villages, the formation of clubs or groups with a public profile – for sports or religious purposes – by certain categories of people can be regarded as provocative insubordination, as political acts provoking violent reactions by dominant castes. Finally, when in "cooperative" villages like Vayalur new associations (such as water-users' associations) were formed by external agencies to promote cooperation, either they remained moribund or existing power structures were reproduced within them. So, contrary to social capital thinking, in the specific context of strong collective action around commons resources in these Tamil villages, the persistence of coordination is not linked to persisting organizations; nor would we expect it to correlate with trust or accountability as functions of the intensity of social interaction.

The historical decline of village collective action and the rise of associations

What about the contrasting case? Are noncooperative villages in the lower catchment characterized by poverty in associational life? In fact, the contrary is the case. Where collective action around the management of irrigation and other commons resources is weak, associationalism abounds. Indeed, if we look at the issue historically (taking the case of lower-catchment village Alapuram), a certain rise in associationalism can be directly linked to the decline of coordinated control of commons resources.

Earlier in this chapter, I described how the growing landed wealth of rainfed cash-crop cultivators in the nineteenth century weakened Maravar-controlled hierarchical systems of public order and common property. Challenges to the old public order involved new forms of caste association initially formed in the context of conflicts over festival honors at regional shrines through which in-migrant cultivators sought to turn growing economic power into durable caste rights and public honor. During the twentieth century, low castes (Dalits) in Alapuram and other lower-catchment villages, who had acquired economic independence through migrant labor, employment, and land acquisition, used an identical strategy, building new informal supravillage networks and castebased associations further to erode coordination based on hierarchical integration (Mosse 1994).[28] Here, once again, the political logic of public rituals that enhance "common knowledge" (about status ambitions) militates against coordination of economic activities (Chwe 2001).

In the 1990s, a plethora of associations – of Dalits, youth, and women – were organizing action around village common properties in Alapuram village. Common properties such as tanks were strategic sites in several ways: first, members of low castes

---

[27] "Kannangudi Process Documentation Report," April 1991.

[28] Significantly, it was only the most numerous and powerful of the four Dalit castes in Alapuram who were able to associate in this way and assert autonomy. Economically weaker Dalit castes could not afford to withdraw from service relations.

(and women) laid claim to these material and symbolic resources as a challenge to upper-caste landlords and contractors; second, because these commons constituted government property (*purumpokkui*, Public Works Department [PWD]), action over them could invoke support from the state (PWD, revenue, or police) for claims to equal access as citizens in face of upper-caste exclusions; and, third, by organizing action on tank repair or water supply, politically ambitious individuals could appeal to common interests and so mobilize the broader constituencies of support that electoral politics demanded.

One conclusion to draw from this scenario is that a simultaneous weakening of hierarchical orders of community collective action and the rise of associationalism (and struggles for autonomy) has characterized the shifting politics of this locality from the mid-nineteenth century. Any discussion of social capital, associationalism, and collective action in the region has to be set in this context. Second, it is important to ask who organizes and associates. Significantly, it is the low castes (Dalits), youth, and women for whom new associations are important and necessary in making claims to resources, asserting rights, or getting support from the state (see Mosse 2005a: 213–15). Typically, more powerful groups do not need to associate in this way to get access to resources or to secure support from the bureaucracy. They rely on informal networks to influence state officials, to broker deals, or to win contracts. When Arulananda, a Dalit man is caught pumping tank water to his dry lands from inside the tank, an influential upper-caste man simply reports the matter to the VAO (village administrative officer), who goes with the village watchman to stop his engine. But when Arulananda understands that, in the same night, upper-caste farmers (the Maravar "president" and his kinsmen) have also been illegally irrigating their cash-crop chillies, he organizes a protest and presents a signed petition to the tahsildar (senior-most subdistrict official).

A third point challenges assumptions linking associationalism (or social capital) with accountability and processes of democratic governance. These associations of the weak do not always seek democratic accountability or transparency from the institutions of government. Rather they petition for authoritative interventions (from the bureaucracy, NGOs, church, or party) in support of specific claims, in local conflicts, or for protection against injustice from powerful individuals in the village. Their concern is not primarily with democratic processes (the pathways to decision-making). Indeed, associations may use nondemocratic means and seek to manipulate an existing personalized order of hierarchy and patronage by appealing to influential persons – tahsildar, district collector, or politician – perhaps to impose on subordinate officers. In water-users' associations, too, mobilization for special pleading and vertical appeals undermines the consolidation of authoritative group decision-making.[29]

Now, the presence of associations among Dalits (or women), self-formed or fostered by NGOs, Dalit movements, political parties, or state agencies, does not make these groups richer than upper-caste men in social capital as a community or household asset. If anything, associations result from the experience of the ineffectiveness of Dalits' existing networks to access services or symbolic resources. Dalits and upper castes may be equally rich or poor in a measure of household social capital, but, as Harriss (2001) points

---

[29]   It is also true, however, that new modes of record keeping and accounting within WUAs challenge existing forms of personal control over institutions and are the source of conflict for precisely that reason.

out, it is not the density of networks but rather their power and reach that matters. When there was conflict over the control of the new water-users' association in the village of Nallaneri, Dalits appealed to local bureaucrats and relied upon support from an NGO working in their hamlet (this was the extent of their "linking social capital"), but the upper-caste Mudaliar faction trying to control the WUA mobilized huge resources for litigation in the dispute and their networks were such that their claims and interests came to be argued for in the chambers of the PWD Secretary in Madras. These accounts show how problematic it is to try to isolate social capital as a form of productive asset from assets of other kinds upon which it depends. It is hard to imagine what it would mean to find, for example, that "social capital is much more equally distributed than physical assets and human capital," as Grootaert and Narayan (2000) do for Bolivia (cited in Grootaert et al. 2003: 23).

In general, a measure of social capital that lifts social relations out of their specific political-economic context for the purposes of quantification cannot avoid flattening out or aggregating unlike things. Moreover, associations have their own history. They come into existence at particular moments in particular ways for specific reasons, perhaps as part of an ongoing struggle. Of course, this also means that conflicts that are provoked by associations at one period of social transition may be resolved by them at another or in the longer term and that in some circumstances certain associations may indeed strengthen collective action around common property. A single-moment survey cannot help but produce a statistical artifact that freezes a dynamic set of relations and permits confused causality or that quantifies social connections in ways that misrepresent their significance (see Harriss 2001).

Democratic Politics, Associations, and Collective Action

There is one final point that I want to make, and this concerns the relationship between collective action, associational activity, and the processes of democratic politics. The social capital policy narrative set in motion by Putnam's (1993) Italian study assumes that vibrant associations not only produce effective community collective action but also foster democratic processes. I have already suggested that associationalism may be compatible with personalized hierarchical modes of decision-making and intervention. It also seems likely that the causal relation is often not from associations to democratic processes but the reverse. In Alapuram, as presumably in a great many Indian villages, the principles and processes of democracy have had a profound effect on collective action and civil association. Alapuram would well illustrate points made by Rudolph (2000) from village studies in northern India, namely, that, on the one hand, electoral competition brings a new associationalism into being, increasingly drawn around the politics of caste and religious identity and increasingly militant, and, on the other hand, "the establishment of democratic institutions at the local level, and [the] channelising of development funds and programs through these, have set in motion processes that tend to deplete – rather than enhance – the pre-existing social capital" (Rudolph 2000: 1764, citing Jayal 1999: 8–9).

In rural India, it would be harder to argue that the social capital of associationalism has produced democratic processes (as Putnam did) than that a particular form of democratic process, including electoral competition and party activity, has generated new forms of association while at the same time disrupting existing forms of community collective action (Rudolph 2000: 1764–5). Political parties have often proved to be powerful pro-moters of social networks. As Jenkins (2001: 259) notes, "to assert that political parties can and ought to remain distinct from the social groups it is their function to reconcile is to assign them a role of dispassionate interest aggregators, shorn of ideology and immune to the pressures of power. There is little empirical justification for such a view." Certainly, during the 1980s and 1990s, electoral processes at different levels in rural Tamil Nadu and the growing importance of identity politics (around caste if not religion) provided the context for further associational activity while weakening older forms of collective action around the commons.

Moreover, as caste and religious identity become more and more central to the wider practices of politics, influencing the terms in which interests are expressed, this begins to appear at the village level in the forms of associations that emerge and the way in which claims to resources are made. So, when Alapuram Dalits write a petition to the tahsildar complaining about uppercaste farmers diverting tank water to dry-land cash crops, they do so in the arresting language of the threat of "caste problems" (*cati piraccinai*). Or, when the PWD Secretary, chief engineer, district collector, and other officials are tele-grammed in the context of a WUA dispute, it is in the language of a threat of "commu-nal riot." And when four jeeps arrive in the village with police and senior revenue officials and a public meeting is organized to resolve matters, the power of both common prop-erty and the discourse of communal identity to evoke a rapid response and bring the state – as a bureaucratic machine of law, order, and justice – into village affairs is clear. In this way, local associationalism intersects with a wider politics of identity in a manner that is mutually enforcing.

Conclusions

This article has involved a conversation between anthropological and economist perspectives on collective action. Important challenges have been posed for anthropology. In particu-lar, how are larger patterns or variations in social outcomes to be explained, how are the effects of different variables to be isolated, and how do observations relate to more gen-eral theory? Historical and ethnographic data have, in turn, offered their own view on the interacting variables and the complex and dynamic "causal patterns" involved (Agrawal forthcoming). Here the question of collective action and the commons is placed within a broader framework of ecological history, governance, and political and economic change that is largely missing from economics frameworks, even those now turning attention to public rituals or symbolic goods as mechanisms of coordination.

The attempt to synthesize the social and the economic in a theory of "social capital" poses questions about the relationship between norms, networks, associations, and col-lective action. But this also introduces unresolved problems: too many different social phenomena are bundled together, and the statistical concept of social capital is unable to grasp the historical dynamic between collective action, associations, and democratic practice. As theory, social capital is too vague about the mechanisms by which social interaction produces values or collective action, and as policy its causal relations are too unidirectional (from associations to collective action or democratic process) to be useful.

Unlike anthropological-historical analyses, economists' models have generalizing and predictive power. They are, in consequence, far more compatible with the policy thinking of governments, donors, and multilateral agencies than the analytical descriptions of anthropologists, whose capacity to generalize or to conceptualize the future is limited (see Appadurai 2004). The strong presence of economic thinking in the centers of policy and power has encouraged the critical observation that economistic models (including social capital) are useful because they are consistent with certain policy priorities in a normative or ideological sense. Thus, game-theoretic models represent community irrigation institutions as internally generated – the equilibrium outcome of structures of incentives – in ways that support neoliberal policies to devolve responsibilities to users, while the emphasis on behavioral change in the community also serves to divert attention away from wider issues of property rights and state policy (Mosse 1999; 2003: 273–6).

World Bank social capital models have been criticized on similar grounds (Fine 1999; Harriss 2001). The concept of social capital is not only accused of encouraging a depoliticized analysis of power relations and social institutions leading to conservative system-sustaining interventions but also of foreclosing the engagement of policy with critical social science (Fine 1999; Harriss 2001). Certainly, the self-history of social capital thinking at the World Bank reveals a series of concessions by anthropologists to economists' epistemology and methodology (Bebbington et al. 2004). Indeed, this social capital discourse reveals the structural marginality of a noneconomist professional group constantly having to persuade those with power (task managers, vice presidents, and regional budget holders) that social relations are important to development (Mosse 2004). The persistent efforts, the strategic collaborations, the compromises, and the publicity (the many inches of website devoted to social capital) are indicators of political weakness and the struggle to achieve respectability for ideas that still command little support internally and have little operational significance. Social capital may, then, in the end, be interesting not for its power to depoliticize the social world but for what it reveals of the structure of unequal power within which conversations between economists and anthropologists have to take place in development institutions. Finally, lest anthropologists succumb to the illusion that power is always located elsewhere and never in one's own domain (Eyben 2003), it is well to recall that, of course, anthropology has its own dubious connections with systems of rule (especially colonial ones). With the turn to community-driven development and the hidden work of anthropologists in shaping these new ventures, the "ethnographic state" (Dirks 2001: 43) may not yet be dead (Tania Li: personal communication).

References

Adams, William, Elizabeth Watson, and Samuel Mutiso. 1997. "Water, Rules and Gender: Water Rights in an Indigenous Irrigation System, Marakwet, Kenya." *Development and Change* 28, no. 4: 707–30.

Appadurai, Arjun. 1981. *Worship and Conflict under Colonial Rule*. Cambridge: Cambridge University Press.

——. 1989. "Small-scale Techniques and Large-scale Objectives." In *Conversations between Economists and Anthropologists: Methodological Issues in Measuring Economic Change in Rural India*, ed. Pranab Bardhan, 250–82. New Delhi: Oxford University Press.

——. 2004. "The Capacity to Aspire: Culture and the Terms of Recognition." In *Culture and Public Action*, ed. Vijayendra Rao and Michael Walton. Stanford, CA: Stanford University Press.

Bebbington, Anthony, Scott Guggenheim, Elizabeth Olson, and MichaelWoolcock. 2004. "Exploring Social Capital Debates at theWorld Bank." *Journal of Development Studies* 40, no. 5: 33–42.

Bourdieu, Pierre. 1977. *Outline of a Theory of Practice*, trans. R. Nice. Cambridge: Cambridge University Press.

Chwe, Michael S.-Y. 2001. *Rational Ritual: Culture, Coordination, and Common Knowledge*. Princeton, NJ: Princeton University Press.

Collier, Paul. 2002. "Social Capital and Poverty: A Microeconomic Perspective." In *The Role of Social Capital in Development: An Empirical Assessment*, ed. Christiaan Grootaert and Thierry van Bastelaer, 19–41. New York: Cambridge University Press.

CWR (Centre for Water Resources). 1990. *Alternative Approaches to Tank Rehabilitation and Management – a Proposed Experiment: Annual Report, 1988–89*. Madras: Centre for Water Resources, Anna University.

Dirks, Nicholas. 1987. *The Hollow Crown: Ethnohistory of a South Indian Little Kingdom*. Cambridge: Cambridge University Press.

——. 2001. *Castes of Mind: Colonialism and the Making of Modern India*. Princeton, NJ: Princeton University Press.

Douglas, Mary. 1987. *How Institutions Think*. London: Routledge & Kegan Paul.

Durlauf, Steven N. 2002. "The Empirics of Social Capital: Some Sceptical Thoughts." World Bank Roundtable Paper, World Bank, Social Development Department, Washington, DC.

Eyben, Rosalind. 2003. "Donors as Political Actors: Fighting the Thirty Years War in Bolivia." IDS Working Paper 183, Institute of Development Studies, Brighton.

Fine, Ben. 1999. "The Development State Is Dead: Long Live Social Capital?" *Development and Change* 30, no. 1: 1–19.

Grootaert, Christiaan and Deepa Narayan. 2000. "Local Institutions, Poverty, and Household Welfare in Bolivia." Local Level Institutions Working Paper 9, Social Development Department, World Bank, Washington, DC.

Grootaert, Christiaan and Thierry van Bastelaer. 2002. *The Role of Social Capital in Development: An Empirical Assessment*. New York: Cambridge University Press.

Grootaert, Christiaan, Deepa Narayan, V. Nyhan Jones, and Michael Woolcock. 2003. "Integrated Questionnaire for the Measurement of Social Capital (SC–IQ)." Social Capital Thematic Group, World Bank, Washington, DC.

Gupta, Akhil. 1998. *Postcolonial Developments: Agriculture in the Making of Modern India*. Durham, NC: Duke University Press.

Harriss, John. 2001. *Depoliticising Development: The World Bank and Social Capital*. London: Anthem.

Hunt, Robert C. and Evan Hunt. 1976. "Canal Irrigation and Local Social Organisation." *Current Anthropology* 17: 389–411.

Janakarajan, S. 1997. "Village Resurveys: Issues and Results." In *The Village in Asia Revisited*, ed. Jan Breman, Peter Kloos, and Ashwani Swaith. Delhi: Oxford University Press.

Jayal, Niraja Gopal. 1999. "Democracy and Social Capital in the Central Himalaya: A Tale of Two Villages." Paper presented at a conference on Democracy and Social Capital in Segmented Societies, Uppsala University, June.

Jenkins, Rob. 2001. "Mistaking 'Governance' for 'Politics': Foreign Aid, Democracy, and the Construction of Civil Society." In *Civil Society: History and Possibilities*, ed. Sudipta Kaviraj and Sunil Khilnani, 250–68. Cambridge: Cambridge University Press.

Krishna, Anirudh and Norman Uphoff. 2002. "Mapping and Measuring Social Capital through Assessment of Collective Action to Conserve and Develop Watersheds in Rajasthan, India." In *The Role of Social Capital in Development: An Empirical Assessment*, ed. Christiaan Grootaert and Thierry van Bastelaer, 85–124. New York: Cambridge University Press.

Krishnan, V. and M. Mohanaraja. 1995. "Social Barriers in Practising Traditional Water Management in Tank Irrigation Systems." *Proceedings of the National Workshop on Traditional Water Management for Tanks and Ponds*, ed. N. V. Pundarikanthan and L. Jayasekhar, 225–35. Madras: Anna University (September).

Li, Tania. 2002. "Government through Community and the Practice of Politics." Agrarian Studies Colloquium Series Paper, Program in Agrarian Studies, Yale University, October 11.

Mosse, David. 1994. "Idioms of Subordination and Styles of Protest among Christian and Hindu Harijan (Untouchable) Castes in Tamil Nadu." *Contributions to Indian Sociology* 28, no. 1: 67–106.

——. 1999. "Colonial and Contemporary Ideologies of Community Management: The Case of Tank Irrigation Development in South India." *Modern Asian Studies* 33, no. 2: 303–38.

——. 2003. *The Rule of Water: Statecraft, Ecology and Collective Action in South India*. Delhi: Oxford University Press.

——. 2004. "Social Analysis as Product Development: Anthropologists at Work in the World Bank." In *The Development of Religion/The Religion of Development*, ed. Ananta Kumar Giri, Anton van Harskamp, and Oscar Salemink, 77–87. Delft: Eburon.

——. 2005a. *Cultivating Development: An Ethnography of Aid Policy and Practice*. London: Pluto.

——. 2005b. "Power Relations and Poverty Reduction." In *Power, Rights, and Poverty: Concepts and Connections*, ed. Ruth Alsop. Washington, DC: World Bank.

Narayan, Deepa. 2002. "Bonds and Bridges: Social Capital and Poverty." In *Social Capital and Economic Development: Well-being in Developing Countries*, ed. Jonathan Isham, Thomas Kelly, and Sunder Ramaswamy, 58–81. Northampton, MA: Edward Elgar.

Narayan, Deepa and Lant Pritchett. 1999. "Cents and Sociability: Household Income and Social Capital in Rural Tanzania." *Economic Development and Cultural Change* 47, no. 4: 871–97.

Narayan, Deepa and Michael Cassidy. 2001. "A Dimensional Approach to Measuring Social Capital: Development and Validation of Social Capital Inventory." *Current Sociology* 49, no. 2: 49–93.

Ostrom, Elinor. 1990. *Governing the Commons: The Evolution of Institutions for Collective Action*. Cambridge: Cambridge University Press.

Ostrom, Elinor, Roy Gardner, and James Walker. 1994. *Rules, Games, and Common-Pool Resources*. Ann Arbor: University of Michigan Press.

Putnam, Robert. 1993. *Making Democracy Work: Civic Traditions in Modern Italy*. Princeton, NJ: Princeton University Press.

——. 2000. *Bowling Alone: The Collapse and Revival of American Community*. New York: Touchstone.

Rao, Vijayendra. 2005. "Symbolic Public Goods and the Coordination of Collective Action: A Comparison of Local Development in India and Indonesia." World Bank Research Working Paper 3685, Development Economics Research Group, World Bank, Washington, DC.

Ray, Debraj. 2004. "Aspirations, Poverty, and Economic Change." BREAD Policy Paper 002, Bureau for Research in Economic Analysis of Development, Cambridge, MA. Available at http://www.cid.harvard.edu/bread/papers/policy/p002.pdf.

Robertson, A. F. 1984. *People and the State: An Anthropology of Planned Development*. Cambridge: Cambridge University Press.

Rudolph, Suzanne Hoeber. 2000. "Civil Society and the Realm of Freedom." *Economic and Political Weekly* May 13, 1762–9.

Runge, C. F. 1986. "Common Property and Collective Action in Economic Development." *World Development* 14, no. 5: 623–35.

Seabright, Paul. 1993. "Managing Local Commons: Theoretical Issues in Incentive Design." *Journal of Economic Perspectives* 7, no. 4: 113–34.

Shah, Esha. 2003. *Social Designs: Tank Technology and Agrarian Transformation in Karnataka, South India*. Delhi: Orient Longman.

Wade, Robert. 1982. "The System of Administrative and Political Corruption: Canal Irrigation in South India." *Journal of Development Studies* 18, no. 3: 287–328.

——. 1987. *Village Republics: Economic Conditions for Collective Action in South India.* Cambridge: Cambridge University Press.

Woolcock, Michael. 1998. "Social Capital and Economic Development: Towards a Theoretical Synthesis and Policy Framework." *Theory and Society* 27: 151–208.

——. 1999. "Managing Risk, Shocks, and Opportunity in Developing Economies: The Role of Social Capital." In *Dimensions of Development*, ed. Gustav Ranis, 197–212. New Haven, CT: Yale Center for International and Area Studies.

6: Culture and Power in the Commons Debate

Amita Baviskar

Introduction

During the workshop "Conversations between Economists and Anthropologists II," it was not surprising that several speakers urged their fellow-participants to pay greater attention to matters of culture in addressing questions around the commons. What *was* unexpected, however, was that the scholars doing the urging were not anthropologists, but *economists*. Pranab Bardhan stressed the importance of incorporating power hierarchies and cultural specificities into analyses of common property institutions. He pointed to growing interest among economists in the maintenance of collective norms. Kaushik Basu suggested further study of the role of "non-economic values" in shaping collective choice. Vijayendra Rao discussed the salience of "symbolic public goods" as resources for building social cohesion. It seemed as if the notorious caricature of economists as irredeemably and irremediably attached to elegantly minimalist models about implausible utility-maximizing individuals had at last been laid to rest.

As Sharad Lélé (ch. 11, this volume) points out, projects around the commons have often been hobbled by the unresolved tensions between practitioners of different disciplines. Economists seeking to prioritize efficiency are at odds with sociologists/anthropologists who want to achieve greater equity. If the quest for equity is interpreted broadly to include greater consideration of the values and interests of subaltern groups, individually and collectively, as they define them, then going by the comments at the workshop, it would appear that economists had crossed over into the anthropologists' camp.

Such a consummation, however devoutly to be wished, seems unrealized on closer examination. The move to construct game-theoretic models that replace an individual with a group – what Sethi and Somanathan (ch. 7, this volume) describe as "methodological collectivism" – still falls far short of addressing the complex interactions between differently situated individuals engaged in collective action. "[T]he process of social choice is [still] viewed as an aggregative one, in which individual preferences are added to one another in arriving at decisions on the substance of social welfare" (Heineman et al. 1990: 71).

In terms of offering insights into collective action, this approach is inherently inadequate – it cannot take account of cultural contexts and the contradictory meanings they produce. Its analytical framework is ill suited to incorporate the inequalities that are central to the shaping of individual and collective choices. As Rayner points out, "these conditions exacerbate Arrow's classical result demonstrating the impossibility of a general procedure for aggregating given individual preferences in a democratic fashion" (Rayner 2003: 5116).

The "symbolic public goods" that Rao (ch. 10, this volume) discusses range from village festivals to knowledge held in common, non-material resources that function rather like "social capital" a la Putnam. But what kind of public goods are these? Festivals are occasions to strengthen relations with the sacred *and* to display temporal power. They may affirm a celebrating community but that solidarity is sought by excluding others or confining them to subordinate positions according to religion, caste and gender. The significance of spiritual reward and of practices of domination, resistance and compromise is embedded in a cultural language whose grammar is very different from the utilitarian principles of economics. If, as Isha Ray (ch. 4, this volume) points out, economists are concerned with outcomes, then adding non-material "goods" may not significantly improve the analytical result as long as the assumptions behind the model into which they are incorporated remain the same. Adding a dash of "culture" and a pinch of "power" to the recipe for understanding collective action around the commons does not take one very far from the familiar terrain of methodological individualism. An anthropological approach requires a more thorough-going theory of social power and inequality, one that transforms the very questions that are considered meaningful for analysis.

The call to re-frame research questions often evokes impatience among those who seek usable recommendations to ameliorate crises around the commons, to whom this appears to be a "merely academic" exercise. Program officers of development agencies and grassroots political activists alike generally seek research that helps address the undoubtedly important issue of "what is to be done" within the frames of their existing institutional goals and processes. The conditions of academic production, especially the dispensations of research funding, have meant that a good deal of work on the commons addresses the direct demands of an audience of development professionals.[1] However, the relationship between academic work that is produced under contract and its sponsors' interests is not always or entirely marked by instrumentalism. For instance, critical analyses of key concepts such as "participation" in ecological management emerged from social scientists who engaged with donor-driven development research questions. How and when research serves to aid, authorize or de-legitimize particular policy initiatives is a subject worthy of more detailed consideration (Mosse 2005). In this chapter, however, I explore a different *scale* of analysis. Here, I propose that a critical social science research that speaks to the development industry needs to be augmented by a form of meta-critique that examines the epistemological bases of institutionally produced knowledge. There is utility, I would argue, in *not* always playing a prescriptive role or confining one's inquiry to the immediate problem at hand, as defined by ongoing initiatives around the commons. Widening

---

[1] Research that is oriented to supporting social mobilization outside the parameters defined by the World Bank or other funding agencies is less voluminous.

the lens to include the political process by which we come to concur on the *definition* of the problem brings to light crucial unexamined assumptions and analytical moves that powerfully shape debates around the commons. Challenging these assumptions and modes of reasoning enables us to recast the commons debate in ways that uphold good anthropological *and* political practice.

Here, I argue that the configuration of resources-interests–identities–actions that is presumed to be at stake in questions around the commons cannot be treated as self-evident. We need to examine the process of cultural production by which "the commons" emerge as objects of analysis and intervention. The emergence of a dominant conception of the commons organizes attention in ways that occlude other, equally valid, ways of understanding what is at stake. I situate this process of knowledge formation and organization dialectically between two contending fields of force:[2] dominant professional development agencies and subaltern social movements, as they negotiate in a world dominated by transnational organizations of capital and government. I show that contemporary meanings of the commons draw upon particular local histories of domination, resistance and compromise, as they are informed by trans-local processes. These histories of contention provide the context for how communities come to be imagined in relation to the commons. In particular, I examine the political implications of a contradictory double move within the commons discourse: invoking the idea of the "global commons" while simultaneously zooming in to fine-tune the micro-practices of particular village groups. These contrary spatial and scalar moves combine to create "the commons effect" – rendering resources and populations manageable by reproducing a powerful set of institutional inequalities.

Hegemony and the Politics of Knowledge

To make these arguments about how cultural power shapes knowledge of the commons, I draw upon Antonio Gramsci's concept of hegemony. As Raymond Williams points out, Gramsci distinguished between "rule" and "hegemony" in defining relations between social classes (1977: 108). "Rule" is expressed in directly political forms and in times of crisis by direct or effective coercion. But the more normal situation is that of hegemony which is "not only the conscious system of ideas and beliefs ["ideology"], but the whole lived social process as practically organized by specific and dominant meanings and values" (Williams 1977: 109). Political legitimacy is achieved when the values and interests of dominant groups appear to be representative of and beneficial to all, such that particular meanings seem to be universally true and applicable.[3] Relations of domination and subordination shape practical consciousness, saturating "the whole substance of lived identities and relationships, to such a depth that the pressures and limits of what can ultimately be seen as a specific economic, political, and cultural system seem

---

[2]   The metaphor is borrowed from E. P. Thompson who used it to address the problem of popular culture within relations of domination (1978: 156).

[3]   Gramsci analyzed how the institutions of state and civil society – the market, schools – serve to disguise and detach the particular interests of the ruling classes such that they appear as generalized interests.

to most of us the pressures and limits of simple experience and common sense" (Williams 1977: 110).

That a given cultural form of domination is internalized does not lead Gramsci to suggest that subaltern groups suffer from "false consciousness." As Williams explains, "a lived hegemony is always a process . . . [I]t does not just passively exist as a form of dominance. It has continually to be renewed, recreated, defended, and modified. It is also continually resisted, limited, altered, challenged by pressures not at all its own . . . [T]he hegemonic [process] has to be seen as more than the simple transmission of an (unchanging) dominance. On the contrary, any hegemonic process must be especially alert and responsive to the alternatives and opposition which question or threaten its dominance. The reality of cultural process must then always include the efforts and contributions of those who are in one way or another outside or at the edge of the terms of the specific hegemony" (Williams 1977: 112–13).

Hegemony, then, is *not* a stable system of ideological consensus secured by dominant groups using culture as an instrument of power. Gramsci did not see hegemony as a "finished and monolithic ideological formation but as a problematic, contested, political process of domination and struggle" (Roseberry 1994: 358). Following Gramsci's emphasis on the *fragility* of the hegemony, William Roseberry proposes that the concept be used "*not* to understand consent but to understand struggle . . . What hegemony constructs . . . is not a shared ideology but a common material and meaningful framework for living through, talking about, and acting upon social orders characterized by domination" (Roseberry 1994: 360–1). That is, a hegemonic process seeks to delimit the *terrain* of struggle, the *terms* of debate.[4] To paraphrase Roseberry, the concept of hegemony is uniquely fitted for an "exploration of the dynamic tension between discursive fields and social fields of force" in an analysis of the commons as a "language of community and contention" (1996: 77). Relevant to the discussion here is another corollary: The hegemonic process is always incomplete and experienced in complex ways; it is not totalizing and cannot fully colonize the life-world of the dominated. This creates a form of *contradictory consciousness*, similar to Pierre Bourdieu's (1977) notion of "misrecognition,"[5] where subalterns struggle to reconcile their lived experience of domination with the subjective framings of identity and interests suggested by hegemonic institutions.

For my purposes here, the concept of hegemony helps to situate "the commons" as emerging from the unequal contestation between development agencies and subaltern movements.[6] Dominant conceptions of the commons invoke historically derived notions of "community" – cultural identities and subjective understandings of collective interests that have material consequences. Development agencies, including states, reinforce these conceptions of community and the commons in their institutional practice, seeking to normalize them so that they come to be experienced as self-evident truths by everyone concerned. In the process, other ways of collectively imagining and acting upon

---

[4]   Also see Crehan (2002: 204).

[5]   Bourdieu uses the notion to illuminate the tensions implicit in exchanges of value between unequally situated actors. The politics engendered in practices of reciprocity modeled on the gift (such as marriage) require the simultaneous maintenance of two conflicting idioms: generosity and calculation.

[6]   The wider context of this struggle is the discourse of development (Escobar 1995), itself produced by the dynamic tensions between post-colonial capitalism and nationalism as emancipatory projects of modernization.

the commons get sidelined, delimiting the terrain of struggle. Imparting legitimacy to particular conceptions of the commons and the communities to which they belong, enables development agencies to authoritatively intervene in their disposition, incorporating some social groups and excluding others. Their practices are modified, or are at least open to challenge and refutation, by groups "outside or at the edge of the terms of a specific hegemony." Hegemonic understandings of the commons are not produced by blunt instruments of coercion, but by subtler acts of persuasion whose success is not guaranteed. The attempt to secure consensus requires alliances between different groups, some accommodation of their differences, and compromises of power (see Li 1999). In the intrinsic uncertainty of this process lies the hope of alternative framings of the commons question that are more socially just and equitable.

Before proceeding with an examination of the commons as a hegemonic cultural formation of the kind discussed above, a clarification is in order. The "cultural turn" towards Gramsci and an analysis of hegemonic processes at work in framing the commons does *not* indicate a move away from a consideration of material resources and processes. Rather, I assume that material and symbolic values and meanings are inseparable. Materiality is apprehended through the senses but is made meaningful by cultural lenses. For instance, the biophysical properties of certain plants and their ability to meet biological demands such as hunger is mediated by cultural modes of appropriation such as extractive technologies, the social relations of production, exchange and consumption.[7] Yet it must also be noted that nature, or the biophysical world, is not infinitely plastic nor amenable to *any* cultural appropriation; its properties both limit and exceed human intentions (Mitchell 2002: 19–53).[8] For Gramsci, hegemony is intimately linked to material relations of domination and exploitation. The process of organizing ideas and subjective understandings both emerges from material relations *and* has profoundly material consequences – people die or lead lives marked by deprivation because of the institutionalized, normalized inequalities of class, caste, race, religion, and gender.

Producing Knowledge about the Commons

What do we mean by the "commons"? Why does "collective action" matter? On which "collectivities" do we focus our analysis? How do particular understandings of commons and communities influence practices on the ground? The term "the commons" immediately evokes a cluster of images and popular meanings that include particular resources such as water, grasslands, and trees, and social groups such as irrigators, pastoralists, and forest-users. Bringing them together is a property regime based on collective rights of usufruct and, variably, control. As I will show below, this common sense understanding proves to be inadequate along all three axes: property regime, resource, and community.

---

[7] For an exemplary account of the cultural construction of a plant, see Mintz (1986). Pollan (2001) offers similar insights on four plants in a more free-wheeling style.

[8] One may, following Latour, describe nature as an "actant," and recognize that agency resides in the non-human world too (Latour 1987: 2004).

The initial spate of research responding to Garrett Hardin's provocation about the "tragedy of the commons"[9] tended to concentrate on relatively small and egalitarian social groups with well-established customary rights to proximate resources such as lobster fishermen in Maine and village irrigation groups in the Nepal Himalayas (McKay and Acheson 1987; Berkes 1989; Ostrom 1990). These groups could visibly demonstrate that they *managed* resources: they worked through committees; distributed tasks and produce; and penalized rule-violators. The Common Property Resources (CPR) researchers' promotion of identifiable "decentralized natural management institutions" was seized by development agencies such as the Ford Foundation and the World Bank as a model to disseminate across the world. If such institutions did not exist or were defunct, the task became to "build capacity" internally and create an "enabling environment" externally (Schroeder 1999). Such a focus on "communities" that manage the "commons" was premised on a clear-cut boundary between the inside and outside – villagers, fishermen, and forest-users ranged against external forces such as the state and the market. Development agencies thus responded to the critique of scholars who sought to re-claim the commons for subaltern groups, but did so by spatializing and simplifying the problem of social inequality and how it should be addressed. Hegemonic ideas about the commons community emerged from this struggle between dominant development institutions and their critics. Their prevalence is evident in the deliberations of the International Association of the Study of Common Property (IASCP); a review of the papers presented at its bi-annual conferences will show that an overwhelming number concentrate on localized communities as the object of analysis, eschewing a wider frame of political economy.

While there are indeed "local institutions" of the sort described above, their relationship with the "outside" proves to be complicated enough to call the boundary into question. Various forms of decentralized management and shared usufruct may be nested within state or public ownership. For instance, while forests may be legally classified as state-owned and state-managed with restricted usufruct rights for proximate dwellers, control may be contested among a range of claimants – forest officials, timber contractors, NGOs, local villagers[10] – acting in collusion or competition (Baviskar 2002; 2001). The state of the resources that these groups manage and use (degraded forests, dwindling river flows) is shaped by prior histories of exploitation and ongoing extraction by non-local groups. The cultural attributes of a village partake of "local" particulars – such as the specificities of soil or topography that both enable and constrain cultural possibilities, but are simultaneously shaped by trans-local circuits of government and economy, education, religion, kinship, and language (see Gilmartin 2003; Ludden 2003). Actors who inhabit multiple subject-positions, and local environments that are profoundly affected by trans-local pasts and presents, challenge us to widen the lens of our analysis. When we do so, other significant actors come into view. As important as the proximate community is the presence of national and international development agencies who discipline local access through the use of repressive and productive power, deploying military and legal authority, creating policies and institutional frameworks, regulating markets, and providing funds.

---

[9]   Also see Olson's 1965 account of the problems of collective action with respect to public goods. This analysis by a political scientist used game-theoretic models and was influential in the CPR field.

[10]   And any one person may well be all of these.

An analysis of the commons must include these actors who are powerful members of the unequal "community" around the commons. These "stakeholders" are not neutral or benign patrons of "local communities," but have their own agenda, including reproduction and expansion of their power. Their operating style is to work behind the scenes, spotlighting the local community while remaining relatively invisible themselves.

The property regimes and resources that are generally considered germane to the analysis of the commons are collectively controlled and used *environmental* resources: water, forests, and pastures in rural areas, and public spaces such as parks in urban places. In the rural context, it is assumed that these resources are valued as part of a complex ecological web (soil–water–biomass–animals), providing long-term ecological benefits that cannot be entirely privately captured. The goal of resource management is *ecological sustainability*, variously defined, as much as equity. This demarcation excludes, say, public sector petroleum companies or private forestry corporations even though they, too, manage environmental resources such as minerals and forests, and represent large groups of citizens or shareholders who collectively control and benefit from these. Why is a corporate body of villagers different from a corporate body of citizens or joint owners? Why is a giant agricultural corporation that farms extensive lands in the US not perceived as a group managing the commons? Just as development agencies devise worldwide programs to reshape villagers' practices around the commons, why do they not focus programmatic attention on changing the operations of Chevron–Texaco or the National Thermal Power Corporation? Surely the practices of these corporate bodies have profound effects on local ecologies as well as communities? When development agencies maintain a separation between different "communities" and concentrate only on one kind, they indulge in a form of misrecognition that enables them to create a manageable world for themselves by eliding the contradictions of their position, even as large corporations continue to shape the conditions of possibility for "decentralized natural resource management."[11] The contradictory positions of national and international development agencies, in their quest to create "the commons" as an object of analysis and action, have been challenged and resisted by different contending groups. I shall now illustrate this by turning to the case of forests in India.

No quest for knowledge is innocent of considerations of power. To think of knowledge as socially produced means that the purpose of inquiry (why we seek to know) is not self-evident or neutral, and nor is the manner of inquiry (how we seek to know). Particular regimes of rule generate particular forms of knowledge (Cohn 1987; Ludden 1992; Scott 1998). For instance, during the Industrial Revolution, the imperative of managing plant species to assure a cost-effective, orderly supply of raw materials for industrial production led to the creation of new social relations where knowledge and rule were inseparable. The new scientific disciplines that systematized natural history, glorified exploration, and "discovery," and established a network for research and experiment across the world (Drayton 2000), re-arranged knowledge of, and relationships between, the natural and social world. The imputation of a certain *order* to nature, the "laws" of evolution,

---

[11]   The boundary between public and private ownership is also blurred by the complexity and dynamism of property relations of ownership, control, management, and use rights. Even at the apparently straightforward level of the village, individual rights to the commons are shaped by relations to private land, and also refracted through relations of class, caste, gender, age, and marriage.

for instance, extended to racial classification, justifying colonial power's re-arrangement of social relations through land alienation and slavery. The notion that knowledge of nature would enable the best possible use of resources, "improving" nature as well as the related lives of colonized subjects, transforming them into industrious peasants and "productive" laborers, continues to persist and inform the commons community.

In the struggles over knowledge and power, the disciplines of forestry and anthropology that emerged as the handmaidens of imperialism[12] were later appropriated and transformed by the project of nationalism. From science at the service of Empire grew science at the service of the independent Nation. The missions of the Indian Forest Service and the Anthropological Survey of India were re-oriented to address the developmental needs of a different "imagined community" (Anderson 1983), even as the relationship of these institutions to subaltern populations displayed, on the whole, a remarkable continuity with the colonial enterprise. The hegemonic ideology of developmentalism demanded the same sacrifices of them and placed similar restrictions: control over forest resources remained with a state primarily concerned with maximizing revenues and facilitating extraction for industrial growth. Development included a civilizational mission of incorporating subalterns more fully into the roles of citizens and proletarians. The hegemony of development was challenged in the late 1970s and throughout the 1980s by a number of initiatives by social movements and rights organizations that Rajni Kothari described as "non-party political formations" (1988). In particular, the proposed 1980 Forest Bill, which sought to further centralize forest management and restrict forest-dwellers' access, sparked a concerted campaign by civil rights groups across the country (Fernandes and Kulkarni 1983). This political mobilization, informed by ongoing movements such as Chipko and other struggles against development agency-led programs such as Social Forestry, inspired a range of social scientists and journalists to produce a body of work that challenged the statist premises of forest policy (Singh 1986; Guha 1989; CSE 1982). However, development agencies stayed away from the populist "forests for the people" manifesto until the 1990s when it seemed to converge with a far more powerful anti-statist project, viz. economic liberalization. Within the neo-liberal framework set by global capitalist organizations and broadly accepted by development agencies, there was a preoccupation with utilitarian concerns such as maximizing efficiency and minimizing waste; decentralizing to cut costs; seeking equity only to the extent that it did not compromise efficiency. This was accompanied by an all-pervasive managerialism, with its concomitant privileging of technocratic expertise (Ferguson 1990). Counter-perspectives from social movements have been incorporated into this field, but often uneasily or in ways that have radically transformed the challenges that such movements pose. Thus social movement critiques that raise issues of democratic practice have been domesticated within the "environment and development" field as a call for "participation." "It seems that the discourse of participation is essentially a managerial discourse, perhaps, even more narrowly, a crisis-management discourse masquerading as a theory of democracy" (Rayner 2003: 5119). Dominant political formations thus structure how knowledge about the commons is produced, circulated and consumed.

---

[12]   On the origins of scientific forestry, see Grove (1995) and Guha (1989); on anthropology and colonialism, Asad (1973); on the political ideologies underlying colonial and post-colonial development, see Cowen and Shenton (1996), Mehta (1999), and Ferguson (1997).

Much of the research on the commons has emerged from the "environment and development" field, dominated by multilateral and bilateral development agencies and the academic and NGO worlds that they underwrite. This context directly influences the process by which certain research areas gain prominence. For instance, the voluminous research on Joint Forest Management (JFM) and Participatory Irrigation Management in India, funded in part by the Ford Foundation and World Bank, mobilized attention towards a set of practices that were relatively minor in scale (albeit "new" and therefore interesting), ignoring the vast forest areas under corporate management (state-owned forest corporations working with private contractors) and bureaucratically run irrigation networks that continued with business-as-usual. In the decade of the 1990s, even as CPR researchers intensified their scrutiny of the micro-practices of Village Forest Committees, large swathes of forests were denotified for "development projects" (Baviskar 2001). If the intention of researchers was to inform public policy (generally narrowly interpreted to mean advising the government or development agencies, as opposed to contributing to a wider debate that includes social activists and organizations of subaltern citizens), they did succeed, but only within the confines of a constrained agenda.[13] This is not to suggest that "big" players conspire to twist the arms of researchers but that social institutions perpetuate their power by socializing subjects to internalize the limits of what is permissible and desirable (Bourdieu 1998: 119). Even a quick analysis of funding trends shows how the boundary between coercion and consent is blurred in the case of research agenda (Baviskar and Saberwal 2001; Ross 2003).

"Our Common Heritage": Hegemony at Work in Creating the Global Commons

Since the 1990s, "the commons" as a category has been expanded to incorporate the "global commons" – seeds, rainforests, oceans, and the atmosphere. From germplasm to the ozone layer, from microbes to the cosmos, the scale of defining the commons in relation to proximate communities has been replaced by a new notion of global environmental resources, communities, and property regimes. How does the discursive move to the "global commons" mark a hegemonic shift? What forms of knowledge and rule does it enable? Since the Rio conference in 1992 (United Nations Conference on Environment and Development) and the establishment of the Global Environment Facility, a transnational framework of negotiating arrangements about managing the commons has come into effect. This institutional framework authorizes international financial organizations, development agencies, and transnational environmental NGOs, among others, to participate in the disposition of resources hitherto controlled (at least nominally) by national governments. Significant for our analysis is the hegemonic process by which arguments are marshalled to legitimize the claims of these powerful groups. Here, I focus in particular on the construction of a new "moral community" around the commons.

---

[13]   I am generalizing across a large body of work. Of course, there are exceptions to this norm; for instance, the work of Nandini Sundar (2001) and K. Sivaramakrishnan (1998) on JFM situates it within a larger, more complex, political context. See also the volume edited by Jeffery and Sundar (1999).

One of the first processes that historically minded anthropologists think of in relation to the commons is their *enclosure*, part of the great sweeping change in property relations that turned peasants into proletarians in Britain (Thompson 1975). The commons were crucial to the subsistence of English peasants who protested fiercely against the institution of draconian laws like the Black Act that cut off their access to resources previously guaranteed. At stake was the notion of a *moral economy*, an ideal that acknowledged and even accepted social inequality but asserted the rights of the local landless poor to the common weal, resources that were held in trust, sometimes by the state. By conceiving of woodlots, game, and fallow fields as nature's bounty, not manufactured by humans and therefore not to be privately appropriated, proponents of moral economy also challenged the ongoing *commodification* of these sources of subsistence and their incorporation into an economy of profit.[14] The concept of moral economy rallied subaltern groups in defence of old ways of life against new social relations that threatened to impoverish them.

Ideas of moral economy continue to saturate contemporary discourses around the commons but, in an ironic reversal, they are brought to bear to disenfranchise subaltern groups.[15] The moral economy of the commons conjures up a collectivity that is greater than the sum of its individual parts. Forests, pastures, freshwater, oceans, climate, and seeds, are not simply resources for proximate groups of users/owners, they are the common property of everyone. In part, this understanding derives from the notion that as "ecological" resources,[16] part of a complex web of physical and biological processes, the commons have a transcendental value that exceeds the present and the proximate, encompassing "other living beings on the planet" or "future generations." The commons are thus endowed with a value that transcends their utility to individual users. This notion of a common patrimony was deployed for colonial and national development, facilitating the state's claim of eminent domain over particular resources. Now transnational organizations also benefit from the particular mode of ownership and appropriation inherent in the notion of the commons. To categorize something as "the commons" is to immediately enable these entities – Northern environmentalists, corporations, the World Trade Organization – to pose as "stakeholders." After all, they too can claim a legitimate role in shaping the future of "our common heritage."

The "common heritage" idea is often promoted by techniques that attribute charismatic qualities to biophysical entities – whales, the Amazonian rainforest (Slater 2002), the western tragopan (Baviskar 2002). Marx's notion of commodity fetishism is useful for understanding how such a representation of the biophysical world works to obscure the social relations that produce it.[17] The social history of a created landscape is concealed,

---

[14] For analyses of contemporary cultural politics around the privatization of biodiversity, see Boal (2001) and Hayden (2003).

[15] It could be argued though that the enclosure movement, rather than pitting moral economy against market economy, represented two opposing sets of claims, *both* of which drew upon moral arguments. The claims of English landlords asserted the *moral* legitimacy of utilitarianism.

[16] Of course, the connection between "ecology" and the commons is historically produced, rather than something intrinsic to the "nature" of the commons. The commons may only signify a particular property regime where the ecological importance of the resource may be irrelevant. Cf. Arvind Rajagopal's work on urban space that imaginatively uses the idea of city streets as commons (Rajagopal 2001).

[17] "The commodity . . . is a very strange thing, abounding in metaphysical subtleties and theological niceties" (Marx 1976 [1867]: 163).

as is the coercive character of conservation (Peluso 1992; Neumann 1998). Arrangements such as the Global Environment Facility of the World Bank enclose species and forest areas and exclude particular users by claiming resources for a universal "mankind" (see Baviskar 2002). Examining one such enclosure in southern Cameroon, Nguiffo pithily sums up the sleight of hand at work: "[T]he 'global commons' are always constructed through the deconstruction of the local commons . . . The interests of 'mankind' are opposed to those of local people, and they are not seen as a part of 'mankind' " (1998: 113). While local access is curtailed, local knowledge is tapped by project managers and researchers as something to be universally shared, under the communitarian rubric of "common heritage."

But such concerns for "common heritage" are rarely asserted for privately owned agricultural lands even though they are also "ecological" resources that sustain other species and on which depends the fate of future generations. We are told that the commons matter because poor people depend on them: up to 25 percent of the household income of poor families in rural India comes from "common property resources" such as land, water and forests (Jodha 1986). But what about the remaining 75 percent, much of it income derived from working on/with privately-owned resources or state projects? As the greater part of poor people's livelihood, surely these should have priority in setting research agenda?[18] The refusal of development agencies to address social inequalities rooted in private property reflects their commitment to maintaining the public/private divide, reproducing a categorization that renders subaltern populations more vulnerable even as they claim to safeguard their welfare. This is achieved by making ecological conservation a priority that supersedes concerns such as immediate livelihoods, and by creating a crisis narrative about ecological degradation that legitimizes the need for managerial expertise. According to Michael Goldman, "In discovering or inventing the *global ecological commons*, and its fragile future, elite Northern scientists and policy-makers also gave birth to the appropriate methods for their understanding (i.e., *global science*) and the character of its inhabitants (i.e., *the global citizen*)" (Goldman 1998: 4). These experts, and the amorphous yet powerful global citizens they serve, effectively rule out alternate ways of framing the commons question, and avoid an examination of their own practices.

Closer to home, the "clean and green Delhi" campaign was launched by middle-class environmentalists who petitioned the Supreme Court to shut down manufacturing industries and demolish squatter settlements (Baviskar 2003). Successfully mobilizing in defence of the urban commons, environmentalists triumphed at the cost of hundreds of thousands of workers who lost their jobs and homes. In a conflict that pitted different sections of urban residents against each other, the more affluent set who claimed to represent the commons as a public good was able to outweigh the "private" privations that environmentalism imposed on the working class. Clean air and green spaces appear to be universally desirable goods, concerns that bind the community at large, while

---

[18]   A commitment on the part of, say, agricultural economists in the 1960s and 1970s to studying access to land and agricultural resources seems to have lost steam in recent decades. The ongoing campaign for access to state/public resources – food and employment, where economists have joined hands with activist organizations like the Mazdoor Kisan Shakti Sangathan, is a welcome move away from the political quietism that marks much of contemporary academia, but it does not go against the current of the unspoken consensus that private property is off limits for public debate, let alone action.

employment and shelter seem to be the limited preoccupation of particular groups. To understand how such a framing of "environmental problems" gains legitimacy, we have to examine the political and intellectual arenas opened and closed by the particular charge invested in the term "the commons."

The surcharged moral weight attached to the commons tilts in favour of authoritative interventions by powerful agents, creating new collectivities whose different discursive practices have material effects. Networks around the commons span different scales, creating articulations between the practices of trans-national organizations, nation-state bureaucracies and NGOs, regional, district, and village-level groups.[19] If the commons have become sites for experiments with decentralization, it is because of the compromises of power. The rights to more valuable forests or agricultural lands are not up for negotiation, only the more economically marginal, interstitial spaces that then lie between regulatory regimes. These spaces serve as laboratories for state and NGO experiments with new management practices (Baviskar 2007) that perpetuate the idea of self-sufficient, ecologically sustainable communities. By becoming sites where state subjects (who seek to manage the environment and the poor, a necessary part of what modern governments do) attempt to garner legitimacy among their various reference publics, the commons become the arena where relations of rule are reproduced and reworked. Yet, in creating the "commons effect," paraphrasing Timothy Mitchell's concept of the "state effect" (Mitchell 1999) – a collective representation of the commons as an isolatable and autonomous object of analysis and action, these networks and the relations between different actors within them are hidden from view by researchers. The spotlight is turned instead on one particular entity – the village community. In the next section, I discuss the hegemonic processes at work in focusing on "local" community, and how the kind of knowledge produced about villagers ignores their contradictory consciousness.

Producing the Village Community: Contradictory Consciousness

Through the discursive moves described above, "the commons" are selectively defined and appropriated, eliding crucial political questions about the control and management of privatized resources. The field of knowledge thus produced focuses overwhelmingly on subaltern village groups; reforming their micro-practices becomes the subject of inquiry and action by development agencies. This is how the terrain of struggle is delimited, and relations of domination and subordination normalized through their effect of shaping practical consciousness. Elite patterns of resource use, and the inequalities intensified by neo-liberalism, are treated as given, even when they are directly consequential in shaping the conditions of life for the poor. The attention devoted to how poor villagers conduct their lives in relation to pastures, water, and trees, is out of all proportion to their economic priorities or the overall ecological significance of these resources. Yet, even within this curtailed sphere of analysis and action, development agencies persist in their misrecognition of subjective interests and the cultural significance of "resources."

---

[19]   This is just one way of slicing the complexity of social action; each of these "levels" is internally differentiated and is formed in relation to others.

In theorizing the village community, the tensions in understanding collective action persist in the shape of classic conundrums that pit the individual versus the collective, agency versus structure. The field of political ecology embraces this dynamic tension by taking as precept Marx's maxim that "men make their own history, but they do not make it just as they please; they do not make it under circumstances chosen by themselves, but under circumstances directly encountered, given and transmitted from the past" (Marx 1963 [1852]: 15). This first step in addressing the individual/collective divide enables an appreciation of how "situated cultural practices and sedimented histories of people and place" (Moore 1999: 658) inform collective action. Yet who are these "people" and what "history" are they making? Scholars have often left these questions unattended, partly because many of them focus on overt conflict around "natural resources" where the collectivities and causes at stake seemed to be self-evident (e.g. forest-dwellers fighting for subsistence versus a state and private companies seeking to profit from timber extraction).[20] On the scale of the everyday, the mundane micro-practices that accrue to make up history, the age-old questions about how powerful inequalities shape collective action persist.

The notion of "moral economy" used in a populist sense to invoke a localized, organic community bound by reciprocity that stands opposed to the state has largely been abandoned by CPR scholars (Agrawal and Sivaramakrishnan 2000; Agrawal and Gibson 2001). There is far greater attention to the processes by which collective identities emerge as contingent and contested, within multiple and overlapping fields of power. The insights from this approach become apparent when we examine the much-researched question of women's participation in Village Forest Committees under JFM. The first attempts to incorporate gender inequalities within the framework of analysis of village communities, assigned women a separate "stakeholder" status, an improvement over previous practice where women were simply assumed to be represented by male heads of household. But the category "women" assumed that all women, regardless of caste and class, age, and marital status, inhabited the same subject position, an assumption that activists worked hard to challenge in their everyday practices (Sarin et al. 1998). Attempting to model patriarchal relations within the household as they impinged on women's participation in JFM committees (whether women would be able to secure management decisions that best represented "their interests": priority to fuel and fodder over commercial species, for instance), some theorists have adopted a "bargaining" model whereby women negotiate from a position of subordination (Agarwal 1994). But this mode of modeling patriarchy assumes that women's interests can be clearly identified in relation to their rights to property and the gendered division of labor. While this model avoids the essentialism of Vandana Shiva[21] and is attentive to the political economy of patriarchy, it does not explain why, even in the absence of patriarchal repression, women so often do not act "in their interests." Rather than imagining interests as given, attached to objective class positions, we have to think of "women's interests" as produced discursively by patriarchal relations (Jackson 2003). Patriarchy as a hegemonic system suggests what "women's interests" might be: being good, loyal wives, and obedient daughters-in-law, not compromising family honor by opposing men. The

---

[20]   And even in such relatively clear-cut cases, there have been sharply divergent perspectives. For instance, Guha (1989), Shiva (1988), and Rangan (2000) offer varied interpretations of the Chipko movement as a peasant, feminist, and regional struggle.

[21]   Which Agarwal has ably criticized (1992).

internalization of these ways of thinking, which are neither forms of "false consciousness" nor entirely coerced by repressive power (after all, the "good" woman is rewarded with praise and respect), is all the more powerful because it is suffused with affect. Love, fear, trust are essential elements of a gendered cultural politics that create subjects with interests. Collective action around the commons is shaped by such perceptions of subjective identities.

Cultural politics suggests that the commons have value within a larger economy of signification which crucially shapes their modes of appropriation. Analysis has generally focused on the use and exchange values of material resources in the commons – grass, water, wood. Value derives from the biophysical properties of these resources as well as the social relations of production within which they are appropriated. But the commons are also resources for collective representations that exceed the concern with immediate material use. This "social life of things"[22] is well illustrated in David Mosse's study of village water tanks in Tamil Nadu where dalits[23] mobilized for representation in the association that managed these bodies (Mosse 2003: 279–82). For dalits, traditionally excluded from institutions controlling the village temple and tank, a place in the water users' association was a form of symbolic capital that mattered, perhaps even more than the material gains from water. As an arena where subaltern aspirations for upward mobility and greater power within a Mudaliar-dominated village caste hierarchy could be pursued, the association's importance exceeded that of the resource it managed. Concerns about honor and respect, crystallized through a region-wide dalit movement, as much as the material practices of cultivation, became central to water management.[24] Following Bourdieu (1998), one must note that expanding the notion of value does not mean that varied elements (honor, water, patronage, votes) can be assimilated into the same matrix. On the contrary, it is precisely their difference and incommensurability that is fiercely guarded (e.g. honor loses its value and is compromised and corrupted if it is "bought," exchanged for money). Multiple hegemonic political formations combine to create contradictory forms of consciousness that complicate the configuration of resources–interests–identities assumed in CPR models. Ignoring this complexity creates sterile models of collective action that are ultimately impotent in redressing either social inequality or ecological degradation. Yet, in their failure, they are successful in reproducing the domination of development agencies.

Conclusion

In this chapter, I examined the process of cultural production by which "the commons" emerge as objects of analysis and intervention. I argued that the emergence of a dominant conception of the commons organizes attention in ways that occlude other, equally

---

[22]   See Appadurai (1986).

[23]   Dalits are members of India's "scheduled castes" – former untouchables whose position at the bottom of the social and economic hierarchy is marked by the experience of being exploited and discriminated against.

[24]   If commons institutions such as water users' associations have multiple intersecting meanings that derive from their embeddedness in wider political formations, sometimes these wider political formations may entirely "take over" the commons. Researchers and development practitioners who search for identifiable institutions that resemble the specialized, rationally organized, decision-making bodies familiar to industrial production are often frustrated when they can't find an "institution" that "manages" the commons. See Fairhead and Leach (1996) and Schroeder (1999).

valid, ways of understanding what is at stake. Development practitioners and scholars are often uneasy with complex representations of the commons, and of the communities around them, since they make it hard to produce general predictive models that are context-proof. Unless compelled by subaltern movements to incorporate dissonant points of view, the development world tends to deal with complexity by attempting to make it manageable through acts of misrecognition and simplification. I have argued here for the political and intellectual importance of attending to the widest connections between power and knowledge in the field of development, and subjecting academic practices to the same searching scrutiny. Critical awareness about hegemonic processes and the forms of consciousness they produce will allow us to situate the commons in a more grounded political frame, a mode of understanding that is crucial for creating a more just and equal world.

References

Agarwal, Bina. 1994. *A Field of One's Own: Gender and Land Rights in South Asia*. Cambridge: Cambridge University Press.

Agarwal, Bina. 1992. "The Gender and Environment Debate: Lessons from India," *Feminist Studies*, 18(1): 119–58.

Agrawal, Arun and Clark C. Gibson (eds). 2001. *Communities and the Environment: Ethnicity, Gender, and the State in Community-based Conservation*. New Brunswick, NJ: Rutgers University Press.

Agrawal, Arun and K. Sivaramakrishnan (eds). 2000. *Agrarian Environments: Resources, Representations, and Rule in India*. Durham, NC: Duke University Press.

Anderson, Benedict. 1983. *Imagined Communities: Reflections on the Origins and Spread of Nationalism*. London: Verso.

Appadurai, Arjun (ed.). 1986. *The Social Life of Things: Commodities in Cultural Perspective*. Cambridge: Cambridge University Press.

Asad, Talal (ed.). 1973. *Anthropology and the Colonial Encounter*. Atlantic Highlands, NJ: Humanities Press.

Baviskar, Amita. 2007. "The Dream Machine: The Model Development Project and the Remaking of the State," in Amita Baviskar (ed.), *Waterscapes: The Cultural Politics of a Natural Resource*. Delhi: Permanent Black.

Baviskar, Amita. 2003. "Between Violence and Desire: Space, Power and Identity in the Making of Metropolitan Delhi," *International Social Science Journal*, 175: 89–98.

Baviskar, Amita. 2002. "States, Communities and Conservation: The Practice of Ecodevelopment in the Great Himalayan National Park," in Vasant Saberwal and Mahesh Rangarajan (eds), *Battles over Nature: Science and the Politics of Wildlife Conservation*. New Delhi: Permanent Black.

Baviskar, Amita. 2001. "Forest Management as Political Practice: Indian Experiences with the Accommodation of Multiple Interests," *International Journal of Agricultural Resources, Governance and Ecology*, 1(3/4): 243–63.

Baviskar, Amita and Vasant Saberwal. 2001. "Fording the Waters: An Institutional History of the Ford Foundation's Programs for Agricultural and Water Resources Development in India." Unpublished report.

Berkes, Fikret (ed.). 1989. *Common Property Resources: Ecology and Community-based Sustainable Development*. London: Belhaven Press.

Boal, Iain. 2001. "Damaging Crops: Sabotage, Social Memory, and the New Genetic Enclosures," in Nancy Lee Peluso and Michael Watts (eds), *Violent Environments*. Ithaca: Cornell University Press.

Bourdieu, Pierre. 1998. "The Economy of Symbolic Goods," in *Practical Reason*. Cambridge: Polity Press.

Bourdieu, Pierre. 1977. *Outline of a Theory of Practice*. Cambridge: Cambridge University Press.

Cohn, Bernard S. 1987. *An Anthropologist among the Historians and Other Essays*. Delhi: Oxford University Press.

Cowen, M. P. and R. W. Shenton. 1996. *Doctrines of Development*. London: Routledge.

Crehan, Kate. 2002. *Gramsci, Culture and Anthropology*. Berkeley: University of California Press.

CSE (Centre for Science and Environment). 1982. *The State of India's Environment: A Citizens' Report*. New Delhi: CSE.

Drayton, Richard. 2000. *Nature's Government: Science, Imperial Britain, and the "Improvement" of the World*. New Haven, CT: Yale University Press.

Escobar, Arturo. 1995. *Encountering Development: The Making and Unmaking of the Third World*. Princeton, NJ: Princeton University Press.

Fairhead, James and Melissa Leach. 1996. *Misreading the African Landscape: Society and Ecology in a Forest–Savanna Mosaic*. Cambridge: Cambridge University Press.

Ferguson, James. 1990. *The Anti-politics Machine: "Development," Depoliticization and Bureaucratic Power in Lesotho*. Cambridge: University of Cambridge Press.

Ferguson, James. 1997. "Anthropology and Its Evil Twin: 'Development' in the Constitution of a Discipline," in Frederick Cooper and Randall Packard (eds), *International Development and the Social Sciences: Essays on the History and Politics of Knowledge*. Berkeley: University of California Press.

Fernandes, Walter and Sharad Kulkarni. 1983. *Towards a New Forest Policy: People's Rights and Environmental Needs*. New Delhi: Indian Social Institute.

Gilmartin, David. 2003. "Water and Waste: Nature, Productivity, and Colonialism in the Indus Basin," *Economic and Political Weekly*, 38(48): 5057–65.

Goldman, Michael. 1998. "Inventing the Commons: Theories and Practices of the Commons' Professional," in M. Goldman (ed.), *Privatizing Nature: Political Struggles for the Global Commons*. London: Pluto Press.

Grove, Richard. 1995. *Green Imperialism: Colonial Expansionism, Tropical Edens and the Origins of Environmentalism*. Delhi: Oxford University Press.

Guha, Ramachandra. 1989. *The Unquiet Woods: Ecological Change and Peasant Resistance in the Himalaya*. Delhi: Oxford University Press.

Hayden, Cori. 2003. *When Nature Goes Public: The Making and Unmaking of Bioprospecting in Mexico*. Princeton, NJ: Princeton University Press.

Heineman, R., W. Bluhm, S. Peterson, and E. Kearny. 1990. *The World of the Policy Analyst: Rationality, Values, and Politics*. Chatham, NJ: Chatham House Publishers.

Jackson, Cecile. 2003. "Gender Analysis of Land: Beyond Land Rights for Women?," *Journal of Agrarian Change*, 3(4): 453–80.

Jeffery, Roger and Nandini Sundar (eds). 1999. *A New Moral Economy for India's Forests?: Discourses of Community and Participation*. New Delhi: Sage.

Jodha, N. S. 1986. "Common Property Resources and Rural Poor in Dry Regions of India," *Economic and Political Weekly*, 21(27).

Kothari, Rajni. 1988. *State against Democracy: In Search of Humane Governance*. Delhi: Ajanta Publishers.

Latour, Bruno. 2004. *Politics of Nature: How to Bring the Sciences into Democracy*. Cambridge: Harvard University Press.

Latour, Bruno. 1987. *Science in Action: How to Follow Scientists and Engineers through Society*. Cambridge: Harvard University Press.

Li, Tania Murray. 1999. "Compromising Power: Development. Culture, and Rule in Indonesia," *Cultural Anthropology*, 14(3): 295–322.

Ludden, David. 2003. "Investing in Nature around Sylhet: An Excursion into Geographical History," *Economic and Political Weekly*, 38(48): 5080–8.

Ludden, David. 1992. "India's Development Regime," in Nicholas B. Dirks (ed.), *Colonialism and Culture*. Ann Arbor: University of Michigan Press.

Marx, Karl. 1976 [1867]. *Capital*, vol. 1. London: Pelican Books.

Marx, Karl. 1963 [1852]. *The Eighteenth Brumaire of Louis Bonaparte*. New York: International Publishers.

McKay, Bonnie and James Acheson. 1987. *The Question of the Commons: The Culture and Ecology of Communal Resources*. Tucson: University of Arizona Press.

Mehta, Uday Singh. 1999. *Liberalism and Empire: A Study in Nineteenth-century British Liberal Thought*. Chicago: University of Chicago Press.

Mintz, Sidney. 1986. *Sweetness and Power*. New York: Penguin Books.

Mitchell, Timothy. 2002. *Rule of Experts: Egypt, Techno-politics, Modernity*. Berkeley: University of California Press.

Mitchell, Timothy. 1999. "Society, Economy, and the State Effect," in George Steinmetz (ed.), *State/Culture: State Formation after the Cultural Turn*. Ithaca: Cornell University Press.

Moore, Donald S. 1999. "The Crucible of Cultural Politics: Reworking "Development" in Zimbabwe's Eastern Highlands," *American Ethnologist*, 26(3): 654–89.

Mosse, David. 2005. *Cultivating Development: An Ethnography of Aid Policy and Practice*. London: Pluto Press.

Mosse, David. 1997. "The Ideology and Politics of Community Participation: Tank Irrigation Development in Colonial and Contemporary Tamil Nadu," in R. D. Grillo and R. L. Stirrat (eds), *Discourses of Development: Anthropological Perspectives*. New York: Berg Publishers.

Neumann, Roderick P. 1998. *Imposing Wilderness: Struggles over Livelihood and Nature Preservation in Africa*. Berkeley: University of California Press.

Nguiffo, Samuel-Alain. 1998. "In Defence of the Commons: Forest Battles in Southern Cameroon," in M. Goldman (ed.), *Privatizing Nature: Political Struggles for the Global Commons*. London: Pluto Press.

Olson, Mancur. 1965. *The Logic of Collective Action: Public Goods and the Theory of Groups*. Cambridge, MA: Harvard University Press.

Ostrom, Elinor. 1990. *Governing the Commons: The Evolution of Institutions for Collective Action*. New York: Cambridge University Press.

Peluso, Nancy L. 1992. *Rich Forests, Poor People: Resource Control and Resistance in Java*. Berkeley: University of California Press.

Pollan, Michael. 2001. *The Botany of Desire: A Plant's-eye View of the World*. New York: Random House.

Putnam, Robert. 2000. *Bowling Alone: The Collapse and Revival of American Community*. New York: Simon and Schuster.

Rajagopal, Arvind. 2001. "The Violence of Commodity Aesthetics: Hawkers, Demolition Raids, and a New Regime of Consumption," *Social Text*, 19(3): 91–113.

Rangan, Haripriya. 2000. *Of Myths and Movements: Rewriting Chipko into Himalayan History*. Delhi: Oxford University Press.

Rayner, Steve. 2003. "Who's in Charge?: Reflections on the Worldwide Displacement of Democratic Judgement by Expert Assessments," *Economic and Political Weekly*, 38(48): 5113–19.

Roseberry, William. 1996. "Hegemony, Power, and Languages of Contention," in E. N. Wilmsen and P. McAllister (eds), *The Politics of Difference: Ethnic Premises in a World of Power*. Chicago: University of Chicago Press.

Roseberry, William. 1994. "Hegemony and the Language of Contention," in G. M. Joseph and D. Nugent (eds), *Everyday Forms of State Formation: Revolution and the Negotiation of Rule in Modern Mexico*. Durham, NC: Duke University Press.

Ross, Eric B. 2003. "Anthropology, the Cold War, and the Myth of Peasant Conservatism." Paper presented at the 102nd Annual Meeting of the American Anthropological Association, Chicago, November.

Sarin, Madhu, with Lipika Ray, Manju S. Raju, Mitali Chatterjee, Narayan Banerjee, and Shyamala Hiremath. 1998. "Gender and Equity Concerns in Joint Forest Management," in Ashish Kothari,

Neema Pathak, R. V. Anuradha, and Bansuri Taneja (eds), *Communities and Conservation: Natural Resource Management in South and Central Asia*. New Delhi: Sage Publications.

Schroeder, Richard A. 1999. *Shady Practices: Agroforestry and Gender Politics in the Gambia*. Berkeley: University of California Press.

Scott, James C. 1998. *Seeing Like a State: How Certain Schemes to Improve the Human Condition Have Failed*. New Haven, CT: Yale University Press.

Shiva, Vandana. 1988. *Staying Alive: Women, Ecology and Survival in India*. New Delhi: Kali for Women.

Singh, Chhatrapati. 1986. *Common Property and Common Poverty: India's Forests, Forest Dwellers and the Law*. Delhi: Oxford University Press.

Sivaramakrishnan, K. 1998. "Co-managed Forests in West Bengal: Historical Perspectives on Community and Control," *Journal of Sustainable Forestry*, 7(3/4): 35.

Slater, Candace. 2002. *Entangled Edens: Visions of the Amazon*. Berkeley: University of California Press.

Sundar, Nandini. 2001. "Beyond the Bounds?: Violence at the Margins of New Legal Geographies," in Nancy Lee Peluso and Michael Watts (eds), *Violent Environments*. Ithaca: Cornell University Press.

Sundar, Nandini. 2000. "The Construction and Deconstruction of "Indigenous" Knowledge in India's Joint Forest Management Programme," in Roy Ellen et al. (eds), *Indigenous Environmental Knowledge and its Transformations: Critical Environmental Perspectives*. Amsterdam: Harwood Academic Publishers.

Thompson, E. P. 1978. "Eighteenth-century English Society: Class Struggle without Class?" *Social History*, 3(2): 133–65.

Thompson, E. P. 1975. *Whigs and Hunters: The Origins of the Black Act*. New York: Pantheon.

Williams, Raymond. 1977. *Marxism and Literature*. Oxford: Oxford University Press.

7: A Simple Model of Collective Action

Rajiv Sethi and E. Somanathan

Introduction

This chapter outlines a theory of collective action in common property resource use. There is now a very large empirical literature on the commons, including numerous detailed case studies as well as a few econometric studies. To the best of our knowledge, however, there is no internally consistent model that broadly conforms to the facts that have emerged from this literature, and that presents comparative static results on when collective action is likely to be successful. The theory outlined here is intended to fill this gap. It is based on the idea that at least some individuals involved in governance and extraction decisions are not motivated exclusively by material self-interest. Specifically, we allow for the possibility that a concern for reciprocity may be an important consideration in such environments. In this respect, our modeling approach is akin to that of Falk et al. (2002), but makes simpler assumptions and is explicit about the effects of different parameters on the prospects for successful collective action.

The empirical literature on the commons agrees on the importance of a number of factors that affect the likelihood of successful collective action. These include small user groups, a high level of dependence on the commons, low monitoring costs, and well-established schemes of punishment. "Beyond this apparently massive consensus there are however a number of important 'shadow zones'" (Baland and Platteau 1996: 289). Referring to the influence of group size and heterogeneity, Poteete and Ostrom (2004: 438) remark that "no consensus has emerged on the exact nature of the relationships or the relative importance of either factor." Agrawal (2003) complains that too many factors that influence the success of collective action have been identified in the empirical literature, that the relations between different factors are not well understood, and that, in the absence of a model, it becomes impossible to sort out which factors really matter.

We argue that the disconnect between theory and empirical work on this problem stems from a formal modeling approach that does not capture one of the important stylized facts of commons management: the importance of a system for sanctioning those who violate agreements.[1] The model in this chapter tranforms a social dilemma into a coordination game by allowing for the possibility that those not adhering to agreements for behaving cooperatively can be punished. The cost of carrying out the enforcement activity is borne by players whose preference for reciprocity induces them to punish violators of agreements even when it is costly to do so. In the model, cooperative behavior will prevail if the prospect of punishment is sufficient to deter those seeking gains from cheating, if the punishment cost is sufficiently low, and if the cost of communicating to coordinate on the efficient equilibrium is less than the expected surplus from collective action. An examination of these conditions then shows which parameters affect the prospects for cooperation and how they interact.

We outline the most common modeling approach taken in the literature and provide some motivation for adopting the alternative taken in this chapter. The next section presents the basic symmetric model and the defining inequalities for the existence of an equilibrium with collective action. We go on to present the conditions for the existence of other equilibria and outline our method for selecting among multiple equilibria when they exist. After this, we discuss the conditions for cooperation prominent in the empirical literature in the light of the model. We go on to generalize the basic model to allow for various kinds of heterogeneity among players and increasing returns before reaching our conclusion.

Review and Critique

Economic analyses of common property typically proceed under the hypothesis that extractors make independent choices with a view to maximizing their material well-being. In a static single-period model, each individual takes the others' actions as given and neglects the implications of their decisions on the payoffs of other extractors. The negative externality in the commons results in a Nash equilibrium with suboptimal extraction levels from the perspective of the group as a whole (Gordon 1954; Dasgupta and Heal 1979).

To explain why cooperation is possible, time is incorporated into the model. The orthodox way to do this is to suppose that there is a future of infinitely many periods. In each period, the players play the game outlined in the previous paragraph. However, rather than maximizing current payoffs, they maximize a discounted sum of payoffs from the current and all future periods. The rationale is that the future matters less than the present because of impatience, the possibility that interest can be earned on resources converted into cash, or uncertainty that there will be a resource to exploit in the future. Now players take as given not just each others' actions in the current period but also the plans made by others for the infinite future. Each player's plan tells her what to do in each period in response to the entire history of play up to that point. The introduction of the future allows players to punish the other players for excessive exploitation by increasing their own future exploitation. The awareness that other players have such a contingent

---

[1]   The books by Ostrom (1990) and Baland and Platteau (1996) show that successful community management of forests, pastures, irrigation systems, and inland fisheries is widespread but far from universal and almost always accompanied by mechanisms for imposing sanctions on violators of agreements.

plan then deters players from harvesting more than their share of the efficient amount. An equilibrium with efficient extraction levels now exists, provided that players do not discount future payoffs too much. Moreover, such an equilibrium need not be based on "incredible" threats of punishment: threats that individuals would not find in their interest to carry out if called on to do so. In other words, there can exist an efficient equilibrium that satisfies the property of subgame perfection.

One difficulty with this modeling approach is that the subgame-perfect equilibrium described above is only one of infinitely many equilibria that exhibit different degrees of resource exploitation. For example, suppose everyone adopts the following strategy: they extract an equal share of the Nash level from the static game in every period no matter what anyone else does. It follows immediately that no single player can gain by deviating unilaterally from his plan at any stage. This is also a subgame-perfect equilibrium, one in which the tragedy occurs in full force. Among other possible equilibria, some are quite outlandish. For example, it is an equilibrium for players to extract an equal share of the Nash level from the static game in every third period, while exercising restraint in other periods unless someone deviates from this rule, in which case everyone switches to the noncooperative behavior in every period.

Since different equilibria will change in different ways in response to changes in underlying parameters, the multiplicity of equilibria poses a problem for the exercise of comparative statics. As a result, comparative statics are sometimes performed on the set of equilibria or by focusing on a chosen equilibrium, usually the best attainable for all players, as, for example, in Bendor and Mookherjee (1987). Unfortunately, the equilibrium set often contains equilibria whose outcomes are very different from each other, while focusing on the best attainable equilibrium requires further justification. We will provide such a justification in the model below, although it is not in the repeated-game framework.

Another problem with the repeated-game approach to explaining cooperation is that it is not robust to noise, for example, in the form of mistakes or experimentation by boundedly rational players. As long as such noise is not negligible, strategies of the kind described above will lead to frequent breakdowns and restarts of cooperation.[2] So far as we are aware, this kind of pattern has not been reported in the empirical literature on common-pool resources. In fact, if, owing to setup costs, it is costly to start cooperating following a noncooperative phase, as is likely in many situations, this explains why attempts to cooperate on the basis of such strategies are not observed.

Economists often interpret equilibria in which exploitation is restrained by repeated-game strategies as "social norms." This interpretation appears somewhat strained. Social norms do not usually take the form of each person implicitly telling the others that if any of them does not conform to the norm, then neither will he. However, in our view, the most serious limitation of the model as a tool for analyzing cooperation in actual commons is that it does away with the need for governance. In fact, as noted above, and as the vast empirical literature on the commons has shown, successful commons management often or even usually has some institutions to support it (Ostrom 1990). These involve rules or norms, with fines or other punishments specified, often explicitly, for violations.

---

[2]   See Bowles and Gintis (2005: ch. 4) for a detailed discussion of why repeated game models cannot explain cooperation in the presence of plausible noise and discount rates.

If the shadow of the future were all that were needed to sustain cooperation, such institutions have no reason to exist. Moreover, the repeated-game approach has not addressed the kinds of questions raised by the reviewers of the empirical literature (Baland and Platteau 1996; Agrawal 2003; Poteete and Ostrom 2004) probably because the model is simply too cumbersome to do so effectively.

One alternative to the standard model is to allow for departures from explicitly optimizing behavior in favor of an evolutionary approach. In Sethi and Somanathan (1996), we postulated that the proportion of players playing different, possibly sub-optimal, strategies would evolve over time under pressure of differential payoffs, with more highly rewarded strategies displacing less highly rewarded ones in the population. A critically important assumption was that social punishments of some sort were available: players, at some cost to themselves, could punish other players who did not exercise restraint in harvesting. Under these circumstances, it was shown that a norm of restraint and punishment can be stable under the evolutionary dynamics. Such norms can be destabilized, however, by parameter changes that make harvesting more lucrative, such as increases in the market price of the resource, or improvements in harvesting technology. While this model gives a better fit to the facts of cooperation in the commons and allows for some interesting comparative statics, it is not tractable when generalized to asymmetrically situated players and is silent as to how a norm of restraint might evolve in the first place.

In this chapter, we outline a new model that attempts to address these problems. It seeks to specify fully the circumstances under which cooperation will be observed and departs from orthodox economic modeling in two ways. First, it assumes that players do not look ahead into the future. This is a simplification made for tractability. Second, it relies on the presence of individuals who do not respond only to material payoffs. Economists have traditionally been reluctant to assume that people behave in ways that are not self-interested. The reason for this is that once such assumptions are allowed in the explanation of behavior, it becomes possible to explain virtually anything, but the explanations will often be vacuous since they end up assuming what they purport to explain. In the past few years, however, a new way of disciplining the behavioral assumptions made in modeling, a combination of evolutionary theory and experimental work, has become available.

The relevant departure from the characterization of people as being motivated solely by self-interest is the idea of reciprocity. Both gratitude and indignation are emotions that are felt in connection with reciprocity, the former being associated with what we may call "positive" reciprocity and the latter with "negative" reciprocity. Experiments with human subjects in the past few years have firmly established that many people display reciprocity that is not motivated by the prospect of future gains. Most relevant to us is the work that has been done with public goods games with punishment opportunities (surveyed in Fehr and Gächter 2000). In these games, subjects play a game in which members of a group each choose how much to contribute to a public good. The experimenter sets the payoffs so that contribution is privately costly but socially beneficial. After each round, players learn how much each of the other players contributed. Usually the others are identified only by numbers, so players never find out what another person actually played. Players then have the opportunity to punish others by lowering their payoffs at some cost to themselves. It is found that even in the last round of such games, when players know there will be no further interaction, some players punish others and do so at considerable cost to themselves. Moreover, the presence of punishment opportunities increases contributions substantially. There have been many experiments by several researchers with variations on this theme in the past few years and they all display these features.[3]

A natural question that one may ask is, why do players behave in this way? Why should preferences for reciprocity have evolved, when it may be costly to indulge such preferences? Sethi and Somanathan (2003) survey a number of mathematical models of how such evolution could have occurred. Essentially, these involve some combination of repetition, commitment, assortation, and parochialism. Here we mention only the basic idea behind the models that use parochialism. This is that people with preferences for reciprocity behave reciprocally with each other and selfishly when they meet people with selfish preferences. As long as people with selfish preferences cannot perfectly mimic those with reciprocal preferences, those with reciprocal preferences can get higher payoffs from cooperating with others like them, and this can more than outweigh their losses when they are fooled by selfish people pretending to be reciprocators.[4]

In fact, there is a good deal of evidence that people are heterogeneous. Some behave opportunistically, cooperating with others when it pays to do so and exploiting others when that is the most privately profitable strategy. Others are reciprocal, or sometimes even unconditionally altruistic. This heterogeneity is also predicted by many evolutionary models. In what follows, we take it as given that some people are "reciprocators," while others are opportunists, and explore the implications for the commons of the interaction between these two preference types.

The Basic Model

There are n players, $i = 1, 2, \ldots, n$, each of whom has access to a common-pool resource. We suppose that some mechanism to monitor resource extraction from the common pool, make rules if necessary, and to levy fines has been set up at some cost. This has, however, to be financed by ongoing contributions, which are observable and voluntary. A failure to contribute may result in punishment, but punishment is costly to impose, and the decision to punish is itself voluntary. Note that we model the punishment of non-contributions to the provision of the public good (in this case, governance) rather than the direct punishment of over-extraction, as in Ostrom et al. (1992; 1994).

---

[3] In addition to the considerable body of work surveyed by Fehr and Gächter (2000), subsequent papers include Bowles et al. (2001), Carpenter and Matthews (2002), Fehr and Gächter (2002), Sefton et al. (2002), Masclet et al. (2003), Page et al. (2005), and Bochet et al. (2006).

[4] The literature on the evolution of reciprocity is now vast; see, e.g., Panchanathan and Boyd (2003), Boyd et al. (2003), and the references cited in both works therein. Although we make no attempt here to endogenize the presence of reciprocators, our model could, in principle, be extended to do so. This is because collective action will be more likely to emerge in groups in which reciprocators have a significant presence, thus raising the average payoffs to reciprocators across a large population composed of many groups. We thank a referee for this observation.

For the time being, let us suppose that all players are identically situated in all respects (this assumption will be relaxed to allow for heterogeneity later). Player i can choose whether to contribute to the public good ($x_i = 1$) or not ($x_i = 0$). The aggregate contribution is denoted $X \equiv \sum_{j=1}^{n} x_j$. This aggregate contribution results in an aggregate benefit of αX, which is shared equally among all players (regardless of their contribution levels). Hence the net benefit to player i arising from any vector $(x_1, \ldots, x_n)$ of contributions is simply $\alpha X/n - x_i$. It is assumed that

$$\alpha/n < 1 < \alpha, \tag{7.1}$$

as is standard in public goods environments. Hence in the absence of punishment, it is individually rational for opportunists to choose not to contribute, although it is efficient for all to contribute.

After contributions have been observed by everyone, each player i can choose whether or not to participate in the collective punishment of all players j with $x_j = 0$. If i punishes, then $y_i = 1$, and if i does not punish, then $y_i = 0$. The total number of punishers, or enforcers, is therefore $e = \sum_{j=1}^{n} y_j$, and, provided that at least one person punishes, the total number of punished individuals is equal to the number of defectors $d = \sum_{j=1}^{n}(1 - x_j)$. Each player who is punished suffers a fixed penalty p regardless of the number of players participating in punishment. This penalty p may consist of partial or total exclusion from the public good or some other social sanction. Finally, the cost of punishing is proportional to the number of defectors (d), and inversely proportional to the number of enforcers (e), with the parameter γ affecting the size of this cost. The material payoff to player i is therefore given by

$$\pi_i(x, y) = \begin{cases} \alpha X/n - x_i & \text{if } e = 0, \\ \alpha X/n - x_i - (1 - x_i)p - \gamma y_i d/e & \text{if } e > 0, \end{cases} \tag{7.2}$$

where $x = (x_1, \ldots, x_n)$ and $y = (y_1, \ldots, y_n)$ are the vectors of contributions and punishments respectively. The first term is i's share of the output αX from the public good. The second term is i's contribution, the third the punishment p (non-zero only if i did not contribute), and the fourth the cost to i of punishing (non-zero only if $y_i = 1$).

We assume that there are two kinds of players, opportunists and reciprocators. There are $0 \leq k \leq n$ reciprocators. Opportunists maximize their material payoffs, and reciprocators maximize utility

$$u_i(x, y) = \pi_i(x, y) + bx_i y_i.$$

Reciprocators therefore experience a "benefit" b if they have contributed and punished noncontributors. We may interpret this as the psychological satisfaction they get from relieving their feelings of anger at noncontributors. Note that reciprocators get no psychological satisfaction from punishing if they are themselves noncontributors, or from having contributed if they do not punish. This game is played every period and it is assumed that players are myopic: they look only at the effect of their actions on current-period payoffs. While this is an extreme assumption, it makes the game simple and tractable, and is no more implausible than the standard hypothesis that players can work out all the future consequences of their actions and those of others. Moreover, in a steady state, the equilibria we identify under myopic beliefs remain equilibria under forward-looking beliefs.[5]

Let $O \subset \{1, \ldots, n\}$ denote the set of opportunists (material payoff maximizers) and $R \subset \{1, \ldots, n\}$ the set of reciprocators. Myopia ensures that opportunists will never punish, and so $y_i = 0$ for all $i \in O$. By contrast, if a reciprocator punishes, then he must have contributed. That is, for any $i \in R$, if $y_i = 1$ then $x_i = 1$.

A strategy or plan for player i is of the form $[x_i, y_i(x)]$ where $y_i(x)$ is an indicator function of the vector of contributions x. For opportunists, $y_i(x)$ is the zero function. We examine the pure-strategy subgame-perfect equilibria of this two-stage game in every period. There are two reasons for this choice. The first is that players playing in a context that is familiar are probably quite good at doing the necessary backward induction. Cosmides and Tooby (1992) present evidence that people are quite good at solving logical tasks in a social context that is familiar while being quite bad at solving logically equivalent problems presented in an unfamiliar context. Second, the best-response dynamics we use below converge rapidly to the subgame-perfect equilibria. We have the following three types of equilibria:

	$i \in O$	$i \in R$
A	Contribute	Contribute, punish if one person defects
B	Defect	Contribute and punish
C	Defect	Defect

In equilibria of type C, there is neither contribution nor punishment. In type B equilibria, opportunists do not contribute, while reciprocators contribute and punish. The equilibria of interest are those of type A, in which all contribute, and, if one person were to defect, all reciprocators punish the defector.[6] The conditions for such a subgameperfect equilibrium to exist are that $k \geq 2$,

$$p \geq 1 - \frac{\alpha}{n} \tag{7.3}$$

and

$$b \geq \gamma \frac{1}{(k-1)}. \tag{7.4}$$

---

[5]   The future can be introduced by allowing p and b to depend on players' discount rates. Punishment can be harsher if there is a future, since exclusion from the public good can be prolonged for several periods. The expected surplus to each player from collective action $\alpha - 1$ can be assumed to be larger for lower discount rates which in turn could raise b, the utility bonus from punishing a defector, since a player may be more emotionally involved with the collective effort when the surplus from it is expected to be high.

[6]   If multiple individuals defect simultaneously, subgame-perfection requires that reciprocators will participate in punishment if and only if this is consistent with utility maximization. We need only consider unilateral deviations, however, in establishing that a particular strategy profile is an equilibrium.

The first of these inequalities states that the cost of being punished (weakly) exceeds the gain from defection. This ensures that all opportunists will cooperate, provided that they expect to be punished for defecting. The second inequality ensures that, in the event that a reciprocator were to defect, it will be an equilibrium (in the resulting subgame) for each of the remaining reciprocators to punish him. Note that we must have $k \geq 2$, otherwise a deviating reciprocator could never be punished. Condition (7.4) implies that $b \geq \gamma/k$, which ensures that, in the event that an opportunist were to defect, it will be an equilibrium (in the resulting subgame) for each of the reciprocators to punish him. Conditions (7.3) and (7.4) together imply that a subgame perfect equilibrium with complete cooperation can be sustained. We go on to discuss their implications and generalizations. First, however, we describe the other possible equilibria and our method of obtaining a unique prediction when multiple equilibria exist. Readers interested only in the practical implications of the model may skim over these next two subsections.

Equilibria with less than complete cooperation

If $k = 0$, then the unique subgame-perfect equilibrium is of type C. If $1 \leq k \leq n - 1$, by contrast, multiple equilibria may exist. Subgame-perfect equilibria of type C with no contributions and no punishments will exist if no reciprocator can gain by unilaterally deviating from a strategy of not contributing to one of contributing and punishing all noncontributors. The payoff at the equilibrium is 0, while the payoff from a deviation of this type is $\alpha/n - 1 + b - \gamma(n - 1)$. Hence an equilibrium of type C will exist if

$$1 - \frac{\alpha}{n} \geq b - \gamma(n - 1). \tag{7.5}$$

Next consider subgame-perfect equilibria of type B, in which opportunists do not contribute and reciprocators contribute and punish opportunists. A necessary condition for such equilibria to exist is that no opportunist can gain by unilaterally switching to cooperation (and thus escaping punishment). Unilaterally switching to cooperation raises by one the total number of cooperators and, hence, causes the provision of the public good to rise by an amount α, which raises each individual's payoff by α/n. In addition, the deviating individual escapes the punishment cost p, and incurs the cost of contribution, which is one. In order for such a deviation to be unprofitable, we must therefore have:

$$p \leq 1 - \frac{\alpha}{n}. \tag{7.6}$$

This ensures that the threat of punishment does not deter opportunists from defecting. In addition, we require that reciprocators have an incentive to cooperate and punish. A sufficient condition for this is the following, which guarantees that a reciprocator would not gain from switching to defection (meaning neither contributing nor punishing non-contributors) even if doing so did not result in punishment from remaining reciprocators:

$$b - \gamma\frac{(n - k)}{k} \geq 1 - \frac{\alpha}{n}. \tag{7.7}$$

This condition is not, however, necessary. Equilibria of type B can also arise if reciprocators believe that switching to defection will result in punishment, and if this belief is warranted given the strategies of other reciprocators. This requires that the following two conditions hold:

$$b \geq \gamma\left(\frac{n - k + 1}{k - 1}\right), \text{ and } b - \gamma\left(\frac{n - k}{k}\right) \geq 1 - \frac{\alpha}{n} - p \tag{7.8}$$

The first inequality ensures that all reciprocators who do not defect have an incentive to punish the one reciprocator who does, provided that they all believe that every non-defecting reciprocator will participate in punishment. The second ensures that a reciprocator will not defect under the belief that he will be punished for doing so. Conditions (7.1) and (7.7) together imply that

$$b \geq \gamma\left(\frac{n - k}{k}\right),$$

which ensures that a reciprocator will not free ride on punishment (while continuing to contribute). This is also implied by the first inequality in (7.8). Hence (7.6), together with either (7.7) or (7.8), is necessary and sufficient for a subgame-perfect equilibrium of type B to exist.[7]

We have so far neglected the case $k = n$. Here equilibria of types A and B are identical, and will exist if and only if (7.3) and (7.4) hold. Except for the non-generic case of $p = 1 - \alpha/n$, equilibria of types A and B cannot coexist if $k < n$. For $k < n$, when $p > 1 - \alpha/n$ complete compliance with the norm of contribution is possible, but when $p < 1 - \alpha/n$ only partial compliance is possible.

These inequalities completely describe when each of the three types of equilibria will exist. They exhaust all generic possibilities for subgame-perfect equilibria, since equilibria must be intragroup symmetric. That is to say, in any equilibrium, since the incentives facing a reciprocator are the same as those facing any other reciprocator, they must take the same action at any stage of the game. This is, of course, true for opportunists as well.

Prediction

Since the model generally permits multiple equilibria, this raises the question of which equilibrium we might expect to prevail in practice. We need to identify conditions under which equilibria of type A will be chosen when these coexist with those of type C, and to perform a similar analysis for the case when B and C coexist. We deal with the coexistence of A and C first.

It may be that (7.4) holds so that all contributing reciprocators will punish a lone defector, but

$$b < \gamma(n - 1), \tag{7.9}$$

[7]   When $k = 1$, (7.7) is inconsistent with (7.5) for generic parameter values so equilibria of types B and C cannot coexist.

so that a reciprocator will not punish if everyone else defects. The latter condition implies (7.5) so an equilibrium of type *C* exists in this case. If, in addition, punishment is strong enough to deter would-be defectors, that is if (7.3) holds, then equilibria of type *A* will exist as well. Notice that the equilibrium payoff to *all* players under *A* is α, which exceeds 1, the payoff from *C*. This raises the possibility that communication among players at the start of each period can allow them to coordinate on the preferred equilibrium.

Suppose the cost to any player of communicating with the other players is c and

$$c < \alpha - 1. \tag{7.10}$$

Therefore, players will soon realize that they are better off agreeing to play *A* as long as (7.10) holds. This alone does not solve the problem of equilibrium selection, since it is also an equilibrium for all commitments to be ignored and for all players to defect. However, such "babbling equilibria" are not observed in everyday experience of coordination problems with pre-play discussion. Experiments on coordination games with two or more players confirm that costless pre-play communication enables players to coordinate on the Pareto-dominant equilibrium (Cooper et al. 1992; Burton et al. 2005; Blume and Ortmann 2007; Charness 2000) even when failure to coordinate involves a considerable payoff loss for those attempting to coordinate and even though the communication permitted in the experiments is extremely sparse. Babbling equilibria seem especially unlikely if communication is at all costly, since in this case only players intending to honor their commitments will bother to make them.[8] For these reasons, we assume that players will coordinate on the *A*-equilibrium when it exists.[9]

We can use (7.7) and similar reasoning to show that if the parameters are such that both *C* and *B*-type equilibria exist, and if the cost of reciprocators communicating with each other is positive but sufficiently small, then we may expect to see only *B*-equilibria in the long run.

It is worth remarking that this setup allows for noise in the sense that if players make mistakes or experiment with new actions now and then, this will not generally result in a change from *A* to *C* equilibria, unless there happen to be simultaneous mistakes by several players. This is a consequence of the static nature of the game, together with subgame perfection. Moreover, if there is such a collapse of cooperation, cooperation may be recovered if the communication cost is sufficiently low. Thus, we would expect cooperation, if it comes into being, to be persistent, although perhaps subject to occasional random crashes.

---

[8]   This method of equilibrium selection amounts to what has been called "forward induction". See Osborne and Rubinstein (1994: 110–15) for a discussion and references to the originators of the concept. This too has been confirmed experimentally by Van Huyck et al. (1993).

[9]   A similar solution to the equilibrium selection problem could be used in a repeated-game model with self-interested players in which each period has a punishment stage following the contribution stage. This could be robust to noise. However, subgame-perfection of efficient equilibria would require strategies that involved an infinite regress of punishments: players who did not punish would need to be punished, and so on. There are also evolutionary approaches to equilibrium selection in repeated games; see especially Fudenberg and Maskin (1990) and Binmore and Samuelson (1992).

We have assumed throughout that the number of reciprocators k and the strength of reciprocity as measured by b are known. However, even if they are not, provided the players' expected values of these parameters (as well as the true values) are sufficiently high, the arguments made above remain valid.

Conditions for Cooperation

The conditions for cooperation to take place in this setup (in addition to $k \geq 2$) are (7.3) and (7.4) together with (7.10). The first of these (7.3), says that punishment must be a sufficient deterrent against non-contribution, the second (7.4) that punishment must be cheap enough to inflict that the psychological benefit of doing so is enough to induce reciprocators to carry it out, and the third says that the surplus to each player from collective action should exceed the per-player cost of communication between players that enables them to coordinate collective action. These are all intuitive. Let us compare them with the conditions for cooperation that have emerged from the commons literature.

Agrawal (2003: 253, table 2) provides a comprehensive list of enabling conditions for successful collective action from three influential books, Wade (1988), Ostrom (1990), and Baland and Platteau (1996) as well as other conditions prominent in the literature. He classifies them as pertaining to resource characteristics, group characteristics, the relation between group and resource characteristics, institutional arrangements, or the external environment. Those pertaining to resource characteristics are small size (of the resource), well-defined boundaries, low mobility, storage possibilities, and predictability. In our model, these factors would matter because they affect the potential surplus $\alpha - 1$ known to be available from collective action.

Group characteristics favoring collective action listed by Agrawal are: (1) small size, (2) clearly defined boundaries, (3) shared norms, (4) past successful experiences – social capital, (5) appropriate leadership – young, familiar with changing external environments, connected to local traditional elite, (6) interdependence among group members, (7) heterogeneity of endowments, homogeneity of identities and interests, and (8) low levels of poverty. Of these, we note that shared norms and past successful experiences emerge as a *consequence* of successful collective action, not a prerequisite. However, if there has been successful collective action in one domain, then the cost of communicating to reach agreement over collective action in another domain may be lowered due to the presence of norms that are transferable from one sphere to another. Clearly defined boundaries for the group are also endogenous: collective action will wholly succeed only if non-contributors can be punished, and the set of contributors defines the group.

In our framework, small group size can influence collective action in several ways. It results in a higher private return to collective action, thus reducing the size of the punishment needed to support it (see [7.3]). It could also be the case that punishment itself is facilitated by small group size since social sanctions will be an effective deterrent only in small groups which are not anonymous. The cost of communication is also likely to be lower for small groups. On the other hand, the cost of punishing someone who violated an agreement could be higher in very small groups (because incurring the enmity of someone in a small community may be very costly) which would make collective action more difficult to sustain (see [7.4]). Increasing returns (discussed below together with heterogeneity and poverty) could mean that small groups may not generate enough surplus to make collective action worthwhile.[10]

Leaders may be those with low costs of communication. Otherwise our model suggests that leadership is not important. Interdependence among group members may increase the effectiveness of social sanctions, but by the same token, also make punishment more costly due to more effective retaliation. Poverty could constrain contributions and thus render collective action impossible. The inequality in the power to punish that may accompany poverty has effects that are discussed below.

Under the heading "Relation between group and resource characteristics" Agrawal lists the following conditions: (1) overlap between user-group residential location and resource location, (2) high levels of dependence by group members on resource system, (3) fairness in allocation of benefits from common resources, (4) low levels of user demand, (5) gradual change in levels of demand. The first two are simply indicators of potential surplus α. The third is a possible outcome of collective action, not a contributor to its success. The fourth and fifth are irrelevant in our model unless they affect α.

Under the heading "Institutional arrangements," Agrawal mentions simple rules, locally devised access and management rules, ease in enforcement of rules, graduated sanctions, availability of low-cost adjudication, and accountability of monitors and other officials to users. Our model indicates that these are all outcomes of collective actions, not prerequisites, with the possible exception of external adjudication which may be exogenous. Finally, under "External environment" Agrawal mentions a low-cost exclusion technology, central governments that do not undermine local authority, supportive external sanctioning institutions, appropriate levels of external aid to compensate local users for conservation activities, and nested levels of appropriation, provision, enforcement, and governance. It is clear that the last is endogenous while supportive external sanctioning institutions are likely to enlarge the expected value of p.

To summarize: our review of the factors listed in the literature as important for determining the success of collective action indicates that many of them are, in fact, endogenous; they are consequences, not determinants, of collective action. In fact, our model suggests that the success of collective action in using common property effectively hinges on whether it is feasible to develop a regulatory mechanism for the commons that ensures a sufficiently large surplus relative to unregulated extraction, whether the cost of communication to establish and maintain this institution is sufficiently low, and whether it is feasible to punish non-contributors enough to deter them at sufficiently low cost. Far from there being too many variables (Agrawal 2003), there are, in fact, relatively few. We have, of course, to qualify this by saying that, as seen above, many factors may affect the parameters α, c, p, γ, and b. But it is much easier to study them if it is understood that their influence is through a small set of parameters and if it is clear how they may be expected to matter.

Finally, it is interesting to note that a cost of communication smaller than the expected surplus (equation 7.10) is not included in Agrawal's list compiled from field studies of

---

[10]   Although we have not explicitly modeled errors (in either the actions taken by individuals or in the perceptions of actions taken by others), the greater possibility of multiple simultaneous errors in larger groups can also adversely affect the possibility of sustained cooperation.

the commons. The possibility of punishment in our model results in a coordination game. The experimental literature clearly shows that communication is critical to whether or not coordination is achieved.[11] We suspect that communication has not received attention despite the experimental literature because it has no role to play in the repeated-game models that are, almost exclusively, the only formal theories of cooperation in social dilemmas.[12]

We point to some more underlying variables that can be expected to influence some of the model parameters. With regard to α, not only must the return to cooperation be high, but it must be *known* to be high by all concerned, or by at least some who are in a position to credibly communicate this information to the others at low enough cost. Reciprocators' utility bonus from punishment b will sufficiently positive only if their emotions are engaged which in turn is likely if the public good provides them with sufficient surplus.

The punishment p has to be effective. Effective punishment will vary from case to case, but the most likely punishment is exclusion from the commons. Whether it is techno-logically and socially feasible may be critical. It will be weak if individuals expect to leave the area soon, so short time horizons and a high probability of migration are not conducive to cooperation. A dense network of social interaction may also favor punish-ment as exclusion can then be used in the domain in which it is cheapest.

From the point of view of empirical testing, it is important to note that the conditions for cooperation are given by inequalities. It follows that cooperation varies *discontinu-ously* with the parameters. Changes in the parameters that are not large enough to reverse any of the inequalities will have no effect. This general point applies to the discussion in the next section as well.

Heterogeneity and Other Generalizations

Consider as a benchmark the homogeneous player case in which (7.3) and (7.4) hold so that A prevails. Now suppose that instead of punishment resulting in a uniform loss p, the effects of punishment vary across players. The material payoffs (7.2) may now be written

$$\pi_i(x, y) = \begin{cases} s_i\alpha(X) - x_i & \text{if } e = 0 \\ s_i\alpha(X) - x_i - (1 - x_i)p_i - \gamma y_i d/e. & \text{if } e > 0 \end{cases} \tag{7.11}$$

where p_i is the cost to player i of being punished, and we are now allowing for a (possibly) nonlinear production function $\alpha(X)$ which describes the output obtained

[11] In fact, even in common-pool resource extraction games in which there is a unique and inefficient equilib-rium involving over-extraction, communication has been found to be effective in raising rents close to the maximum in experimental situations, even in the absence of punishment (Ostrom et al. 1994) and even with heterogeneous extractors (Hackett et al. 1994). The almost ubiquitous presence of punishment mechanisms in the field, however, suggests that communication without punishment would not be sufficient to stabilize co-operation in settings in which interaction takes place for much longer periods than in the laboratory.
[12] Explicit punishments are also unnecessary in repeated-game models of cooperation in social dilemmas but, unlike the ease of communication, they cannot be easily overlooked in the field.

as a function of total contributions. As before, we initially fix the share s_i accruing to player i at $1/n$.

Suppose for simplicity that now there are just two possible values of p, namely p_l and p_h and that (7.3) holds for p_h but not for $p_l < p_h$. Suppose $p_i = p_l$ for n_l players and k_l reciprocators and $p_i = p_h$ for the remaining $n - n_l$ players and $k - k_l$ reciprocators. Those players i with $p_i = p_l$ are little affected by punishment and will find it optimal to defect since

$$p_l < 1 - \frac{\alpha(X)}{n}, \tag{7.12}$$

In the period following this, there may be too few reciprocators who have contributed to punish the players with $p_i = p_h$ at reasonable cost, that is,

$$b < \gamma\left(\frac{1}{k - k_l - 1}\right).$$

Furthermore, the free-riding of some players will lower the returns to the others, possibly making it not worthwhile for them to contribute even if they were to be punished, that is,

$$p_h < 1 - \frac{\alpha(X_h)}{n},$$

where $X_h = \sum_{j=1}^{n-nl} x_j$ denotes aggregate contributions by those players i with $p_i = p_h$. Notice that this inequality is more likely to hold if the production function $\alpha(\cdot)$ displays increasing returns. Thus, heterogeneity in susceptibility to punishment especially in combination with increasing returns, may lead to collective action becoming infeasible.

The model so far fixed both the shares of the public good accruing to each player, and the contributions. However, if side payments are possible or, equivalently, contributions can be varied continuously so that the distribution of the surplus $\alpha(X) - X$ from the public good may be changed (within limits) without affecting the total surplus, then it becomes easier to achieve cooperation. This would be the case, for example, if the production function $\alpha(\cdot)$ were such that there exists a surplus-maximizing total contribution X^*, players are not wealth-constrained, and punishment is a sufficient deterrent on average. A precise statement of this fact is in the appendix.

In this case, the players may, after discussion and bargaining, agree on a vector of contributions leading to a total contribution of X^* and that ensures that the necessary inequalities for successful collective action hold. Heterogeneity in susceptibility to punishment, can be taken into account in the division of the surplus by giving players with less susceptibility to punishment larger shares of the surplus, while still leaving all players with a share of the surplus large enough to motivate them to incur the cost of enforcement when necessary. This may be exactly what is happening when elites take the initiative to organize collective action as, for example, in Wade (1988). Heterogeneity, at least within limits, is not as inimical to collective action as one might think. Poteete and Ostrom's (2004) survey of collective action in forest management provides some empirical support for this view.

Irrigation systems and fisheries have heterogeneous returns to collective action because of hetergeneity of location and landholding in the former case and of skills and capital equipment in the latter. As outlined above and in the appendix, contributions can be tailored to take such heterogeneity into account. Those with low returns from collective action can be asked for correspondingly lower contributions. This suggests that it may not be heterogeneity of returns but, rather, other factors that explain why collective action so often seems absent in these contexts.[13] When irrigators are from different villages and fishermen from different ports, high communication costs and inability to punish may explain the failure of collective action.

We have discussed heterogeneity power and the returns to collective action, but the literature on heterogeneity has mostly focused on other dimensions, with wealth being the most important. It will, however, be immediately obvious to the reader that the model suggests that an important reason why wealth and poverty might matter is because they result in heterogeneity of power. Wealthy people, particularly in small communities, are typically less vulnerable to social sanctions than poor people, and more able to impose penalties on others. Wealth has probably received more attention than power in the literature simply because it is easier to measure. Of course, as mentioned earlier, it also matters because it can constrain contributions. This is the aspect of wealth that has received theoretical attention (Baland and Platteau 1997; 1998).

Heterogeneity of power may actually favor collective action in some circumstances. To see this, let us allow the punishments p_i to depend on the entire vector y_{-i} (so that the effect of punishment on i depends on the number and identity of the particular individuals who choose to punish i). As a benchmark, suppose, first, that the parameters are such that punishment is not an effective deterrent even when all individuals punish. That is, for all players i

$$p_i(1, \ldots, 1) < 1 - \frac{\alpha}{n}.$$

Now suppose, instead, that there exists a group of powerful persons I, who can effectively punish the others J (but not each other), if at least one of the others take part in enforcement, say by monitoring defection. We need both the powerful and the weak for enforcement. Otherwise, if the weak were not needed, the powerful would be able to coerce the weak and leave them worse off. The powerful need to be given shares large enough that the *private* returns to contribution for them are high enough to induce them to participate, even though they cannot be punished. Suppose that for all $j \in J$,

$$p_i(y_{-j}) > 1 - s_j\alpha$$

if at least one component y_i of y_{-j} is 1 for some $i \in I$, and at least one component y_l of y_{-j} is 1 for some $l \in J$. Suppose also that the cost of punishment depends on the identity

[13]   As pointed out by Baland and Platteau (1998) there may be asymmetric information about the returns to collective action and this could hinder transfers to compensate low returns. This problem should not be exaggerated, however. In small communities much of the relevant information is easily found out. Even when it is not, good design could reduce the extent of the problem. For example, if equal saleable input quotas are allocated to fishers to increase the catch to effort ratio in a fishery, then low-skill fishermen who may have a lower return from the quota could raise their return by selling to higher-skill fishermen.

of the punishers so that if at least one member from each group punishes, then the punishment cost is less than b. Finally, suppose for all $i \in I$,

$$s_i \alpha > 1.$$

Now all the inequalities necessary for an A-equilibrium are in place provided the communication cost $c < 1 - \alpha$. For this to be a Pareto improvement over a situation with no contributions it is necessary that $s_j \alpha n > 1$. Clearly there are many configurations of the parameters such that these inequalities hold. However, if the weak did not have something to offer, for example, by way of help in monitoring, then it is unlikely that the powerful would allocate a share to them that would make them better off than they would have been under the unregulated outcome.

It is often observed that elites take the lead in the management of common property resources and appropriate the lion's share of the benefits. As Baland and Platteau (1998) point out, this is not always a Pareto-improvement over an unregulated outcome because the poor may be worse off. Whether or not this actually occurs has to be assessed on a case-by-case basis.

Conclusion

We hope that the model presented here will prove useful as a framework for empirical research into the issue of when collective action in the commons will be successful. It can be adapted to particular situations by suitable modeling of the production function, punishment technology, and so forth.

What policy implications can we draw from this theory? If outside intervention to help spur collective action in the commons is to be successful, it has to ensure that enforcement of contributions (or other non-defection) is both effective and cheap. Lowering the cost of communication about such issues may be the role that outside agencies can play. They may do so by helping participants see that collective action has been successful in similar circumstances elsewhere, or simply by initiating and facilitating the process of discussion on the issue. They may need to provide information about the benefits of collective action in cases where this is not clear to the participants. Of course, this will only work if the underlying conditions are favorable. This is less likely when players are transient so that exclusion has little force, or when exclusion is not possible for some reason, or when there is a set of powerful players who cannot be punished and whose private returns cannot be made high enough to make it attractive for them to participate. Legal reforms that allow for community enforcement or allow the state to lend force to community enforcement may be called for in some cases. Care needs to be taken, of course, to see that this does not result in an expropriation of the poor. Insisting that the process of legal change require the consultation and consent of all groups would make this less likely.

We have not addressed some potentially important issues. What factors make it likely that bargaining over the division of the surplus will end in agreement? How does history affect the proportion of reciprocators, or does it not? We leave these interesting but challenging questions to future research.

Appendix

In this appendix we show that heterogeneity in the returns to collective action (as captured by the shares s_i of the surplus from the public good) and in susceptibility to punishment does not change the prediction of an efficient outcome if players' communication costs are sufficiently low, transfers unconstrained by wealth are possible, and punishments are effective on average. Note that using the general payoff function (7.11) and allowing for heterogeneous susceptibility to punishment, the conditions (7.3) and (7.10) for an efficient A-equilibrium to prevail are replaced by

$$s_i \Delta\alpha + t_i \geq \frac{X^*}{n} - p_i, \quad \text{for all } i = 1, \ldots, n, \tag{7.A1}$$

$$\sum_{i=1}^{n} t_i = 0, \tag{7.A2}$$

and

$$c_i < s_i \alpha(X^*) - \frac{X^*}{n} + t_i \quad \text{for all } i = 1, \ldots, n, \tag{7.A3}$$

where t_i is a transfer received by player i out of the total contributions, $\Delta\alpha = \alpha(X^*) - \alpha(X^* - X^*/n)$ is the increase in surplus that is generated when all players rather than all but one player contribute, and c_i is player i's cost of communicating with the other players. Equation (7.A1) says that the (possibly negative) increase in a player's payoff when he contributes rather than defects plus the (possibly negative) transfer he receives conditional on contributing should be at least as much as his contribution less the damage from being punished. The condition (7.4) that requires that punishing not be too costly is unchanged. If, on average, punishment is a sufficient deterrent, meaning that

$$\bar{p} \geq \frac{X^*}{n} - \frac{1}{n}\Delta\alpha, \tag{7.A4}$$

where $\bar{p}$ denotes the average of p_i, then it is straightforward to check that if we set

$$t_i = \left(\frac{1}{n} - s_i\right)\Delta\alpha + \bar{p} - p_i,$$

then (7.A1) and (7.A2) are satisfied. Of course, for the efficient outcome to prevail we also require (7.A3) to hold. Note that transfers tend to make up for inequality in returns.

References

Agrawal, Arun (2003). Sustainable Governance of Common-pool Resources: Context, Methods, and Politics. *Annual Review of Anthropology*, 32: 243–62.

Baland, Jean-Marie and Jean-Philippe Platteau (1996). *Halting Degradation of Natural Resources: Is There a Role for Rural Communities?* Oxford University Press and FAO, Oxford.

Baland, Jean-Marie and Jean-Philippe Platteau (1997). Wealth Inequality and Efficiency in the Commons. Part I: The Unregulated Case. *Oxford Economic Papers*, 49(4): 451–82.

Baland, Jean-Marie and Jean-Philippe Platteau (1998). Wealth Inequality and Efficiency in the Commons. Part II: The Regulated Case. *Oxford Economic Papers*, 50(1): 1–22.

Bendor, Jonathan and Dilip Mookherjee (1987). Institutional Structure and the Logic of Ongoing Collective Action. *American Political Science Review*, 81: 129–54.

Binmore, K. G. and L. Samuelson (1992). Evolutionary Stability in Repeated Games Played by Finite Automata. *Journal of Economic Theory*, 57: 278–305.

Blume, Andreas and Andreas Ortmann (2007). The Effects of Costless Pre-play Communication: Experimental Evidence from Games with Pareto-ranked Equilibria. *Journal of Economic Theory*, 132: 274–90.

Bochet, Oliver, Talbot Page, and Louis Putterman (2006). Communication and Punishment in Voluntary Contribution Experiments. *Journal of Economic Behavior and Organization*, 60: 11–26.

Bowles, Samuel and Herbert Gintis (2005). A Cooperative Species: Human Reciprocity and its Evolution. Book manuscript, Santa Fe Insitute, Santa Fe, NM.

Bowles, Samuel, Jeffrey Carpenter, and Herbert Gintis (2001). Mutual Monitoring in Teams: Theory and Evidence on the Importance of Residual Claimancy and Reciprocity. Mimeo, Middlebury College, Dept of Economics.

Boyd, Robert, Herbert Gintis, Samuel Bowles, and Peter Richerson (2003). The Evolution of Altruistic Punishment. *Proceedings of the National Academy of Science*, 20: 123–43.

Burton, Anthony, Graham Loomes, and Martin Sefton (2005). Communication and Efficiency in Coordination Game Experiments. In John Morgan (ed.), *Experimental and Behavioral Economics*. Elsevier, Amsterdam, pp. 63–85.

Carpenter, Jeffrey and Peter Matthews (2002). Social Reciprocity. Working Paper 29, Middlebury College, Dept of Economics.

Charness, Gary (2000). Self-serving Cheap Talk: A Test of Aumann's Conjecture. *Games and Economic Behavior*, 33: 177–94.

Cooper, Russell, Douglas V. DeJong, Robert Forsythe, and Thomas W. Ross (1992). Communication in Coordination Games. *Quarterly Journal of Economics*, 53: 739–71.

Cosmides, Leda and John Tooby (1992). Cognitive Adaptations for Social Exchange. In John H. Barkow, Leda Cosmides, and John Tooby (eds), *The Adapted Mind*. Oxford University Press, New York, pp. 163–228.

Dasgupta, Partha and Geoffrey M. Heal (1979). *Economic Theory and Exhaustible Resources*. Cambridge University Press, Cambridge.

Falk, Armin, Ernst Fehr, and Urs Fischbacher (2002). Appropriating the Commons: A Theoretical Explanation. In Elinor Ostrom, Thomas Dietz, Nives Dolsak, Paul C. Stern, Susan Stonich, and Elke U. Weber (eds), *The Drama of the Commons*. National Academy Press, Washington, DC, pp. 157–91.

Fehr, Ernst and Simon Gächter (2000). The Economics of Reciprocity. *Journal of Economic Perspectives*, 14: 151–69.

Fehr, Ernst and Simon Gächter (2002). Altruistic Punishment in Humans. *Nature*, 415: 137–40.

Fudenberg, Drew and Eric S. Maskin (1990). Evolution and Cooperation in Noisy Repeated Games. *American Economic Review: Papers and Proceedings*, 80: 274–9.

Gordon, H. Scott (1954). The Economic Theory of a Common Property Resource: The Fishery. *Journal of Political Economy*, 62: 124–42.

Hackett, Steven, Edella Schlager, and James Walker (1994). The Role of Communication in Resolving Commmons Dilemmas: Experimental Evidence with Heterogeneous Appropriators. *Journal of Environmental Economics and Management*, 27: 99–126.

Masclet, David, Charles Noussair, Steven Tucker, and Marie-Claire Villeval (2003). Monetary and Nonmonetary Punishment in a Voluntary Contributions Mechanism. *American Economic Review*, 93(1): 366–80.

Osborne, Martin J. and Ariel Rubinstein (1994). *A Course in Game Theory*, MIT Press, Cambridge.

Ostrom, Elinor (1990). *Governing the Commons: The Evolution of Institutions for Collective Action*, Cambridge University Press, Cambridge.

Ostrom, Elinor, Roy Gardner, and James Walker (1994). *Rules, Games, and Common Pool Resources*, Ann Arbor, University of Michigan Press.

Ostrom, Elinor, James Walker, and Roy Gardner (1992). Covenants with and without a Sword: Self-Governance is Possible. *American Political Science Review*, 86: 404–17.

Page, Talbot, Louis Putterman, and Bulent Unel (2005). Voluntary Association in Public Goods Experiments: Reciprocity, Mimicry, and Efficiency. *Economic Journal*, 115: 1032–53.

Panchanathan, K. and Robert Boyd (2003). A Tale of Two Defectors: The Importance of Standing for Evolution of Indirect Reciprocity. *Journal of Theoretical Biology*, 224: 115–26.

Poteete, Amy R. and Elinor Ostrom (2004). Heterogeneity, Group Size and Collective Action: The Role of Institutions in Forest Management. *Development and Change*, 35(3): 435–61.

Sefton, Martin, Robert Shupp, and James Walker (2002). The Effects of Rewards and Sanctions in Provision of Public Goods. Working Paper, University of Nottingham.

Sethi, Rajiv and E. Somanathan (1996). The Evolution of Social Norms in Common Property Resource Use. *American Economic Review*, 86: 766–88.

Sethi, Rajiv and E. Somanathan (2003). Understanding Reciprocity. *Journal of Economic Behavior and Organization*, 50: 1–27.

Van Huyck, John B., Raymond C. Battalio, and Richard O. Beil (1993). Asset Markets as an Equilibrium Selection Mechanism: Coordination Failure, Game Form Auctions, and Forward Induction. *Games and Economic Behavior*, 5: 485–504.

Wade, Robert (1988). *Village Republics: Economic Conditions for Collective Action in South India*, Cambridge University Press, Cambridge.

8: Revisiting Demsetz

Contextualizing Community–Private Ownership in Western India

Pranab Mukhopadhyay

Introduction

A discussion on commons involves a property rights framework and therefore in a conversation between economists and anthropologists, one is compelled to encounter Demsetz who has drawn as much on the work of anthropologists as he has of economists to set up his theory of property rights.[1] Demsetz (1967) sets out the economic rationale for the existence of common property and under what circumstances private property rights would replace them (state of technology, market-access and resource value). We will briefly re-visit his work before taking up questions in our own geographical proximity – in Goa, India. In the following section we examine the literature on property rights, redistribution and sustainability. We then describe the dynamics of colonial state extraction, its impact on rural governance structures followed by changes that occurred in the post colonial period before discussing possible explanations for the change in property rights regime in Goa. We conclude with a discussion on the policy implications in the context received theories of common vs. private property and sustainability.

Property rights: common and private

Demsetz (1967) draws on the anthropological studies of private property evolution among American Indians in the sixteenth and seventeenth centuries. He finds a direct link between the growth of commercial trade in fur and the establishment of private land rights among Native Americans who had traditionally managed hunting grounds as common

---

[1] In this schema he precedes a line of distinguished economists who have used anthropological insights to illustrate outcomes in economic theory (see Ray: ch. 4, this volume).

property. Commercial trade raised the value of furs and led to increased hunting. Free hunting, which was previously for self-consumption, now catered to an external market, leading to hunting beyond individual needs of the tribe. This necessitated the creation of private hunting grounds by an arrangement akin to a seasonal allotment system.

Private ownership, however, developed only in those geographical areas where it was economically viable to establish private hunting grounds. Not all areas had extensive supply of fur producing animals (which had a high market price). Some had grazing species requiring large grazing lands for survival. In these cases, the cost of private ownership of land outweighed the benefits and they displayed less developed forms of private land ownership (Demsetz 1967: 353).

The argument suggests that common property will not be able to internalize all the externalities which establishment of private property can. Communal property would not be able to follow a "pay-to-use-the-property" system just as policing expenses may be too high to follow a "pay-him-not-to-use-the-property" system (Demsetz 1967: 355). He concludes that the existence of a certain form of property rights is linked to: (1) existent technology, and (2) market access and values – which for reasons of convenience we will call the Demsetz conditions.[2]

These conditions, however, leave open spaces: Can commons exist even with changes in technology, market access or market value of products? Can communities preserve common property by "pay-to-use-the-property" system or find frugal ways to follow a "pay-him-not-to-use-the-property" system. Can non-market, non-technological changes cause a conversion of common property to private property?[3] And when commons are converted to private property under non-Demstez conditions does it lead to better ecological outcomes?

At this point we propose to link up the debate of common v. private property with another debate in economics which also has ecological traces – heterogeneity and sustainability. Does asset re-distribution (specifically land or tenancy reforms) lead to an increase in efficiency and cooperation (sustainability) among agents?

Land reforms: efficiency, equity, and sustainability

Asset redistribution, especially land reforms, evokes immense passion in the social science discourse as it does in the arena of electoral politics. The traditional studies in asset distribution are largely linked to land issues because in agrarian societies land has an extra-economic value (Bhaduri 1973).

One view which has received support opines that small farms and productivity are inversely related (monotonically). This empirical observation therefore creates the justification for land (tenancy) reforms on the grounds of both efficiency and equity gains (Banerjee 1999; Bardhan 1973). Farm Management Studies in India as well as other countries have found

---

[2]   See also Deininger and Feder (1998) for a similar argument.
[3]   The inherent instability of common properties has been suggested by Hardin (1968) and the limits of collective action (that would be required to maintain common properties) has been posed by Olson (1965). However, Ostrom (2000) points out that despite such strong arguments suggesting failure of commons and collective action, the world around us has numerous instances to indicate the contrary.

the inverse relationship to be empirically valid (Berry and Cline 1979; Besley and Burgess 2000).[4]

The argument revolves around empowerment of asset-less families who farm the land with family labor as opposed to the landed (or absentee landlords) who till the land with the assistance of farm labor (who could be either wage labor or share-croppers). Agency theory suggests that transaction costs (incentive, monitoring and supervision) in non-family based farms could be fairly high, especially in the case of absentee owners and therefore such production systems would have low levels of efficiency (Deininger and Binswanger 1999; Ray 1998).

In a non-family based system, where tenants or sharecroppers are involved, there is constant bargaining between the tenant and landowner over share of produce and distribution of risk. Technology and the mechanism of surplus extraction by the state is a crucial determinant in the balance of power between cultivators, tenants, land owners and the state apparatus.[5]

As the burden of risk is shifted on to the tenant/cultivator, the economy would move to a low-level equilibrium trap. The sharecroppers would put in less effort and the expected output would be lower. In such circumstances, a move from tenant-based farming to owner-based farming is expected to improve yields (and productivity) justifying land reforms (Banerjee, Gertler, and Ghatak 2002). This also ties in well with the property rights school argument that ownership provides adequate incentive for the owner to optimize production and reduce "easy-riding" (Coase 1960).

Equity, privatization, and sustainability

Much of this literature, however, does not examine the impact of redistribution on ecological sustainability and the problem of institutional transition.[6] When the mode of asset re-distribution is by administrative fiat or by populist political measures, the resultant situation could induce incentive problems. While on normative grounds asset re-distribution may be desired, what is of concern is the ecological consequences especially in fragile zones when common property is privatized and endogenous institutions are replaced by new inorganic ones in which the incentives for conservation may not be optimally configured (Jodha 1986; Mukhopadhyay 2005b).[7] The utility maximising behaviour of lobby groups to use the democratic state with universal franchise to further its own goals needs to be brought into this analysis of CPR.

---

[4]   Assunção and Braido (2005), however, find that the empirical observation of inverse relationship is weak when input use is accounted for while testing for productivity gains.

[5]   Evidence from India suggests that the emergence of a monetized economy and a shift in the revenue collection in monetary units during the colonial era changed the character of risk sharing between the state (through its intermediary revenue collectors) and the cultivator. There was a shift from a system of risk and product sharing to monetary rent where the tenant/cultivator bore the entire risk while the landowners (and the exchequer) through a fixed rent ensured their own revenues (D'Souza 2002).

[6]   There are exceptions like (Holden and Shiferaw 2002) who argue that security of tenure is a pre-condition for agents to undertake conservation measures.

[7]   This is similar to what Agrawal (ch. 3, this volume) refers to as the romantic view of commons where an apolitical framework of analysis is used. Role of social institutions such religion and caste could impact on cooperative behaviour because there are side-payments involved (Ray ch. 4, this volume).

This is familiar domain for social choice theory – assume that group A and B are contesting to achieve goal X. By themselves they would not be able to achieve it unless they enlist the support of group C who are not interested in outcome X per se but would like to achieve outcome Y which is currently not on either A or B's agenda. Outcome Y however would require institutional change and therefore needs either A or B to push for it. Group B, presumably the new comer in this business promises outcome Y for group C if they support them (B) in achieving X.[8] So both B and C go home happy with respective outcomes X and Y to the detriment of A. If institutional reform and change in property rights regime can be achieved by legislative fiat then all a significant group has to do is ally with another one (with which it has no apparent conflict of goals) to achieve its desired outcome at no economic cost to either group. Political processes involving universal franchise can therefore be used for democratic reform but these need not necessarily lead to long run ecologically sustainable outcomes.[9]

The effect of such changes is compounded when there are exit opportunities. For example, after land redistribution or tenancy reform alternative economic opportunities may emerge which could entice the farmer off the field. Agriculture may no longer provide sufficient incentive to the new beneficiaries while the old owners stand disenfranchised (Mukhopadhyay 2005b). If there are high initial costs for the collective good then small farmers in the presence of an imperfect credit market would face a low productivity cycle – the so-called Olson effect (Baland and Platteau 1997). It could defeat the very purpose of tenancy reform – to increase efficiency of farm output due to reduced incentives of the gainers in farming. The effective land area under agriculture may also decline along with the potential increment in productivity. It might impede adoption of new technology and thereby reduce the long run growth in agriculture. Two possible consequences of reform could be reduction in (potential)[10] output and conservation.

Dayton-Johnson and Bardhan (2002) suggest that the relationship between inequality and conservation could be non-linear – an "inverted-U" – similar to the expanded notion of the "Kuznets" curve. When wealth is more equally distributed we might witness greater cooperation subject to a threshold. Those below a given threshold level of wealth will have a dominant strategy of non-cooperation while others above the threshold level would cooperate if they find others adopting a cooperative strategy. A cooperative outcome would fail if the proportion of those below the threshold is high (Baland and Platteau 1997). Sethi and Somanathan (ch. 7, this volume) suggest that cooperative outcomes are more likely when group size is bigger because the number of reciprocal agents (as opposed to utility maximizers) would be greater thereby increasing the possibility of achieving a critical mass of co-operators.

---

[8]   It is being assumed that there is no conflict in the achievement of X or Y.

[9]   When seen in conjunction with Olson's (1965) argument that emergence of collective action, especially in large groups is difficult if not impossible, it is no surprise that an existent equilibrium disturbed by exogenous factors could have an adverse impact on collective effort.

[10]   We use term the potential because in the new scenario there may not be an actual decline in output. However, due to non-adoption of new technology, the potential gain in production is compromised and the economic loss, therefore, is the non-attainment of a feasible higher output. The lower financial strength of new beneficiaries could also affect the amount spent on soil conservation thereby affecting long term sustainability.

Would a change in ownership in any way alter outcomes? A large part of the redistribution debate relates to reallocation of assets or goods in the individual domain even if mediated by the state. But is a similar effect to be expected if this redistribution involves common property? What happens to sustainability when we move to greater homogeneity by privatising common property?

Contrary to received wisdom (at that time) on commons, Demstez (1967) and Alchian and Demsetz (1973) argued that even when there are externalities, privatization is an efficiency enhancing measure.[11] Owners of the resource would be able to internalize all the costs and benefits. Much of the external costs, which are not accounted for under community ownership, will be internalized under private ownership – especially individual ownership.[12] If there is a polluting agent in the neighborhood, then as long as there are property rights protecting the resource being polluted, the cost of that pollution would be internalized. The Coase theorem informs us that it does not matter what the initial allocation of resources or assets is, whether a state or market exists or not, because rational individuals will reach an efficient outcome by a process of bargaining, as long as transaction costs are low.[13]

As far as the management of natural resources is concerned, especially in developing countries, experience shows that privatization may not always lead to efficiency gains, especially when contracts are incomplete, or there are non convexities (Seabright 1993; Grossman 2001). Even when property rights allocation is secure in private hands, if the private discount rate exceeds the social discount rate, degradation would proceed quicker than socially desirable (Dasgupta and Maler 2004). Under such conditions, a self-governing local community with commons might have a more efficient production locus than if private property rights are established (Ostrom 1990).[14]

We explore these issues in the context of the agrarian transition in Goa in the last four decades and study a traditional village institution called the *communidade* (or *gaunkari*), and its role in maintaining ecological sustainability[15] in Goa, a small coastal state in India. We take a bird's-eye view of four and a half centuries of colonial rule (1510–1961), four decades of post-Independence phase and attempt to understand the impact of institutional change on preservation of public works that contribute to soil conservation.[16]

---

[11] "If private rights can be policed easily, it is practicable to resolve the problem by converting communal rights into private rights. Contrary to some popular notions, it can be seen that *private* rights can be socially useful precisely because they encourage persons to take account of *social* costs" (Alchian and Demsetz 1973: 24, emphasis in original).

[12] This is in contrast to the arguments posed favoring social cost benefit analysis as a superior method of ranking projects than private cost benefit analyses which do not account for externalities that projects may create.

[13] Coase (1960) becomes relevant since Arrow–Debrue outcomes hold in the absence of externalities.

[14] Agrawal (ch. 3) and Ray (ch. 4) in this volume summarize the extensive literature on the conditions necessary to sustain collective action and the interested reader is referred to these papers.

[15] By ecological sustainability we imply the maintenance of recovered lands in their current status of agricultural land use and by conservation we imply undertaking protective measures (embankment maintenance) from unintended flooding by tidal waters (similar to Holden, Shiferaw, and Wik 1998).

[16] Goa was a Portuguese colony till 1961 whereafter it joined the Indian union. In 1987, Goa received statehood (after being a Union territory in the interim period).

Communidades *as a land management institution*

Land management in rural Goa has traditionally been the responsibility of a community institution called the *communidade* (or *gaunkari*) one of the oldest endogenous resource management institutions (not dissimilar to the village republics in many other parts of India, e.g., Wade 1992).[17] These village-level organizations owned the cultivable lands of the village and leased them out to individual cultivators by periodic auction. The highest bidder would acquire the right to till the auctioned parcels for the period of the lease (Pereira 1981).

The land leases were transferable by inheritance but there were restrictions on transfer by sale or change of land use for purposes other than contracted with the *communidade* at the time of the lease (which constitutionally had to be agricultural).[18] As tax demands from the colonial state increased, as probably did the demographic pressures, the barren and uncultivated lands on the periphery of the village were leased out for a fixed rent. In some areas after 25 years, the lessee was entitled to ownership of the land. The perceived reason for this is on the one hand to provide an incentive to the farmer to develop the land and on the other to allow the village to increase the area of productive land (D'Souza 2000: 114).

The *communidade* supervised all the lands of the village under the jurisdiction of the village associations and the rents collected were used for public works. Surplus rent was distributed equally among all *gaunkars* as dividends (*jonos*). Membership to the *communidade* was, however, bounded on two counts: gender (male) and descendence. Only male descendents of all original settler families were entitled to be *gaunkars*. A major part of their assets were the lands (*khazans*) recovered by reclamation from marshes and the tidal waters with the help of *bunds* (embankments).[19]

In later years the *gaunkars* allowed inclusion of other skilled and semi-skilled persons in the *communidade* for community development. Those who financially helped the *gaunkars* were called "interested participants with limited interest" (*accionistas*). Others were also absorbed as groups or communities and given rights over certain earmarked lands (*componentes*) and could be of either sex. This presumably was permitted on two strategic counts: one to give the institution social stability and also to keep membership from falling below the minimum required.[20]

---

[17] The traditional village organization of Goa was called the *gaunponn* – *gaun* (village) and *ponn* (organization), and renamed as *communidades* by the Portuguese. The *communidades* were responsible for construction and maintenance of roads, drainage and irrigation systems, public security as well as judicial and religious institutions (Pereira 1981). The *communidade* system was substantially different from the the *zamindari* or *jajmani* system seen in the British part of colonial India.

[18] The sale of *communidade* land apparently could take place only by way of public auction of its entire property and assets when the respective *communidade* became bankrupt, other exceptional circumstances, or when the membership fell below the minimum required (Pereira 1981).

[19] In 1967, the total land area owned by the *communidades* was estimated to be 36,624 hectares. The amount of reclaimed (*khazan*) lands was estimated to be 18,000 hectares. Of this, the *communidades* owned 6,386 hectares while private ownership was about 2,500 hectares. The remaining 9,000 hectares belonged to either religious institutions (temples and churches) or the government. The *communidades* also controlled 440 hectares of rivulets in seven talukas (GoG 1967a: 306; 1992: 26).

[20] A cluster of villages, for purposes of administrative efficiency was organized into a *Mahal* which was supervised by a judge and a council. In Tiswadi e.g., the *mahal* council consisted of 8 villages and in Salcete it consisted of 12 villages. Some believe that before villages became independent units, the *mahals* acted as the lowest tier of administrative unit (Velinkar 2000: 130).

There is little known about the origins of the *communidades* and the early history is unclear. In the pre-Portuguese period the *communidades* are believed to have enjoyed considerable autonomy in administrative, financial as well as judicial powers. Two possible reasons could be cited for the autonomy enjoyed by these local institutions. First, most pre-colonial rulers were not based in Goa and so indulged in revenue farming, which were also auctioned as a tax on gross produce. The *communidades* were only responsible for fulfilling the tax demands of the ruler and were left untouched in their mode of functioning thereby acquiring relative autonomy.[21] Second, these rulers did not last long enough to change the basic character of these institutions or interfere with its internal functioning.[22] The Portuguese colonization lasted for 450 years (1510 to 1961) and had significant impacts on the *communidades*.[23]

In the next section we discuss how the fortunes of Portuguese colonial rule impacted on the *communidades*.

---

[21] Over time as the complexity of the *gauponns* increased so did the rules and regulations. From customs and conventions emerged a set of rules and regulations called "Mandavoli." It set up the rents, irrigation charges, distribution of rents, personal share of each *gaonkar*, grants for temples, and areas constituting each *vangor* (clan). It is said that in the early times, every decision of the *gauponn* was taken unanimously. If there was a single dissenting voice (veto), the item was dropped. However, subsequently, this veto power seems to have been eroded by fresh regulations issued in 1745 (Velinkar 2000: 129).

[22] A brief summary of the different kingdoms which ruled over Goa and Konkan is listed below (Xavier 1993).

Until mid-thirteenth century: Kadamba rule

Mid-thirteenth century to 1294: Yadavas (of Devagiri) who conquered the Chalukyan Empire
1294 to 1367: Allauddin's invasions into South India
1367–1469: Vijayanagar empire brings Goa under its fold
1469–1488: Bahamani kings (Mohammed Shah III)
1488–1510: Adil Shah (Split in Bahamani dynasty, Adil Shah gets Goa)
1510–1961: Portuguese colonial rule.

Old conquests

1510 March 1: A. de Albuquerque takes over Goa. Yusuf Adil Shah retaliates and takes back Goa.
Nov. 25: A. de Albuquerque retakes Goa. Initial conquered area: Island of Goa and the 4 adjacent islands of Chorao (earlier name Chudamani), Divar (Dipavati), Vamsin and Jua.
1543: Bardez and Salcete added to Portuguese control

New conquests

1763: Ponda (from the Marathas)
1764: Kepem and Canacona (from rulers of Sonda)
1781–8: Pernem, Sattari, and Bicholim (from Bhonsales of Sawantwadi).

[23] The financial obligations of the *communidade* apparently were limited till they sought help from the Kadamba rulers to stop infiltration of Muslim invaders by the sea route in 1054. In return they agreed to pay the sovereign a protection tax called *coxi vordo* – tax given of free will [GoG 1964: 23]. During the phase when Goa came under the Bahamani dynasty (1469–1510), there seems to have been a steady rise in imposition of land taxes. In fact, when Afonso Albuquerque was seeking support for his campaign against Adil Shah, he promised to bring down the taxes if the local population helped him (de Souza 1981: 120). Soon after establishment of the Portuguese reign, Afonso Mexia (Superintendent of Revenues and Taxes) through the *foral* of 1526 established a fixed rent for the 31 villages of Tiswadi which had to be collectively paid. The responsibility of payment lay with the 8 main villages who had to pay up even if there was default by other villages. In case any village defaulted on the payment, the land lease of the village was auctioned but the *communidades* did not lose their land ownership rights and could reclaim their right to auction lands by payment of full dues (D'Souza 2000: 112).

The colonial era (1510–1961)

The transition in *communidades* has to be understood in the context of the politics of colonization and inquisition – demands for administrative revenue and support for religious institutions.[24] Afonso Albuquerque established the Portuguese reign in 1510 and it lasted till 1961 – about 450 years.[25] The Portuguese empire followed a rigorous religious policy in all its colonies during 1540–1640 as part of its arrangement with the Roman Catholic Church and the main support for the new Christian institutions came from the state.[26] Through the sixteenth century to mid-seventeenth century the Portuguese sea-borne empire controlled the sea trade between Asia and Europe.[27] The revenues it earned as customs duties in Goa were able to substantially contribute to its liabilities for meeting church expenses.

After the mid-seventeenth century the colonial government went through a difficult financial period. Portugal lost its sea supremacy to the Dutch, leading to a decline in revenues from customs duties. It was also engaged in frequent wars with other rulers on the

[24]   This found reflection in most policies of the government including internal administration of the *gaunkaris*. Interference in the functioning of the *communidades* (in 1573) went to the extent of forbidding *gaunkars* (of Salcete) to convene meetings or pass resolutions without the presence of Christian *gaunkars* (Xavier 1993: 67). Some authors like D'Costa (undated: 46), assert that the emergence of private individual property in Goa was a contribution of the Portuguese colonial policy. While there is insufficient evidence to support this assertion, it is more likely that the proportion of private property expanded during the Portuguese colonization. The first attempt by Afonso de Albuquerque to integrate the Portuguese into the Goan society was by way of encouraging inter-marriages between Portuguese soldiers and widows of slain Muslim and Hindu soldiers. In addition to the land grants, Albuquerque is said to have gifted a horse and a house. Prior to this private property was said to be limited to the house plot (Xavier 1993: 7). While he did not interfere in the working of the *gauponns*, he allowed those villages which made land grants to these couples to forgo their *coxi vordo* (voluntary contribution to the king). The second big boost to private property rights came during the period of the Inquisition. The state confiscated (1) all temple lands, (2) private lands of those who did not convert to Christianity, and (3) Christians who did not conform to the edicts of the Inquisitorial authority. One part of the confiscated lands went to Christian missionary institutions as private property grants. A second part was given to new converts to seek their cooperation. A third part was allocated for tenancy.
[25]   The Portuguese occupation can be divided into two distinct phases, separated by almost two centuries. The sixteenth-century occupation (Old Conquest) of 3 *talukas*: Ilhas, Salcete, Bardez; and eighteenth-century occupation (New Conquest) of 6 additional talukas: Pernem, Sanquelim, Ponda, Sanguem, Quepem, and Canacona.
[26]   In 1540 all the temples of Ilhas taluka were destroyed and soon after the Portuguese governor wanted to take over these lands in Ilhas taluka for the financial support of the new Christian organizations that emerged in Goa. The temples were important beneficiaries of *Communidade* lands. The then Acting Governor of Goa called for a consultation with the leading *gaunkars* of Ilhas regarding the future of the temple lands. The temple lands earned about 2,000 (silver) *tangas brancas* and obviously attracted the attention of the revenue offices of the colonial government. The *gaunkars* suggested that since these lands belonged to the village *communidades* the lands should revert to the respective villages. In February 1545 the Governor, Martin Afonso de Souza transferred ownership of these lands to the College of St Paul. The apparent reason was that these temple lands were not taxed. The villages however remained saddled with the payment of the tax of the now confiscated temple lands despite losing their temple lands. However, a settlement was reached whereby the lands remained with the village but the rent was passed on to the Catholic institutions for their maintenance (Xavier 1993: 123).
[27]   In 1574, the total land revenue of the Portuguese colony (Old Conquest areas of Island of Goa, the *talukas* of Ilhas, Bardez, and Salcete) was 88 million *reis*. Of this amount, 15.5 million was spent on churches. Interestingly, there seems to be no evidence of any religious tax till 1640. By 1707, we find evidence of villages being forced to meet expenses of church repairs. In 1745, a half *tithe* was re-introduced in addition to the existing taxes. Shastry (1987: 38) points out that earlier when this half *tithe* was imposed on village communities, they protested. The half tithe was repealed but an additional tax of 5 percent was introduced on the quit rent (*foro*).

mainland. Both these contributed to the decline in financial capability of the colonial government in Goa. It is during this time that we see an increasing financial reliance of the government and the Church on village communities (Shastry 1987: 35; de Souza 1981: 119). By the mid-eighteenth century the colonial government had taken control of the finances of the *communidades* and no expenditures could be undertaken without sanction of the government except for funds allocated to "divine cult and church repairs" and for emergency repairs of the embankments (*bunds*). The *communidades*, in order to maintain their control over lands and meet the tax demands had to resort to borrowing both from members of the village as well as outside which led to the creation of a category of *associantes* who were not necessarily *gaunkars* but now acquired a stake in the financial well-being of the *communidade* with the issue of shares that earned dividends.[28]

There was constant acrimony between the state and the church too regarding the distribution of resources that each could get from the village communities.[29] The local government would often complain to the crown that churches were undertaking unnecessary repairs and imposing the costs on the villages which were therefore unable to pay state dues. The extensive tax imposed and the massive withdrawal of resources from the *communidades* in the eighteenth century left them severely indebted.[30]

---

[28]   *Communidades* raised money and resources from *gaunkars* as well as *foreiros* (later settlers who could not participate in the village administration) and were issued *tangas* (shares) in exchange for the loans. These shares were non-transferable till the seventeenth century (GoG 1964: 25). Based on the decree of 1880 (and Regulamento 1882 executed in 1888), all alienable claims on *communidades* such as *tangas, melagas, arqueiras*, etc. (different forms of *interesses*, financial interests or claims) were converted into shares of only one type having a nominal value of Rs. 20 in 1882 (GoG 1967a: 43 and Pereira 1981: 41). Shareholders still did not get equal status as *gaunkars* in village affairs especially in leasing of *communidade* plots which at that time could only be leased by the *gaunkars*. In 1904, under pressure from the *culcharins* and *cuntocares* (outside shareholders who were not original descendants of *gaunkars* but admitted to the *communidade* later), the government issued a new code whereby they acquired equal status with the *gaunkars* as regards lease of plots belonging to *communidades* (GoG 1967a: 43, 53). In June 1735 the Portuguese government issued new rules by way of which non-*gaunkars* (outsiders: *cuntocares*) were allowed to bid for the lease of paddy fields but only through the *gaunkars*. In case of disputes between the *communidades* and their members, the government would adjudicate.

[29]   The reasons for acrimony were also because the state government suspected that the church officials were colluding with groups of *gaunkars* who used this route to siphon off monies of the *communidades* for their own betterment. Being assigned for "divine cult," this money was not taxed by the state nor could the allocation be questioned. This phenomena became so widespread that in 1711 a vice-regal order was passed whereby all village resolutions dealing with financial allocations had to be approved by the Viceroy's office. This was ratified by the King of Portugal in 1719 (Shastry 1987: 41–2).

[30]   The Island of Goa had an accumulated debt of more than 425,000 *ashrafis*. The annual interest was estimated to be 21,000 *ashrafis* while their annual income was estimated at 155,000 *ashrafis* (Shastry 1987: 43). Even though the *communidades* faced impoverishment, the church organizations became increasingly prosperous. In 1759, some of the church organizations gave loans totalling 350,000 *xerafins* to the General Assemblies of village communities as well as individual village communities to meet their tax obligations to the colonial state by mortgaging their lands (de Souza 1981: 123). Trading was banned as far as the religious orders were concerned. However, under guise of exchanging surplus, members of the church engaged in trading and this helped the church accumulate large assets. But due to restrictions on their trading activities, they concentrated their efforts on the domestic economy – especially the village lands. The Jesuits were able to substantially increase the output of the lands they cultivated. The church had three sources of revenue: (1) endowments and legacies including its profits from shares it held in the *communidades*; (2) profits from participation in trade; (3) profits from farming.

As *communidades* became economically burdened with increasing taxation *gaunkars* started trading on communal lands. They framed rules whereby the communal lands could only be leased to *gaunkars*. They would then acquire tenancy rights over these fields at nominal charges and sub-let them at higher rents (called *Alca*). A whole set of "middle-men" emerged who survived on *Alca* and 90 percent of the land came under tenant cultivation (D'Costa undated: 51).[31]

Data available for the decade prior to implementation of the Tenancy Acts indicates that these institutions were able to disburse dividends to their members after allocating for embankment maintenance (GoG 1967b: annexure no. 8, 22–3). In the next section we take up the transition of the land management system in the post-colonial period.

The post-colonial period (1961–)

Goa joined the Indian union in 1961 and this marked a significant departure in the dynamics of local governance that followed. Over time, the structure of the village had changed and the number of tenants and laborers had increased in the village and therefore the *communidade* as a village unit of governance had become non-representative. Decision-making in a democracy could not justify the sustenance of a non-representative institution to manage village affairs involving both *gaunkars* and non-*gaunkars*. The *panchayat* system, which was prevalent in the rest of India when Goa joined the Indian union, was introduced in Goa in 1963–4 and this encroached upon the jurisdiction of the *communidades*. The *panchayat* was designated to be the local government institution in place of the *communidades*.

Issues of land distribution (security of agricultural tenure) became significant, especially after Goa joined the Indian union in 1961. The demands for land reform and "land to-the-tiller" were made part of the change in the institutional structure of governance. The popular elected government riding on a wave of reformist agenda abolished the annual auction of lands owned by the *communidades*.

It legislated to give security of tenancy rights, stopped eviction of tenants and gave the *Mundkars* the right to buy their house sites (the Goa, Daman, and Diu Agriculture Tenancy Act 1964, the Goa, Daman, and Diu Mundkar (Protection form Eviction) Act 1975).[32] To

---

[31]   By 1735 (*Regiment*) there is evidence of existence of arbitrators which is indicative of disputes regarding rents (D'Souza 2000: 117). The *Assento da Relacaco* (1786) records discussion about conflict resolution between the crown and village communities. These disputes must have been quite widespread as the Decree of 1836 abolished the post of Village judges (which ended all judicial powers of the *communidades*) and placed judicial responsibility on the district judge (D'Souza 2000: 118). The dynamics of the village organizations is reflected in the series of official notifications that were issued. After the Regiment of 1735 and the *Assento* of 1786 came the *Regiment of* 1871 (8 articles), Decree of 1880, Regulations of 1886 (465 articles), Code of Communidades 1905 (750 articles), Code of 1933 (873 articles) and finally the Code of 1961 (660 articles). In 1905 the agrarian chambers were abolished and the powers of the chambers were transferred to the Administrator of village communidades (D'Souza 2000: 118–20).

[32]   According to the Royal Decree of 1901 (24 August) the *mundkar* is defined as "an individual residing in a dwelling settled in another's rural property mainly with the aim of cultivating or for looking after the property" (quoted in GoG 1967a: 283). The *munddcarato* system prevailed largely as a verbal agreement between the landlord and mundkars and sometimes as unwritten conventions followed over generations. Properly drawn up contracts were rare (GoG 1967a: 282).

substitute the *communidade* and its responsibilities with a new beneficiary institution, formation of a Tenant's Association was made mandatory as per the Tenancy Act (1964) and Rules and Regulations (1975). These laws completely altered the relations between the state–local governments and the power structure within the village. The role of the *communidade* declined as its financial powers were withdrawn. There are at present 223 *communidades* in Goa however they are a mere shadow of their past.

The Tenants Associations, which on the other hand were state engineered, did not deliver in terms of provision of public goods – maintenance of embankments for soil conservation. Of the 138 Tenants' Associations reviewed by the Agricultural Land Development Panel in 1992, the majority were found to be defunct (GoG 1992). Unfortunately, the *panchayats* which have universal membership have no direct incentive to take over the agrarian tasks of the *communidades* nor do they have the financial buoyancy (Mukhopadhyay 2005d). This resulted in reduced maintenance of the embankment structures even though the state decided to institute a special agency for overseeing the same.[33] In the post-colonial period there has also been a large out-migration from rural Goa especially to the Gulf which has impacted on land use and maintenance (Mukhopadhyay 2005b; 2005c).

The consequence of the institutional change simultaneous with the exit of *gaunkars* from the agrarian management system has led to:

1 greater homogeneity and privatization in land ownership due to the tenancy legislation, which may be desirable on normative grounds (Mukhopadhyay 2005b);
2 decline in the maintenance of public works leading to salinity effects and fallowing of land indicating sustainability problems (Alvares 2002; de Souza undated; GoG 1992; 2000; Mukhopadhyay 2005a; 2005b; TERI 2000) – an undesirable consequence which could undo the positive social benefits that homogeneity might have generated.

4 Imperative for Institutional Change

The question that crops up then is, why did the property rights regime undergo change in Goa in the immediate aftermath of liberation from colonial rule? Demsetz (1967) had identified three factors which determine the switch from community ownership to private ownership: technology, market access and value of the resource. In the interregnum of transition from colonial to independence none of these seem to have changed.

We must qualify our statement here. Land values must have changed in the period between 1510 to 1961. Since there were no major changes in technology of production in the first half of the twentieth century – till the time of the Green Revolution – there is no reason to believe that productivity would have gone up and therefore land values. In fact, post securitization of tenure we do not see adoption of modern agrarian technology in

---

[33] The Soil Conservation Division created in 1969 was responsible for overseeing the maintenance of embankments (GoG 1992: 55). The expenditure (in current prices) on embankments by this division has gone up from Rs 0.69 million (in 1962) to Rs 4.16 million (in 2000) however, in real terms, the actual expenditure on embankments has actually declined (Mukhopadhyay 2005b).

Table 8.1 *Taluka*-wise distribution of tenants and *gaunkars*[a]

No.	Talukas	No. of tenants in 1963	Resident gaunkars and shareholders	Total no. of registered gaunkars and shareholders
1	Tiswadi	6,025	3,457	8,870
2	Salcete	11,017	4,956	12,473
3	Bardez	9,494	14,128	25,003
4	Mormugao	1,601	790	2,090
5	Ponda	1,350	1,357	2,321
6	Bicholim	641	1,022	1,290
7	Pernem	41	0	0
8	Quepem	165	85	107
9	Sanguem	146	80	106
10	Canacona	67	63	133
11	Satari	4	29	38
	Total	30,551	25,967	52,431

[a] Pernem is a peculiar case because all the *communidades* of Pernem forfeited their lands and there is no inscription of *gaunkars* in this *taluka*. During the Portuguese colonial rule, Pernem was the territory bordering the Maratha lands and the charge of the entire land area in this *taluka* was given to the Ranes to protect thereby disenfranchising the *communidades*.

Source: GoG 1967b: annexure 6, pp. 18 and 19

Goa in the same manner as in other parts of rural India where Green Revolution technology allowed quantum leaps in agricultural production. In terms of market access, there could not have been any major changes either since Goa was a trading post which in the first place brought the Portuguese to *Goa Dourada*. So Demsetz conditions do not seem to be the reasons why the commons were privatized.

What then could possibly explain this need for shift in the property rights framework? The answer probably lies in the changed procedure of government-formation – from colonial to electoral democracy. In the post-1961 era, with elected governments becoming the order of the day, any political party would rationally seek to corner the largest number of votes. The issue which seemed to carry the day in Goa at that time was related to landownership.

Is this a mere conjecture or is there evidence to back this claim? The distribution of tenants vis-a-vis Gaunkars in Goa prior to enactment of the Tenancy Act (1964) presents an interesting picture (table 8.1). In 1963, on the eve of Tenancy legislation, the number of resident *gaunkars* and shareholders (25,967) happens to be much smaller than the number of tenants (30,551) aggregated across the state.[34] In fact, if one were to exclude just

---

[34] The *talukas* which are exceptions to this are Bardez, Ponda, and Bicholim. In Ponda and Bicholim, however, the difference is marginal.

one taluka (Bardez) from these calculations, then the tenants add up to 21,057 and resident *gaunkars*/shareholders are only 11,869 (just about 50 percent of the tenants).[35]

Electorally, the political compulsions for land reform become strategic.[36] Beneficiaries of the land reform also included the *mundkars*, for whom data was not available (since they worked on private lands) and therefore are not enumerated here. The number of potential beneficiaries, therefore, is actually larger than the tenants' numbers indicate. It is no surprise that the Maharashtrawadi Gomantak Party (MGP) which brought in these changes had an unbroken run of electoral wins for seventeen years.[37]

Is this of any consequence to the discussion on the commons? In contrast to Demsetz who suggested that changes in market access/values and technological change push the move from common property to private property, in the case of *Gaunkaris*, possibly it was the imperative of electoral politics that drove the establishment of private rights over community lands and had little to do with technology or market values. As suggested by Agrawal (ch. 3, this volume) it had more to do with the external social and political institutional changes which were critical in determining the shift in property rights regimes in Goa.

Discussion

This chapter brings to fore a few issues that have been of concern to "commons" studies. First, the Demsetz conditions do not close all the factors that determine regime change. The overarching social and political framework can be crucial in determining what kind of property rights regime would prevail. Second, equity enhancing measures while desirable for economic, ethical or moral grounds needs to be carefully examined when it is being done by dismantling an organic institution and by privatising common resources which require contribution from members or users for its sustenance. A simple foisting of new institutions even if democratic may face the classic collective action problem that the literature is well aware of. In Goa, the parcelling of lands earlier managed by a community institution led to negative ecological outcomes. The new owners of the land have been unable to replace the *Communidades* in their task of coastal zone management. This could be due to factors caused by lack of prior history of cooperation. In the euphoria of asset distribution, institutional incentives were not studied, as cooperation was expected to automatically emerge among beneficiary farmers. This demonstrates that emergence of collective action is difficult even when homogeneity is achieved, if appropriate institutional mechanisms do not evolve simultaneously and organically.

---

[35]   One must point out here that in table 8.1 the total number of registered gaunkars and shareholders outnumber the tenants. Does that nullify our argument? It must be remembered that the tenant enumeration is only of a single male person in the tenant household. For the *gaunkars* though, every male member of the family is listed. So, if every household is assumed to have had at least two or three male members then the number of tenant beneficiaries becomes much larger. The number of tenant beneficiaries then is greater than the *gaunkars* (even when we include the non-resident members).

[36]   The population in 1961 was 0.58 million.

[37]   In the current political scenario, MGP has lost its electoral charm amongst its constituencies. In the last decade they have become increasingly marginalized with an emergent BJP (a rightist nationalist party) taking over their traditional support base. The number of representatives they were able to send to the state assembly have also declined considerably.

References

Alchian, A. A. and H. Demsetz (1973) "The Property Rights Paradigm," *Journal of Economic History*, 33(1): 16–23.

Alvares, Claude (ed.) (2002) *Fish, Curry and Rice*, Mapusa: Goa Foundation.

Assunção, J. J. and L. H. B. Braido (2005) "Testing among Competing Explanations for the Inverse Productivity Puzzle," http://www.econ.puc-rio.br/pdf/td500.pdf, accessed October 25.

Baland, J. M. and J. P. Platteau (2003) "Economics of Common Property Management Regimes," in K. G. Maler and J. Vincent (eds), *Handbook of Environmental Economics*, North Holland: Elsevier, 127–90.

Baland, J. M. and J. P. Platteau (1997) "Wealth Inequality and Efficiency in the Commons I: The Unregulated Case," *Oxford Economic Papers*, 49: 451–82.

Banerjee, A. (1999) "Land Reforms: Prospects and Strategies," Working Paper 99–24, Department of Economics, Massachusetts Institute of Technology, October, http://papers.ssrn.com/paper.taf?abstract_id=183711

Banerjee, A., P. Gertler, and M. Ghatak (2002) "Empowerment and Efficiency: Tenancy Reform in West Bengal," *Journal of Political Economy*, 110(2): 239–80.

Bardhan, P. K. (2001) "Distributive Conflicts, Collective Action and Institutional Economics," in G. M. Meier and J. E. Stiglitz (eds), *Frontiers of Development Economics*, New York: Oxford University Press.

Bardhan, P. K. (1973) "Size, Productivity and Returns to Scale: An Analysis of Farm-level data in Indian Agriculture," *Journal of Political Economy*, 81: 1370–86.

Berry, R. A. and W. R. Cline (1979) *Agrarian Structure and Productivity in Developing Countries*, Baltimore: Johns Hopkins University Press.

Besley, T. and R. Burgess (2000) "Land Reform, Poverty Reduction, and Growth: Evidence from India," *Quarterly Journal of Economics*, May: 389–430.

Bhaduri, A. (1973) "A Study in Agricultural Backwardness under Semi-feudalism," *Economic Journal*, 83: 120–37.

Borges, C. J., O. G. Pereira, and H. Stubbs (2000) *Goa and Portugal: History and Development*, XCHR Studies Series 10, New Delhi: Concept Publishing Co.

Coase, R. (1960) "The Problem of Social Cost," *Journal of Law and Economics*, 3: 1–44.

Dasgupta, P. and K. G. Maler (2004) "Environmental and Resource Economics: Some Recent Developments," Working Paper 7–04, Special Issue, South Asian Network for Development and Environmental Economics (SANDEE), Nepal, http://www.sandeeonline.org/, accessed October 25.

Dayton-Johnson, J. and P. K. Bardhan (2002) "Inequality and Conservation on the Local Commons: A Theoretical Exercise," *Economic Journal*, 112(481): 577–602.

D'Costa, Adelyne (undated) *Social Change in Goa*, Margao: Timblo Printers.

Deininger, K. and H. Binswanger (1999) "The Evolution of the World Bank's Land Policy: Principles, Experience, and Future Challenges," *The World Bank Research Observer*, 2(4): 247–76.

Deininger, K. and G. Feder (1998) "Land Institutions and Land Markets," December, backg-round paper, Development Research Group, http://www.worldbank.org/html/dec/Publications/Workpapers/wps2000series/wps2014/wps2014.pdf, accessed October 25.

Demsetz, H. (1967) "Towards a theory of Property Rights," *American Economic Review*, *Papers and Proceedings*, 62: 347–59.

de Souza, Luis (undated) "Breached Bunds a Threat to Farming and Water Security in Divar," *Firday Balcao*, 3(6), Goa Desc, www.goadesc. org/balcao/topic_environment.htm, accessed October 25, 2005.

de Souza, T. R. (1981) "The Voiceless in Goan Historiography," in John Correia-Afonso, *Indo-Portuguese History: Sources and Problems*, Bombay: Oxford University Press, pp. 114–31.

D'Souza, Carmo (2000) "The Village Communities: A Historical and Legal Perspective," in Borges et al., pp. 111–23.

D'Souza, R. (2002) "Colonialism, Capitalism and Nature: Debating the Origins of Mahanadi Delta's Hydraulic Crisis (1803–1928)," *Economic and Political Weekly*, 37(13).

GoG (1992) *Report of the Agricultural Land Development Panel*, Panaji: Revenue Department, Government of Goa.

GoG (1967a) *Aspects of Agricultural Activity in Goa*, vol. 1, Panaji: Government Printing Press.

GoG (1967b) *Aspects of Agricultural Activity in Goa: Annexures*, vol. 2, Panaji: Government Printing Press.

GoG (1964) *Report of the Goa Land Reforms Commission*, Government of Goa, Daman and Diu, February, Panaji: Government Printing Press.

Grossman, H. I. (2001) "The Creation of Effective Property Rights," *American Economic Review*, 91(2): 347–52.

Hardin, Garrett (1968) "The Tragedy of the Commons," *Science*, 162.

Holden, S. T. and B. Shiferaw, (2002) "Poverty and Land Degradation: Peasants' Willingness to Pay to Sustain Land Productivity," in C. Barrett, F. Place, and A. A. Aboud (eds), *The Adoption of Natural Resource Management Practices: Improving Sustainable Agricultural Production in Sub-Saharan Africa*, New York: CAB International Publishing.

Holden, S. T., B. Shiferaw, and M. Wik (1998) "Poverty, Market Imperfections, and Time Preferences: Of Relevance for Environmental Policy?," *Environment and Development Economics*, 3: 105–30.

Mukhopadhyay, P. (2005a) "Now That Your Land Is Mine . . . Does It Matter?" *Environment and Development Economics*, 10(1): 87–96.

Mukhopadhyay, P. (2005b) "Heterogeneity, Commons and Privatisation: Agrarian Institutional Change in Goa," South Asian Network for Development and Environmental Economics, Kathmandu, Working Paper 14–06.

Mukhopadhyay, P. (2005c) "Tourism and its Economic Impact on Women in Goa," report submitted to the Goa State Commission for Women, Panaji: Government of Goa.

Mukhopadhyay, P. (2005d) "Rural Self Governance in Goa: Financial Feasibility or Fragility," Working Paper, Department of Economics, Goa University.

Olson, M. (1965) *The Logic of Collective Action*, Cambridge, MA: Harvard University Press.

Ostrom, E. (2000) "Collective Action and Social Norms," *Journal of Economic Perspectives*, 14(3): 137–58.

Ostrom, E. (1990) *Governing the Commons: The Evolution of Institutions for Collective Action*, New York: Cambridge University Press.

Periera, Rui Gomes (1981) *Gaunkari, the Old Village Associations*, vol. 1, Panaji: Printwell Publishers.

Ray, D. (1998) *Development Economics*, New Delhi: Oxford University Press.

Shastry, B. S. (1987) "Sources of Income and Items of Expenditure of the Churches in Goa (c. 1510–1800 A.D.): A Note," in B. S. Shastry (ed.), *Goan Society through the Ages*, New Delhi: Asian Publication Services, pp. 35–47.

Seabright, P. (1993) "Managing Local Commons: Theoretical Issues in Incentive Design," *Journal of Economic Perspectives*, 7(4): 13–34.

TERI (2000) "Population, Consumption and Environment Interrelations: A Tourist Spot Scenario," New Delhi: Tata Energy Research Institute (TERI Project Report 97EM50).

Velinkar, J. (2000) "Village Communities in Goa and Their Evolution," in Borges et al. (eds), 124–32.

Wade, R. (1987) *Village Republics: Economic Conditions for Collective Action in South India*, Cambridge: Cambridge University Press.

Xavier, P. D. (1993) *Goa: A Social History (1510–1640)*, Panaji: Rajhauns Vitaran.

9: Scale and Mobility in Defining the Commons

Vyjayanthi Rao and Arjun Appadurai

Common Paradoxes

As anthropologists, we are struck by the self-evident nature of definitions of the commons in the literature about the commons. Such definitions often view the commons as aggregations of local situations but fail to take into account the conditions under which these commons appear *as* commons within the lives of communities. While the politics of resources considered at a larger, abstract level is indeed the very raison d'etre for the study of the commons, there is not enough attention to the circumstances under which commons arise, disappear and mutate into other kinds of property resources. The aggregation of these kinds of events into definitions of the commons enables a different sort of window into understanding the commons. To illustrate what we mean by this, we would like to turn to a specific example drawn from fieldwork in India.[1] In this example, we see that all sorts of conditions are brought to bear not only on the politics of resource use but in the volatility of the definition of the commons itself.

In March 1981, several villages along the banks of the river Krishna had to be evacuated by force. The village sites were about to be submerged by the reservoir waters of the Srisailam dam whose construction had just then been completed, more than fifteen years after it began, damming the river at the eponymous town of Srisailam in Andhra Pradesh, an ancient and important pilgrimage centre. More than one hundred villages in Mahbubnagar and Kurnool districts were affected and eventually about one hundred and fifty thousand people were displaced in some fashion – some lost their homes, some lost farmlands and many lost both. As the dam was being constructed, the AP State Department of Archaeology and Museums prepared to "rescue" and salvage a number of

---

[1] This example is drawn from the fieldwork on which Vyjayanthi Rao's dissertation, "Ruins and Recollections: On the Subjects of Displacement" is based.

historic monuments from the submergence zone. The rescued monuments were historic exemplars of monumental Hindu temple architecture, constructed in the individual villages by various imperial and local powers as acts of piety and displays of power. The temples were first dismantled and later reconstructed, not within the villages reconstructed after submergence, but in specially designated temple compounds located at various scenic spots along the banks of the Srisailam reservoir.

One particular village within this submergence zone – itself a historic site because it had once served as the seat of a large Hindu jagir (small territory granted by a Moghul ruler to an army chieftain in recognition for military service) paying tribute to the Hyderabad Nizam – was unique because it simultaneously became the site of all of these multiple transactions. After submergence of their village site, the villagers, not wishing to be relocated by the government to areas some distance away from the original site, led an initiative to purchase lands from neighboring villages and to reconstruct their houses only two kilometres away from the old site. The Department of Archaeology and Museums meanwhile also decided to construct a temple compound around this reconstructed village. The compound was created by moving about forty temples, belonging to a particular period, dismantled from various villages around the submergence zone into a designated area at the edge of the reconstructed village. In the heart of the new settlement, somewhere between the archaeological compound and the new settlement, a large rocky expanse of land was left over as the only land that had lain within the original revenue boundaries of the submerged village. A sixteenth-century Sri Vaishnava temple, which had been at the spatial heart of the submerged village site was also selected for transplantation by archaeologists but unlike the other temples, it was not moved away from the village in its spatially reconstituted form. Driven by a sentimental politics, this temple was reconstructed by archaeologists on this left-over portion of village space at the behest of the erstwhile ruling family of this zamindari (territory belonging to a zamindar, or tax-collector, appointed by the sovereign authority; the system, prevalent in Moghul India was perpetuated by the British during their rule).

The lands that had made space, within the original village sivar – or boundary in the revenue sense but also in a ritual sense – for the monumental village temple were appropriated by the Andhra Pradesh State Religious Endowments Department. Prior to submergence, although the lands are designated as charai – or grazing lands – on a revenue map of the village prepared just after the merger of the princely state of Hyderabad with the Indian Union in 1948, they had been cultivated by generations of harijan (lit. "children of god" – a term used by Gandhi to refer to untouchable communities) families with the permission of the zamindar.[2] These families were amongst the poorest in the village. After submergence, when most of the cultivable lands within the village sivar disappeared, these families appeared to have escaped the fate of the other villagers. Yet, they now found themselves caught in the net of the law of eminent domain. Their lands were claimed for the temple reconstruction on the grounds that they were common lands, a category that had not existed in practice prior to the submergence. These farmers found themselves reclassified as "squatters" and "illegal occupants of village lands," losing the rights gained, through conditions of near bondage, to cultivate and have exclusive access to "common" resources.

---

[2]   The use of the term harijan here is following local usage by the subjects themselves.

In this instance, a number of important issues pertaining to the commons can be noted. First, through customary sanction, village-level arrangements provided access to resources for the poorest groups. These arrangements were, of course, connected to various illiberal practices for the extraction of labor but nonetheless constituted an arrangement for managing the commons. The commons themselves were recognized *as* commons only through such arrangements. There was no such thing as free and open access in the strict sense. The law of the commons as such was an artifact of distributive practices. The claims made by the state's religious endowments department over these lands followed a different logic, invoking the commons as a space over which the law of eminent domain applied. Applying this classificatory logic further meant dispossessing the families who had been cultivating these lands for generations without the compensation that was paid to all other cultivators, both landowners and tenants. Thus the disappearance of the village ironically meant the recognition of commons as commons where perhaps none had existed before.

In recent years, fundamental and perhaps catastrophic changes have taken place in the landscape within which resources in general, not to speak of common property resources have been viewed. The above example of the use of the law of eminent domain is just one of them. The symbolic transformation of the value of land, both rural and urban, including the exchange of rural landholdings for urban real estate value, the shift from small farmers undertaking commercial farming to the institutionalization of industrial agriculture and the shift of land resources out of agriculture altogether and into other kinds of "culture" – aquaculture etc. is but a small part of this landscape of changes. The darker side of just these changes involves increasing rural poverty and immiseration, an epidemic of suicides amongst farmers across central South India and massive environmental degradation. These transformations are a small part of the increasing privatization of bio-resources on the one hand and the traffic in such resources across regions on the other. Our discussion of "approaches to understanding collective action on the commons" will be situated in the context of this landscape. One of the key questions that we raise in this chapter concerns these movements of resources – across sectors and regions. In so doing, the chapter builds on the spirit of the conversation proposed by the conveners.[3] The focus of our observations, however, will rest on the methodological problem of capturing these movements and the location of the commons *in the landscapes created by these movements*.

Alongside, it is also necessary to keep in view the transformed landscape of policy-making in India. The explosive growth of cities, for example, is a key factor accompanied by various kinds of "exchanges" and conversions of resources within an altered infrastructural economy. We argue that while the issue of the commons is certainly one about measuring the extent and nature of such resources, their use and their conservation/protection, it also contains within it, albeit spectrally, broader problematics of the relationship between resource distribution and management, collective identities and units of analysis. Moreover, the whole problem of the measurement of their extent and nature is itself tied up to this larger problematic, as the first example of the Telangana

---

[3]   The authors are referring to the "Conversations II" workshop held in Goa, India (August 2003).

village shows. The "commons," by their very nature, engage overlapping spatial and territorial formations, indeed create overlaps between communities and interests, between states and communities and so on. Thus, the best methods for understanding the social, cultural and collective implications of the commons might also turn out to be eclectic and diverse. We begin by briefly summarizing the relationships between disciplinary positions and ideas about and definitions of what constitutes the "commons," followed by some of specific methodological questions and conclude with a section focusing on the various factors that anthropologists need to address in order to account more fully for the transformations of the small-scale worlds in which they have typically worked. This section is thus not so much of a dialogue between anthropologists and other disciplines as a checklist of the factors that might impinge on what counts as properly anthropological constructs in the contemporary moment. It is hoped that further research along these lines will be helpful in opening up the dialogue between and across disciplines.

What's Common about the Commons?

Even a cursory look at the literature on the commons reveals an apparently extraordinary diversity of positions, definitions etc. While there are necessarily correspondences between disciplinary affiliations and intellectual positions (and even political positions) on what constitutes the commons, there are also intradisciplinary divergences. Especially considering the fertile climate that now exists for interdisciplinary methods, it is fairly common to find practitioners of one discipline espousing the methods or conclusions of another whilst challenging the dominant assumptions of their own disciplines. Yet worries about the limits of another's methods are also equally present: it is not uncommon, for example, for political scientists to call for more intensive "field-studies" of the kind that anthropologists are thought to undertake whilst at the same time worrying about how the data thus collected might be aggregated, collated with and corroborated against a range of other data sets and information obtained through other designs.[4] We suggest, in other words, that unlike in the 1980s, there may exist today, a greater ecumenical spirit in terms of the provenance and purchase of different kinds of "data."

Debates internal to various disciplines have, by now, produced factions within disciplines that apparently adhere to one or another side of binary oppositions, depending upon point of view, point of departure and desired terminus. Thus, there are ecologists for whom conservation is the central disciplinary problem and others who adopt a more "protectionist" stance. There are economists committed to market intervention and privatization of resources in the service of more efficient management of scarce resources while others are equally committed to inducing "cooperation" through incentives. Likewise, the question of the state as an active agent in carving out common and free

---

[4] See Chopra (2001) for an example of such ecumenical practice in relating different kinds of data and different conceptual frames to one another in her argument about measuring commons and "wastelands" at the national level.

access resources as "properties" of specific communities as against other, more local and more decentralized institutions of allocation and management of access has formed an important focus of internal distinctions within political ecology/political science. In anthropology, these problems have appeared closely tied to the problem of method and of units of analysis. In particular, the problem of defining the locus of community has been a preoccupation for anthropologists of South Asia for at least half a century.

The commons, and specifically the development of social movements around the protection and allocation of common resources have raised the question of the "natural" loci of community, collective action, shared meanings and interests. Whereas earlier seminal debates were conducted around the village as the "natural" unit of sociological and anthropological analysis, more recent work has complicated this analytic debate by suggesting that fieldwork can and should be undertaken at the "awkward" scale that exceeds villages but still focuses on the processes by which localities are produced (Appadurai 1996). We will turn to some empirical examples of field-sites constituted around common resources that raise questions about the very idea of what counts as a common resource a little further on.

For the moment, it is important to note that these debates and transformations within communities of academics and researchers are important to track precisely because of the implications that these positions and points of departure have for the policies that are produced around them. The relationship between massive state intervention and the publication of the *Tragedy of the Commons* in the late 1960s is now well known. As the conveners have pointed out, subsequent anthropological evidence "corrected" the assumption that the management of the commons could only be achieved through state regulation or other forms of external coercion by providing evidence around the hypothesis that communities had developed various practices and institutions for achieving the same ends. Yet in terms of possible policy implications, these conclusions have tended to operate sometimes with far too "romanticized" a notion of community, failing to take into account heterogeneity, complexity and the interests of the various actors involved. As Bonnie McCay, for example, has demonstrated, the question of what measures should be taken to protect or otherwise manage common resources are determined in part by the definitional frameworks that determine what counts as the "commons." In her reading of the history of policy, McCay makes the point that our theories and hypotheses themselves have an effect on the management of the commons when they become hegemonic paradigms in the framing of policies (see McCay and Acheson 1987).

However, while these issues are critical to bear in mind for any inter-disciplinary dialogue to bear fruit, a broader epistemological issue remains implicit in these broadly political arguments. This may be thought through in terms of the problem of measurement and information design and its effects on the constitution of our objects of inquiry and our conclusions. To put it more simply, before agreeing on action to be taken in regard to the Commons, it is also necessary to understand how we decide epistemologically what constitutes the Commons. In the following section, we pay particular attention to the distinction formulated by Appadurai in 1984, between distributional and relational analyses as we attempt to think the question of what's common about the commons from a specifically methodological angle. In the final section, we turn to some specific challenges facing anthropology and, by extension, its dialogue with the social sciences.

The Politics of Information Design: Anxieties and Opportunities

A central preoccupation of the earlier round of conversations[5] was the problem of measurement in all its dimensions: what was being measured, why it was being measured (or, how we decide on what was to be measured) and the interpretation of measurement. Appadurai makes the point that there fundamentally are two approaches to measurement, viz. those that focus on the distribution of outcomes and those that focus on the "relational dimension of the processes which lead to these outcomes." This argument is further tied to an observation that large-scale and aggregative techniques tend to be especially designed to measure the distribution of outcomes and lead to distributional analyses. Further, in these kinds of studies, there is also a basic assumption of the relationship between scale and the generalizability of the hypothesis. On the other hand, there are also genuine difficulties in aggregating a number of small-scale and intensive studies that tend to focus on relational dimensions and processes to arrive at large-scale generalizations. Problems with measurement reflect epistemological issues at the deepest levels, where there is no agreement about whether or not certain aspects of social life are even quantifiable.

In regard to the commons, we may have to include an additional methodological layer to this argument, having to do with information generation and the design of data sets in relation to one another to get a better handle on the issues. It is necessary to acknowledge – especially in regard to an object as self-evidently shaped by inter-connection and overlapping interests and groups – that there can emerge a form of research practice (not only among professionals but also among the "actors" themselves) that is not so much dependent upon primary data collection as upon constructing relationships between existing data sets of "information." Of course information is never neutral and is always permeated by the assumptions that lead to its production in the first place. Moreover, access to information differs significantly among groups, individuals and communities. Yet, the lengthening temporal horizon of the post-colonial state's practices of governmentality and the increasing penetration of various forms of media make available an archive of information, sometimes appearing to be "raw" but more often than not, evidently designing reality. This may, on occasion, lead to creative cross-cutting at the conceptual level, displaying a certain virtuosity in bringing together, for example, geographic information from the vantage of satellites together with legal regimes and data on economic opportunities. Such creativity is not uncommon in the worlds of environmental activism.

One notable example of this kind of flexible measure is the concept of the "Ecological Footprint," developed by Mathis Wakernagel and William Rees, a "planning tool" designed to "translate sustainability concerns into public action" (Wakernagel and Rees 1995). They explain it as follows: "The Ecological Footprint concept is simple, yet potentially comprehensive: it accounts for flows of energy and matter to and from any defined economy and converts these into the corresponding land/water area required from nature to support these flows. This technique is both analytical and educational. It not only assesses the sustainability of current human activities, but is also effective in building public awareness and assisting decision-making" (p. 3). What is precisely

---

[5] The reference here is to "Conversations I" in Bangalore.

interesting about this mensurational concept for our purposes here is that the concept is designed as a *popular* research tool, yet incorporates "scientifically" rigorous techniques and available "information."

In regard to anthropology in particular, the two sets of developments – first, the changes at the empirical level some of which we observed at the beginning of the chapter and second, the possibilities of the democratization of research practices through the increasing spread of the *means* of documentation – change the landscape within which our objects are constructed. What are the consequences of this transformation and why should they matter? In this concluding section, we will try to deepen this question further and suggest some possible avenues for further conversation.

Sizing up the Commons: Anthropological Subjects and Objects

As interpreted by Appadurai in 1984, the macro-micro dialectic across the social sciences might be characterized in multiple ways. He observes that economic measures of rural poverty were, by and large, characterized by an expansive, national geography while anthropological measures mapped micro-terrritories and micro-events. He suggests that the interpretation of micro-events of entitlement or failure of entitlement could lead, via *relational* analyses, to an expanding palette of explanatory possibilities. Conversely, economic analyses, despite focusing on the collection, aggregation, and standardization of large amounts of information (or by sampling across large amounts of data), ultimately work by using distributional patterns to *narrow* down the possible explanatory choices to the ones most frequently encountered and thereby more general. The relationship between scale and the generalizability of a proposition is therefore inverted in the two approaches. For this reason, anthropological anxieties have often centered on the question of the representativeness of the object of observation in relation to the object of inquiry.

There have been several lines of internal critique and debate, too many to list here (including the demonstration of an isomorphism between certain spatial productions, identity and cultural difference) which point to the possibilities of involution inherent in this approach. In particular, as anthropology's subjects become literally or figuratively mobile and unmoored from particular micro-territories, the scalar dimensions of the worlds they inhabit change in multiple ways. First, in terms of physical space itself, migration for work or pleasure or for participation in collective action maps out larger and larger terrains. This transforms the very scale of the geographies created by following relational processes. If earlier the coherence of the village as an agrarian economy depended upon demonstrating relations as close the village level as possible, now relational analyses routinely take global processes and their impacts on observational sites into account (see, for example, Gupta 1997).

Second, in terms of (re)designing information, expansive and indeed sometimes explosive scales of information availability also contribute to the transformation of the scale of social life at the level of the locality and indeed in distilling the "phenomenological" quality of locality from the swirl of representations via the social practice of the imagination (Appadurai 1996). These latter changes are beginning to have interesting repercussions for the already complex histories of interactions between state territorialities and local rights. On the one hand such "research" and design practices provide the ammunition for communities of interest to confront the state while on the other hand, the state's own practices of democratic decentralization in the matter of resource access and management could also have hidden and sinister implications for the survival and well-being of local communities.

A third level of scalar transformation pertains to new regimes of value and meaning within which common resources are now embedded. Such regimes enable the "conversion" of resources such as water and rivers from principally agricultural infrastructure to playing a crucial role in the spatial and cultural formatting of cities. A case in point are the events surrounding the sudden filling of the Sabarmati river, which had run dry for decades, in Ahmedabad city limits in August 2002.[6] This flooding effected the creation of a Hindu symbolic geography for the city closely connected to the BJP government's desires to re-format the city's cultural landscape. The re-filling of the river was in turn made possible by the construction of the Sardar Sarovar dam over the Narmada, a project conceived to harness the river's waters for multiple purposes, including provision of drinking water and irrigation. As is well known, the dam's construction led to one of the largest social and political protest movements in recent Indian history, which was squarely centered on making visible the exclusions that were being effected in so harnessing a common resource.

In an earlier moment, one of the key questions in the relationship between culture and economy was about the relationship between contracting relational scales at the geographic level to be consistent with the scale of the observer and the generalizability of the hypothesis. Today, we take the largeness of scale and the awkwardness of the angle at which it sits vis-à-vis the scale of the observer for granted and ask, instead, how can we read locality from this constant murmur of the global? Second, how do we factor in the relationship between empirical "facts," regimes of value and the availability of "information" to those whom we study? Often, the apparently spectral production and disappearance of common resources appears to be as closely tied to the ideologies and regimes of value as it is to empirical events of degradation creating the possibility of multiple explanatory chains vis-à-vis an apparently singular phenomenon. Finally, in all this, one of the singular challenges for anthropologists remains the possible disappearance of a central disciplinary value – viz. cultural diversity – under the weight of the tensions between the concerns of markets and exclusionary politics on the one hand and those of "development" on the other.

This appears as a key outcome of the culture–economy relationship, which in turn has been the central preoccupation of this chapter refracted through the particular lens of the commons. Why should this concern us? To conclude, we quote from Appadurai's essay (2002) on cultural diversity:

> Cultural diversity is the critical link between the intangible and the tangible dimensions of development. Tangible development can be measured in terms of human health, economic capabilities, commodity flows and physical guarantees of security and productivity. Intangible development consists of the spirit of participation, the enthusiasm of empowerment, the joys of recognition and the pleasures of aspiration. Although these intangible measures of development may seem obvious, overlooking them has often created massive

---

[6] For this example, Vyjayanthi Rao thanks architect Kanu Agrawal who has completed a master's thesis on the cultural politics of urban design in contemporary Ahmedabad at the Yale School of Architecture.

failures in the worldwide effort to develop poorer economies and transfer life-sustaining technologies. Cultural diversity provides the key link between these two crucial dimensions of development, themselves fundamentally indivisible, by guaranteeing the survival of multiple visions of the good life, and of a large range of ties between material and moral visions of well-being. Many development projects have failed because they have failed to make the link between these dimensions, or have tried to impose a single vision of human betterment and material well-being. (Appadurai 2002)

Crucial to this interpretation of cultural diversity is the possibility of a method versatile enough to follow the multiple threads of data streams to create more diverse relational pictures. We began by questioning the self-evidence of the commons as an open and freely accessible resource and asked what constitutes the commons *as* being in common (or not). In other words, our analysis did not start with a "measurement" issue while assuming that the commons are self-evidently those resources that support the poor, although they have the potential to do so. As we have stressed throughout, the issue of the commons and the production, deployment, disappearance and re-creation of the commons (each of which we take not to be self-evident) both as an empirical event in various local contexts as well as a discursive event, is a crucial site for raising the key questions of anthropology as well, concerning cultural diversity, rather than cultural identity and its politics. The politics of cultural identity tend to operate with a romantic notion of community while the notion of cultural diversity leaves open the tie between creativity in designs for living and the "natural" boundaries of groups producing those designs. This aspect emerges especially clearly in the focus on the contemporary conditions under which we conceptualize and deal with the commons. We hope that in focusing on cultural diversity in relation to the commons in this manner, we have opened up at least some space for a dialogue across disciplines.

References

Appadurai, Arjun, 1989. "Small-scale Techniques and Large-scale Objectives," in P. Bardhan (ed.), *Conversations between Economists and Anthropologists*. New Delhi: Oxford University Press, 250–82.

Appadurai, Arjun, 1996. *Modernity at Large*. Minneapolis: University of Minnesota Press.

Appadurai, Arjun, 2002. "Cultural Diversity: A Conceptual Platform," *UNESCO Declaration on Cultural Diversity*, Cultural Diversity Series 1. Paris: UNESCO.

Chopra, Kanchan, 2001. "Wastelands and Common Property Land Resources." *Seminar* 499. New Delhi, March.

McCay, Bonnie and Acheson, James M. (eds), 1987. *The Question of the Commons: The Culture and Ecology of Communal Resources*. Tuscon: University of Arizona Press.

Rao, Vyjayanthi, 2002. "Ruins and Recollections: On the Subjects of Displacement." Dissertation submitted to the University of Chicago.

Wackernagel, Mathis and Rees, William E. (eds), 1996. *Our Ecological Footprint: Reducing Human Impact on the Earth*. Ilustrated by Phil Testemale. Gabriola Island, BC; Philadelphia, PA: New Society Publishers.

10: Symbolic Public Goods and the Coordination of Collective Action

A Comparison of Local Development in India and Indonesia

Vijayendra Rao

Symbolic Public Goods

Most economists think of common property as physical – a plot of land, a body of water, a forest – and as bounded within geographic space. In this chapter, building on work in social theory, I argue that common property can also be social – defined within symbolic space.[1] People can be bound by well defined social circles, creating agglomerations that have characteristics similar to common property. I call these circles and agglomerations "symbolic public goods" and make the case that such constructs are central to understanding collective action. Typically, when anthropologists discuss the functioning of CPRs, they contrast indigenous, local, meanings with routinizing state-level bureaucratic apparatuses, which circulate at the national and transnational level. However, national-level symbolic institutions can also percolate downward – shifting local constructions of identity and social organization and changing the incentives for collective behavior. As development policy becomes increasingly decentralized, this "production of locality" (Appadurai 1997) plays a central role in shaping the institutions of decentralization. Thus symbols can have important tangible, material outcomes. The point is illustrated by a comparative analysis of constructions of nationalism in India and Indonesia, and the significant impact that they have had on local development and public service delivery.

Economists and social theorists think very differently about collective action.[2] Economists, at least since Olson (1965), have believed that when individuals make

---

[1] I am attempting here to inform economists' notions of public goods and "signaling" with the work of social theorists such as Arjun Appadurai and Pierre Bourdieu, who locate economic action within social and cultural arenas, to achieve a better understanding of collective behavior. In doing so I also rely on Michael Suk-Young Chwe's recent attempts to bring game theoretic notions to bear on social theory.

[2] See Bardhan and Ray (ch. 1, this volume) and Rao and Walton (2004) for more on this divide and ways to bridge it.

decisions about whether to participate in collective activities, a reasonable approximation of how these decisions are made can be provided by rational choice models of materially driven individual behavior. Typically, economic models focus on the costs and benefits of participation: How large a share of the collective good will the agent obtain by participating? Is it worth the loss in income and time? The power of game theory is then applied to examine how these choices are made strategically with others in the group. Such models can result in a range of outcomes, from Olson's "free-rider problem" to Hardin's "tragedy of the commons," with the cards stacked against reaching an efficient outcome.

Later scholars, such as Ostrom (1990), have tried to correct this. Basing themselves on field observations that demonstrate the success of collective action in a variety of settings, they allow for social institutions which generate norms, impose sanctions and improve the incentives for collective action. Usually, these scholars have incorporated socially derived incentives that affect individual choices by explicitly modeling the sanctions that are imposed by communities, or/and have incorporated the effects of "social norms" directly into the preference set.

A second approach followed by economists who incorporate social effects has made the models dynamic, allowing for repeated interactions with the same group of actors. Under these circumstances, individuals have to consider how their behavior today may generate a reaction by others in their community tomorrow. So long as individuals value payoffs in the future more than payoffs today, and expect to interact on a regular basis, cooperative outcomes will ensue, and these may become "habit forming" (e.g. Seabright 1997; Bardhan and Dayton-Johnson 2002).

A third approach looks at the evolution of norms of cooperation (e.g. Sethi and Somanathan 1999). Under certain circumstances, societies may evolve so as to select individuals who have a strong desire for collective activity, weeding out "mutants" who are more narrowly self-interested. This provides an explanation of why norms of communal living may be internalized in some societies. The logic here is Spencerian – the core value is consumption, everyone is maximizing their economic welfare, and those who do this inefficiently are eliminated.[3]

Much of social theory follows a more collectivist logic, emphasizing views derived from Durkheim rather than Spencer, and in some ways all of it is about group action – though not necessarily about collective action in the strict sense. Communities can "think" (Douglas 1986). Social norms, identity, "culture," etc. are collectively determined – with individuals, subservient to the collective will, tied into the larger goals of the potlatch. This finds its ultimate expression in the structuralism of Lévi-Strauss, who emphasizes meaningful communication in trying to uncover the linguistic and symbolic structures that facilitate human interaction within society. A parallel stream of thinking, initiated by Weber, emphasizes the role of history, social organization, and what economists call "path dependency," i.e. considering a broader set of motives than those focused narrowly on consumption. Talcott Parsons (it is interesting to note that both Weber and Parsons were originally trained as economists) attempted to integrate Durkheim and Weber by carving out a role for individual agency within this larger structural frame, and this has been taken by Geertz and others into the realm of symbolic anthropology. Here, the goal is to uncover

---

[3]   See Baland and Platteau (2003) for a review of the literature on the role of institutions in collective action.

the inner symbolic logic of cultures and communities: to understand via "thick description" the strategies that are used to make up the economic and symbolic exchanges that create a meaningful community.

Another movement integrating structure and agency is Bourdieu's notion of practice theory, which focuses more on "what people do rather than what they say." The idea here is to see how human action is embedded within a general realm of *habitus* – the set of durable principles – practices, beliefs, taboos, rules, representations, rituals, symbols, etc. that provide a group of individuals with a sense of group identity and a consequent feeling of security and belonging.[4] For Bourdieu, cultural markers within habitus, provide a way of classifying hierarchal relationships between groups – not only classifying *other groups*, but for members of a group to differentiate *themselves from others*. By positioning a group within the social hierarchy, culture affects the sense of the possible. For those at the high end of the hierarchy, it provides the means to maintain their high position; while for those at the low end it limits aspirations, creates discrimination, and blocks mobility. Bourdieu argues, therefore, that culture is a form of capital and situates symbolic action in the center of the struggle for power and domination within groups.

This divide between economic and social theory provides an entry point for this chapter. Economists emphasize material rationality and methodological individualism, and social theorists, as methodological holists, tend to be far more concerned with how social organization is structured and contested.

Recent work by economists has attempted to bridge this divide. An important effort is the work of Michael Suk-Young Chwe (1999; 2001), which demonstrates how collective action has to distinguish between *structure* and *strategy*. Chwe's basic argument goes as follows: Most models of collective action assume, implicitly, some pre-existent "common knowledge."[5] That is, when a group of individuals plays a collective action game, whether static or dynamic, it is assumed that individual A knows the payoffs, information sets, costs, incentives, possible moves, etc. faced by individual B. Individual B, in turn, knows all this about individual A, and further knows that individual A knows everything about individual B. Individual A, in turn, knows that individual B knows that individual A knows, and so on. This common knowledge assumption then permits games of strategy to be played with a common understanding of the rules of the game – everyone knows what everyone else is playing. For instance, a cricket player persuaded to play baseball will be quickly confused – enough to not be able to understand or appreciate the skill, strategy, and actions of the other players. It is this aspect of coordination and common understanding that common knowledge attempts to capture – it plays a coordinating function that is a precondition for collective activity and collective cannot occur in its absence. Common knowledge is arguably the core concept behind such amorphous notions such as "social capital" which figure prominently in the discourse on development collective action, and have come under some criticism (Mosse: ch. 5, this volume).

---

[4]   This is my imperfect account of Bourdieu's definition of *habitus*: "a system of durable, transposable dispositions . . . principles which generate and organize practices and representations that can be objectively adapted to their outcomes without presupposing a conscious aiming at ends or an express mastery of the operations necessary in order to attain them" (Bourdieu 1990; 1998).
[5]   Also see Bardhan (1993) on this point.

Chwe goes even further, arguing that much of what we call "culture" is about the generation of common knowledge (Chwe 2001) – about turning "weak" ties into "strong" ones (Granovetter 1973). Public rituals, sites and events, such as festivals, celebrations, churches, temples, even the Olympic Games, help people to build a sense of community. In this sense, Chwe is simply borrowing from symbolic anthropology. Victor Turner (1982), for instance, describes festivals as "generally connected with expectable culturally shared events." He suggests that when a social group celebrates a particular event it "celebrates itself" by "manifesting in symbolic form what it conceives to be its essential life." Thus, festivals and other such shared collective things serve to build social cohesion by reinforcing ties within a community. David Mosse (1997), in work examining the management of common property resources in Tamil Nadu, makes a similar point.[6] He argues that both symbolic and material interests matter in collective action, and that "Tanks, like village temples, are public institutions expressive of social relations, status, prestige and honor." They are not only physical inputs but also "repositories of symbolic resources."

Thus, in order to understand collective action it is crucial to understand its social context via the common knowledge generating processes that underlie it. Yet such processes are themselves the product of strategy and contestation. They can take a variety of forms – Intangible processes of identity formation such as "nationalism," physical entities like mosques and temples, and periodic ritual events like festivals. All these share characteristics of public goods – in the sense that they can be simultaneously "non-rival," or capable of being simultaneously "consumed" by many individuals; and sometimes "non-excludable," wherein it is not possible to deny anyone access to the good. For these reasons, I will call all such goods *symbolic public goods*." There are important cases where excludability may be built into the consumption of the good, in which case they might more accurately be described as club goods.

An important function of symbolic public goods (henceforth SPGs) is coordination – to generate common knowledge. There are all manner of public goods and activities that serve this purpose, and many have both symbolic and material functions. This is true in particular of common property resources, which serve an important material purpose but are also often sacred spaces or symbols of royal or colonial power. But separating these functions permits the identification of two linked but separate sources of strategic behavior. Some public goods – such as village festivals – may be more uniform in their symbolic function, while others, such as a clinic or a school, may be more hybrid. I will, therefore, call public goods that have a primarily symbolic function "uniform;" and those that have a mixed function "hybrid." "Pure" might have been a better adjective than "uniform," but it could be confused with the "pure" in "pure public goods," the latter being completely non-rival and non-excludable. Therefore, SPGs may be either uniform or hybrid and, at the same time, pure or impure. All are, I would argue, essential to an understanding of the role of "community" in collective action.

Such SPGs are often repositories of memory and identity – testaments to major binding events in the community. In this sense they may be closely linked to the evolution of social norms and may serve as the symbolic embodiment of those norms – i.e. the public acknowledgement of a shared perspective. Norms need reinforcement mechanisms.

---

[6]   See also Mosse (ch. 5, this volume).

Identity is not some fixed and exogenously provided entity which people either choose or inherit, as economic models tend to assume (e.g. Akerlof and Kranton 2000). It represents strategic interactions within a community that are usually embedded within SPGs. A feeling of kinship or commonality with another person needs to be expressed and reinforced in concrete ways in order to be stable. This could happen via reciprocal gifts when only two people are involved, or, when the size of the network increases and gifts are not enough – it needs a potlatch – a whole system of gift exchanges with coded and structured meanings may come into being. When such a system of exchange serves a purely material purpose within, for example, an expanding economy, it will quickly transit into a market-based system (e.g. Kranton 1996). However, communities cannot exist in the absence of common knowledge and the exchanges could also be purely symbolic – strengthening networks and establishing "trust." When the network becomes dense enough via intensified interaction, or becomes large enough via increased membership size – systems of reciprocity become embodied within SPGs which serve as repositories of collective identity and historical memory.

Communities are not, of course, always formed through tedious evolutionary processes. They can be created far more quickly. A major exogenous event – e.g. a terrible famine or a devastating war – can bring people together to cope with the hardship that ensues. A church or temple may be built to mark the event, an annual commemoration or celebration which serves to reinforce a group's sense of community may be instituted. SPGs thus play an important role in establishing the structures and rituals that help define collective identity. In a stable equilibrium they define the "conjuncture"[7] of social life and are associated with what Appadurai (1997) calls "pragmatic" rituals that help reproduce and reify communities. But, as Appadurai argues, it would be a mistake to view this in a static context because communities themselves can be "produced." Shifts in the relative power of groups, or in information technologies, or in the nature of the state can result in the formation of new SPGs that compete with existing forms to establish new circles of power. So, SPGs may be the result of endogenous decisions and their construction a potent method of rallying people into a movement by forming a dense, cohesive network. This is particularly true when the value signaled by the SPG resonates deeply with a large enough group of people. Several examples come to mind: consider for example the calculated imitation of classical Roman martial rituals and architecture symbolically used by the Nazi party to express nationalist imperial pride (Burleigh 2000), or the construction of the Petronas towers in Kuala Lampur in the heyday of the East Asian "miracle." In more micro settings, the construction of large and flashy churches by evangelical American Protestants in certain poor areas of developing countries serve as potent symbols associating a religion with the promise of wealth and mobility.

In other words, SPGs are not only symbols of established power, they can be volleys shot in an attempt to acquire power. The (sometimes literal) construction of a SPG results in the symbolic construction of a community, and this process of construction generates power by establishing control over a body of people. Power is not only acquired by constructing a new SPG, it can also be the result of power dynamics within it. Moving up

---

[7]   This is a crude inversion of Alfred Marshall's use of this word to describe the social context of economic behavior.

or down in the hierarchy of an SPG's power structure is closely associated with status mobility. Thus, SPGs can result in publicly observable competitive expenditures that can be quite substantial – for instance in the celebration of temple festivals (Rao 2001). As in a competitive potlatch, this can sometimes be a sustaining equilibrium wherein a high level of expenditure on symbolic activities is essential to maintain status within the community. Thus, games of social status may be symbolically acted upon with actions involving public or club goods (Basu 1989; Bloch, Rao, and Desai 2004). Not all communities may be centered on one SPG. Just as identities can be varied and overlapping, so can communities and their binding symbols. And nor do only individuals compete for status within the context of one SPG: the same village may have competing sources of symbolic power and social status. SPGs can, in this way, prove to serve as the fulcrum around which endogenous coalitions of individuals are formed within a community.

SPGs can, as is obvious from the discussion above, both unite and divide. A well defined geographic area can have several intersecting SPGs within it. These can in turn sometimes cooperate and sometimes compete to create a logic of overlapping communities and identities. A village, for instance, may be a "community" in one sense with SPGs – common land, a well, a post-office – that span its population cohesively and thus help define a space of common knowledge within which individuals act. But these individuals may also be subdivided into several other communities – for instance, by religion. Consider a village with Hindus and Muslims, with their associated SPGs (temples and mosques) and rituals. The Hindus may themselves be subdivided by caste and become identified by caste-specific SPGs (e.g. caste associations, caste-specific wells and shrines), and the Muslims by different types of mosques (e.g. an old mosque constructed by a long-forgotten zamindar, newer mosques constructed by newly wealthy and radicalized migrants to the Gulf).

SPGs are, in these ways, centrally related to the acquisition and maintenance of power. And the actions that involve the creation or construction of a new SPG can be potent signals of a new power dynamic. But sometimes the publicly observable destruction of a SPG serves as a signal for the formation of a new one: think of the symbolic destruction of the Babri Masjid and its effectiveness as the signal of a new, muscular Hindu nationalism; or the World Trade Center. Thus, in situations of asymmetric information, such as when a new and relatively unknown group wants to communicate a shift in its political intentions, or when a newly wealthy family wants to demonstrate its wealth and thus use its new-found economic status to acquire social leverage, the construction (or destruction) of an SPG can serve as a very effective signal.

While SPGs are collectively defined, strategy and contestation within them depend on individual agency. But individuals can also drive *resistance* to them: if the control of an SPG is indicative of elite status, less powerful individuals who have reason to disagree or oppose such elites (but who do not have the physical and symbolic resources to create competing SPGs) may react with what Scott (1995) calls "weapons of the weak." Instead of abiding by the rituals of SPG participation, they may "foot-drag," abscond, hide, and otherwise decline to participate in a manner both subversive and less than overt. Such resistance too can help define a community of the disenfranchised via its relatively invisible rituals and symbols.

For instance, in Suharto's "New Order" Indonesia, young women often expressed their opposition to his dictatorial authority – which was for a long time dedicated to obstructing organized Islam – by covering their heads with a *jilbab* (*hijab*), causing this headgear to become a fashionable symbol of resistance to Suharto's rule (Hefner 2000).

Conversely, women in Iran often wear designer clothes and make-up under the *chadors* imposed upon them by Islamic authorities. Such covert forms of resistance can lead to social movements – in Indonesia wearing the *jilbab* became a symbol of the pro-democracy movement that ultimately led to Suharto's resignation; and the sartorial resistance in Iran could well augur a similar result. Note that when the rules and rituals of SPGs are blatantly and overtly violated, this can – as with SPG destruction – be a signal of power. The satyagraha movement in India used symbolic resistance against SPGs associated with British rule as a central element of its strategy. And the South Indian sandalwood smuggler Veerapan's legend was built on his ability to blatantly violate conservation laws while eluding the police.

In short, as much as SPGs "create" communities, they do not supplant or suppress individual agency. In fact, individual action plays an important role in how SPGs are strategically positioned, interpreted, and consumed.

I will now briefly illustrate the salience of SPGs by comparing the very different local development and decentralization strategies followed by India and Indonesia. Data for this comes from several rounds of fieldwork, collaboratively conducted with several co-authors, in Java, Kalimantan, Sulawesi, Karnataka, Kerala, Andhra Pradesh, and Tamil Nadu over several rounds since 2002.[8]

Links to Local Development

Development is fast decentralizing and development agencies and government are increasingly relying on the presumed power of collective action to increase "voice" and equitably deliver public services (Bardhan 2002). The "Community Driven Development" (CDD) portfolio of the World Bank for instance has risen from $250 million since the mid-1990s to more than seven billion dollars today. Much of the justification for this has come from the premise that tapping into a community's "social capital" is "empowering" for the poor. Critics have contended that this emphasis on community development can result in the capture of resources by elites (Abraham and Platteau 2004), which has led to an increased focus on the role of inequality on collective action (Bardhan and Mukherjee 2003; Bardhan and Dayton-Johnson 2002).

Other critics have begun to ask what "participation" really means and whether "participatory development" is, in fact, leading to the empowerment of the poor (Mosse 2001; Mansuri and Rao 2004). A crucial issue here is not just inequality of wealth in a community, but social heterogeneity and the consequent inequality in power (Abraham and Platteau 2004). The empirical evidence on the impact of social heterogeneity is mixed, with the evidence suggesting that it is bad, irrelevant, or even good for collective action (Mansuri and Rao 2004). The role of heterogeneity and inequality in collective action, and the extent to which community-based approaches are truly participatory and empowering, depends crucially on how well collective action is coordinated. This requires an understanding of the critical role of SPGs, the distribution of status and power within the

---

[8]   My co-investigators in Indonesia are Vivi Alatas, Victoria Beard, and Menno Pradhan. In India they are Radu Ban, Tim Besley, Monica Dasgupta, and Rohini Pande.

village and communities that they represent, and the distribution of control within them. The relative impact of inequality and social heterogeneity may work via the mediating influence of SPGs.

India and Indonesia are both culturally and geographically diverse countries that achieved independence within two years of each other. They have had centuries of social and economic exchange. They have important cultural similarities. Yet they have followed very different strategies of political and economic development, with Indonesia turning increasingly autocratic soon after independence – till its turn towards democracy at the end of the Suharto era in 1998. India, on the other hand, has been a stable democracy since its independence, with a vigorously independent election commission. Both countries have begun to increasingly decentralize since the 1990s, with Indonesia devolving powers to state and district governments, and India doing the same to village and district panchayats (governing councils) which are elected.

Both countries have survived ups and downs in their economies, but as of 2001 their per capita incomes were very close with India's at PPP $2,570, compared to PPP $2,990 in Indonesia.[9] Yet Indonesia has been far more successful in providing public services to the poor. One indicator of this is that while 76 percent of children complete primary school in India, 91 percent complete it in Indonesia, even though India spends 7.2 percent of its GNP on primary education, while Indonesia spends only 3.2 percent. Such stark differences in human development indicators occur for health as well, with India spending 0.9 percent of GNP on health while Indonesia spends 0.6 percent, yet India's under-5 mortality rate is 93 and Indonesia's is 45. Indonesia has therefore not only been more effective at providing public services, it has also been far more efficient. What accounts for this stark difference in performance? I argue below that SPGs have played an important role.

Collective Action and Community Development in Indonesia

Any discussion of Indonesian society has to start with the research of Geertz and his monumental work, *The Religion of Java*, which laid out many of the themes that have played a central role in understandings of Javanese culture. Geertz's writings may have even shaped how Indonesia's nationalism, with its strong Javanese flavor, has been articulated and imagined.

Geertz outlined several competing categories of groups, ideologies, and cultures within rural Javanese society. The first was the existence of three major sub-traditions – the Abangan – who are nominally Muslim but stress a more traditional form of Javanese religion consisting of rituals such as the *slametan* – more on this later – spirit beliefs, magic and sorcery. Next, the Santri – pious Muslims who tended to be the more wealthy traders who identified with the ulema and so emphasize pilgrimage to Mecca, prayers, the Fast, and such things. And finally the Prijaji, upper-class Javanese who derive their identity from Hindu–Javanese courts of the pre-colonial period, and who identify with the Ramayana, the Mahabharata, and other traditions that derive from Hinduism and Buddhism.

---

[9]   All data in this paragraph are from the World Development Report 2004.

Geertz's village was defined by interactions between these groups and the sub-groups within them. For instance the Santri were further subdivided into Mohamadiyas, who were Islamic reformists intent on modernist social change while keeping within Islamic traditions; and the more conservative Nahdatul Ulama (NU), who believed in establishing a political presence for Islam within Indonesia while connecting to the larger Islamic world. Neither, however, were Wahhabi. They represented a more civil version of Islam derived from Indian (primarily Gujarati) traders who had introduced the religion to Indonesia.

Applying the idea of SPGs to these groups and assessing their implications for collective activity, we should first note that the Prijaji barely figure in the politics of Geertz's village, where the primary action is between the Abangan, Mohamadiyas, and NUs. The Abangan's main SPG is the tradition of the *slametan* – a ritual where a group of people (almost always male heads of households) get together to sanctify an auspicious event – a birth, a funeral, etc., where, typically, a village elder recites some religious (Koranic) versus, others make ritualized speeches, and a meal is begun but not completed (people take the food home and consume it later). *Slametans* are required for so many activities that there is a reciprocity associated with them. One has to belong to the *slametan* circuit to belong to the community, and this can be a very expensive proposition.

The Santris, on the other hand, socialize primarily through prayer meetings and Koran reading groups. To quote Geertz: "For the santri, the sense of community – of *ummat* – is primary. Islam is seen as a set of concentric social circles, wider and wider communities – spreading away from the individual *santri* where he stands: a great society of equal believers constantly repeating the name of Prophet, going through the prayers, chanting the Koran."

The Islamic community is centered around mosques and prayer groups. Santris in Geertz's reading of his village, were the globalized community. Links via commerce and religion connected them closely to the world outside the village. They were also – via the Mohamadiya – the modernizers; and, via the NU, the democratizers. The NU were themselves in conflict with the Mohamidiya. They were far more keen to modernize the education system and force Indonesia into the modern world, but wary of direct political engagement.

Geertz's interpretation of rural Javanese life has been refined somewhat by more recent scholarship. In particular, anthropologists (Beatty 1999) have argued that the Santri do not represent a subtradition as much as a smaller group within a larger Islamic world; and that the *slametan* is not a pre-Islamic ritual but is based much more on Sufi traditions within Islam (Woodward 1988). The division, it is argued, is not between Abangan and Santri but between Kejawen (the pre-Islamic Javanese culture which subsumes both Abangan and Prijaji) and the more recent Islamicizing trends personified by the Santri. Since almost everyone in Java is Muslim, this is really a subdivision within Islam, and not really a chasm between Islam and other traditions.

Post-colonial Indonesia was dominated by upper-class Muslim Prijaji and its history in the decades following independence can be seen as being primarily about the "Javanization" of the country (Ricklefs 2001). The ideological basis of Javanese or Kejawen belief is that social interaction is "collective, consensual and cooperative,"[10] as

---

[10]   Bowen (1986: 545).

exemplified by the *slametan*. Bowen (1986) argues, in an important article, that much of this is expressed in the term *gotong royong* or mutual assistance. This term has become the framework for Indonesian nationalism and the basis for construction of a national tradition. Sukarno, the "father" of Indonesia, attempted to use the notion to unify the diverse Islamic, non-Islamic, Nationalist and Communist groups in the new country by calling for a spirit of *ke gotong royong* (or *gotong royong*-ness). *Gotong royong* provided a form of cultural legitimacy to state control.

With Sukarno's ouster in a coup in 1967, his successor Suharto's "New Order" economic policy had, especially in its initial phases, a two-pronged strategy – to lay policies in place that would enable high rates of growth, and to pass on the benefits of that growth to the rural poor. Part of the reason for this was a genuine desire on Suharto's part to help the rural poor – he saw himself as a son of farmers – but it was also part of a calculated strategy to minimize the influence of the left, whose rise had been tolerated by Sukarno but which Suharto was determined to suppress (Hefner 2000). An important element in this strategy was to dictatorially force the spirit of *gotong royong* into hamlets and villages around the country. *Gotong royong* became a key element in strategies for developmental interventions in rural areas, and particularly in the mobilization of rural labor. In order to protect the political and cultural unity of the Indonesian state, it had to be strongly authoritarian, and development had to proceed in a cooperative and collaborative manner. By the early 1970s the term *gotong royong* had been complemented by the Sanskrit word *svadaya* or self-help and mobilizing *svadaya gotong royong* was central to the implementation of development policy (Bowen 1986).

As Sullivan (1992) demonstrates in his detailed ethnography of local development in a Javanese community, the combination of an autocratic state and the principle of *svadaya* resulted in a form of forced labor. In order to be a good Indonesian, one had to contribute labor and cash for development projects. Collective action was the norm, not the exception. It was very straightforward to mobilize: grants received by the village headman (*kepala desa*) were low because they assumed that the mismatch between the size of the funds and the expected cost of the proposed project would be locally mobilized. The headman whipped up contributions from the community which were actively mobilized by ward leaders – *kepala dusun* in rural areas, *RW/RT* in urban areas. Everyone was expected to contribute free labor – otherwise people felt they could easily be labeled unpatriotic or uncooperative and consequently face social, political, material and even physical sanctions. It is never wise, in a dictatorship, to disobey the wishes of the dictator – and decentralization in pre-*reformasi* Indonesia was essentially a set of concentric circles of dictatorial rule justified by appealing to a sense of forging a strong Indonesia united by the beliefs of *gotong royong* and *svadaya*. There was no choice except to participate. Bowen and Sullivan both point out that this model had much more to do with patterns established during the Japanese occupation of Indonesia than traditional Javanese traditions.

In this manner, nationalism was the symbolic public good constructed by Indonesian political leaders, deploying "imagined" traditional beliefs that made the individual subservient to the community. It is not surprising that Benedict Anderson conceived of "imagined communities" largely from his deep understanding of Indonesian history (Anderson 1991). Since most of this was undertaken in the context of a military dictatorship – there being not much room for individuals to dissent – it laid the foundation for the coordination of collective action.

Suharto's two-pronged strategy had spectacular results for over two decades, with very high rates of growth and substantial improvements in the living standards of the poor. As we have seen, these improvements in living standards were achieved in a cost-effective way by, in effect, taxing the poor in the name of community participation. In other words, under Suharto's dictatorial rule there was a suppression of freedom, an implicitly regressive tax structure, but also, relative to India, excellent consequences for human development. There was also a sharp increase in corruption and cronyism, and, ultimately, this led to the creation of an economy based on shaky macro-economic foundations. The East Asian crises which started in 1997 shored up anti-Suharto and pro-democracy forces in Indonesia, leading to his ouster in 1998 and to the emergence of a democratic order which has culminated in the subsequent political defeat of Sukarno's daughter Megawati Sukarnoputri.[11]

Along with democracy has come a concerted effort to decentralize the political and fiscal authority of state and district governments. At the village level, this has had several implications for SPGs. The authority of the *kepala desas* and *lurahs* is increasingly questioned. But, as recent survey data demonstrates, the spirit of *gotong royong* has by no means disappeared. Rather, it has been so deeply institutionalized that not abiding by it is sensed by people as a violation of a communitarian ethic, which remains even now part of the foundation of what it means to be a good Indonesian. A recent survey shows that levels of participation in public goods construction remains high at 47 percent, and 59 percent of respondents say that they participate primarily because of "tradition" or "obligation." This has real consequences – 37 percent of the cost of village public goods are contributed by the community, with 60 percent coming from the government.[12]

However, life is far less dictatorial now, and other important political players have emerged to compete with state authority. Much of this can be seen in the profusion of mosques all over the countryside – some with shiny stainless steel domes, others painted blue or white, some with particularly large loudspeakers attached to their minarets,[13] others, more traditional, made of stone and brick with large tree-lined courtyards. As Hefner (2000) shows, much of the resistance to Suharto was led by Islamic groups – in particular by NU and the Mohamediya. To compete with these movements, Suharto attempted to create a "regimist Islam" with state-funded mosques staffed by government employees belonging to the Ministry of Religion. Often, all three types – NU mosques, Mohamediya mosques and "Golkar"[14] mosques – exist in Indonesian villages, with competing spheres of authority. In addition, immigrants to Malaysia or the Gulf signal their new-found wealth by building their own mosques. And neighborhoods get together sometimes to construct community mosques – which are usually more in the nature of small prayer rooms. Even though these are physical entities, they symbolize different symbolic spaces

---

[11]   Her first name was given her by an Indian – Biju Patnaik a close friend of Sukarno. Patnaik had participated in Indonesia's war of independence as a fighter pilot, and went on to become one of India's most prominent and colorful politicians.

[12]   All data from UPP2 Evaluation baseline survey 2004.

[13]   Some Imams are particularly proud of their loudspeakers. I went to interview one in an empty but large mosque in the middle of the afternoon. The Imam insisted on conducting the entire interview – which was mainly about the role of the mosque in local development activities – speaking directly into the live microphone, presumably to demonstrate to the neighborhood that he was important enough to be interviewed by a World Bank official.

[14]   Golkar was Suharto's political party. It remains an important force in Indonesia.

– political alignments, religious differences, and even personal conflicts. Mosque prayer groups are often the site of development activity – arenas where the beneficiaries of targeted programs are decided about or where a new project that requires volunteer work is publicized. Mosques are also, often, the site of political activity, attracting charismatic speakers who attempt to mobilize their flock towards one political position or another.[15] In addition to such religiously driven SPGs, there are alternative sources of secular authority. These include NGO-driven credit circles, women's groups, and governing councils associated with different development schemes that are specially designed to counter traditional government authority structures with more decentralized and accountable institutions.

Interestingly, donor agencies – particularly the World Bank – in a radical departure from practice, have structured some of their Indonesia assistance in a manner that takes cognizance of SPGs. This was done consciously via a series of Local Level Institution studies that attempted to measure the level of "social capital" in Indonesia. In effect, these surveys (not unsurprisingly) uncovered the extent to which *svadya gotong royong* played a role in the life of Indonesian communities. Legitimized by this, there was a conscious attempt to design projects that tried to steer community participation in a less dictatorial and more accountable direction via the multi-million dollar World Bank-assisted rural-focused Kecamatan Development Project (along with Urban Poverty Project, its urban counterpart: see Guggenheim 2005) that journalists have lauded as "stars" of the World Bank's portfolio (Mallaby 2004). While previous projects had attempted to build on participatory institutions, they had largely placed authority in the hands of local officials and thus worked within the institutional confines of the New Order regime – with the associated negative externalities of corruption, cronyism and graft. KDP's logic was to attempt to retain the spirit of *svadaya gotong royong* but create new spheres of authority within SPGs who were more associated with reform: such as elected village committees and watchdogs drawn from local journalists and NGO workers.[16] Thus, an SPG optic was consciously employed to remake the approach of local development so that it was better aligned with the spirit of the Indonesian reform movement. This represents an important attempt to make development more ethnographically informed and place the design of interventions squarely within cultural contexts.[17]

This style of development works because it has a long-term horizon, careful monitoring, constant learning by doing, all of which go against the myopia inherent within old-style development. Old style development is technocratic: predicated on excessive reliance on a "model" – either based on a "best-practice" framework (a project design that worked wonders in one place would have the same impact another), or on methodologically individualist rational-choice modeling that is totally ignorant of symbolic,

---

[15] Note that while I am focusing on divisions within Islam, in some parts of Indonesia churches, both Catholic and Protestant, may also play a role, and in other parts Hindu temples and Buddhist viharas may provide alternative sources of authority.

[16] A quantitative analysis of the LLI data show that a household's participation in village government SPGs has an adverse effect on the voice and participation of neighboring households – demonstrating the "chilling" effect of SPGs that have their origins in the New Order (Alatas, Pritchett, and Wetterberg 2002).

[17] Not surprisingly, KDP's founding "task manager," Scott Guggenheim, was trained as an anthropologist. He has a written a fascinating account of KDP's origins, its struggles, and current mode of operation (Guggenheim 2005).

social and cultural logic. Bringing in an SPG optic reveals the real challenge of development, its role as an agent of cultural and political change. Dealing with these challenges,
which have always been present but rarely confronted, requires a new way of doing
development that is more decentralized, more difficult, more honest, and – arguably –
more sustainable.[18]

Democracy and Local Development in India

India's nationalist SPG is rather different, and so is its experience with local development.
Unlike Indonesia its democratic roots date back at least to the Montagu-Chelmsford
reforms of 1919 (which provided for regular elections to governing bodies and the
federal, state and local levels), and to the consequent creation of political parties competing for political power. Also, unlike Indonesia, India's struggle for independence
was dominated by Gandhi's nonviolent satyagraha movement. Armed resistance, while
symbolically important, was never at the center of power.[19] Despite the trauma surrounding
the partition of British India into India and Pakistan, when India achieved independence
in 1947 the army was subservient to political authority. The Indian constitution, written
by lawyers trained in the US and UK, was predicated on making India a "sovereign, social-
ist, secular, democratic republic."[20] India's first prime minister Jawaharlal Nehru, was deeply
influenced by Soviet models of development, but was also a democrat to the core. In Nehru's
India, as in Sukarno's Indonesia, state action was the key, and included centralized planning to promote economic growth and equitable development. But Gandhi held deeply
held beliefs that the key to India's problems lay in village *swaraj* – village self-rule (Gandhi
1962), i.e. in devolving power to autonomous village councils and making them self-sufficient.
The parallels with *svadaya gotong royong* are obvious and not necessarily coincidental.

In India the economic model largely failed but the democratic model worked – at least
at the federal and state levels. Elections were, and continue to be, run by independent
election commissions, and the results are viewed as fair as those in any Western democracy. But at the local level democracy, till recently, was not institutionalized. Even though
most state constitutions mandated regular elections and varying degrees of fiscal authority to village government, elections were rarely held and local governments were, for the
most part, toothless (Matthew and Buch 2000).

Gandhi's vision of village swaraj led three states to attempt early democratic reforms
at the local level in the 1970s and 1980s: West Bengal in the east, and Karnataka and
Kerala in the south.[21] In order to institutionalize and spread democratic decentralization
to the rest of the country, two amendments to the Indian constitution – the 73rd and
74th – were passed in 1993. Among other goals, they mandated that elections to local

---

[18]   As an ironic illustration of a clash of civilizations within the changing culture of development institutions
KDP's success has caused it to be categorized it as "best-practice," with its final design pitchforked into entirely
different cultural contexts. Viewed through the optic of SPGs, the illogic of this becomes starkly obvious.

[19]   Subhash Chandra Bose, a former president of the Indian National Congress, formed the Indian National
Army that attempted to liberate the country in collaboration with Japanese forces during World War II.

[20]   Preamble, Constitution of India.

[21]   For well-documented studies of these state-level movements see Leiten (1996) for West Bengal, Crook and
Manor (1998) for Karnataka, and Isaac and Franke (2000) for Kerala.

village councils or panchayats be systematized and supervised by independent election commissions and that they be given more fiscal authority and political power. Another important innovation was that *gram sabhas*, or village assemblies, be held at regular intervals throughout the year. These are open meetings which anyone in the village is free to attend in order to discuss budgets, development plans, the selection of beneficiaries, and to interrogate village panchayat and local administrative officials on any issue. A third key aspect is that seats on panchayats, including the position of the panchayat president (*pradhan* or *sarpanch*) be reserved for Scheduled Castes and Tribes (according to their size in the village population), and women (a third of all seats in the panchayat and all presidencies, on a rotating basis). I will not attempt here to evaluate the impact of the 73rd amendment – several research projects are attempting to examine this[22] – but will briefly illustrate how thinking about democratic decentralization in India via an SPG lens can provide some useful insights. I will focus on the South Indian states of Kerala, Karnataka, and Andhra Pradesh.[23]

In the early 1980s the newly elected Janata government in Karnataka passed legislation experimenting with setting up structures of local governance. These later became the foundation of the 73rd amendment – including regular elections, the institution of *gram sabhas*, reservations for Scheduled Castes and Tribes, and women. This experiment largely ended in 1991 with the election of a Congress-led government in the state.[24] With the passage of the 73rd amendment, regular elections to panchayats continue to be held, but panchayats have very small budgets and limited fiscal authority. In Kerala, on the other hand, a series of Communist governments increasingly decentralized authority to local governments. The momentum of this process was vastly increased in 1996, when the Left Democratic Front passed legislation mandating that 40 percent of total state expenditures be disbursed by local government institutions. This was accompanied by a concerted effort to introduce participatory democracy, not just by ensuring that *gram sabhas* were regularly held, but via links with "planning seminars" held at the ward, village, block and district levels to determine the allocation of budgets. A left-led People's Campaign for Decentralized Planning facilitated this process by supervising and disseminating information about decentralized planning. Consequently, Kerala's panchayats have considerably more clout than those in any other part of the country (Isaac and Franke 2000). However, in recent years Kerala's decentralization has seen serious setbacks as a consequence of the LDF's loss of political power, coupled with a serious budget deficit in the state government's finances (Sethi 2004).

Andhra Pradesh (AP), on the other hand, has tried to undermine the power of panchayats for almost ten years under the tenure of the Telugu Desam (Telugu National) party. The state, however, has also had a long history of decentralization: a series of legislations since 1958 have attempted to empower panchayats. Panchayats in AP were controlled, largely, by the Congress Party. Consequently, when the Telugu Desam (Telugu Nation) party, led by Chandrababu Naidu, came to power in 1995 it instituted the Janmabhoomi (birth land)

---

[22] See Chattopadhaya and Duflo (2004), Bardhan and Mookherjee (2005), Besley, Pande, and Rao (2004b), Chaudhuri, Harilal, and Heller (2004).

[23] It is important to keep in mind that these states are relatively more developed and egalitarian than those in north India. The analysis here would therefore be very different than if my data were Bihar or UP.

[24] Though, ironically, it was a Congress-led government in the center that passed the 73rd and 74th amendments.

program. This attempted to give power to administrative rather than political authorities by making them directly answerable to villagers via *gram sabhas* unassociated with panchayats. Panchayat elections were not held till 2001, and their authority was further undermined with the formation of various village "users groups" which had budgetary authority under the Janmabhoomi program. This is a nice example of how a new government that wants to demonstrate the irrelevance of SPGs constructed by its predecessor can signal this by creating fresh SPGs that displace the old; Naidu's Janmabhoomi program was introduced with a great deal of fanfare (press releases, public meetings, posters and manuals printed on high-quality paper) supposedly heralding the dawn of a new era of "good governance." Thus, of the three states, AP has made the least progress in implementing the 73rd amendment – but with the Telugu Desam's recent electoral loss this is likely to change.

The *gram sabha* is a particularly important SPG introduced via panchayat reforms. In Kerala, which has high levels of literacy and political awareness, *gram sabhas* have become active institutions for the incorporation of public grievances into the planning process. In Karnataka and Kerala, on the other hand, *gram sabhas* are largely seen as yet another type of top-down development intervention – representing the power of the state to disrupt existing power relations. For this they are both resented and manipulated by entrenched elites – and used and appropriated for private benefit by disadvantaged groups. When *gram sabhas* were first introduced in Karnataka in 1993, many *pradhans* found them threatening and did not hold them, or made then ineffectual by holding them at unannounced times, or staged them in the panchayat office instead of in a public area (Crook and Manor 1998). This unsanctioned violation of government authority was an important signal of their local power. In more recent data we find that, when they are held, *gram sabhas* largely serve to identify and allocate benefits targeted to mandated groups such as Scheduled Castes and Tribes (SC/STs). Not surprisingly, they are most often attended by SC/Sts, and those SC/STs who attend them are also more likely to benefit from programs (Besley, Pande, and Rao 2004c).

In an interesting demonstration of the hold that the village swaraj/democracy SPG has on Indians, democratically elected panchayat-like structures are often spontaneously formed in squatter settlements in slums (Jha, Rao, and Woolcock 2007). Squatter settlements, of course, are not officially sanctioned and therefore do not fall within formal institutions of governance. Yet, in work in Delhi slums, we found that immigrant squatters would have regular elections for members of panchayats and would also elect a pradhan. The elections were generally perceived as fair even though they were organized by members of the community. Candidates were usually affiliated with political parties, and the winning candidate had electorally legitimized authority. This elected pradhan largely functioned as an intermediary between slum-dwellers and agents of the state – helping constituents obtain "ration cards," voter identification cards, and other tokens of citizenship. They also helped them get access to jobs in government offices, and tried to persuade bureaucrats to provide public services – such as water trucks and toilets – to the slum. Thus, even thought they had no fiscal authority they re-imagined existing SPGs to find a way to improve access to the state.[25]

---

[25] Appadurai (2004) describes a very different use of SPGs in Mumbai by slum-dwellers who strategically used rituals such *sandas melas* (toilet festivals) to bring their utter lack of sanitation facilities to the attention of government authorities and international organizations.

Thus, in India, as in Indonesia, power is largely a matter of controlling and accessing the apparatus of state. But unlike Indonesia, the strategies in India for manipulating power come via control of the political process. Therefore, electoral turnout is very high – about 70 percent for village panchayat elections (Besley, Pande, and Rao 2004b). Public goods are almost entirely centrally funded – with only 24 percent of households claiming that have made any contribution towards their provision (about half the percentage in Indonesia). Public goods, such as schools, roads and clinics, are therefore hybrid SPGs – symbols of the largesse of the state rather than "owned" by the community. As a result, they represent opportunities for private appropriation – manifested in high levels of absenteeism by schoolteachers, medical workers, and other state employees, and in corruption by panchayats when giving contracts. With the exception of Kerala, panchayats have very small budgets. Their funds are largely acquired from a small house tax, and petty taxes which validate transactions such as land sales. Most of a panchayat's budget is currently derived from programs with targeted beneficiaries – such as housing for SC/STs and food for work programs – over which *pradhans* have very little discretion. Yet, success in panchayat elections is a stepping-stone to higher elected office, and *pradhans* can control relatively lucrative contracts for village public goods. High positions in panchayats are, therefore, rather highly valued, and panchayat elections are often very competitive, being structured around the same party-based competition prevalent in state and national elections (even though some states officially ban party affiliations in panchayat elections). Despite this, panchayats do manage to get things done, often by acting as intermediaries to divert state government projects and funds to their villages. And *pradhans* provide public goods in a manner entirely consistent with the incentives of electoral competition – tending to take more care of their own constituents, heir home village, and their caste (Besley, Pande, and Rao 2004a).

It should be apparent that the "nationalist" SPG in India is based on notions of liberty and universal franchise, coupled with Gandhian beliefs about village self-sufficiency. These have succeeded in bringing democracy and political competition to the lowest levels of government and given democracy deep roots. Yet, with the exception of Kerala, state panchayats do not yet have much financial power: the provision of public goods remains largely with officials at higher levels of government. Consequently, panchayats tend to be viewed as symbols of state government rule and are manipulated for private benefit. This lack of fiscal decentralization and the consequent symbolic lack of "ownership" of public goods, as well as the lack of accountability at local level, makes the delivery of public services very inefficient. An SPG lens would suggest that public policy should strengthen panchayat institutions to allow for greater local level control, which would then increase both symbolic and political accountability and improve the efficiency of public service delivery.

To briefly conclude: The comparison between India and Indonesia suggests a different kind of equity–efficiency trade-off. Indonesia chose a vision of nationalism that emphasized local participation, in a manner that may have regressively taxed the poor. It was also coercive, and, being enforced by the power of military dictatorship, helped abrogate individual liberty. But it did result in the efficient delivery of public services. India chose a different path. It emphasized democracy and universal franchise even in village government. This, for the most part, resulted in inefficient public service delivery, keeping India well behind Indonesia in human development indicators despite similar levels of per capita income.

An understanding of symbolic public goods provides a useful way of understanding why Indonesia and India had diverged so much, and also suggests some avenues for public action. It is crucial to understand how symbols of nationalism play a role in local governance and community action. These can have important material implications. On the other hand, material objects – such as mosques, temples, and less obviously, schools and clinics – also serve a symbolic purpose. Understanding their symbolic meaning can contribute towards a better appreciation of how communities function, and of how to make public service delivery more effective and inclusive. However, these meanings can change – and sometimes change very quickly – both because they can be explicitly manipulated in contests for power, but also because they are influenced by the external political and economic environment. This ability of SPGs to change can provide guidance on how shifting their symbolic functions can lead to more effective, and equitable, local development.

Local development in Indonesia would be foolish to ignore the obvious advantages that can be gained from harnessing the value of participation. But the challenge is to do this less coercively, more inclusively and with greater electoral accountability. This is the task that KDP has taken on. Local development in India would be negligent if it ignored the tremendous achievement of thriving democracies at the village level. But these village governments need to be given fiscal teeth so that public goods can be brought within the purview of power exercised by locally accountable governments. But democracy needs to be "deepened" in the sense of giving excluded groups, such as slum dwellers and women, avenues to improve their access to the apparatus of government, and to external sources of support. The strategic use of SPGs – such as forming informal panchayats in urban areas, or accessing gram sabhas to improve access to public services, is one avenue. But these new SPGs can be threatening to existing power structures and have thus not been effectively institutionalized. This is where public action can make a difference by using fiscal and legislative means to strengthen institutions of voice, while using alliances with civil society groups, as was done in Kerala, to shore up the ability of gram sabhas to fulfill their potential to make panchayats more accountable and inclusive.

References

Abraham, Anita and Jean-Philippe Platteau, 2004. "Participatory Development: Where Culture Creeps In," in V. Rao and M. Walton (eds), *Culture and Public Action*, Stanford: Stanford University Press, ch. 10.

Akerlof, George and Rachel Kranton, 2000. "Economics and Identity," *Quarterly Journal of Economics*, 115(3): 715–53.

Alatas, Vivi, Lant Pritchett, and Anna Wetterberg, 2002. "Voice Lessons: Local Government Organizations, Social Organizations and the Quality of Local Governance," World Bank Policy Research Paper 2981, March.

Anderson, Benedict, 1991. *Imagined Communities: Reflections on the Origins and Spread of Nationalism*, revd edn, London and New York: Verso.

Appadurai, Arjun, 1997. "The Production of Locality," in Arjun Appadurai, *Modernity at Large: Cultural Dimensions of Globalization*, Delhi: Oxford University Press, ch. 9.

Appadurai, Arjun, 2004. "The Capacity to Aspire: Culture and the Terms of Recognition," in V. Rao and M. Walton (eds), *Culture and Public Action*, Stanford: Stanford University Press, ch. 3.

Baland, Jean-Marie and Jean-Philippe Platteau, 2003. "Institutions and the Efficient Management of the Commons," mimeo.

Bardhan, Pranab, 1993. "Symposium on Management of Local Commons," *Journal of Economic Perspectives*, 7(4): 87–92.

——. 2002. "Decentralization of Government and Development," *Journal of Economic Perspectives*, 16(4): 185–205.

Bardhan, Pranab and Dilip Mukherjee, 2003. "Political Economy of Land Reforms in West Bengal 1978–98," mimeo, Boston University.

Bardhan, Pranab and Jeff Dayton-Johnson, 2002. "Inequality and Conservation on the Local Commons: A Theoretical Exercise," *Economic Journal*, 112(July): 577–602.

Bardhan, Pranab and Dilip Mookherjee, 2005. "Political Economy of Land Reforms in West Bengal 1978–98," mimeo, May.

Basu, Kaushik, 1989. "A Theory of Association: Social Status, Prices and Markets," *Oxford Economic Papers*, 41(4): 653–71.

Beatty, Andrew, 1999. *Varieties of Javanese Religion: An Anthropological Account*, Cambridge: Cambridge University Press.

Besley, Tim, Rohini Pande, and Vijayendra Rao, 2004a. "Politics as Usual? Local Democracy and Public Resource Allocation in Rural India," mimeo.

——. 2004b. "Panchayats and Resource Allocation in South India: A Report," mimeo.

——. 2004c. "Participatory Democracy in Action: Survey Evidence from Rural India," mimeo.

Bloch, Francis, Vijayendra Rao, and Sonalde Desai, 2004. "Wedding Celebrations as Conspicuous Consumption: Signalling Social Status in Rural India," *Journal of Human Resources*, 39(3): 675–95.

Bourdieu, Pierre, 1990. *The Logic of Practice*, Stanford: Stanford University Press.

——. 1998. *Practical Reason*, Stanford: Stanford University Press.

Bowen, John R., 1986. "On the Political Construction of Tradition: Gotong Royong In Indonesia," *Journal of Asian Studies*, 45(3): 545–61.

Burleigh, Michael, 2000. *The Third Reich: A New History*, London: Pan Macmillan.

Chattopadhayay, Raghabendra and Esther Duflo, 2004. "Women as Policy-makers: Evidence from a Randomized Policy Experiment in India," *Econometrica*, 72(5): 1409–43.

Chaudhuri, Shubham, K. N. Harilal, and Patrick Heller, 2004. "Building a Local Democracy: Evidence from Kerala, India," *World Development*.

Chwe, Michael Suk-Young, 1999. "Structure and Strategy in Collective Action," *American Journal of Sociology*, 105(1): 128–56.

——. 2001. *Rational Ritual: Culture, Coordination and Common Knowledge*, Princeton: Princeton University Press.

Crook, Richard C. and James Manor, 1998. *Democracy and Decentralization in India and West Africa*, Cambridge: Cambridge University Press.

Douglas, Mary, 1986. *How Institutions Think*, Syracuse: Syracuse University Press.

Gandhi, Mohandas K., 1962. *Village Swaraj*, Ahmedabad: Navjivan Trust.

Geertz, Clifford, 1976. *The Religion of Java*, Chicago and London: University of Chicago Press (reprint).

Granovetter, M., 1973. "The Strength of Weak Ties," *American Journal of Sociology*, 78(6): 1360–80.

Guggenheim, Scott, 2005. "The *Kecamatan* Development Project, Indonesia," in Anthony Bebbington, Scott Guggenheim, Elizabeth Olson, and Michael Woolcock (eds), *The Search for Empowerment: Social Capital as Idea and Practice at the World Bank*, Hartford: Kumarian Press.

Hefner, Robert W., 2000. *Civil Islam: Muslims and Democratization in Indonesia*, Princeton and Oxford: Princeton University Press.

Isaac, T. M. Thomas and Richard W. Franke, 2000. *Local Democracy and Development*, Delhi: Leftword Books.

Jha, Saumitra, Vijayendra Rao, and Michael Woolcock, 2007. "Governance in the Gullies: Democratic Responsiveness and Community Leadership in Delhi's Slums," *World Development*, 35(2): 230–46.

Kranton, Rachel, 1996. "Reciprocal Exchange: A Self-Sustaining System," *American Economic Review*, 86(4): 830–51.

Leiten, G. K., 1996. *Development, Devolution and Democracy: Village Discourse in West Bengal*, Delhi and London: Sage Publications.

Mallaby, Sebastian, 2004. *The World's Banker*, Council of Foreign Relations Books, Harmondsworth: Penguin.

Mansuri, Ghazala and Vijayendra Rao, 2004. "Community-Based and -Driven Development: A Critical Review," *World Bank Research Observer*, 19(1): 1–39.

Matthew, George and Nirmala Buch, 2000. *Status of Panchayati Raj in the States and Union Territories of India*, Delhi: Concept Publishing Company.

Mosse, David, 1997. "The Symbolic Making of a Common Property Resource: History, Ecology and Locality in a Tank-irrigated Landscape in South India, *Development and Change*, 28: 467–504.

Mosse, David, 2001. " 'People's Knowledge,' Participations and Patronage: Operations and Representations in Rural Development," in Bill Cooke and Uma Kothari (eds), *Participation: The New Tyranny*, London: Zed Books.

Olson, Mancur, 1965. *The Logic of Collective Action: Public Goods and the Theory of Groups*, Cambridge: Harvard University Press.

Ostrom, Elinor, 1990. *Governing the Commons: The Evolution of Institutions for Collective Action*, Cambridge: Cambridge University Press.

Rao, Vijayendra, 2001. "Celebrations as Social Investments: Festival Expenditures, Unit Price Variation and Social Status in Rural India," *Journal of Development Studies*, 38(1): 71–97.

Rao, Vijayendra and Michael Walton, 2004. "Culture and Public Action: Relationality, Equality of Agency and Development," in V. Rao and M. Walton (eds), *Culture and Public Action*, Stanford: Stanford University Press, ch. 1.

Ricklefs, M. C., 2001. *A History of Modern Indonesia since c. 1200*, 3rd edn, Stanford: Stanford University Press.

Scott, James C., 1995. *Weapons of the Weak: Everyday Forms of Peasant Resistance*, New Haven and London: Yale University Press.

Seabright, Paul, 1997. "Is Cooperation Habit Forming," in Partha Dasgupta (ed.), *The Environment and Emerging Development Issues*, New York: Oxford University Press and WIDER.

Sethi, Geeta, 2004. *Report on Fiscal Decentralization in India*, Washington, DC: World Bank.

Sethi, Rajiv and E. Somanathan, 1999. "The Evolution of Social Norms in Common Property Resource Use," *American Economic Review*, 86(4): 766–88.

Sullivan, John, 1992. *Local Government and Community in Java: An Urban Case-study*, Singapore: Oxford University Press.

Turner, Victor, 1982. "Introduction," in Victor Turner (ed.), *Celebration: Studies in Festivity and Ritual*, Washington, DC: Smithsonian Institution Press.

Woodward, Mark R., 1988. "The *Slametan*: Textual Knowledge and Ritual Performance in Central Javanese Islam," *History of Religions*, 28: 54–89.

11: Interdisciplinarity as a Three-way Conversation

Barriers and Possibilities

Sharachchandra Lélé

Introduction

The title of this book suggests that the main disciplinary divide in research on CPRs is between economists and anthropologists. But the two alternative expansions of the term "CPRs," viz., common property resources and common-pool resources, highlight the social and the biophysical dimension of the problem respectively (Stevenson 1991). The starting point of this chapter, therefore, is that interdisciplinarity in the context of CPRs has to be (at least) a three-way conversation between economists, anthropologists and natural scientists.[1] Implicit in this point of departure is also the idea that having this conversation and eventually a collaboration of some kind is desirable[2] and to some extent possible. The question therefore is not "whether" but "how." Answering this question requires a comprehensive understanding of the different barriers that prevent this three-way conversation from being a productive one. I believe that the barriers include not just differences in epistemology and method that have been well-debated in other chapters of this book and elsewhere, but differences of other kinds as well. I suggest a four-dimensional categorization of these barriers, and then discuss the form and relative importance of each in the different sides of the conversational triangle using various illustrations. Finally, I suggest a few practical ways of overcoming these barriers. These discussions, illustrations and suggestions draw as much upon my personal experience in crossing disciplinary

---

[1] In this chapter, I use the term "natural scientists" as shorthand for natural scientists (e.g., ecologists or biologists), physical scientists (e.g., soil scientists, atmospheric scientists, or environmental chemists), and engineers of all kinds. Similarly, I include the humanities under the rubric of the "social sciences." By calling for a three-way conversation, I assume that the "natural sciences" can be treated as a relatively homogeneous block compared to the social sciences.

[2] Embedded here is a question of "desirable for whom." I shall argue later on that interdisciplinarity is desirable (and its quality or adequacy can be judged) only where there is an expressed societal need to address a particular pressing problem.

boundaries and conducting interdisciplinary research on forests, watersheds and forest-watershed linkages as upon the examples available in the CPR or broader environmental studies literature.

Barriers to "Interdisciplinarity"

At the outset, I would like to point out that the terms "discipline" and "interdisciplinarity" are slippery ones that can themselves become an obstacle to understanding the issue at hand. Conventionally, "a discipline is a body of knowledge or branch of learning characterized by intersubjectively accepted content and methods" (Kockelmans 1979). When the content (or subject matter) is distinctly different, the separation seems "obvious." Thus, the broad grouping of learning into the disciplinary "blocks" of social and natural sciences seems to correspond well with our intuitive sense that understanding how human beings behave is a distinctly different exercise from trying to understand how the non-human world functions. It is usually assumed that this major difference in subject matter is correlated with (and perhaps causative of) differences in epistemology and method, notions of rigor and adequacy of proof, and so on. Hence C. P. Snow's famous description of these two blocks as "two cultures" that do not, and almost cannot, communicate with each other.

Within these two blocks, however, disciplinary boundaries do not mean the same thing. In the natural sciences, it is true that the differences in subject matter are getting increasingly blurred – e.g., where does "physical" end and "biological" begin? However, there is an underlying belief that disciplines represent different (complementary) areas of inquiry. In the social sciences, on the other hand, the logic behind disciplinary boundaries seems much more confusing.[3] We were told that anthropologists study culture, economists study behavior in the market, and political scientists study behavior in the political arena (such as electoral politics). But increasingly, economists are studying all of these phenomena, and anthropologists have expanded far beyond the study of exotic tribes to examine behavior in all spheres of contemporary society. Methodological differences are also getting blurred, with political scientists using game theory extensively and sociologists becoming highly quantitative. On the other hand, the sub-discipline of Marxist economics would seem much further away from mainstream (neoclassical) economics than the approach of many political scientists and even some anthropologists! Perhaps the time has come to "forget disciplines, think scientific communities" (Lélé and Norgaard 2005). But given that most of us are brought up with the disciplinary labels, I will continue to

---

[3] As Jasanoff (2002) points out, "disciplines" are not natural categories. They have histories and their names, content, and boundaries develop and change. In a hilarious, if apocryphal, illustration of this point, she quotes Jose Luis Borges' mention of a "certain Chinese encyclopedia" in which it is written that "animals are divided into: (a) belonging to the Emperor, (b) embalmed, (c) tame, (d) sucking pigs, (e) sirens, (f) fabulous, (g) stray dogs, (h) included in the present classification, (i) frenzied, (j) innumerable, (k) drawn with a very fine camel-hair brush, (l) et cetera, (m) having just broken the water pitcher, (n) that from a long way off look like flies! Without going to this extreme, the Gulbenkian Commission on the Restructuring of the Social Sciences (1996) has argued that the disciplinary separations in the humanities and social sciences have always been idiosyncratic and reflect a splintering that has been detrimental to their development.

use the major disciplinary categories or blocks (the "natural" and the "social" sciences) as a starting point, identifying the inconsistencies and subtleties as I go along. Similarly, I shall use the label of "economics" and "anthropology" loosely, sometimes as representative of the "quantitative" and the "interpretive" social sciences respectively and sometimes as representing alternative explanations of human behavior that economics and non-economics social sciences offer.

The terms "interdisciplinarity," "multi-disciplinarity," and "trans-disciplinarity" are also a source of confusion (Kockelmans 1979). Broadly speaking, multi-disciplinarity is recognized as simply the juxtaposition of the findings of different disciplines, without any attempt to reconcile or merge them. Interdisciplinarity and trans-disciplinarity are seen as "stronger" efforts to link or merge existing frameworks or develop entirely new ones. Note, however, that "simple juxtaposition" might seem adequate in some contexts (when the subject matters are complementary) but not in others (when the subject matter is the same). For the sake of brevity, I shall use the term "interdisciplinarity" as shorthand for all three versions–multi-, inter- and trans-disciplinarity – through most of this chapter, and delve into the subtle differences only towards the end.

Moving from the semantic to the substantive,[4] I propose four broad types of barriers to interdisciplinarity. First, there is the problem of values being embedded in all types of inquiry and at all stages: in the choice of questions, theoretical positions, variables, and style of research. But certainly most natural scientists, and even many social ones, are loath to acknowledge the presence of value judgments in their work. Furthermore, in the context of contentious social issues such as "sustainability," "environmental degradation," or "sustainable development," decision-makers call on scientists to provide "objective" advice, making such acknowledgment even more difficult. Consequently, scientists may "talk past each other" in ways that no amount of theoretical or methodological flexibility can resolve.

Second, researchers in different disciplines or sub-disciplines may study the same phenomenon but differ in their theories or explanatory models (and underlying assumptions). In the case of complex phenomena, it is not easy to prove the superiority of one theory over another in a particular case. Maintaining allegiance to one's school of thought may come to seem more important than openly exploring which explanation seems to work better in a particular context. This seems to be the case particularly within the social sciences, but it is also true for ecology.[5] On the other hand, sciences that have developed at the borders of the social–natural divide (e.g., agronomy in the natural sciences or agricultural economics in the social sciences) are required to make some assumptions about the processes that intrude from the other side (e.g., the decision-making process of the farmer or the nature of agro-ecosystems, respectively). These disciplinary assumptions about the "other" half of the system are usually simplistic, but not easily abandoned, creating a barrier even when the subject matter is on the face of it quite distinct and complementary.

---

[4] While acknowledging the link between them.

[5] The level of complexity of ecological phenomena, and hence the under-determinacy of the science, resembles the situation in the social sciences. "Ecology . . . is more empirically and theoretically underdetermined than many other sciences . . . [it is characterized by a] bottom-up, case-study approach in ecological method, rather than a top-down, hypothetical-deductive approach . . . in part, because of the uniqueness and historical character of many ecological phenomena" (Shrader-Frechette and McCoy 1993: 109).

The third type of barrier is the one that has been most emphasized in the literature on interdisciplinarity: the differences in epistemology and hence in specific methods, notions of adequate proof, and so on. As Bauer puts it, "Scientists (and engineers) believe implicitly in certain absolute truths, and further believe that given enough time and effort the ultimate truth can be found, whereas for some philosophers, sociologists and other [social scientists] there is no absolutely determinable truth" (Bauer 1990). These differences may exist even between disciplines within each disciplinary block. Certainly a major difference between the approaches of anthropologists and economists is their differing perception about the objective versus subjective nature of knowledge and whether it is the context-specific or generalizable. Within the natural sciences, although positivism generally reigns supreme, scientists studying complex processes such as those in ecology have grappled with the question of how much is really knowable through reductionist models and experimentation (see, e.g., Botkin 1992).

Finally, the manner in which society interacts with and organizes academia influences the production of interdisciplinary research. As Schoenberger (2001) and others have pointed out, the relative importance or "validity" of a direction of inquiry or approach is not determined simply by some "objective" recognition by academics of its ability to "generate more valid knowledge than another." Forces at work within the larger society outside academia shape the perceived importance of a particular discipline or of a particular kind of interdisciplinary crossing. This generates differences in attention to (and resources commanded by) different disciplines[6] and consequently conditions behavioral patterns, such as arrogance or defensiveness, amongst their practitioners. Society also influences the institutional arrangements within academia that create incentives (or otherwise) for interdisciplinary knowledge production.

The differences in normative concerns, models, methods, and societal recognition are obviously not randomly distributed but significantly (though not entirely) correlated with each other. Values and models co-evolve (Lélé and Norgaard 1996), and certain models are only amenable to certain methods (and vice versa). And academia and society at large seem to accord greater respect to certain ways of doing science over others: currently, quantitative approaches seem to hold sway. Interdisciplinary conversations and crossings will generally have to grapple with a package of barriers simultaneously.

I shall now discuss what form and importance the different barriers take in the context of each of the sides of the triangular conversation around CPRs. Given, however, that the issues that arise in natural scientists conversing with economists overlap substantially with those that arise in their conversations with anthropologists, I shall divide the discussion into two major sections, viz., the problem of linking the natural sciences to the social sciences or to particular streams within them, and then the question of linking or reconciling the streams within the social sciences.

Linking the Natural to the Social

The main difficulties in natural scientists conversing with social scientists appear to revolve around the refusal of natural scientists to recognize the value-laden nature of applied

---

[6] Schoenberger (2001) calls this "the social relations of knowledge production," and she elucidates this concept with much greater sophistication than I have done here.

science and the hidden assumptions that each disciplinary block carries about the other area. Issues of methodology are relatively easily worked out (partly through selective linkages), although practical difficulties in linking the two inquiries remain. Societal biases towards the natural sciences are, however, strong, especially in developing countries, even as the need for social science input in CPR management is being increasingly recognized in policy circles.

The value-laden nature of science

The belief in value-neutrality is strongest and most pervasive in the natural sciences (including engineering). Natural scientists "essentialize" certain dimensions of natural phenomena and equate the preservation of these dimensions as "good" CPR (or environmental) management, without realizing that the choice is actually a social one. Take the example of tropical forest management. Tropical forests contribute a variety of benefits, but these benefits flow to different groups in society. Some of the benefits, such as fuelwood, fodder, leaf manure, timber, and minor produce, may flow to communities living close to the forests, while watershed services flow primarily to those living in the plains downstream, and carbon sequestration benefits accrue to the entire global community. Different ways of managing forests yield different mixes of benefits. Dense, undisturbed forests yield high levels of biodiversity and watershed services, but little by way of tangible products. Carefully managed, lopped forests might yield high levels of fuelwood, fodder, and leaf manure, but reduced levels of biodiversity and medium levels of watershed benefits. Monocultural timber plantations, on the other hand, would maximize timber production at the expense of most other benefits. Some of the benefits generated by forests, such as fodder or fuel, may also be obtained to some extent from non-forest land uses, such as coffee plantations or croplands. Thus, prioritizing forests over other land uses, and certain forest management systems over others, means valuing certain benefits and certain beneficiaries over others. When one decides which mix of benefits is best, one is deciding how the diverse needs of different sections of society and of present versus future generations should be valued. This decision is essentially a social or political one. Science can illuminate this social debate by generating clearer estimates of the trade-offs and complementarities between different benefits, but science cannot "objectively" settle the debate.[7]

Unfortunately, debates in forestry have often been fruitless because of the refusal of the participants to recognize this point. The debates are really about what should be the goal of forest management, not about which method of forest management will or will not achieve a particular goal. For instance, in the Western Ghats region of India, after the British takeover of the forests, there was a major debate as to the appropriateness of the local practice of lopping or pruning forest trees for obtaining leaf manure and fuelwood. British foresters were up in arms against this practice:

---

[7]   Note that judgments about what is socially valuable (what kind of forest should be sustained over what period of time) are almost inextricably linked to the subjective choices of the dependent variables, the likely set of independent variables, the functional form of the model, and the scale of analysis. That these are value-loaded choices becomes clear when one thinks of how different ecologists might respond to the question, "What constitutes a good forest?" The chances are that community ecologists might define this as a highly diverse forest, whereas ecologists of the Odum energetics school might define it as a highly productive forest.

The kind of [*soppinabetta*][8] that meets one at every turn . . . consists of open forest of mutilated stems from which the branches have been lopped close to the trunk, on which fresh shoots are allowed to remain for [a few years] . . . The induration, impoverishment and degradation of soil are necessary consequences . . . such land must become utterly barren. (MacGregor 1894)

In contrast, a British agricultural chemist appointed to inquire into the state of Indian agriculture noted the same practice with approval:

I saw cultivators lopping around their own fields . . . Nor were the trees ruthlessly destroyed . . . some trees are most usefully grown for pollarding. (Voelcker 1897)

Clearly, what is "good silviculture" in the eyes of the agriculturally-oriented expert is not so in the eyes of the forester.

The forester MacGregor had predicted that "ruin and desolation will be the outcome of the present state of things." Foresters and ecologists in post-independence India seemed to concur (Gadgil 1987a; Reddy et al. 1986). However, subsequent rigorous field studies showed that even a century after these dire predictions, the extent of barren land was limited and the productivity of the intensively lopped forests was much higher than estimated earlier. Often (though not always) it was sufficient to meet the harvesting pressures. Where forest was in the form of pure grasslands, it was more often than not the result of conscious manipulation by farmers interested in promoting fodder growth than the result of poor management (Lélé 1994; 2000). Rather than being a scientific judgment about what harvesting and management practices are sustainable, the foresters' criticisms seem to be driven by their underlying value judgment that such intensive or different use of forests was inherently undesirable.

But natural scientists are generally uncomfortable with the idea that "sustainable resource management" or more generally "environmentally sound development" is not a self-evident, value-neutral concept. They have attempted to hang on to the cloak of value neutrality in different ways. For instance, in the context of ecosystems, some scientists argue that sustaining biodiversity automatically sustains all other products and services. Or that concepts such as "ecological integrity" or "natural capital" are somehow fundamental and so do not involve value judgments. Or that one can somehow "objectively aggregate" the subjective notions of environmental soundness into an environmentally correct Gross Domestic Product or Ecological Footprint or Global Sustainability Index. In this, they have been abetted by policy-makers, who also prefer to cloak their decisions in the armor of scientific-ness so as to escape facing awkward questions about the values they are espousing. But it can be easily shown that such sleight of hand does not get rid of value judgments. Each of these concepts is relevant only with respect to a particular choice of what is ultimately of value, or particular notions of how disparate values within society should be aggregated (see Lélé and Norgaard 1996 for a detailed discussion; Rykiel 2001).

---

[8]   *Soppinabetta* is the Kannada term for forests over which farmers are given rights for harvesting leaf-manure, fuelwood, etc.

When one attempts to link the natural to the social (either individually or collectively), such hidden value judgments can cause serious problems. If social scientists are insensitive to the value judgments embedded in the natural science, they may take the natural scientists' assessment at face value, as an objective assessment of the quality of resource management, and end up going astray in the analysis of social cause of this quality. For instance, in the case of the heavily used forests in the Western Ghats, Nadkarni et al. (1989) assumed that the forests were degraded (à la MacGregor) and then struggled to explain why these individually controlled forests suffered a tragedy that is supposed to be restricted to the "commons" (Lélé 2000).

On the other hand, when social scientists do point out the possible ways in which natural science may be value laden, natural scientists are likely to become upset and defensive. For instance, in a program aimed at exposing social scientists to basic hydrology that I co-organized,[9] the hydrology expert introduced the concept of "groundwater potential" and "sustainable utilization." The latter was defined as the situation in which groundwater extraction does not exceed the rate of groundwater recharge. At this point, an economist pointed out that this definition was debatable, because if communities living in the upper part of the watershed (typically where most of the rain falls and recharge occurs) were to extract the entire recharge, it would leave no water for downstream communities or for base flow in the river. The hydrologist took quite some time to understand the empirical point being made and, even then, insisted that the official definition of sustainable utilization was "correct."

Hidden assumptions about the other

Prima facie, one might not expect to encounter a clash of models between natural and social scientists, because their models are (supposed to be) about distinct parts of reality. But research on CPRs cannot be *purely* natural or *purely* social. Natural scientists have to characterize human intervention in biophysical processes before attempting to model its impact. Social scientists have to make assumptions about how natural processes are to be represented in the analysis of social cause and effect. Out of some combination of ignorance, convenience and arrogance, the tendency has been to represent the "other" part of reality by drawing upon the set of assumptions that have become embedded in their own traditions, rather than upon cutting edge research from the "other."

Natural scientists have often been the first to point out environmental problems of enormous social consequence. Naturally, they participate in, and often lead, societal efforts to address these problems. Charged with providing policy recommendations, they have to make judgments about how society works. They do not have adequate training to do this, but they are perhaps emboldened to do so by their position and are likely to adopt simplistic models of social dynamics. As an article in Nature put it, "Few of us know much about the dynamics of the cosmos, but we all know plenty about human nature – or at least we think we do" (Anonymous 2005: 1003). So some natural scientists have applied models of biological carrying capacity to human systems (e.g., Pandey and Singh

---

[9]   "Hydrology for Social Scientists," a cross-disciplinary exposure program organized on behalf of the Indian Society for Ecological Economics in December 2001 in Bhopal.

1984; Kessler 1994), even though, unlike animals, human beings constantly innovate, respond to resource scarcity by varying their levels of consumption, and import materials across most system boundaries. Similarly, the concept of "demand-supply gap" has been repeatedly used in the literature on fuelwood scarcity, wherein "demand" is calculated on the basis of "per capita requirement times the number of people" and the per capita requirement is a constant, not dependent upon the price of fuelwood or the cost of its collection. This ignores a basic economic maxim that, at equilibrium, supply must generally equal demand and that demand cannot generally be estimated without knowing what the price is (see Masera 1994).

The above may be seen as examples of explicit disciplinary crossings that failed, rather than of hidden assumptions by natural scientists about the other. However, there are several examples of models that more implicitly "biologize" the causal analysis. For example, analyses of rangeland degradation in the Sahel have tended to focus exclusively on stocking rates, ignoring the major influence of rainfall and the complex relationship between grazing and rangeland productivity. Consequently, degradation is seen simply as resulting from the imbalance between livestock population and range resources. And the growth of livestock populations is treated solely as a biological process, controlled by herd demography and range productivity. A host of predator-prey models were developed and used to question the ecological sustainability of Sahelian pastoral systems, with tragic consequences for pastoral communities (for a detailed exposition, see Turner 1993). The same is the case with studies of deforestation. When forest ecologists use simplistic production-harvest comparisons to establish the fact of deforestation, they are implicitly highlighting the quantity consumed and quickly inferring that the size of the human population is the problem (e.g., Singh et al. 1984), rather than (say) the method or timing or form of extraction and therefore the question of forest rights. But as in the case of the Sahelian rangelands, where it was the timing of grazing that was a crucial factor (Turner 1999), qualitative factors are often as or more significant than quantitative measures of extraction when it comes to forest degradation. In the Western Ghats, for instance, individual and exclusive forest rights, social status and economic purchasing power combine to enable elite farmers to reduce their degrading pressure through a combination of tactics that include adopting gobar-gas technology, stall-feeding cross-breed cattle and investing in fencing. On the other hand, middle peasants and landless households are unable to make these transitions and appear to cause more degradation (Lélé 1993a; 2000). Simple technical solutions advocated by ecologists (e.g., Gadgil 1987b) could not and did not work.

Belittling or over-simplifying the other is, however, by no means the preserve of the natural sciences alone. Many social science theories and their adherents have tended to ignore or underplay the constraints imposed by natural resources and processes on human actions. Even today, many economists continue to use arguments based on economic models that assume an infinite substitutability among resources through technological change (e.g., Lomborg 2001). For others, such as hard-line Marxists, technology matters but is entirely determined by social structure, so it is not necessary to understand the relationship between technologies and environmental systems.

A more specific case is that of the models of renewable resource dynamics being used in resource economics. Several decades ago, economists adopted the logistic growth model to depict the relationship between the standing stock and the natural rate of growth of a resource. Though very convenient to analyse, this model (and its variants) seems applicable to only certain kinds of resources under very special circumstances, and patently inapplicable to many other resource-use situations, such as grazing in annual grass-lands or leaflitter extraction from forests where changes in standing stock of the biomass that is being extracted do not directly affect future production of that biomass (Lélé 1993b). While there is now some recognition among economists of the complex relationship between forest stock and the flow of ecosystem services of different kinds, in the routine practice of economic modeling (such as in adjusting GDP estimates for environmental degrada-tion) they tend to revert back to simple stock-based indicators.

Epistemologies and methods: practical issues

Much has been said about the epistemological differences between the two disciplin-ary blocks (the "two cultures" of C. P. Snow). Most natural scientists certainly continue to perceive the social sciences as being "qualitative" and hence "less rigorous." As the Gulbenkian Commission's report puts it, during the nineteenth century, the disciplinar-ization and professionalization of knowledge was accompanied by its division into two domains. This division "took on the flavour of a hierarchy, at least in the eyes of natural scientists – knowledge that was certain (science) versus knowledge that was imagined, even imaginary (what was not science)" (Gulbenkian Commission on the Restructuring of the Social Sciences 1996: 5).

But amongst the social sciences, economics (or at least its mainstream) took it upon itself to become as naturalistic (i.e., quantitative and mathematical) as possible. Consequently, natural scientists have shown a greater willingness to collaborate with economists than with other social scientists. And yet, other approaches such as political ecology and ecological anthropology are flourishing, suggesting that individuals have made the necessary crossings, giving the lie to the seriousness of the qual–quant divide. Sufficient exposure to the "other" might be enough to clear the misconceptions that give rise to this particular barrier.

I believe that more than the misconceived qual-quant divide, it may be practical issues in combining natural and social research that inhibit cross-disciplinary work. Under-standing environmental change caused by human actions (e.g., the effect of deforestation on hydrology) requires sampling across different intensities of human-induced environ-mental changes (e.g., watersheds with different levels of deforestation), keeping other variables (e.g., rainfall and soils) constant. But to understand how these environmental changes affect human communities and, more important, what factors influence human response to environmental change, researchers need samples wherein the extent of environ-mental change is similar (e.g., similarly deforested watersheds) and only one social factor varies (e.g., the strength of collective-action institutions). Finding adequate samples of such situations in the real world is virtually impossible (Kiran Kumar et al. 2006), and studying even limited samples may require enormous resources. Moreover, ecolo-gical or biophysical data collection often requires more equipment and human resources than the collection of socio-economic data. At least in my experience, estimating the effects of grazing practices on grass production or of fuelwood extraction practices on forest regeneration or measuring streamflow and associated hydro-meteorological par-ameters was much more time and resource consuming than conducting even large sample household surveys. All of this can lead to tensions within interdisciplinary projects about which questions to prioritize and how to practically make the linkages.

Using "nested" designs, where the biophysical research is conducted in a carefully chosen subset of socio-economic units (e.g., individual farm plots or forest plots with a larger sample of households or villages) or with careful simulation of typical resource management practices (e.g., clipping experiments to simulate the effects of grazing on grassland productivity – see Turner 1992) is one approach that might work in some situations. Recent advances in remote sensing and geographical information system (GIS) techniques have also opened up the possibility of relatively rapid assessment of ecological conditions across a large number of socio-economic units (Liverman et al. 1998), although the limitations of these techniques also need to be kept in mind (Lélé et al. 1998; Lélé 2001).

Socialization and organization

There are significant differences in the manner in which society treats the two disciplinary blocks. These differences are reflected in the incentives and support provided, attention paid to, and hence attitudes cultivated. In most countries, the natural science-social science divide is reinforced early on. India is perhaps an extreme case, where students are forced to choose between "science" and "arts" as early as the eleventh year of schooling and where exposure to the arts, humanities and social sciences in the undergraduate science or engineering degree programs is minimal and the undergraduate courses in the social sciences completely bereft of the "natural." But I believe this pattern is true in most developing countries that were ruled by the British. For instance, at an international conference on biomass energy resources which was attended mostly by natural scientists and engineers, I noticed that those from south Asia and Africa tended not to engage with or even see the socio-political dimensions of various issues, whereas those from Latin America were more comfortable and willing to do so. The liberal arts approach to education in the United States may be at the other end of the spectrum, but the divide is present even there.

More than just lack of exposure to the "other," it is the clear signals of superiority or inferiority communicated by society to the practitioners (and by them to their students) that are a problem. Many societies, especially Asian ones, are constantly telling students that "science" is superior to "arts."[10] This signal is reinforced at the undergraduate stage by the half-hearted manner in which the social sciences are taught in most professional courses in these countries. Naturally, the social sciences are seen as irrelevant, boring and non-rigorous. Conversely, the social scientists, because they supposedly were not good enough to get into the "science stream," are often in awe of the natural sciences. At least two senior Indian social scientists have told me that they believe that a person with an undergraduate in the natural sciences can still become a social scientist, but not vice versa.[11] Part of this aura of superiority certainly stems from the general myth that natural sciences are quantitative and hence more rigorous. But part of the aura of the natural sciences stems from their much greater capacity to predict phenomena accurately and to increasingly

---

[10]   The message may be meant to convey only that "a science education is more likely to give you a secure job than an arts education" but the resulting bias is unfortunately more sweeping.

[11]   Again, this may not be a universal phenomenon but, rather, specific to countries where, as mentioned above, undergraduate programs are more narrowly conceived and provide less exposure to the interpretive social sciences and humanities.

manipulate these phenomena with enormous dexterity to generate benefits for human-kind, at least in the short run. That social processes are enormously more complex and unpredictable than biophysical ones is conveniently forgotten.

The belief of the superiority of the natural scientists is so deep-rooted that whenever social problems have the slightest technical dimension, politicians have traditionally called on only technicians – the natural scientists – to help solve them. Until the latter half of the 20th century in the developed world, and more recently in the developing world, most governmental committees on natural resource management were constituted solely of natural scientists and engineers. The Intergovernmental Panel on Climate Change was initiated by (and its leadership is dominated by) natural scientists, even though the origins and impacts of climate change are ultimately highly social. One may attribute part of this to simply the pioneering role played by natural scientists in identifying such crises. Certainly, recent years have seen some attempts by policy-makers to pay more attention to the social dimension of environmental problems. But even as late as 2003, when the Government of India set up a National Forest Commission, it was headed by a retired judge and included activists (both social and wildlife), an eminent botanist, two foresters and a bureaucrat, but no social scientist (economist or non-economist). Moreover, the biases inbuilt into the Indian educational system do not seem to be changing at all, and the increasing importance being given to mathematics and computers in the US schools does not bode well for the future of liberal arts education.

Economists and Anthropologists: The Bigger Divide

The differences between economists and anthropologists have been characterized by some as differences between the quantitative and the interpretive social sciences, and hence as arising from this difference in epistemology and method. This suggests that a merging of methods will provide fuller insights into what is essentially the "same problem" being investigated – poverty (as in *Conversations I*: (Bardhan 1989)) or CPR degradation (as in this book). But as I have argued at the outset, disciplinary differences are multi-dimensional and interrelated, and simple labels are inadequate to capture them uniquely. Disciplines, sub-disciplines and schools within them conceive or characterize problems differently and explain them in different ways. These implicit differences in normative concerns and explicit disagreements over models of human behavior seem to be bigger barriers to interdisciplinary conversations within the social sciences. A streak of hegemonism similar to the hidden assumptions that natural scientists have about social phenomena makes these differences even more difficult to resolve.

Differing normative concerns

One would expect social scientists to be quite aware of the idea that all knowledge of reality (and therefore nature) is socially constructed and therefore value-loaded. But even within the social sciences, the recognition of how one's science is "value-loaded" varies across disciplines. Mainstream economists are most prone to holding illusions of value-neutrality. For instance, mainstream welfare economists aggregate costs and benefits imposed by a particular policy change on different members or sections of society to come up with a measure of net change in aggregate social welfare. In the textbooks on welfare economics, it is admitted that such aggregation actually requires "prior agreement on the social welfare function" so as to determine the relative weights to be given to the impacts felt by different members or sections (which is a social and political process). It is accepted that market prices will not reflect marginal social values if (for instance) income is not evenly distributed (Broadway and Bruce 1984: 292). Classic texts on applied welfare economics such as Dasgupta et al. (1972) suggest that while deriving and using different relative weights for each individual would be very difficult, common weights can be assigned to groups of individuals with similar incomes, and the effects of different weighting schemes can be explicated. In practice, however, virtually all valuation studies and benefit–cost analyses use market prices for the aggregation exercise without any differences in the weights assigned to the rich and the poor. No attempt is made in these studies to point out that the choice of weights is arbitrary, or to do a sensitivity analysis by changing the weights (see Howarth 2001, for an exception). Yet, most practicing economists insist that their benefit–cost analysis provides an "objective" basis for decision-making, when in fact decisions based upon such benefit–cost analysis reflect a one-rupee-one-vote approach.[12] The pervasive discourse about "getting prices right" is another illustration. The belief that there is one right price contradicts basic economic theory, because different distributions of rights, or income, result in different combinations of efficient market prices.

Other social scientists are less likely to insist that their position is value neutral, but they are nonetheless rarely explicit about what values they espouse, and thus end up talking past each other. This problem is likely to be more acute in a discussion on CPRs than on, say, poverty alleviation (the subject of *Conversations I*) because CPRs are an inherently more multi-dimensional and hence more contestable phenomenon. In a detailed review of the literature on CPRs, Menon (1999) has pointed out how different streams in this literature talk past each other because their underlying normative concerns are different: the collective action stream focuses on efficiency improvements in resource management (e.g., Ostrom 1990), the environmentalist stream focuses on "ecological prudence" or sustainability (e.g., Gadgil and Guha 1992), and the poverty stream focuses on the impacts of CPR degradation on the poor (e.g., Jodha 1986). One can detect a reasonable correlation between these three streams and their disciplinary/sub-disciplinary roots: the collective action stream being linked to the rational-choice folks in political science, the environmentalist approach having strong links with the natural sciences, and the poverty focus being characteristic of old-school economists and sociologists.

Of course, this correlation is by no means 100 percent. Some differences are sub-disciplinary and others are at the level of individuals. Kanbur (2002) argues that the

---

[12]   The textbook by Broadway and Bruce blandly states that "much of the literature in cost–benefit analysis, and most of the issues we wish to deal with here, are involved with using 'efficiency' criteria for project evaluation. Consequently, we shall assume for the purposes of this chapter that the economy can be treated as if all persons are identical, so that no distributive weights are needed"! Others argue that if the aggregate benefit minus cost of a particular policy or project is positive (when measured in the conventional manner) then, by the Hicks–Kaldor compensation criterion, that policy is clearly Pareto-improving and hence socially desirable. This ignores the fact that there could be policies that are not Pareto-improving (as they involve making somebody worse off) but that could be considered socially more desirable, i.e., Pareto optimality may not be the preferred criterion for decision-making.

perception of neoclassical economists being unconcerned about distributional consequences is not correct. He says it is just that they strongly believe that distributive issues
are best achieved through "income transfers" by the state rather than by choosing
"inefficient" projects. To me, this is still evidence of the weak commitment of neoclassical
economists to distributive justice and an indication of how values correlate with models,
because income transfers do not question the status quo on property rights.

In any case, the fundamental problem remains: that much of academic debate on the
commons starts off on the wrong foot by not explicating what each participant's normative concerns and priorities are, and an equal failure to recognize how their individual
models make it difficult to accommodate other normative concerns. As Menon and Lélé
(2003) point out, this failure to clarify the normative concerns in the beginning and also
to actually measure these ultimate variables of interest (rather than some proxy such as
"institutional persistence") has led to much confusion in the debate on which institutional
arrangements are likely to be most "successful" in CPR management.

Models: explicit disagreements and moving targets

All social science disciplines are ultimately attempting to understand the same phenomenon,
viz., human behavior. At the cost of some simplification, one might say that each social
science discipline makes different assumptions about the key driver(s) of human behavior: e.g., some believe it is an eternal quest for income or profit maximization, others
believe it is a quest for power, while yet others believe behavior is highly conditioned by
cultural norms and value systems that differ across communities. These basic assumptions are prima facie mutually incompatible, and disagreements within the social sciences
are therefore extremely deep-rooted. Note that one is using the term "disciplines" very
loosely here. The differences in causal models may correlate better with sub-disciplines,
rather than disciplines. That is, there are "materialists" within economics as well as sociology, and there may be economists who allow for the role of cultural factors.

Research on CPRs or environmental issues in general clearly shows these fundamental
differences in causal explanations, whether one correlates them to disciplinary or sub-
disciplinary categories. Neo-classical economists insist that the problem lies in missing
markets or improper setting of prices of resources and pollutants (Repetto 1986; Pearce
1998). Political economists focus on the fact that different economic classes have differential access to natural resources and that the material consumption and pollution by the
powerful classes comes at the cost of the less powerful (e.g., Agarwal 1985; Blaikie 1985).
Institutionalists explain resource degradation in terms of the failure of institutions to solve
free-rider problems (Hanna and Munasinghe 1995). Eco-feminists have argued that environmental degradation is related to the domination of women by men (Mies and Shiva
1993), while ecological anthropologists have argued that it is related to how human beings
perceive their relationship with nature (Merchant 1989).[13] In the "Conversations II"
workshop also, several anthropologists insisted that human behavior is driven largely
by a cultural politics, not a material one. Similarly, David Mosse's chapter (5) in this
book is an attempt to sift through competing explanations for the presence and absence

---

[13]   Given the vastness of this literature, the references given in this paragraph are purely indicative, not
comprehensive.

of functioning community institutions for minor irrigation tank management in Tamil Nadu, south India. He rejects the explanation of institutional economics, viz., that the institutions exist where the material benefit–cost calculus of collective action is positive, by showing how an explanation based on tanks as a symbol of power in a caste-based society has greater explanatory power, explaining the failure of institutions even where the material benefit–cost calculus is favorable.

In such a situation, what does interdisciplinarity mean? That depends upon how one sees the relationship between these explanatory perspectives and reality. One approach would be to think of each of these as partial explanations, i.e., explaining part of the problem. This would mean that the apparently competing explanations can coexist, and even be reconciled as part of some kind of meta-theory of human behavior. Indeed, it has been argued that the social sciences *were* in fact one single holistic science inquiring into "the nature and varieties of humankind" till the mid-nineteenth century when this inquiry "split into separate and [unequal] specialities and disciplines." [It was at this point that the] "severance of social relations from the economic, political and ideological contexts in which they are embedded and which they activate was accompanied by the assignment of the economic and political aspects of human life to separate disciplines" (Wolf 1982, quoted in Harriss 2002). It should therefore be possible, in theory, to restore this holism – an ambition that fields like "development studies" and perhaps "gender studies" (Jackson 2002) seem to be based upon.

Certainly an acknowledgment that one's explanation may be partial would be a good beginning towards better explanations. But merging the entire set of explanations seems rather difficult. Simply running multiple regressions with all these variables on large datasets, which is the methodological response of economists and rational choice theorists, seems inadequate because the variables do not simply operate at the same scale or are linked to each other through more complex chains or do not seem to emerge from any linearizable model. Nevertheless, as Mosse's chapter suggests, it might be possible to collect data at different scales to test different explanations and the relations between them. But this would require some kind of a "meta-theoretical procedure" for choosing between explanations in a specific context. To use the example of Mosse's chapter (5) again, one should not insist that caste-based social relations will explain the presence or absence of collective action institutions around CPRs in every context. For instance, in the Himalayas where caste-based conflict is known to be much less of an issue (though not entirely absent) and the material conditions favoring collective action much stronger, one would have to allow for the possibility that caste-based social relations do not turn out to be very significant determinants of the presence of collective action, although they might yet influence the distribution of benefits. This would clearly require extensive training in or familiarity with different social science theories, without absorption of the dogmas of each so that one is open to alternative explanations to begin with.

Even if the goal of holistic, multi-dimensional explanations seems far-fetched at present, the importance (and difficulty) of getting individual disciplines or models to state their assumptions clearly and accept their limits should not be underestimated. Indeed, I believe that the difficulty in interdisciplinarity within the social sciences lies not so much in the fact that different disciplines or sub-disciplines have competing models for the same phenomenon, but that at least some disciplines refuse to stick to a clear causal model which can be the basis for a meaningful debate. The major culprit here is the sub-discipline of neo-classical economics. In its typical hegemonic style, it claims to have long ago abandoned the model of human beings as strictly "profit-maximizing" or "consumption-maximizing" and moved to a "utility maximizing" framework, which creates room for incorporating all other models of human behavior. This claim has only limited validity. First, even though the utility function approach allows for (say) altruism to be part of the person's rationale, other assumptions about what constitutes "rational" behavior (e.g., that people maximize not satisfice, a la Herbert Simon) as well as the tendency to equate rigor with mathematical models limit the capacity of economics to actually represent diverse behavioral situations. Second, in practice, most analysts eventually write the utility function in terms of consumption or imputed income or some other simple material benefit. I would argue that economics as a theory of human behavior has some explanatory power only when it is cast in such concrete terms; once material considerations are replaced with "utility," it is impossible to predict human behavior since utility is unmeasurable and could mean different things to different individuals. It would therefore be easier to hold a meaningful conversation if economists were to state their causal model at the outset, rather than to act as if any causal model is welcome but then impose a particular method of data collection and hypothesis testing that might rule out most non-material explanations. This is also the essence of Harriss's critique of the distortion of the concept of social capital through economistic analysis (Harriss 2002).

Epistemology and method

The above is not to suggest that the epistemological and methodological divide between the interpretive and the quantitative social sciences (what Kanbur calls the "qual–quant" divide – see Kanbur 2001) has been bridged. I shall, however, not dwell on it here. One reason is that it has been more exhaustively treated by the other chapters in this book and by others elsewhere (e.g., Kanbur 2002). But another reason also is that the focus on the qual-quant divide seems to have distracted us from the more fundamental questions of rigor (Harriss 2002), viz., the realism of the assumptions that are necessarily made when theory and data are forced to be articulated through, and hence "reduced" by, the quantitative method of economics. As Kaushik Basu said in the "Conversations II" workshop, economists tend to ignore phenomena or processes that cannot be put into a mathematical form. Unless this rigidity in neoclassical economics is weakened, one cannot hope for a truly interdisciplinary exploration. What will remain then is the hegemonistic approach of economists, where anthropological methods of *data collection* alone are used to "thicken" the explanations of economic models (Vijayendra Rao: ch. 10, this volume).

Thus, promoting genuine interdisciplinarity within the social sciences will require a methodological (and theoretical) pluralism that ecological economists have been arguing for (Norgaard 1989) and neoclassical economists have been consistently opposing (hence the rejection of ecological economics by hard-nosed "environmental economists," especially in the USA). This applies to the hard-core political ecologists or others as well – see, e.g., Vayda (1996).

Academic organization and social standing

One would have expected that, even if natural science undergraduates do not get exposed to the social sciences and vice versa, there would be significant exposure to disciplines within the same block. Unfortunately, the situation within the social sciences does not seem to be much better – cross-disciplinary exposure, especially across the econ-anthro divide, is limited and the hostility palpable (Karanth 2002; Guha 2002). Moreover, as in the case of the natural–social divide, policy-makers seems to value economists more than anthropologists, especially in developing countries, if one goes by the proportion of funds provided for the two categories of social sciences.[14] And the clout of economists, or neoclassical economists to be precise, in the international donor community needs no highlighting, notwithstanding the inclusion of some anthropologists and sociologists into the World Bank. It would be hard to estimate how much of this difference in the social standing of different social science disciplines and sub-disciplines is due to the qual–quant divide and the layperson's belief that quantitative is more rigorous, and to what extent it is due to the fact that the neoclassical economists' overriding attention to efficiency and their models that (for instance) deify markets are aligned with the interests of the powerful actors in society today. As mentioned earlier, these things come in packages. The fact remains that this situation aggravates the disciplinary divides.

What the Econ–Anthro Divide Means for the Links with the Natural Sciences

With the above analysis of the differences within the social sciences in mind, we can re-examine the social-natural linkage to see how the barriers may vary depending upon which kind of social scientist the natural scientist is conversing with. To the extent that non-economists are somewhat more sensitive than economists to their own value positions, I speculate that anthropologists may be able to detect the value judgments of natural scientists more quickly and flag these issues early on in a conversation as compared to economists. For instance, the fundamental problem with the colonial concept of "scientific forestry," viz., that it is scientific with respect to a particular socio-political objective of forestry, was flagged by Ramachandra Guha, a sociologist-cum-historian (Guha 1985). And to the extent that the method of anthropologists requires spending much more time in the field, one should and does find that anthropologists are generally more sensitive to and careful in representing the biophysical context of a problem. The emergence of ecological anthropology (e.g., Vayda and McCay 1975) and political ecology (Blaikie and Brookfield 1987) as major streams within the non-economics social sciences before the emergence of ecological economics (Costanza 1989) is an indication of this phenomenon.

It is therefore ironical that, when natural scientists or engineers attempt to cross boundaries and engage with the social aspect of environmental problems, they generally tend to adopt the economics perspective (e.g., Perrings et al. 1995). This seems to follow from their "natural" affinity with the quantitative and mathematical treatment in modern neoclassical economics.[15] The exceptions are those within ecology that still adhere to the

---

[14] For instance, most of the institutions supported by the Indian Council for Social Science Research are dominated by economists.

[15] But it also might be reinforced by the increasing support being provided to ecological or environmental economics (as compared to, say, political ecology) by the state and by donor agencies – a phenomenon that may have more to do with affinities in values and models than the inherent worth of this particular interdisciplinary crossing.

natural history approach (rather than mathematical modeling), who then seem to find it easier to talk to anthropologists (e.g., Maffi 2001).

Conclusion: Ways around the Barriers

Conversations between economists and anthropologists have tended to get bogged down in the question of whether interdisciplinarity is possible at all. In the context of CPRs, by emphasizing the inextricable biophysical dimension and thereby calling for a three-way conversation, I have tried to push the debate from "whether" to "how." I have tried to provide a bird's-eye view of the barriers to such interdisciplinarity in practice, which include not just differences in epistemology and method but perhaps more serious ones of value judgments, models and social standing. While the many examples of interesting social-natural integration provide us with hope, the height and multiplicity of the barriers, especially within the social sciences, may make us pause. Thus, before concluding how one might get around these barriers, it might be worth briefly re-examining the assumption we began with, viz., that some amount of interdisciplinarity is desirable and feasible. If the barriers are as significant as described above, one would be justified in asking whether the game is worth the candle. In response, one may begin by noting that interdisciplinarity is not an end in itself. It is necessary only when one wants to understand a problem "comprehensively," which in turn is necessary only when the ultimate motivation behind the research is a wish to bring about some lasting *change*, i.e., in a problem-solving context. In the "Conversations II" workshop, David Szanton narrated how efforts by the US Social Science Research Council to promote interdisciplinary research worked only when there was a concrete and pressing social problem to focus on. Kanbur (2002) makes essentially the same argument when discussing how to promote interdisciplinarity in development studies. And CPR degradation is clearly an important and urgent social problem with an inextricable biophysical component. A three-way conversation is therefore necessary. And based upon the preceding discussion, some suggestions may be made to make such a conversation more fruitful.

Clearly, the first and foremost requirement is for researchers to be much more self-reflective about the value judgments embedded in their work. Given that they are trying to contribute towards "solving" socio-environmental problems, it is essential that they ask what "problem" it is that they are trying to solve and what concerns underpin this problem definition and influence their choice of variables of interest and causal models. For instance, rather than taking collective action as "obviously good" and thereby making it the dependent variable every time, they might ask who benefits from collective action and who does not (such as those owning land in the command area of an irrigation tank and those who do not), what concerns might not be met simply because collective action occurs (such as the biodiversity concerns of a community beyond local forest users) and which of these concerns may be legitimately brought into the picture. Rather than give such issues the usual short shrift (the mandatory opening paragraph that goes something like "tropical deforestation is a matter of concern because . . ."), researchers should take them up as seriously as questions of theory and methods. And when working in teams, significant amount of negotiation will be required to figure out which concerns should be addressed in the particular inquiry; otherwise it will be hard to maintain the motivation required for what can be an exhausting effort.

Second, researchers will have to examine and unlearn the hidden assumptions one makes about the "other," and re-learn the more nuanced explanations that the other disciplinary block has about its area of inquiry. When working across the natural-social divide, this would lead to biophysical models that are better informed about the nature of social interventions in ecosystems and the social values derived from them, and social models that better reflect the complexities of biophysical systems. In either case, the choice of "linking variables" – variables that link the critical social aspect of natural processes to the critical natural aspect of social practices – would be crucial. Forest ecologists studying the impact of fuelwood collection on forests would then presumably distinguish between differences in harvesting practices, such as the ratio of green wood to deadwood extraction or the girth of saplings felled, rather than simply focusing on "tonnes of biomass" (for details, see Lélé 1993a). Hydrologists would identify exactly which portion of streamflow or infiltration is socially useful to which community, rather than giving gross values for the variables. And political scientists would presumably be more sensitive to the ecological dynamics of a resource before trying to link group size or other variables to the presence of collective action. This "multi-disciplinary" form of research would eventually lead to more "interdisciplinary" insights that actually modify the individual disciplinary models to some extent. For instance, anthropologists working in the Sahel have contributed as much as ecologists to the overturning of the "equilibrium" model of grassland ecosystems in favor of the "disturbance" model (see Mace 1991).

Adequately linked multi-disciplinarity is not, however, a useful model for integrating economic and anthropological research. This is because their insights, when independently arrived at, are more likely to be conflicting than complementary. Even if concerns are notionally the same (such as poverty alleviation), the assumptions and value judgments inextricably tied to their models introduce significant differences in nuance and emphasis. Much more openness, exchange of methods and ideas and a strong belief in pluralism will be required before much progress can be made. Notions of rigor tied exclusively to quantitative analysis will have to be loosened up, and economists would have to begin spending much more time in the field. Anthropologists would have to be more willing to make specific recommendations for policy and/or action than they do today, while economists would have to think twice before they crank out the next set of generalizations for policy-makers. Given the difficulty (if not impossibility!) of such crossings happening on a large scale, interdisciplinarity here might be restricted to a few selective crossings by individuals, rather than the possibility of team work that might exist (and be essential) across the social–natural divide.[16]

This is not to suggest that shared concerns, greater self-reflectivity, and cross-disciplinary exposure will suffice. To promote interdisciplinary research at large, changes at the individual- and team-level must be complemented by major institution-level changes in curricula, incentives, evaluation criteria, and accountability. These may not be in the hands of individuals who seek to do interdisciplinary work; however, some of these constraints could be eased at the outset of major interdisciplinary projects (e.g., by getting parent institutions to agree that the outputs that emerge should not be evaluated by conventional

---

[16]   Even for such multi-disciplinary teams spanning the social–natural divide to function, I have found that having one truly "interdisciplinary" person who knows enough about each discipline to be able to "communicate" with each of the disciplinary specialists is very useful.

disciplinary or departmental standards). Eventually, society at large will have to realize the importance of generating a truly interdisciplinary understanding of CPRs and provide the necessary pressure, institutional space and recognition for carrying out these efforts rigorously.

References

Agrawal, A., 1985, "Politics of environment II," in A. Agarwal and S. Narain (eds), *The State of India's Environment 1984–85: The Second Citizen's Report*, Centre for Science and Environment, New Delhi, pp. 362–80.

Anonymous, 2005, "In praise of soft science," *Nature*, 435(7045): 1003.

Bardhan, P. K., ed., 1989, *Conversations between Economists and Anthropologists: Methodological Issues in Measuring Economic Change in Rural India*, Oxford University Press, Delhi.

Bauer, H. H., 1990, "Barriers against interdisciplinarity: implications for studies of science, technology and society," *Science, Technology & Human Values*, 15(1): 105–19.

Blaikie, P., 1985, *Political Economy of Soil Erosion in Developing Countries*, Longman, London.

Blaikie, P. and H. Brookfield, eds, 1987, *Land Degradation and Society*, Methuen, New York.

Botkin, D. B., 1992, *Discordant Harmonies: A New Ecology for the Twenty-first Century*, Oxford University Press, New York.

Broadway, R. W. and N. Bruce, 1984, *Welfare Economics*, Blackwell, Oxford.

Costanza, R., 1989, "What is ecological economics?," *Ecological Economics*, 1(1): 1–7.

Dasgupta, P., A. Sen, and S. Marglin, 1972, *Guidelines for Project Evaluation*, United Nations Industrial Development Organization, Vienna and New York.

Gadgil, M., 1987a, "Depleting renewable resources: a case study from Karnataka Western Ghats," *Indian Journal of Agricultural Economics*, 42: 376–87.

Gadgil, M., 1987b, "An operational research programme for integrated development of microcatchments in Uttara Kannada district: a proposal," Technical Report 49, Centre for Ecological Sciences, Indian Institute of Science, Bangalore.

Gadgil, M. and R. Guha, 1992, *This Fissured Land: An Ecological History of India*, Oxford University Press, Delhi.

Guha, R., 1985, "Scientific forestry and social change in Uttarakhand," *Economic and Political Weekly*, 20(45–7): 1939–51.

Guha, R., 2002, "Barriers to inter/trans-disciplinary research," in S. Lélé, G. Kadekodi, and B. Agrawal (eds), *Interdisciplinarity in Environmental Research: Concepts, Barriers and Possibilities*, Indian Society for Ecological Economics, New Delhi, 34.

Gulbenkian Commission on the Restructuring of the Social Sciences, 1996, *Open the Social Sciences: Report of the Gulbenkian Commission on the Restructuring of the Social Sciences*, Stanford University Press, Stanford.

Hanna, S. and M. Munasinghe, eds, 1995, *Property Rights and the Environment: Social and Ecological Issues*, Beijer International Institute of Ecological Economics and the World Bank, Washington, DC.

Harriss, J., 2002, "The case for cross-disciplinary approaches in international development," *World Development*, 30(3): 487–96.

Howarth, R. B., 2001, "Climate rights and ecological modeling," in D. C. Hall and R. B. Howarth (eds), *The Long-term Economics of Climate Change*, Elsevier, Amsterdam

Jackson, C., 2002, "Disciplining gender?," *World Development*, 30(3): 497–509.

Jasanoff, S., 2002, "Reading between the lines: the disciplines and the environment," in S. Lélé, G. Kadekodi, and B. Agrawal (eds), *Interdisciplinarity in Environmental Research: Concepts, Barriers and Possibilities*, Indian Society for Ecological Economics, New Delhi, pp. 3–5.

Jodha, N. S., 1986, "Common property resources and rural poor in dry regions of India," *Economic and Political Weekly*, 21(27): 1169–81.

Kanbur, R., ed., 2001, *Qual–quant: Qualitative and Quantitative Poverty Appraisal – Complementarities, Tensions and the Way Forward*, Cornell University, Ithaca, NY.

Kanbur, R., 2002, "Economics, social science and development," *World Development*, 30(3): 477–86.

Karanth, Gopal, K. 2002. "Economics and sociology: staying on or merging the borders – reflections on the social side of the boundary," in S. Lélé, G. Kadekodi, and B. Agrawal (eds), *Interdisciplinarity in Environmental Research: Concepts, Barriers and Possibilities*, Indian Society for Ecological Economics, New Delhi, 44–6.

Kessler, J. J., 1994, "Usefulness of the human carrying capacity concept in assessing ecological sustainability of land-use in semi-arid regions," *Agriculture, Ecosystems & Environment*, 48(3): 273–84.

Kiran Kumar, A. K., A. Menon, and I. Patil, 2006, "Methodological challenges of social science research on land use change and watershed services: insights from the Western Ghats," in J. Krishnaswamy, S. Lélé, and R. Jayakumar (eds), *Hydrology and Watershed Services in the Western Ghats of India*, Tata McGraw-Hill, New Delhi, 249–64.

Kockelmans, J. J., 1979, "Why interdisciplinarity?" in J. J. Kockelmans (ed.), *Interdisciplinarity and Higher Education*, Pennsylvania State University Press, University Park,

Lélé, S., 1993a, "Degradation, sustainability, or transformation: a case study of villagers' use of forest lands in the Malnaad region of Uttara Kannada district, India," Ph.D. thesis, University of California, Berkeley.

Lélé, S., 1993b, "Private property rights and forest preservation in Karnataka Western Ghats, India: Comment," *American Journal of Agricultural Economics*, 75: 492–5.

Lélé, S., 1994, "Sustainable use of biomass resources: a note on definitions, criteria, and practical applications," *Energy for Sustainable Development*, 1(4): 42–6.

Lélé, S., 2000, "Degradation, sustainability or transformation?," *Seminar*, 486: 31–7.

Lélé, S., 2001, " 'Pixelising the Commons' and 'Commonising the Pixel': Boon or Bane?" *Common Property Resource Digest*, 58: 1–3.

Lélé, S. and R. B. Norgaard, 1996, "Sustainability and the scientist's burden," *Conservation Biology*, 10(2): 354–65.

Lélé, S. and R. Norgaard, 2005, "Practicing interdisciplinarity," *Bioscience*, 55(11): 967–75.

Lélé, S., G. Rajashekhar, V. R. Hegde, G. P. Kumar, and P. Saravanakumar, 1998, "Meso-scale analysis of forest condition and its determinants: a case study from the Western Ghats region, India," *Current Science*, 75(3): 256–63.

Liverman, D., E. F. Moran, R. R. Rindfuss, and P. C. Stern, eds, 1998, *People and Pixels: Linking Remote Sensing and Social Science*, National Academy Press, Washington, DC.

Lomborg, B., 2001, *The Skeptical Environmentalist: Measuring the Real State of the World*, Cambridge University Press, Cambridge.

Mace, R., 1991, "Overgrazing overstated," *Nature*, 349(6307): 280–1.

MacGregor, J. L. L., 1894, "Letter No. 6237 of 1893–94 from the Conservator of Forests, Southern Circle, to the Commissioner, Southern Division," Government of Maharashtra (Archives).

Maffi, L., ed., 2001, *On Biocultural Diversity: Linking Language, Knowledge, and the Environment*, Smithsonian Institution Press, Washington, DC.

Masera, O., 1994, "Socioeconomic and environmental implications of fuelwood use dynamics and fuel switching in rural Mexico," Ph.D. thesis, University of California.

Menon, A., 1999, " 'Common property studies' and the limits to equity: some conceptual concerns and possibilities," *Review of Development and Change*, 4(1): 51–70.

Menon, A. and S. Lélé, 2003, "Critiquing the commons: missing the woods for the trees?" *Common Property Resource Digest*, 64: 1–4.

Merchant, C., 1989, *Ecological Revolutions: Nature, Gender, and Science in New England*, University of North Carolina Press, Chapel Hill.

Mies, M. and V. Shiva, 1993, *Ecofeminism*, Zed Books, London.

Nadkarni, M. V., S. A. Pasha, and L. S. Prabhakar, 1989, *The Political Economy of Forest Use and Management*, Sage Publications, New Delhi.

Norgaard, R. B., 1989, "The case for methodological pluralism," *Ecological Economics*, 1(1): 37–57.

Ostrom, E., 1990, *Governing the Commons: The Evolution of Institutions for Collective Action*, Cambridge University Press, New York.

Pandey, U. and J. S. Singh, 1984, "Energy-flow relationships between agro and forest ecosystems in Central Himalayas," *Environmental Conservation*, 11(1): 45–53.

Pearce, D., 1998, *Economics and Environment: Essays on Ecological Economics and Sustainable Development*, 2nd edn, Elgar Publishers, Cheltenham.

Perrings, C. K., K.-G. Mäler, C. Folke, C. S. Holling, and B.-O. Jansson, eds, 1995, *Biodiversity Loss: Economic and Ecological Issues*, Cambridge University Press, Cambridge.

Reddy, A. N. Y., D. Sarmah, P. Pande, G. B. Narvekar, B. S. Gouda, and K. Yekanthappa, 1986, "Integrated approach for eco-development of Uttara Kannada district," mimeo, Office of the Conservator of Forests, Canara Circle, Karnataka Forest Department, Dharwad.

Repetto, R., 1986, *Economic Policy Reforms for Natural Resource Conservation*, World Resources Institute, Washington, DC.

Rykiel, E. J., 2001, "Scientific objectivity, value systems, and policymaking," *BioScience*, 51: 433–6.

Schoenberger, E., 2001, "Interdisciplinarity and social power," *Progress in Human Geography*, 25(3): 365–82.

Shrader-Frechette, K. S. and E. D. McCoy, 1993, *Method in Ecology: Strategies for Conservation*, Cambridge University Press, New York.

Singh, J. S., U. Pandey, and A. K. Tiwari, 1984, "Man and forests: A Central Himalayan case study," *Ambio*, 13(2): 80–7.

Stevenson, G. G., 1991, *Common Property Economics: A General Theory and Land Use Applications*, Cambridge University Press, Cambridge.

Turner, M., 1992, "Life on the margin: herding practices and the relationship between economy and ecology in the inland Niger delta of Mali," Ph.D. thesis, University of California.

Turner, M., 1993, "Overstocking the range: a critical analysis of the environmental science of Sahelian pastoralism," *Economic Geography*, 69(4): 402–21.

Turner, M., 1999, "Spatial and temporal scaling of grazing impact on the species composition and productivity of Sahelian annual grasslands," *Journal of Arid Environments*, 41(3): 277–97.

Vayda, A. P., 1996, *Methods and Explanations in the Study of Human Actions and Their Environmental Effects*, CIFOR/WWF Special Publication, Centre for International Forestry Research and World Wide Fund for Nature, Jakarta, Indonesia.

Vayda, A. P. and B. J. McCay, 1975, *New Directions in Ecological Anthropology*, vol. 4, Annual Reviews, Inc., Palo Alto, CA.

Voelcker, J. A., 1897, *Report on the Improvement of Indian Agriculture*, Office of the Superintendent of Government Printing, Calcutta.

12: Feminism Spoken Here

Epistemologies for Interdisciplinary Development Research

Cecile Jackson

Introduction

Research policy increasingly emphasizes interdisciplinary and multidisciplinary research, which is valued for its problem-solving qualities and for delivering accountability, yet the institutional and conceptual obstacles can seem ever greater as disciplines assert themselves in competition for resources. This chapter argues that one of the drivers of successful interdisciplinary research is a shared politics of progressive social change; feminist epistemology demonstrates how shared values allow disciplines to converse and cooperate, through the subjectivities of researchers. It also suggests that feminist epistemologies offer a set of conceptual advances for overcoming old problems between disciplines, particularly anthropology and economics,[1] such as different ideas about individuals and persons, which are important for development studies. The arguments made for the value of feminist epistemologies are relevant to all development studies research since a mark of this field is its distinctive concern for social justice on a global scale. Feminist epistemologies have some good answers to the question of what it is that makes politically engaged research – on poverty and wellbeing, voice and governance, resource access and control, social exclusion and inequality – stronger than research which pretends to neutrality.

Development research has not been immune to androcentric knowledge practices and over the last few decades feminist epistemologies within gender analysis have decentred the orientations to male interests and lives in the ways that poverty is defined, how class and status are identified, how labour and leisure are bounded, and how productive work

---

[1] The terms economics and anthropology of course can make no pretence at comprehensive coverage, given the diversity within disciplines, and refer largely to that area of development economics represented by Sen, where the bridge between the disciplines has the smallest area to span, and to a reflexive strand of social anthropology.

is understood and valued. But it is arguable that gender analysis of development has been taken up largely at the level of categorical comparisons of women and men rather than integrating the deeper changes needed in rethinking what constitutes knowledge of development. Human well-being is conceptualized in ways which start from an assumed male subject and men remain the norm against which women, the deviant gender, are measured. For example, instead of asking why women are less self-interested than men, we could be asking why men are so self-interested, or instead of asking why girls have lower self-esteem than boys we could be asking why boys are conceited (Anderson 2005: 201). Of course, mere table-turning is not the point; the point is that no one gender should set the norm for humanity.

The coming together of disciplines requires motivation, and what I seek to do here is to first look at this as a cooperation problem, then, after a brief overview of feminist epistemologies, to discuss some strengths of these approaches as a vehicle for disciplinary conversation and intercourse.[2]

Are Economists from Mars and Anthropologists from Venus?

If the metaphor of kinship describes the relationship between disciplinarity and interdisciplinarity, so that disciplinarity is to lineage as interdisciplinarity is to marriage (Jackson 2002; Strathern 2004: 45–6), then one could look at cooperation between partners as disciplines, and the obstacles and rewards that this bears. Sen's cooperative conflict approach (1990) offers a device to pinpoint how the different interests and perceptions of economists and anthropologists produce unsatisfactory outcomes, even when these obstacles can be overcome. This model suggests that bargained outcomes reflect the power of the party with the greater degree of self-interest, the more highly valorized contribution to knowledge, and the stronger position in the event of cooperation failure. Thus one would ask about the actual and perceived self-interest of each party, their actual and perceived contributions to a partnership, and their actual and perceived breakdown positions in the event of cooperation failure.

In relation to perceived and actual self-interest – the extent to which each discipline sees itself as self-contained and independent of other disciplines, and the extent to which this is actually so – both anthropology and economics have clear and self-sufficient identities with autonomous bodies of theory, and would not see the well-being of their discipline as dependent on the well-being of the other. But economics has a willingness to colonize other disciplines, and an assumed ability to absorb a much greater terrain than anthropology would claim, seen for example in their takeover of the concept of social capital (Fine 2001). Economics arguably faces less internal questioning and angst over how to define itself, what its scope is, what the boundaries are between it and other social sciences, compared to anthropology which is given to continuous soul searching, doubt and selfcritique (indeed, to some, this is one of its most attractive features).

---

[2]   Multidisciplinarity is usually taken to mean work which is closely aligned to that of other disciplines on the same subject whilst interdisciplinarity refers to that which integrates disciplines within one analytical framework. Too much can be made of this distinction; here I use the latter term to cover a range of such engagements.

On actual and perceived contributions, setting aside adjudicating on actual contributions – which has been done extensively elsewhere – what is the perception amongst economists and anthropologists of their contribution to development studies knowledge? Economists display considerable certainty and readily accept their pre-eminent position, whilst anthropologists tend more to a position which, whilst asserting the value of their insights, is simultaneously self-critical and anxious, for example, of the complicity of anthropology in the project of colonialism, and concern about development as neo-colonialism. Ambivalence about deeper involvement in the development establishment, and in practice and policy, also marks anthropology, although this is not simply a lack of the self-esteem of economics, but a disposition in which the margins are quite a good place to be.

In relation to actual and perceived breakdown positions, one may ask how much do economists need anthropologists and vice versa? When cooperation cannot overcome differences, then what threat points exist? "Divorce" or the failure to "marry" leaves anthropologists with potentially constrained funding (whilst bilateral development agencies may not necessarily favour economics in funding decisions, multilaterals certainly fund more research in economics than in other disciplines), although possibly with higher social status amongst other anthropologists, since interdisciplinary partnerships so frequently position anthropology in a service role. The threat available for anthropologists to wield over economists appears even weaker; failure to cooperate with anthropologists would carry few apparent costs.

A cooperative conflicts approach might suggest then that economics is the stronger partner whose preferences are more likely to be reflected in outcomes. But a bargaining approach seeks to explain outcomes with reference to the gains to individuals from cooperation, whilst interdisciplinary feminist research is possibly an example of another kind of pathway to cooperation based on other kinds of gains. In an extended framework of "gains," the researcher's identities and subjectivities motivate a different kind of calculus, in which the gains are not only material or social status. A willingness to put in the extra effort and invest time in understanding how other disciplines approach your subject, and further, risking the disapproval of senior colleagues and the loss of disciplinary identity by publishing across these boundaries, may be as much an act driven by conviction and a set of moral values, as a calculus of gain. If this is a calculus, it is one in which self-accountability, a sense of doing the right thing, is the main pay-off. Of course a social accountability exists too – to those academic communities of solidarity (Benhabib 1995: 246) which we all inhabit, be they explicitly feminist, or simply a taken-for-granted orientation to social justice. This is a very different kind of accountability to the societal accountability by which researchers have to justify the value of the work they do at public expense. Self-accountability and social solidarities also create incentives for, and gains from, interdisciplinary cooperation.

To be a woman social scientist with no interest in gender relations is fairly anomalous, both because of the individual lived experience of gender and because of the implicit solidarity of the community of women that exists by virtue of the subaltern nature of (some) womanhood – even if this is only latent. Whilst perhaps only a minority of women academics might selfidentify as feminist, a feminist sensibility seems to me nearly universal in the everyday alertness to gender as a differential, marking actions, speech and meanings. But should we feel faintly embarrassed by these sensibilities, and defensive about them because they suggest bias, or should we explicitly recognize them in order to achieve a superior "objectivity" and, as I suggest below, celebrate them for motivating interdisciplinary and multidisciplinary understandings of gender relations and gender justice?

Feminist Epistemologies

The starting point for feminist research of all hues is the case for the multiple exclusions of women from science, as respondents and researchers, and the male biases of research in which men have been the unmarked representatives of humanity, have commanded discourses of power, dominated the practice of science and produced knowledges bearing the particular stamp of male identities and interests. The project of formulating research perspectives and practices which overcome these failings has involved debate and innovation across the spectrum from research techniques to epistemologies.[3] Methods are based on historical traces, listening or observing; feminists can use any method, but how they use them may be distinctive. They see significance in different things than a non-feminist, using the same method, might. In methods based on testimony, questions of who is spoken to, how they are spoken to, what expectations are held about who can speak on behalf of others, and what can be voiced, how meanings are understood, and what status speech has as evidence, are all distinctive concerns in the feminist application of mainstream methods of interviewbased data collection. The project of recovering the voices of women in historical records faces particular problems from the silencing effects of subaltern status. Feminist applications of research methods also usually transcend the qualitative – quantitative divide, and can be located in economics, demography, geography and other fields where quantitative methods are deployed – an important characteristic for interdisciplinary interchanges.

At a higher level of abstraction are feminist methodologies,[4] such as the expansion and reformulation of Marxist political economy to understand women's exploitation in wage labour, or feminist political ecology, which puts the elements of political ecology as theory, through a gendered lens (Rochleau 1995). But our focus here is on feminist epistemologies[5] which emphasize the validity of knowledges based on lived experience, and on gender identity. There are a number of feminist epistemologies, which can only be sketched here, following the conventional distinctions made by Harding (1987).

Feminist empiricism suggests that a feminist knowledge includes women, and therefore is more complete. This stance does not reject science but says that male bias can be eliminated by doing better science, by stricter adherence to the norms of science. This is perhaps the stance which is least critical of science, but nevertheless subverts the ideology of science insofar as it recognizes the intrusion of social identities into the practices

---

[3]   Methods are techniques for gathering evidence, methodologies are theories and analysis of how research should proceed, and epistemologies are theories of knowledge, or what could be thought of as justificatory strategies. There are no feminist methods of research, but there are feminist methodologies and epistemologies.

[4]   Methodology concerns itself with how theories are applied in particular research. Marxist political economy is a methodology, since it tells you what things you need to know about in order to apply that theory (ownership of means of production, social relations, class differentiation and so on).

[5]   Epistemology is a theory of knowledge, and an answer to the question of how we know what we know. It is interested in what counts as knowledge and who can be a knower. Epistemologies work as justificatory strategies, based on, for example, appeals to God, custom, observation, reason or authority.

and findings of scientific endeavours. Feminist standpoint as an epistemology has been much debated. It suggests that if knowledge is socially constructed then it is unavoidably gendered, since gender is a major form of social differentiation in all known societies. Women and men know different things and in different ways. But further, since the subordination of women is a general feature of human societies (albeit in different spheres, manners and degrees, and not excluding the gendered vulnerabilities faced by particular groups of men) these knowledges are devalued relative to those of hegemonic masculinity. The project of revaluing women's knowledges leads many feminists into opposition to methodologies and methods built around both the assumed male subject and the male researcher. Feminist post-structuralist epistemology is distinguished by a focus on the cultural and on gender as a performance, an emphasis on power residing in the ability to frame discourse, rather than to command material resources, and a rejection of universalism in favour of relativistic positions on say, gender equity.

In the selective discussion that follows I have had to skate over many important debates and disagreements in feminist epistemologies, perhaps suggesting a misleading impression of unity, but I hope to have focused on areas of substantial agreement for the purpose of showing why feminist epistemologies are so useful for understanding poverty and inequality and what degree of adjacency exists with (some kinds of) economics. Dilemmas and disagreements which I have had to bypass include the compatibility of feminism with post-modernism (Benhabib 1994); the critique of feminists from developing countries and women of colour (Mohanty et al. 1991); the relationship to science and kinds of empiricism; questioning of the value of reflexivity (Patai 1994); the potentially exploitative quality of empathy and intimacy with respondents (Stacey 1991); and the ethical issues of advancing academic careers on the basis of the lives of the deeply disadvantaged.

What I do next, however, is to comment on some elements common to much feminist epistemology, which seem to me likely to strengthen interdisciplinary development research. In using the terms feminist epistemology or methodology I do not of course imply that all feminist researchers use these approaches, only that the political logic of social justice for women has produced attention to a set of issues which enriches individual disciplines and offers valencies across them. What do these epistemologies have to offer in the project of bringing economists and anthropologists into closer and more constructive conversation? I first make two points relating to researchers and the conduct of research, and then suggest three areas where the substantive content of development research is enhanced by feminist epistemologies.

Feminism, Positionality, and Objectivity

> Feminist objectivity is about limited location and situated knowledge, not about transcendence and splitting of subject and object. (Haraway 1991: 189–90)

Feminist epistemologies are marked by the pro-women stance of feminism, a position of doing research for women. This is clearly very distinctive since it does not accept the ideal of value-free objectivity. Thus a key question is "how is it that politicized research produces more complete and less distorted research results?." The question also has broad relevance since most development research is based in a set of values – that poverty and inequality are bad – and thus also needs to engage with how an explicit social justice orientation strengthens research, rather than constituting "bias."

Given the pro-women stance of feminist research, and the weight given to women's voices, the question of whether this simply amounts to "bias" or if, on the contrary, it can be justified as conducive to better knowledge and understanding, is important. Feminists argue that it is precisely the subject position of women, with particular kinds of social experiences, that makes feminist knowledge less distorted, or "truer." The answer to why feminist knowledge is stronger is not only because it includes women, and thus works with a fuller representation of humanity, but also because women have superior access to experience which includes that of being subordinated. To have a feminist standpoint is to have that understanding of life which comes through the struggles of being disdained and disadvantaged.

There are clearly problems of potential essentialism in giving an uncritical epistemological privilege to any social group, and in the implication that "because a woman says it, it is true," or that there are "women's ways of knowing." Essentializing women in the face of evident variations amongst them in relation to the experience of subalternity is problematic, and is discussed further below. For example, India provides plentiful examples of women expressing views that are racist and sexist, and furthermore, epistemological privilege of this sort dodges the issue of how women understand and articulate their own interests, and does not allow for any kind of "false consciousness" or mystification. Many gender analysts would have a problem with the idea of epistemological privilege in its most naked form, and would prefer a recognition of positionality and the gender politics of knowledge which is, however, self-critical.

One of the consequences of feminist values is the attention to positionality, and situated knowledges, since we understand the subordination of women as grounded in social structures which, whilst certainly changing over time, tend to reproduce relations of inequality of varying kinds and severity. What follows from a recognition of positionality in relation to knowledge is a distinctive awareness of how the marginality of women has distorted and compromised the claims to objectivity of mainstream social science. For example, for sample surveys to represent a given population, each member must have an equal chance of inclusion, an equal ability to "speak," and an equal ability to be understood. But these conditions often do not apply to women who are largely excluded by virtue of not being household heads (surveys still usually interview household heads and use the household as the unit of analysis), who experience muteness by virtue of the maleness of dominant social discourses (Ardener 1975), and who face interlocutors with greater social distance from them than male respondents do (the majority of research assistants and researchers are men and language distances are greater, so that women are even less clearly "heard" than poor men).

Added to this is the failure of science to address issues of context, that is, the absence of objectivity in the ways research questions are arrived at, weighted and ranked, and supported. Thus Sandra Harding (1991) has argued that standpoint theory has a "strong" objectivity compared to the "weak" objectivity of science, since the latter only applies to research methods and the context of justification, rather than the deeper question of how problems are defined and hypotheses fashioned in the first place – in other words, to objectivity in the context of discovery. A feminist awareness of values and biases in this context offers an enhanced objectivity compared to an assumption of a neutral context of discovery (Rose 1994: 93). As well as the context for the definition of research questions, the context of investigation is also subject to unconscious bias. Elizabeth Anderson uses the example of double-blind, multi-centre, placebo-controlled testing of drugs, which is used precisely to exclude the effects of values and biases, to make the point that "feminist empiricist epistemology . . . produces arguments of the same type as those already accepted by our knowledge practices" (Anderson 2005: 191). These practices are used to ensure that bias is eliminated, and in a similar way feminist attention to context seeks to remove gender biases, conscious or not, from knowledge claims, and indeed involves raising the standards for evaluating methods of data collection and interpretation. Thus feminist epistemology is an explicitly political enterprise, but one that is justified by epistemic values, such as reason and empirical adequacy, to which science "already declares its allegiance" (p. 192).

Does this aspect of feminist epistemology drive a wedge between its followers and development economists? It should not, since these are the procedures of good science, and also since the gap between these ideas and mainstream social science may be narrowing. Recently Amartya Sen discussed what he calls positional objectivity thus, "The nature of objectivity in epistemology, decision theory, and ethics has to take note of the parametric dependence of observation and inference on the position of the observer" (Sen 2003: 463). This is not to describe the "simply subjective" and arbitrary, but a set of beliefs which appear from the location of the observer, and the information at hand, to be true. Positionally objective beliefs may of course be right or wrong, but in discussing the latter Sen links this to the Marxian term "objective illusion" and remarks that "an objective illusion . . . is a positionally objective belief that is, in fact, mistaken" (p. 470), giving the example of self-perception of high morbidity in Kerala despite actually low morbidity. High literacy and extensive public health services make Keralites more aware of health threats and preventative actions, and therefore their positionally objective assessment is of high morbidity. Sen argues that the persistence of gender inequalities within families involves objective illusions, when for example, the locations of observers places them in cultural frames which normalize, say, excess mortality of girls. Thus he is accepting as objective a class of views and perceptions which would have been seen as merely subjective until recently.

Furthermore, if one was to turn the searchlight of positional objectivity around onto economists and social scientists themselves, one would see that such researchers work not with a complete objectivity, but with one constrained by their own positionalities (of gender, class, race) and objective illusions. So what then is subjectivity? Sen seems to see this as a residual – for that which cannot be specified as positionally objective (p. 475) – and he defines it as "special mental tendencies, particular types of inexperience, or constrained features of reasoning" (p. 475), which is quite delicious in its connotations, when applied to researcher subjectivities. I next discuss other, more positive, ways of considering researcher subjectivities. But first let us pause to note that the decades of engagement of feminists with ideas of objectivity have not arisen through debates within disciplines but rather as a consequence of both looking across at androcentrism in science and of the commitment to doing research for women (Harding 2005: 218). In other words it is the politics of feminism which drives interdisciplinarity and epistemological progress.

Feminist Reflexivity, Researcher Subjectivities, and Interdisciplinarity

The term reflexivity comes from the ethno-methodological tradition in sociology and refers to the fact that, in describing something, we do not stand apart from it, separate from the order already existing around us. Rather, we are part of that order and create it by talking about it, and as researchers we create the reality we seek to describe. At a practical level this means that when we ask a question of a respondent there are many ways in which the answer given is dependent on what that person thinks about the researcher, the research, the possible consequences of particular responses and so on. Therefore the researcher must always be aware of how perceptions of herself or himself alter the research. For example, in research with Chicana women the same questions elicited more openness about discrimination when asked by a Chicana woman researcher than by an American woman, while respondents were more open about sex with the American than with the Chicana researcher (Tixier y Vigil and Elsasser 1976). Feminists have taken up this insight and argued for its recognition, most obviously in how the gender of the researcher influences research, but this also holds for class, race, age, language groups and other social divisions. This is obviously very relevant not just to gender researchers but to all development studies researchers, who, whether we are researching our own cultures or others, are all likely to be – relative to our respondents – rich, foreign, educated, urban, ethnically other, temporary, and ignorant of local knowledge.

Feminist reflexivity is also a political stance. It places the researcher on the same critical level as her subject matter. The researcher is not posed as objective, value-free and neutral but as having a subjectivity and a positionality, that is, a social, cultural, political, and economic location. It is a self-consciousness that constantly examines one's own self in interaction with "respondents." This self critical introspection and analysis of one's self as researcher and one's impact on research processes, respondents and findings, and the politics of positionality, requires the researcher to explicitly recognize the social relations which enable some parties and disadvantage others, and which foreground some interpretations and silence others, and this is precisely what produces strong objectivity.

Feminist epistemologies are, of course, not the only ones which consider positionality and subjectivity, but they are perhaps the most notable in the sub-field of social science concerned with development. Participatory research epistemology has frustratingly offered great potential to take this forward (Cornwall 2000) but mainstream participatory research practice has remained resolutely unaware of the deeper politics of speech (Narayan 2000). Michael Drinkwater, from a position grounded in critical hermeneutics and research focusing on natural resource management in southern Africa, argues that the concept of agency is not yet generally applied to the researcher, and draws on Gadamer in particular to argue that improving self-knowledge improves the ability to understand others (Drinkwater 1992: 374) and that the personal histories we take into encounters with others can be both enabling and inhibiting. For example, "enabling prejudices" are those that establish common ground across widely diverse social and cultural locations, such as western academic researcher and Indian farm worker. Being a mother of three constitutes just such a bridgehead between my world and those of women I study.

Inhibiting prejudices, however, are those which might make assumptions based on my particular lived experience, for example that education and employment are empowering for women. What must happen is a gradual understanding of other reasonings and knowledges, not by empathizing, or substituting one view for another, but by analysis which transcends the particular towards a larger whole, a kind of dialectical "tacking" between local detail and larger structural pictures, as Geertz describes it (Drinkwater 1992). Proper understanding derives from neither imposition of researchers' views on the subject of study nor abject acceptance of the views of the researched. The process of engagement allows meaning to emerge, meet scrutiny, revision, and expansion. It must be a critical engagement, in which the researcher as sceptical interpreter must be visible and open.

Subjectivities are at play in how we evaluate research too, for there are personal factors which influence the degree to which we find research results convincing, and interpretations believable. Male bias can raise the burden of proof for research on gender matters. In a recent evaluation of the policy impact of the intrahousehold research of IFPRI, several male researchers registered surprise that when presenting findings on these issues to development institutions, the level of evidence considered necessary to make a point was considerably higher than in research without a gender focus (Jackson 2005).

Feminist reflexivity also produces effects on language and, I suggest, a predisposition towards interdisciplinarity. Hilary Rose (1994: 95) points out that the emphasis on organic intellectuals in feminist epistemologies is also an emphasis on writing accessibly, and the importance of communicating to other women and men across the well-guarded disciplinary fences. Disciplines depend on specialist languages, and boundaries and expertise are maintained with particular vocabularies which establish exclusivity and insider status. But the politics of feminism question the superior expertise of the researcher, insist on equalizing researcher and subject, and thereby call into question languages which exclude. Feminist theorists have been strongly criticized when they theorize in ways which "ordinary women" find hard to follow (Patai 1988): I cannot think of any other analytical field with a similar emphasis.

Understanding one's positionality, which has a formal and structural connotation, is one thing, but a further step is acceptance of the personal subjectivities of researchers. Sen's definition above has rather negative connotations – arbitrariness, special mental tendencies, particular kinds of inexperience, constrained reasoning – which suggest inconsistency, irrationality and ignorance. However, a sociological understanding of subjectivity is that it is "an amalgam of both psychological dispositions developed out of . . . unique biographical circumstances and the habits, customs and orientations that reflect . . . involvement in particular social groupings" (Layder 1997: 27), and thus it inevitably both enables and constrains knowledge. Or for psychologist Mahoney, subjectivity is anchored to a particular position in the social and cultural grid, and yet faces continually conflicting histories and interpretations which have to be negotiated and which move and motivate through their emotional impact (Mahoney 1996: 609). Feminist epistemologies emphasize experience based knowledges, and shared experience as the basis of cross-cultural solidarities, and therefore bring into focus the significance of our own academic biographies. It is a feature of feminist authorship that accounts of personal experience are integrated into published work and not frowned upon as compromising "objectivity."

The willingness to expose the personal enables insight into the academic cultures which resist multidisciplinary intercourse and interdisciplinary research. Lawson (1995) writing about geography, perhaps the closest to an interdiscipline which exists, discusses the strong and power-laden divisions between researchers with quantitative and qualitative methods foci and how these work against the ability to separate technique from ontological positions. The intellectual cultures which establish the habitus of successive generations of researchers include not only collective and hierarchical evaluations of journals with different characters, and levels of funding won by colleagues (which is much greater for projects with large surveys and associated forms of analysis – or more "scientific" technical activity requiring technology and laboratory analysis), but also the no less powerful observations of the methods and identities of invited speakers, and responses to these speakers, reactions to job candidates and so on (Lawson 1995: 455).

The legitimacy, in feminist epistemologies, of personal experience in shaping understanding, coupled with the attempt to minimize the separation of researcher and researched (and therefore the requirement to examine one's own subjectivity and not only that of respondents) means that researchers are more explicit about their own predispositions and feelings. Thus, for example, feminist researchers have been willing to expose and discuss the contradictions of researching for women yet also deceiving to some extent those women in fieldwork (for instance, by pretending to be married); the problem of disliking women respondents with sexist and racist views; and the discomfort of the underlying power differentials between researcher and researched (Wolf 1996).

Personal experience also lies at the heart of multi and interdisciplinary interchange which operates very much through researchers as persons. Marilyn Strathern (2004: 17) asks "what makes knowledge (able to) travel?," and suggests that practices which make knowledge portable include the patenting of processes, the creation of products (publications) and of projects such as research programs. But the elemental knowledge-carrier is the person, as individual researcher: "persons ferry knowledge about, drawing on quite different aspects of their own biographies, in ways that might be quite unpredictable" (p. 25).

The question of whether and how feminist epistemologies produce better knowledge is usually argued in relation to the value of knowledge "from below," and the enhanced objectivity following from recognition of situated knowledges, as the preceding section suggests. But less discussed, and just as important, are two further points suggested here: first, that feminist solidarity, across class and education divisions, predisposes us to languages which include, and that feminist values produce a willingness to invest in crossing disciplinary boundaries, the better to understand, in the round, the position and condition of women and the character of gender relations; and that feminist epistemologies emphasize researcher subjectivities in ways which enhance the portability of knowledge from one field to another. It is the important role of interaction between feminists, as much as feminist methodology per se, which fosters disciplinary interchange and stands as an object lesson for researchers conducting interdisciplinary research on development issues.

Having considered epistemological points relating to the conduct of research and the understanding of the position of the researcher, I will now make three points which aim to suggest the positive insights for interdisciplinary development research which derive from feminist epistemology, although they share deep roots with older disciplinary traditions. These deal with an awareness of essentialism, a recognition of the politics of speech, and a position on methodological individualism and the person.

Essentialism and Kinds of Rationality

Sen defines rationality as "the discipline of subjecting ones choices – of actions, values and priorities – to reasoned scrutiny" (Sen 2003: 4). He dismisses earlier definitions of rationality as internal consistency of choice, as intelligent pursuit of self-interest or as maximization in general, and criticizes rational choice theory for its "almost forensic quality, focusing on the detection of hidden instrumentality, rather than acknowledgement of direct ethics" (pp. 28–9). The basis of this reasoned scrutiny may be very much broader than social science has generally accommodated under the term rationality, and it opens the space for inclusion of feminist notions of rationality.

Feminist epistemologies lay great emphasis on women's experiences – unlike traditional social science research – and some take this emphasis on women's experiences to mean that only women can "know" about women's position and perspective. Others take this further to suggest that we can consider kinds of knowledge which are distinctive to women. In ecofeminism this appears in terms such as "women's ways of knowing" which may have a biological basis or a social basis. Critics argue that this is "essentialist," being based on a belief that women share some essence of woman-ness, out of time and place, which leads them to shared understandings, although it is fairly meaningless to speak of women as a single transhistorical social category (Agarwal 1991; Jackson 1993; Leach 1992).

The familiar debates between ecofeminists and feminist political ecologists in developing country contexts have focused on common property resources (CPRs) – for example, the Chipko movement and how it has been understood (Rangan 2000). But it is not only ecofeminists who consider that women have distinctive forms of knowledge, and maternal thinking has been proposed as a distinctive kind of thinking which derives from the labour of mothering (Ruddick 1989). Some call this an ethic of care, and thus Rose (1994) considers that the social practices of women, grounded in the caring parts of the economy, in child care and care of the sick and the elderly, gives rise to distinctive knowledges which value love and care, and are more emotional in character, adopting a "constrained essentialism" in making this case. For Rose, masculinist knowledge is characterized by an emphasis on cognitive and objective rationality, and she maintains that women's knowledges introduce another dimension. For example, when women primatologists came into the study of primates they clearly took a more empathetic and emotional approach to their subjects; Jane Goodall formed strong relationships with her apes and Diane Fossey also had very protective relationships with them, and this kind of connectedness to their research subjects formed part and parcel of their insights into primate behaviour. This is not irrational, but an expanded idea of the rational which rejects a dualist opposition with the emotional.

There are other forms of knowledge than the rational, and the emotional is a significant element in how we know, what we choose to find out about, the claims of knowledge, and how knowledge is legitimized. The emotional is an element in our lived epistemologies. When I first read the paper by Gloria Goodwin Raheja (1996) on women's speech practices in rural north India, I wept. The paper analyses proverbs and songs sung when women leave their natal homes to move to their husband's homes on marriage – often distant and where they will be lower status "strangers" in their marital homes. The lines "Call me back quickly, mother/Beg with folded hands" touch me enormously because they chime with my own experience of exile and loss. I feel them to speak truthfully and display an epistemological position which says "I believe this to be true because my own life experience tells me so." The other thing that happens with these lines is that they move me to identify with someone apparently very different to me – a rural north Indian woman. Such emotions are another kind of bridgehead across the divides of difference, and the bedrock of a feminism which recognizes both difference and commonality. It is also a bridgehead to epistemologies in the humanities and thereby draws further disciplines into the project of understanding gender relations and gender justice.

The point for development studies researchers in general is that we all undoubtedly have subterranean feelings about what is true and what is not. This is part of recognizing one's own values and how they affect your research. Research cannot be value-free, nor is it desirable to simply adopt a pro-women feminist stance (which compromises the critical), but we should be self-consciously aware of our values, and that Sen's "reasoned scrutiny" should admit knowing by feeling, as one kind of knowledge to triangulate with others.

Women and Speech, Voice and Choice

Voice is treated rather simplistically in most development economics, in relation to choice and decision-making and participation, and indeed bargaining in general. Speech equates to power, and interests are expected to be expressed directly and without mediation. But these assumptions seem much less secure in the light of feminist theorizing of the nature of testimony, speech and the politics of voice and choice, and thus "decision-making." Here feminist epistemology makes a truly great contribution, with clear implications for participatory approaches to research and development. The importance of including women in participatory research consultations is quite broadly recognized, and this first step opens out many further questions. Testimony is one of the primary ways in which we come to know, yet the ability to speak, make testimony, is often taken for granted to be independent of social identity. People are expected to give different testimony depending on social identity, but the ways those identities constrain the act of speech as well as its content are rather less recognized in development research, although this is researched intensively in feminist sociolinguistics (for example, Eckert and McConnell-Ginet 2003) where interruptions, use of standard speech forms, directness and other qualities of speech display (context dependent) gender differences.

Two notable differences in the treatment of women's voices in development studies is the conflation of individual voices with collective representation, and the recognition of "false consciousness." Women seem to be taken to speak for the collectivity of women in ways that male voices do not. Since men remain the unmarked gender male voices are not expected to speak for their kind as a gender but in differentiated voices of class/ethnicity. Women, however, are much more commonly treated as an undifferentiated group in which their gender identities are given more weight than that of class or ethnicity. This may be related to the other difference: the idea of false consciousness, in development research, is almost entirely discussed in relation to women's perceptions of their value (Kandiyoti 1998; Sen 1990). What women say about themselves and the social relations of gender is much more readily put down to the mystification of gender inequality, as compared to what men say – in relation to either gender or other social relations such as class – despite the origins of the term in marxist thought. The implication is that women's speech is more "socialized" than men's, and less reliable as an expression of their interests.

However, the point on which I want to focus here is the question of speech and silence. Edwin Ardener remarked on the treatment of women in anthropological monographs that they are both present, in being spoken about but silent, as he says, like the cows of Nuer. He observes them to be more difficult respondents: "women giggle when young, snort when old, reject the question, laugh at the topic" (Ardener 1975: 2), and his main explanation is that women are silenced (muted) by inhabiting vocabularies formed by male interests and dominance, through which their particular world views are not easily expressed. Others of course have also commented on the problem of speech for the sub-altern (for example Spivak 1988), and researchers have seen the need to triangulate speech and testimony with other kinds of expression, such as myth and stories, in order to "hear" what women are saying. The implication for interdisciplinary development studies research is that what women say in interviews is affected both by their social location, and by their relationship with language and direct speech as one means of conveying information and expressing interests.

Another kind of response to the question of mutedness is to rethink what silence means (Jackson 2005). For example Rajan (1993) argues that it is a mistake to associate speech with power and agency and silence with weakness and passivity: silence can also express power and certainly resistance. Silence can signify the powerful party, in for example, job interviews, confession, therapy, and it can constitute punishment – being sent to Coventry, or solitary confinement. It can also signify resistance. Understanding the meanings of silence, starting from Winnicott's view that "silence can be an active protest against intrusion rather than a passive, submissive position," leads Mahoney (1996: 613) to an analysis of how flawed communication produces agency. The anger of imperfect communication, and communication failures, motivate a sense of agency and resistance, which her theory of power locates in the delicate balance between being heard and not heard, speaking and not speaking: "The struggle of interpersonal relations, far from obscuring one's own sense of agency . . . actually may set the conditions that give rise to it" (p. 615). Silence, or not communicating, can be an effective reaction to a sense of being controlled.

Mahoney argues that, for the developing child, "Perfect communication is as threatening as absence of communication, because it obscures the difference between subject and object and threatens to annihilate the subject's sense of agency and creativity in the world" (p. 614). Since girls are raised with a greater expectation of relational orientation, the intrusions of intimate others who do not allow them to withdraw, "produces a socially compliant subject and communication itself becomes linked to a sense of being controlled, to producing a response demanded by the other." Silence can be then a resistant response for girls, which allows a stronger sense of the authentic inner self: "power and defiance within the intimate relationship constitute the essential ground for experiencing a self that feels authentic" (p. 618). Too much communication and compliance leads to feeling false and not "real," and the imposter syndrome, whereby successful women can often feel deeply fraudulent, as a consequence of their compliance. This account of the importance of resistant silence and imperfect communication to subjectivity, selfhood and agency casts a different light on the assumed value for women of unmediated speech and perfect communication in intimate relations. At the same time, as Rajan concludes in her analysis of the silence of Indian wives, and their refusals to accuse husbands even whilst dying from burn injuries after "bride burning" attacks by husbands: "In the feminist practice of 'reading' silence, our caution must be neither to pronounce definitively that 'the subaltern cannot speak' nor to romanticise silence as the subaltern's refusal to speak" (Rajan 1993: 87–8).

Therefore feminist approaches to testimony are marked by awareness that people have differential abilities to "speak" and to "hear," that reliance on direct speech alone, as evidence, is unwise, and that speech is not to be equated with power and silence with weakness.

Social Relations of Gender and Gender Personhood: The Social and the Individual

Ideas about individuals, persons and selves are culturally and historically varied, and not necessarily in expected ways, such as an assumed transition from more collectivist notions to more individualist ones.[6] These differences stand between the disciplines too and methodological individualism has long been seen as a major obstacle dividing economics from "social" social sciences. Feminist epistemologies offer a model of the person which is particularly useful at a moment when economics is possibly opening up to an expanded and more social version of the individual, and, conversely, sociology and anthropology are intensifying interest in personhood and agency, beyond the controlling effects of social structures.

The individualist[7] mode of thought characteristic of modern western societies, and the individual inhering within it, is one who chooses, decides, evaluates and calculates, and who thinks and acts as an autonomous selfdirecting agent relating to other such men – and men they clearly are (Midgeley 1984). "[F]or many liberals and neo-classical economists he becomes no more than a calculating machine interacting with others in the marketplace on the basis of revealed preferences" (Lukes 1993: 298–9). By contrast the individual characteristic of anthropology has been one who is completely identified with and by social roles, who operates and practises within an accepted social framework,[8] and whose identity is given by this framework so that "who I am is answered both for me and for others by the history I inherit, the social positions I occupy, and the 'moral career' on which I am embarked" (p. 299).

---

[6]   Carrithers et al. (1993) point out the similarity between the concept of the self in fifth-century India and nineteenth-century Germany.

[7]   Individualism is a particular western concept of the person; it is defined by MacFarlane as "the view that society is composed of autonomous, equal units, namely separate individuals and that such individuals are more important, ultimately, than any larger constituent group. It is reflected in the concept of individual private property, in the political and legal liberty of the individual, and in the idea of the individual's direct communication with God" (MacFarlane 1978: 5).

[8]   Carrithers et al. (1993) argue that important lines of thought in nineteenth and twentieth-century France laid moral value on the collective; that individualism was coined as a pejorative term; that the cult of science represented the collective as real and of cognitive value; and that Durkheim found the designs and purpose of collectivities everywhere he looked. Mauss lies within this tradition, for ultimately "underneath the real value and the real determining power lies with the collectivity; so all mois are personnes" (Carrithers et al. 1993: 239). So the emphasis on the social determination of the person has a particular historical context, as indeed does the emphasis on the individual as standing outside of society.

The individual has been conceptualized very differently in economics and anthropology. Disciplines are also divided by different takes on intention and the question of what motivates the self. As Martin Hollis (1993: 227) points out:

> Individualism relies on a "self" in each actor, which gives shape to his real motives and, in combination with others, accounts for the dynamics of a social system. Yet this self is threatened in two directions. If it reduces to a Humean bundle of preferences, which are then traced to socialisation and hence to the system itself, it vanishes into the system it was meant to explain. If it is a Hobbesian core, so private and so much at a distance from its public, legitimating masks that the real man is impenetrable, it vanishes from scientific enquiry. The puzzle is how to avoid this two-way vanishing trick.

Thinking about women's motivation and agency requires a notion of the self which reflects socialization but also recognizes the unique, biographical woman who engages creatively with the social, cultural and discursive resources available in any particular subject position. Feminist epistemologies offer a means to overcome this split between the autonomous individual in economics and the socialized individual in anthropology. The Enlightenment roots of feminism, and the potential gains from the individualist project for women, whose socially given roles conferred limited power and considerable sub-ordination within the social contract, has been in tension with the critique of the male template of the person in Enlightenment (Jackson 1996), but nevertheless there is a strong element of individualism in feminist thought and projects. At the same time, it is the social-ized individual which is both important to understandings of the reproduction of gender cultures and the mystifications of gender inequalities which lead women to accept their positions, and yet is also challenged by notions of women's agency. Feminist epistemologies foster disciplinary interchange through inhabiting this ground between the conventional methodological individualism of economics and the tendency to social structural deter-minism of much sociology, and focusing on the overriding need to understand women's agency in ways which are not simply given by either. These are, of course, stereotypes of disciplines but it is broadly true that economics has emphasized the individual, and sociology and anthropology the social, in their favoured explanations. Feminist economics and anthropology in the 1970s and 1980s crossed these divides with a concept of the person embedded within social relations of constraint, which was used to great effect to deconstruct the treatment by economics of the household as a single undifferentiated unit governed by a benevolent dictator, and currently it is engaged in deconstructing "community," where this is treated as undifferentiated and equitable. These have been key contributions to understanding CPRs and collective action (Cleaver 1999; Kothari and Cooke 2001). This epistemological position rejected the idea that a household head (generally male) could represent, or speak for, household members (often female). The consequent deconstruction of household and community works not only by examining gender dif-ferentiated interests and outcomes, but also by sustaining a view of the person which is simultaneously individual and social, invested with agency but also constrained by social relations, and experiencing well-being which is both personal and conditional on the well-being of significant others.

It is in feminist anthropology that the teasing apart of individuals, selves and persons has made most progress, following in that area of the discipline mapped out by Mauss's 1938 essay on the person and the self, in which he argued that the self is a universal self-awareness of body and spirit, but declared his interest in not the sense of self but the social history of the concept of self, and how it has evolved under different societies (reprinted as Mauss 1993). The primary interest in anthropology has been in the social processes and institutions which form persons, and to a lesser extent, selves, whilst feminist anthropology has analysed gender differentials in personhood (Moore 1988; Strathern 1988). Thus, for example, La Fontaine (1993: 130) connects notions of the person to the nature of authority in society[9] and argues, in relation to three societies in Uganda, Ghana, and Kenya, that:

> most Lugbara women and some Lugbara men are not persons . . . [t]he personhood of women among the Tallensi women is of a lesser order than that of men for women lack the domestic and lineage authority of men . . . [and] for the Taita . . . the full range of ritual powers is not open to women so that they reach the limits of their achieved personhood sooner than men.

Although this overly social perspective has been criticized, Taylor (1993) reminds us that self-knowledge depends on language, which must be interactional, and therefore we cannot see persons as anything other than formed in relation to other persons, that is, in social environments. The most personal and individual aspects of the self are social because of language, and cannot be simply interiorized and individualized. The positionality of the person, discussed above, is always plural and never singular, and thus the experiencing individual is multiply located and socially engaged. As Henrietta Moore writes, "Experience is . . . intersubjective and embodied; it is not individual and fixed but irredeemably social and processual" (Moore 1994: 3). The individual is profoundly social in many ways – identities are socially constructed, experience is socially relational, personhood develops through social interaction, and persons are not, in all cultures, bounded from other persons in the ways they are in the west (Strathern 1988). Women are, however, individuals and have powers as such which are not simply given by social roles and relations. Feminist interests in power and the capacity to change structures of authority such as patriarchy leads us to a special interest then in the individual as much as the "person" – in this anthropological sense.

These seem to me richer ways of thinking about individuals, persons, agency and social change, in development research. What common ground might there be across disciplines, and particularly in economics? In his critique of rational choice theory Sen (2003: 33) discusses how self-interest is seen in characterizing rationality, and distinguishes three elements within the idea of self-interest: that a person's welfare is selfcentred and depends only on her own consumption; that her only goal is to maximize her own welfare; and that her choices are based entirely on pursuit of her own goals. By contrast he argues that "[t]he reach of one's self is not limited to self-interest maximisation" (p. 37), that "rationality cannot be entirely captured by the systematic pursuit of given goals and

---

[9] The terms person, individual and self are sometimes used interchangeably, but La Fontaine clarifies usage as follows: "If the self is an individual's awareness of a unique identity, the 'person' is society's confirmation of that identity as of social significance. Person and individual are identified in contrast to the self" (1993: 124). Radcliffe-Brown (1952) distinguishes the individual, as the biological organism and object of empirical study, from the person, as a complex of social relationships.

does require some kind of critical scrutiny of the goals themselves" (p. 40), and that "[w]e may choose to impose on ourselves certain behavioural constraints on grounds of social custom" (p. 40). This amounts to a significant step towards the ideas of persons and selves in other disciplines. What is rational, for Sen, are choices formed not around self-interest alone but arrived at through a process of scrutiny, not necessarily reasonable. It allows, then, for a person to be guided by values which constrain the pursuit of personal object-ives, and by thinking based not on the individual person but on group membership, and therefore constitutes a notion of the person which is much closer to that which anthro-pologists adhere to.

Conclusion

Obstacles to interdisciplinary interchange within the academy are well known, such as the increasingly formal character of mainstream economics which excludes many with-out the requisite technical skills, or offers only a limited participation (skip the algebra and models and take the figures on trust), the political economy of disciplinary power and the social relations of disciplines, sketched out here through a cooperative conflicts metaphor. Against this I have suggested that feminist values have propelled interdiscip-linarity by providing the motivating force to overcome these enduring obstacles, and that the content of feminist epistemologies provides both important insights in its own right to social scientists researching development, and a means of drawing disciplines closer at this moment when economics appears to be receptive to expanded concepts of what is objectivity and rationality, and to the fundamentally social character of the individual.

References

Agarwal, B. (1991) *Engendering the Environment Debate: Lessons from the Indian Subcontinent.* East Lansing, MI: Centre for the Advanced Study of International Development, Michigan State University.

Anderson, E. (2005) "Feminist Epistemology: An Interpretation and a Defense," in A. Cudd and R. Andreasen (eds), *Feminist Theory: A Philosophical Anthology*, pp. 188–209. Oxford: Blackwell Publishing.

Ardener, E. (1975) "Belief and the Problem of Women," in S. Ardener (ed.) *Perceiving Women*, pp. 1–19. London: Malaby Press.

Benhabib, S. (1994) "Feminism and the Question of Postmodernism," in *The Polity Reader in Gender Studies*, pp. 76–92. Cambridge: Polity Press.

Benhabib, S. (1995) "Cultural Complexity, Moral Interdependence, and the Global Dialogical Community," in M. Nussbaum and J. Glover (eds), *Women, Culture and Development: A Study of Human Capabilities*, pp. 235–58. Oxford: Oxford University Press.

Carrithers, M., S. Collins, and S. Lukes (1993) (eds), *The Category of the Person: Anthropology, Philosophy, History*. Cambridge: Cambridge University Press (first published 1985).

Cleaver, F. (1999) "Paradoxes of Participation: Questioning Participatory Approaches to Develop-ment," *Journal of International Development* 11(4): 597–612.

Cornwall, A. (2000) "Making a Difference? Gender and Participatory Development." IDS Discussion Paper 378. Brighton: University of Sussex, Institute of Development Studies.

Drinkwater, M. (1992) "Visible Actors and Visible Researchers: Critical Hermeneutics in an Actor-Oriented Perspective," *Sociologia Ruralis* 32: 367–88.

Eckert, P. and S. McConnell-Ginet (2003) (eds), *Language and Gender*. Cambridge: Cambridge University Press.

Fine, B. (2001) *Social Capital versus Social Theory: Political Economy and Social Science at the Turn of the Millennium*. New York: Routledge.

Haraway, D. (1991) *Simians, Cyborgs, and Women: The Reinvention of Nature*. New York: Routledge.

Harding, S. (ed.) (1987) *Feminism and Methodology*. Bloomington, IN: Indiana University Press; Milton Keynes: Open University Press.

Harding, S. (1991) *Whose Science? Whose Knowledge? Thinking from Women's Lives*. Milton Keynes, UK: Open University Press.

Harding, S. (2005) "Rethinking Standpoint Epistemology: What is 'Strong Objectivity'?," in A. Cudd and S. Andreasen (eds), *Feminist Theory: A Philosophical Anthology*, pp. 218–36. Oxford: Blackwell Publishing,

Hollis, M. (1993) "Of Masks and Men," in M. Carrithers, S. Collins and S. Lukes (eds), *The Category of the Person: Anthropology, Philosophy, History*, pp. 217–33. Cambridge: Cambridge University Press.

Jackson, C. (1993) "Women/Nature or Gender/History? A Critique of Ecofeminist 'Development'," *Journal of Peasant Studies* 20(3): 389–419.

Jackson, C. (1996) "Still Stirred by the Promise of Modernity," *New Left Review* 217: 148–54.

Jackson, C. (2002) "Disciplining Gender?," *World Development* 30(3): 497–509.

Jackson, C. (2005) "Strengthening Food Policy through Gender and Intrahousehold Analysis: Impact Assessment of IFPRI Multi Country Research." Impact Assessment Discussion Paper 23. Washington, DC: International Food Policy Research Institute.

Kandiyoti, D. (1998) "Gender Power and Contestation: Rethinking 'Bargaining with Patriarchy'," in C. Jackson and R. Pearson (eds) *Feminist Visions of Development: Gender Analysis and Policy*, pp. 135–52. London: Routledge.

Kothari, U. and B. Cooke (eds) (2001) *Participation: The New Tyranny?* London: Zed Books.

La Fontaine, J. (1993) "Persona and Individual: Some Anthropological Thoughts," in M. Carrithers, S. Collins and S. Lukes (eds), *The Category of the Person: Anthropology, Philosophy, History*, pp. 123–40. Cambridge: Cambridge University Press.

Lawson, V. (1995) "The Politics of Difference: Examining the Quantitative/Qualitative Dualism in Post-Structuralist Feminist Research," *Professional Geographer* 47(4): 449–57.

Layder, D. (1997) *Modern Social Theory: Key Debates and New Directions*. London: Routledge.

Leach, M. (1992) "Gender and Environment: Traps and Opportunities," *Development in Practice* 2(1): 12–22.

Lukes, S. (1993) "Conclusion," in M. Carrithers, S. Collins, and S. Lukes (eds), *The Category of the Person: Anthropology, Philosophy, History*, pp. 282–301. Cambridge: Cambridge University Press.

MacFarlane, A. (1978) *The Origins of English Individualism: The Family, Property and Social Transition*. Oxford: Blackwell.

Mahoney, M. (1996) "The Problem of Silence in Feminist Psychology," *Feminist Studies* 22(3): 603–25.

Mauss, M. (1993) "A Category of the Human Mind: The Notion of Person, the Notion of Self" (first published 1938), in M. Carrithers, S. Collins, and S. Lukes (eds), *The Category of the Person: Anthropology, Philosophy, History*, pp. 1–25. Cambridge: Cambridge University Press.

Midgley, M. (1984) "Sex and Personal Identity. The Western Individualist Tradition," *Encounter* 63(1): 50–55.

Mohanty, C., A. Russo, and L. Torres (eds) (1991) *Third World Women and the Politics of Feminism*. Bloomington, IN: Indiana University Press.

Moore, H. (1988) *Feminism and Anthropology*. Cambridge: Polity Press.

Moore, H. (1994) *A Passion for Difference: Essays in Anthropology and Gender*. Cambridge: Polity Press.

Narayan, D. (2000) *Voices of the Poor: Can Anyone Hear Us?* New York: Oxford University Press for the World Bank.

Patai, D. (1988) "Who's Calling Whom Subaltern?," *Women and Language* 11(2): 23–6.

Patai, D. (1994) *Professing Feminism: Education and Indoctrination in Women's Studies.* Oxford: Lexington Books.

Radcliffe-Brown, A. (1952) *Structure and Function in Primitive Society: Essays and Addresses.* London: Cohen and West.

Raheja, G. (1996) "The Limits of Patriliny: Kinship, Gender and Women's Speech Practices in Rural North India," in M. Maynes, A. Waltner, B. Soland, and U. Strasser (eds), *Gender, Kinship, Power: A Comparative and Interdisciplinary History*, pp. 149–76. New York and London: Routledge.

Rajan, R. (1993) Real and Imagined Women: Gender, *Culture and Postcolonialism.* London: Routledge.

Rangan, H. (2000) *Of Myths and Movements: Rewriting Chipko into Himalayan History.* London: Verso.

Rochleau, D. (1995) "Maps, Numbers, Text, and Context: Mixing Methods in Feminist Political Ecology," *Professional Geographer* 47(4): 458–66.

Rose, H. (1994) *Love, Power and Knowledge: Towards a Feminist Transformation of the Sciences.* Cambridge: Polity Press.

Ruddick, S. (1989) *Maternal Thinking: Towards a Politics of Peace.* Boston, MA: Beacon. Stacey, J. (1991) "Can there be a Feminist Ethnography?," in S. Gluck and D. Patai (eds), *Women's Words: The Feminist Practice of Oral History*, pp. 111–19. New York: Routledge.

Sen, A. (1990) "Cooperative Conflicts," in I. Tinker (ed.), *Persistent Inequalities*, pp. 123–49. Oxford: Oxford Univesity Press.

Sen, A. (2003) *Rationality and Freedom.* London: Belknap Press/Harvard University Press.

Spivak, G. (1988) "Can the Subaltern Speak?," in Cary Nelson and Lawrence Grossberg (eds), *Marxism and the Interpretation of Culture*, pp. 271–311. Urbana, IL: University of Illinois Press.

Strathern, M. (1988) *Gender of the Gift: Problems with Women and Problems with Society in Melanesia.* Berkeley, CA: University of California Press.

Strathern, M. (2004) "Commons and Borderlands." *Working Papers on Interdisciplinarity, Accountability and the Flow of Knowledge.* Oxford: Sean Kingston Publishing.

Taylor, C. (1993) "The Person," in M. Carrithers, S. Collins, and S. Lukes (eds), *The Category of the Person: Anthropology, Philosophy, History*, pp. 257–81. Cambridge: Cambridge University Press.

Tixiery Vigil and N. Elsasser (1976) "The Effects of Ethnicity of the Interviewer on Conversation: A Study of Chicana Women," in B. DuBois and I. Crouch I (eds), *Sociology of the Language of American Women*, pp. 161–9. San Antonio, TX: Trinity University Press.

Wolf, D. (1996) "Situating Feminist Dilemmas in Fieldwork," in D. Wolf (ed.), *Feminist Dilemmas in Fieldwork*, pp. 1–55. Boulder, CO: Westview Press.

Commentaries

Commentary 1: Social Norms and Cooperative Behavior

Notes from the Hinterland between Economics and Anthropology

Kaushik Basu

Literal and Social Meanings

John Bon Jovi has a well-known song that goes, "It's been raining since you left me."

The popular Bengali singer, Anjan Dutta, on the other hand, has a song that says, (my translation), "The clouds bring no rain, when you are not around."

I can see some over-trained social scientists having difficulty understanding these lyrics. If you treat human preferences as idiosyncratic (some like rain, some do not), as economists often do, then it is not clear whether John Bon Jovi is lamenting the fact of his girl-friend having left him or celebrating it.

To understand the song, one needs to recognize that rain is not just a matter of individual preference, but has *social* meaning and *shared* significance. So it is meant to be understood that John Bon Jovi is referring to the gloom and depression associated with rain.

A social scientist who understands this but no more will be able to appreciate the Bon Jovi song, but will be in a quandary when he or she is then made to listen to Anjan Dutta's lyrics. If that is what John Bon Jovi means, then is Anjan Dutta trying to tell us about the relief he feels when he is left alone by his girlfriend? The answer of course is no (as a shrewd observer would no doubt surmise, if from nothing else, from the fact that the joy of one's girlfriend not being around is not quite the stuff of poetry). Social meanings are often relative; they can vary across collectivities. A person brought up in India *knows* that rain is associated with beauty and romance, and its absence, denotes gloom and bereavement.

Evidently, to *understand* both these lyrics one needs to understand not only the literal meanings of terms and expressions but also their contextual and social significance. This is analogous to the way in which anthropology can enrich economics. Economics is very good with the literal. The literal is also usually formalizable; something that, in principle, a computer can deal with. Economics, with its heavy reliance on deductive reasoning, is well equipped to deal with this. But in analyzing human behavior and crafting policy that can influence human behavior, it is important to go beyond the formal and the literal. There is much that is intuitive, that comes from a *feel* for the society one is dealing with. This is what anthropology can bring to the table of economic policy making.

In this commentary I will illustrate this point with the problem of incentive compatibility and the organization of cooperative behavior among human beings. But before that I want to make a comment on formal and informal knowledge.

The Acquisition of Knowledge

Economists go to great lengths to emphasize the importance of acquiring knowledge "correctly" – the use of deductive logic must be flawless and we must not generalize to everybody from knowledge gained from small and biased samples. At one level one cannot dispute this. But, at the same time, to dismiss other informal ways of acquiring knowledge, which may be at variance from the economist's method would be a mistake. This can be illustrated with a simple example.

Consider a child who tells you that the teacher was happy with him, because she smiled a lot after reading his essay. If you asked the child how he knew from the smile that the teacher was happy, he would probably say that he knew this from his experience with his parents and friends (a smile from them was usually followed up with other kinds of indications of happiness).

Now, if you were a stickler for precision, you would have no option but to admonish the child for picking up information from a small and biased sample and generalizing to the world. But it should, at the same time, be evident that if you do not allow a child to pick up information in this scientifically flawed manner, the child will grow up to be a very ill-informed person. A little thought should make it evident that each of us learns vastly more from ascientifically acquired information than from scientifically acquired information.

I am not saying this to discourage the formalism that economists strive to achieve, but almost as a statement of paradox – to make us aware that even though we may not fully understand how, "wrong" methods of picking up information do, typically, end up informing us well.

Though I say that we may not fully understand how, there may be an evolutionary route for explaining this, which I had hinted at in my book, *Prelude to Political Economy*. It is conceivable that the "wrong" method of picking up information, namely the one that children use, may, through a process of natural selection, end up coinciding with where the right method would take us to. That is, the domains where we do use small and biased samples to pick up information could be domains where the biased sample yields the same information as the full sample or a randomized draw from the full sample.

As with all evolutionary arguments, this is not fool-proof but only suggestive. It is after all possible that what natural selection does is give us wrong information, but one which nevertheless enhances our survival chances. For example, if there were two potential beliefs about rabid dogs – that they like to tickle human beings mercilessly and that they do not like to do so (they just walk away from human beings). Then, having the former belief, which would make us run away from rabid dogs, could come to be a shared belief among human beings, because those without such a belief would eventually die out. The belief would be wrong but useful and, moreover, it would be so widely shared that no one should realize it is wrong.

As this example shows, it is therefore entirely possible that what we take to be "information" is actually collective delusion, but of a kind that is helpful to increase survival. In fact, when I look around myself I do feel I can spot several wrong but widely-shared beliefs. But let me not go into examples of such beliefs as I have no wish to get into trouble with the religious right.

Commons and Common Interests

One of the major problems that confront economic policy makers – maybe *the* most major problem – is the organization of collective behavior. The problem of the commons, which pertains not just to the maintenance of the village pond and grazing ground but global environmental policy, pollution control, and the use of non-renewable resources; the problem of development; and the problem of governance are all instances of the problem of collective action.[1]

Economists have been striving to design interventions which bring individual incentives in alignment with the collective interests of mankind. We have been greatly concerned with the "commons" problem, the fear that a group of people free to graze their cattle on common land will graze the land down to barrenness, to their own collective detriment. We therefore try to impose charges, or work out penalties or give rewards so that the action that is in each person's self-interest is also the ideal action from the collective point of view.

When some government program fails, such as when government-employed, tenure-assured teachers fail to teach diligently or play truant from school, we economists say that that is only natural. A teacher does what is rational from his self-interested point of view. The flaw is in the bureaucratic system that fails to align individual interest with collective interest. Economists have gone out of their way to try to devise incentive systems for bureaucracies, which solve the free-rider problem.

I do not want to diminish this effort, since economics has had some remarkable successes. Yet, to be obsessed with this method and not to recognize that human behavior has social foundations, which, even if we cannot fully formalize (like the child's method of acquiring knowledge discussed above), play an important role and makes many collective action problems very different from what we depict it to be using formal game-theoretic models.

If we step back from our textbooks and look at the world from a distance, we will realize that, just as there are plenty of examples of the commons problem, there are also many examples where, mysteriously, the commons problem does not arise. The family refrigerator is rarely kept locked, but it does not get cleared out by the first person who happens to chance upon it. In offices people leave doors open when they go out for lunch, but books and stationery do not vanish, or, if one were to be more precise, they more often do not vanish than do vanish.

The number of instances where not-working would have no consequence on the worker's salary or tenure, but the worker works nevertheless, is large. Not to try to understand

---

[1]   See, for instance, Ostrom 1990; Bardhan 1993; Hoff and Stiglitz 2001; Rao 2004.

these mysterious mechanisms which make people behave in social ways, even when that is not in their own interest (excepting in the tautological, and therefore trivial, sense of defining whatever one does as being in one's self interest), is a major failure of economics and a major handicap in understanding why some societies have done so well and some so poorly.

It may be true that successful economies have more incentive-compatible organizations, but I believe that even more importantly successful economies are ones where individuals are more prone to work in society's common interest *even when that is at divergence with their self-interest*. And anthropology is the discipline that can potentially help us understand the latter better, and that is the source we need to draw upon to design more successful policies.

I do not know the details of where this kind of inquiry will end up, but I know that this can potentially explain more phenomena than the method of narrow individual rationality can. All that I wish to do in the remainder is to suggest what may lie behind our widely observed incentive-incompatible behaviors.

Two important considerations that economists usually omit can explain why we may need to look beyond narrow individual incentive compatibility. In all models created by game-theorists, economists and, recently, some political scientists, each individual is supposed to have a feasible set of actions, or strategies, open to him, and he chooses the one that is best from his own point of view.

First, there is a rather abstruse philosophical criticism of this approach. In most real situations (outside of actual games like chess or hex, though even for this there may be some questions) there are no well-defined sets of actions open to individuals. One can see this in some practical contexts. Think of a village moneylender, choosing a plan of how to lend to some poor peasants in a village. In economics, we typically think of him as deciding what interest rate to charge, and maybe set some limit on how much to lend and, in the event of a default, whether to take the person to court or the local panchayat.

Sophisticated economists may object to this and say, why does he simply have to choose one interest rate? He can think of schedules of interest rates (the rate varying with the amount being borrowed) and then choose one *schedule*. This is a genuine criticism but what most theorists fail to realize is that this route of criticism actually is endless. After all, the lender cannot only choose between different schedules of interest rate, but also between whether to be threatening while making the offer or friendly, whether to give the threat to the borrower alone or the borrower's wife as well. And as for what happens in the event of a default, the options open to him seem endless. One cannot only take the person to court or to the panchayat but also hit him on the head, give him a moral lecture and so on. And not only is it endless, but it may not even constitute a set.[2]

Second, human beings are innately socialized creatures. They have a sense of social norms and integrity (this, I am aware, can vary across people). So actions that are technically feasible may not be actually feasible simply because they lie outside of one's consideration. If we ask an economist why she does not pick pockets while traveling by bus even when they see wallets bulging and half out of fellow travelers' pockets, it is possible that she will tell you that he does not do so because the gains are likely to be smaller

---

[2]   This is so in the sense that the collection of possibilities may give rise to the Russell paradox of sets. I have discussed this in Basu (2000).

than the expected cost. Such an answer shows more than anything else the corroding power of over education in economics. The truth, for most human beings, is that they simply do not think of doing so. It is beyond consideration for most people. Our social norms and sense of integrity are sufficiently hardwired in most of us that for lots of actions we do not have to think and then reject. We simply reject.

One may be tempted to say that this is still no reason to go beyond selfish utility maximization; it is just that we need to broaden the definition of what constitutes self-interest. But there is one big difference. Social norms and culture are society-dependent. The actions that a Trobriand Islander considers unusable for reasons of social norms may be quite different from what a British Islander considers beyond the pale of human use and what a Trobriand Islander would himself consider unusable if his society was in a different equilibrium. I have no doubt that in some groups, pockets are not picked only when the expected cost of doing so exceeds the expected benefit.

In India, there is currently a lot of soul searching about why there is so much teacher absenteeism from school. This is often thought to be because the jobs of teachers are secure. It is almost certainly true that if we could put in place a system by which too many missed classes would lead to a loss of job, absenteeism would go down. But at the same time, there is an undeniable matter of norm. It is now an acceptable norm among teachers that it is okay to miss class. There is very little stigma attached to such behavior. In the US, lots of professors have tenured jobs but they do not start to miss classes because of this. What monitors their behavior is not a formal system of punishment but social norms and stigma, which are often internalized and self-monitored, so that missing a class without adequate reason is simply not an action that is considered. So, while in today's India one may need to use economic incentives to get teachers to school, once the new situation has persisted for a while there should be no further need for economic incentives.

The realization, more than two hundred years ago, that much of the order that prevails in society can come about from individuals pursuing their own selfish ends, was stunning indeed. It has rightly been epitomized in lengthy monographs and pithy theorems. But to go over to the other extreme and assume that the order and collective efficiency that we see occur invariably because of individual incentive-compatible systems is to handicap our understanding of not just society and polity but also the economy.

References

Bardhan, P. (1993), "Symposium on the Management of Local Commons," *Journal of Economic Perspectives*, vol. 7.

Basu, K. (2000), *Prelude to Political Economy: A Study of the Social and Political Foundations of Economics*, New York: Oxford University Press.

Hoff, K. and Stiglitz, J. (2001), "Modern Economic Theory and Development," in G. Meier and Stiglitz, J. (eds), *Frontiers of Development Economics*, New York: Oxford University Press.

Ostrom, E. (1990), *Governing the Commons: The Evolution of Institutions for Collective Action*, Cambridge: Cambridge University Press.

Commentary 2: Sociologists and Economists on "the Commons"

Erik Olin Wright

Economists and Sociologists are surprised by very different things.[1]

For an economist, a well-maintained commons is a puzzle, something that cries out for an explanation. Since people are *naturally* rational self-interested actors always trying to minimize their contributions to public goods, it is surprising when they robustly cooperate with each other. A well-protected commons thus calls for an elaborate explanation. Somehow the incentive structure must be such that individuals experience real costs when they defect from cooperation and abuse the commons. Perhaps this is an iterated prisoner's dilemma with no known termination date, so something like tit-for-tat enforces compliance. Perhaps the participants in the commons recognize the potential for a tragedy of the commons and therefore, in good Hobbesian fashion, hire an enforcer to punish violators. But then, who guards the guardian? How is the collective action problem of regulating punishments solved? As a last resort, when all else fails, the economist might reluctantly invoke norms, values, and culture as part of the explanation. The appeal to norms is reluctant since the explanation seems lazy and circular – people cooperate because they hold cooperative norms. How do we know they hold cooperative norms? Because they cooperate. So, to avoid the taint of circularity, something like evolutionary game theory is invoked to explain how cooperative norms could develop from the interactions among naturally rational self-interested actors.

For a sociologist, a devastated commons is a puzzle. People are naturally social actors, born and raised in a web of social relations infused with norms and values. Cooperation is an intrinsic feature of human sociability, part of what makes social reproduction possible. Because of the naturalness of norm-regulated sociability, sociologists have invented

---

[1] In the spirit of a "think piece" this chapter will make broad statements about "economists" and "sociologists." I do this with some trepidation since there are many sociologists who place interests and incentives at the center of their analyses in a manner very much like economists, and a few economists who treat norms and values as something other than simple elements of preferences.

a special term for the condition of normlessness – "anomie." The atomized, rational, self-interested actor who acts in all contexts solely on the basis of implicit calculations of self-directed incentive-based costs and benefits is pathological, and when this occurs as a general characteristic of a social setting, an elaborate explanation is called for. What explains the failure of socialization to norms of cooperation and social responsibility? Why have the values which underlie norms of sociability and cooperation lost their potency? There must be some force at work which is corrosive of value-laden sociability, which has narrowed the scope of the collective "we" of actors' identities so that they readily defect from cooperative solutions to collective problems. Perhaps the culprit is "the market," which contributes to a long-term transformation of culture from more collectively oriented norms of cooperation and obligation, to norms of competition and individual pursuit of self-interest. In any case, what especially needs to be explained is the low level of cooperation around the protection of a common-use resource.

More broadly, I think the contrast between economists and sociologists can be described this way: economists assign a privileged place to self-interested rational action in their micro-level explanations of social phenomenon, and thus give central weight to the problem of incentives in explaining variations across contexts. Sociologists, in contrast, deploy a menu of forms of action of which rational action is one, but only one, type of social action. In contemporary sociological analyses a variety distinct modes of social action are seen as significant: self-interested rational action, normative action, moral action, habitual action, and creative action, to name some of the more important types. Normative action means following particular rules of behavior that, typically, vary considerably from social context to context. Moral action infuses such rules with beliefs about what is right and wrong, not just proper and improper. Habitual action is action that requires little or no conscious choice: actors more or less follow internalized scripts. Creative action is action in which the actor does not have clear, specified goals to which appropriate means are chosen (as in the model of rational action), but rather engages in pragmatic problem-solving interaction with others in which ends and means co-evolve, and ends are discovered and transformed through such interaction.[2]

These forms of action overlap and interact; they are not hermetically sealed modules in the subjectivities of actors. For example, normative action defines some social contexts as settings within which the economists' favored self-interested rational action is entirely appropriate, but other settings in which such action is inappropriate. On the other hand, the incentive structures that frame rational action can, under certain circumstances, cross thresholds in which individuals choose to violate norms which they would otherwise find binding (as suggested in the aphorism "everyone has a price").

Of course, there are some ways of construing the idea of self-interested rational action – especially when it is framed as "utility maximization" or "preference satisfaction" – in which every conceivable form of action can be viewed as simply a subtype of a generic

---

[2]   The precise theoretical status of these different forms of social action varies across traditions of sociological theory. Max Weber draws a fairly sharp distinction between instrumentally rational action and what he calls value-rational action as two forms of individual action. Emile Durkheim sees instrumental rationality as itself a result of a particular kind of individualistic value system. Hans Joas, a contemporary theorist, elaborates a refined inventory of forms of action, drawing heavily from the pragmatist tradition of social theory. The common thread in these various treatments is that individual action is irreducibly heterogeneous.

process utility maximization. Why do people follow norms and abide by moral codes? They follow norms because of the psychic costs of shame for violating them; they follow moral codes because of the "guilt fines" of acting immorally. A rational cost–benefit calculation of the consequences to the individual therefore explains action on the basis of both norms and moral codes. Most sociologists reject this amalgamation on the grounds that the cognitive processes, emotional states and behavioral patterns linked to these modes of social action do not all involve a process of "maximization" in any subjectively meaningful sense, nor are they all subjectively oriented to enhancing individual satisfactions (except in a tautological sense in which "satisfaction" is defined in such a way that everything one does must enhance satisfaction otherwise one wouldn't do it). Sociologists, therefore, broadly work within a framework of action in which qualitatively different modes of social action are not reducible to any singular form of action, while economists generally adopt a framework in which utility maximization or some close cognate is treated as a satisfactory general model of all forms of action.

This contrast in the models of action has direct bearing on how the problem of incentives in the analysis of the commons figures in the characteristic analyses of economics and sociology. In economics incentives play a pivotal role in solving empirical puzzles over the commons because of their direct impact on choices. In particular, the likelihood of punishments for violating rules governing the commons impacts directly on the choices by actors to cooperate with the protection of the commons or to act individually in ways which are collectively destructive to the commons. The variations across settings, then, are primarily in how positive and negative incentives are organized, how information around incentives is acquired, how violations of the commons are monitored, how the sanctions associated with such violations are imposed, and so on.

Incentives would also figure prominently in sociological analysis, but they would play two quite different roles, with different logics and dynamics. As with the treatment of incentives in economics, one role for incentives in sociological analysis is the direct impact on behavior via individual calculation of costs and benefits of different courses of action. But sociologists also see the issue of rewards and punishment as playing a crucial, distinct role in the social production and reproduction of norms and values, not just the direct reward structure faced by actors in making their choices. This is essentially Emile Durkheim's view of the ways in which norms and moral codes are infused with a kind of social sacredness that give them weight in people's subjectivity. The issue here is both one of *socialization* – how are norms and values effectively inculcated as serious, internalized regulators of behavior? – but also of *normative maintenance* – how are people told that particular norms and values are of deep *shared* importance to the members of the community in which they live? Rituals, punishments, and certain kinds of publicly visible rewards all serve to symbolize such shared salience. This is not because punishments instill mass fear of sanctions for violation of the norms in question, but because punishments publicly affirm both the moral salience of the norm in question and the shared, collective commitment to the norm.[3] When such norms and moral codes are effectively

---

[3]   It is important to stress the two components here: salience and shared commitment. Norms vary in their salience, in the moral weight that backs them up, and in the extent to which they are shared within a given community. The *public* quality of norm-affirmation is critical for instilling and communicating this collective quality.

infused with such shared, collective salience, then actors cooperate out of duty and commitment, not because of an ongoing calculation of how best to maximize their individual self-interests.[4]

For a sociologist, then, the devastation of a commons would be, in the first instance, interpreted as a failure of the social mechanisms of inculcation and reproduction of norms and values, rather than mainly a failure of the immediate incentive structure of rewards and punishment individuals confront in making choices about compliance with protecting the commons. Many possible causes could explain such erosion of normative regulation. Rapid geographical and social mobility can increase the density of people in a community whose actions affect the commons but who have not been socialized into the specific normative order needed to protect the commons. Such mobility could also lead to a breakdown of the social networks through which informal sanctions affirm the collective commitment to these norms. Increasing heterogeneity in a community can erode a sense of collective identity, which in turn can undermine cooperative norms to the extent that such norms typically include a specification of the relevant categories of people with whom one normatively cooperates (as opposed to the category of people with whom one cooperates simply for rational-instrumental reasons). Erosion of cooperative norms with respect to the commons could also be tied to erosion of social classification systems about which domains of action require cooperation. One of the critical features of normative action in general is the definition of those social contexts for which given norms are binding. An erosion of the social classification system which signals to people which contexts are appropriate for selfish action and which are not could therefore lead to a collapse of cooperation. This is how markets might impact on the commons: the triumph of markets in the mundane economic life of people erodes the distinction between private and public normative contexts of action, and thus could make it harder to consistently evoke commons-protecting norms and values. None of these kinds of issues are likely to play much role in a self-interested rational-actor model of the fate of the commons.[5]

The contrast in underlying models of action in economics and sociology also bears on what is the most obvious, striking contrast between sociology and economics (on virtually every topic, not just the problem of the commons): the level of mathematical formalization expected in the standard piece of economics is orders of magnitude greater than in the standard piece of sociology, even in cases where sociologists do quantitative research. This is not because economists care more about causation than do sociologists and thus feel compelled to elaborate rigorous formal models of the interconnections and feedbacks among an array of causal processes. Sociologists also try to identify causal

---

[4]   To translate this point into the conventional language of economists in which values/norms are simply elements of preferences, punishments affect the formation of preferences, not simply the cost–benefit calculations of actors given fixed preferences.

[5]   There are some specific contexts in economics analyses in which some of the causal processes listed here would have some relevance. When the problem of the commons is seen as an assurance game, one of the key issues is satisfying the information conditions for cooperation – i.e. people need to be assured that the vast majority of people in a community share the assurance game preference order in which universal cooperation is preferred over individual defection. High levels of social and geographical mobility and the erosion of local social networks could all interfere with such information conditions. The sociological analysis adds to this an argument about how such mobility and heterogeneity might affect the preferences themselves rather than simply the knowledge of actors about each other's fixed preferences.

mechanisms and figure out effective research strategies for studying them. They key issue here, I think, is the degree of simplification embodied in the underlying assumptions that economists and sociologists feel is acceptable.

The self-interested rational actor model allows for a simple, powerful mathematical representation of choice and action. Such models were initially developed for the relatively straightforward contexts of market behavior in which rational, self-interested action is undoubtedly a pretty good first approximation for many issues (although even in the pure market context, as economic sociologists like to point out, norms play an important role – the "noncontractual foundations of contract" to quote Durkheim's formulation). When challenged that the simplifying assumptions underlying such models are radically unrealistic, economists either say that the simplifications are strictly heuristic – that they enable one to formalize the models and see how much we can learn from them – or that, for the problem at hand, they are tapping the most important causal processes. In either case, the simplified action model of utility maximization under constraints is viewed as a sound basis on which to build both theoretical and empirical analyses.

If one believes that good social explanations should be based on a multi-dimensional concept of social action involving a variety of irreducible, interacting modes of action none of which is generically privileged, then the problem of mathematical formalization becomes much more difficult. Action is not simply the result of choice, it is also the result of habit; choices are not simply based on maximization of utility, they are also governed by norms and moral commitments; and ends are not always given prior to action, but develop through pragmatic social interaction. With that level of complexity as one's starting point, sociologists have generally preferred to elaborate their theoretical ideas discursively rather than formally. In general, they are profoundly skeptical that knowledge of real-world problems generated by simplified one-dimensional views of social action will be meaningful. They thus opt for explanations that will be messier and less precisely specified than those of economists, but – in their view – resting on more plausible assumptions about how people really act and live their lives.

There is clearly a trade-off between these two ways of theorizing social action and studying specific social phenomena. The purported greater realism of sociological explanations often brings in its wake an ad hoc quality loaded with complexity and contingency, but not much by way of systematic theoretical argument. Economists offer precise, rigorous elaborations of a limited number of causal mechanisms that enable them to make quite specific predictions about the choices people will make and the actions they will take under specifiable conditions. Sociologists invoke a more realistic menu of logics of action, but are characteristically vague in how they think about the interactions among these models of action. Given the general unwillingness (or inability) to formalize these interconnections, the result is a style of analysis with highly developed concepts and relatively underdeveloped theory. Economists, on the other hand, work with a much thinner set of concepts, but deploy them in more rigorous, systematic theoretical elaborations.

I see no general basis for choosing between the thin conceptual menu with analytically rigorous theory in economics and the elaborate conceptual menu with analytically casual theory in sociology. Interesting, novel insights that change the way we think about the world are tough to get in either configuration.

Commentary 3: CPR Institutions

Game-theory Constructs and Empirical Relevance

Nirmal Sengupta

Among its points of inquiry, the goals of the workshop "Conversations II" included "how theoretical methods and field-based methods can best be blended." For anthropology, research method itself is field based. Economists at the most talk of field experiences. Once in a while, experiences from the field are put to use for modifying theory. Unlike anthropology, where this is a regular occurrence, economics does not have many such examples of theory building. Theories of the commons are one area where facts from the field have contributed to modification of economic theory and models. This provides an excellent opportunity for studying the field-based methods of economists. In this chapter I describe the development of rational choice modeling of collective action on the commons, suggesting why some matters were accepted, some rejected, and some others are still awaiting judgment. The first section is about the emergence of game theories of commons as a field-based method. The second section lists a few questions raised in the field indicating the need for modifying game models in specific directions. The concluding section introduces, apart from summing up, certain recent efforts of theorizing in these directions. I will describe the evolutions through my personal experiences, in order to provide a lively picture. Many of us, who have been associated with the development of CPR theories from the very beginning, have gone through similar experiences.

The Beginning

Theory of collective action

In the early 1970s, while making a perspective plan for the state of Bihar, I had a chance to move a little away from input–output tables, matrix inversion and computer simulations. I was required to assess the local resources that might be used for making a development plan for the state. I went around the state talking to people, to know more about local resources. And this is the wonder; I did actually find some promising but neglected resources. The local people talked of many resources; for the present study I mention only one of these, an irrigation system of Bihar. The people in this area would show me some rudimentary embankment structure and mention the name *ahar*. I could not follow why they were important. But I started collecting information on their potential as resources. Gradually I learnt that there were about ten thousand *ahars* in that region. Together, they stored as much water as a major dam, and had made south Bihar (Magadh) *immune to both flood and famines*.[1] At the same time, these were not listed in irrigation statistics. The officials had not the slightest idea of their potential. This is not very surprising. Most CPR were "discovered" from field experiences, though they were very much in existence. Local genetic resources are now being "discovered" though the local people have known these all along.

In due course I learnt[2] that there were several traditional irrigation and water management systems of comparable importance. No doubt systems like the *ahar-pynes,* deserve to be developed and extended. But how? What exactly should we do? If government was so negligent that the official data did not even show their existence, then how were these surviving? How were these indigenous systems being managed? The basic question that I had in the 1970s was one of management.

How were these traditional irrigation systems managed? The colonial government had a simple answer for all such questions – *zamindars* (landlords) manage anything and everything in their domains. From a reading of these records I published an article in 1980 naively suggesting that the *zamindars* constructed and maintained[3] *ahars* and *pynes*. This fitted nicely with the reigning theory of that period, that of the Asiatic mode of production further vulgarized by the Oriental despotism thesis of Wittfogel. In essence, these theories postulated that authorities like *zamindars* were essential for the construction and management of irrigation systems. My field experiences however, stood in sharp contrast. The *zamindars* were there no more after the abolition of *zamindari*. The present authority, the government, did not even know of their existence. There simply was no effective authority to lend support to the Wittfogelian thesis. But the system survived.

By then serious doubts about the role of despotic (even benevolent) authorities in irrigation had started creeping in. Fieldwork by anthropologists (e.g. Leach 1961; Glick 1970; Mitchell 1973; Hunt and Hunt 1976) had highlighted the role played by user communities in management. In my 1980 article I had mentioned those only in a footnote. In another five years CPR institutional theories appeared in full vigor and lent support to the possibility of management without despotic authority. Around that time Hardin wrote his famous article (Hardin 1968) about management of CPRs, predicting that systems like *ahars* and *pynes* were merely awaiting their tragedies. His Hobbesian recommendation parallels that of the Asiatic mode and Wittfogel's. But the simple argument of the new theory of the commons was that the continuing existence of those systems, which could not last as per Hardin, were pointers to alternative systems of management.

---

[1]   As per government reports. I wrote about this system in Sengupta (1980). A detailed account is now available in my book (Sengupta 2001).

[2]   I did a study of the so-called traditional irrigation systems all over South Asia, published as "Irrigation: Traditional vs. Modern" and later, a book (Sengupta 1993). The IIMI (before it became IWMI) used to publish a bulletin of *Farmer Managed Irrigation Systems* all over the world, which too reported several locally important irrigation systems.

[3]   This article is now frequently cited in environment history studies, unfortunately missing the corrections that I did later (e.g. Sengupta 2001).

Theory building

The theorization of the field experiences followed two different courses, largely aligned to disciplines. One group of scholars looked primarily to habitat, cultural practices, belief systems and worldviews for explanation of sustainable CPR management by small communities. They were primarily sociologists and anthropologists (e.g. McCay and Acheson 1987; Berkes and Folke 1998), though distinctive by their stress on resources, ecosystems, technology and property relations. Economists and political scientists (e.g. Ostrom 1990; Bardhan 1993; Baland and Platteau 1996) were caught up by the contradictions in the then-existing collective action theories in their disciplines. Contesting the then-prevalent notion that common interests lead to group organization and collective action, Mancur Olson (1971) had shown that voluntary collective action was next to impossible. Economists and political scientists working on CPRs had to engage themselves primarily in developing alternative theories that would explain observed collective action phenomena. Given the context, the merit of this exercise is beyond question. But the established discourse of collective action theory was formal, universalist and essentially reductionist. It could not embrace symbolism.

The formal models of collective action that developed to explain CPR situations consisted of costs and benefits to individual actors, incentives and penalties. A third stream of theorization should also be mentioned. This is the "moral economy" approach (Scott 1976). The moral economy approach is based on a small community's need to cope with risk and its collective dependence on local resources, often institutionalized in religion, folklore, and tradition. This stream brings in the political perspective, which is missing in the other two.

The practical implications of these three streams of theorizing are different. The symbolic cultural theories are directed more at ecological interpretations. The political anthropology approach interprets political actions. Both of them may facilitate collective action on CPRs in the way of identification of potential areas/villages/systems but cannot suggest what can be done for securing cooperation if the congenial conditions are not met. The rationality-based approaches on the other hand, try to find suitable conditions – or "principles" following Ostrom (1990) – that can be replicated in all situations. Mosse (2003: 16) suggests that the rationality-based approach finds favour in participatory programs and the like. However, I feel that this approach did not have much success in programs, in spite of being favoured, because of inherent weaknesses of the theory. In the next section I discuss these weaknesses.

Some Questions

In spite of his doomsday prediction Hardin did lay the foundation for a rigorous game-theory formulation of the commons. I feel that without this initial stress CPR studies would have shown the same lethargy that other empirical fields show about theory. In the next few years game theory models of commons were further developed (e.g. Ostrom, Gardner, and Walker 1994; Baland and Plateau 1996), largely out of efforts to modify models to field realities. The success of a model is in the explanations it provides through its implications. In this section I will only introduce several questions that have been raised.

Process theory

To a pure theorist the only importance of cases of collective action in traditional commons was to counter Hardin's thesis of the "tragedy of commons." To others, there were questions of practical significance. What should one do about the cases of still working traditional commons, like that of the *ahars* and *pynes*? Should we leave good management alone? Is there a reason to intervene even though performance is good? And if so, how do we intervene? Game theory or any other economic theory had explanations for the occurrence of collective action, but no leads regarding necessary and desirable policies. Community organizers with sociology or social work backgrounds were engaged to foster water users' associations. Economists were not invited for the task, and rightly so. Economists direct their energy to finding equilibrium. They have little to say about the way to the equilibrium.

Both symbolic and moral economic approaches used norms, customs and culture as explanantia for participatory actions. The rational-choice approach made remarkable progress while treating those as explananda. The change should have enabled the rational choice approach to suggest ways of internalizing norms for better participation. Unfortunately, theorists are pleased just to show that normative equilibrium will exist at the end of an evolutionary path. Evolutionary game theory has nothing to say about the process of evolution, about the disequilibrium state that exists before reaching the equilibrium, whether it is possible to facilitate evolution of norms and steer evolutionary paths in desired directions (viz. Sengupta 2001: 55–69). That would have permitted a role for facilitating agencies. There is an interesting contrast between the two branches of game theory. Mechanism design postulates the existence of conscious designers while rejecting processes in favor of a single-shot solution; evolutionary games admit process but deny a role for a conscious designer.

Transition

In promoting traditional irrigation systems another serious question should be answered. Can techniques be separated from their social basis? In indigenous knowledge research this is now a hotly debated question. Brouwer (1997) drew a distinction between indigenous knowledge system (IKS) and indigenous technological knowledge (ITK), arguing that IKS delineates a cognitive structure in which theories and perceptions of nature and culture are conceptualized. It includes definitions, classifications and concepts of natural, social, economical and ideational environments. Is it possible to conserve and promote ITK like that of *ahar-pyne* irrigation, without extending support[4] to IKS? When colonial intervention was the popular explanation for the degradation of traditional knowledge, and traditional social settings were considered glorious, arguments were made in favour of promoting IKS. Even today it is argued (e.g. Agrawal 1995) that from a development perspective it is difficult to conceive why a working system may need intervention. But a different perspective may demand intervention. Even if performance of a traditional commons is good, it may be supporting highly inequitable distribution and so deserve change.

---

[4]   Current IK researchers are divided over this issue. Indigenous peoples' movements insist that conservation of indigenous genetic knowledge is closely linked with land rights of the communities.

Also, in a rapidly changing modern world it is less likely that traditional/indigenous institutions will survive long. How should the old CPR associations be transformed?

Economics has never bothered about such questions. In fact, questions like these would not arise in conventional economic analysis. Anthropologists went to distinct societies, first to study their economies and cultures, and also to understand the transition process from old to new institutions. As globalization has proceeded, and local communities are rapidly being transformed, anthropology and sociology have moved more into studying the transition process and its implications. Economics, with rare exceptions, was not interested in primitive societies and their institutions. Those were regions meant just for market extension. Reorganization of collective action on the commons would involve institutional transition in developing countries. The question is whether economics has a suitable theoretical framework for this. My answer is "no." In game theory models a well-performing traditional institution is in equilibrium. It can change in just one way – by deteriorating.[5]

The scale of CPR

Another problem that has arrested the growth of empirically meaningful theory is the artificial scaling of CPRs. It is true that CPRs are more important for the poor and in traditional societies. It is one thing to admit their importance in certain spheres, but another to restrict the analytical subject to that sphere. One major bias was to conceive of CPRs exclusively as technologically primitive, pre-modern, small-scale phenomena. Olson (1971) celebrated the role of small communities in collective action. Baland and Platteau's (1996) influential work relegated CPRs to small groups alone. Even if I leave aside the "commons" in Brundtland's "Our Common Future," there arc rich materials which shows the inappropriateness of binding CPRs to small scales. Keohane and Ostrom (1995) demonstrated the value of comparing collective action problems at vastly different scales, from local arrangements to international regimes. No doubt, at the village-level, CPRs often assume critical importance for the livelihood of the rural poor, for reasons ranging from employment opportunities to risk minimization. No doubt, attention to these will help the poor. But does it mean that one has to take a static view? Should the commons remain as local as in the past? Or should they extend and increase in scale?

In some distant past the region around the Tamiraparani river in south India had only a few small tanks. As technology developed the tanks were connected to rivers by construction of dams (anicuts) on rivers, which enriched their water supply. In the nineteenth century modern technology was used to construct anicuts in more difficult sections of the river, connecting more tanks. In the twentieth century massive reservoirs were constructed

---

[5] Lately, this problem of equilibrium analysis has drawn some attention. Evolutionary biologists have suggested that speciation occurs in punctuated equilibrium. Aoki (2001) has used the punctuated equilibrium approach in economics. Towards this end I have used (Sengupta 2001) the theory of self-organization, now known as a part of complex system analysis, which suggests that phase transition in non-linear dynamic systems may generate systemic (equilibrium) evolution in a punctuated form. Here the scope of study is the state away from equilibrium (i.e. disequilibrium). Under some conditions a system far away from the equilibrium may develop a different evolutionary process leading to a different equilibrium. This may be explained as the same ITK existing under different IKS (equilibrium) and under some conditions the collective action may move away from one IKS to another. In other words, new forms of participatory organization are able to support old technology.

to stabilize the supply. Finally, a few decades back, two hydropower stations were added, making it a multipurpose project. The Tamiraparni irrigation system now irrigates 35 thousand hectares not only through its channel systems but also through 179 tanks in its command area. Three reservoirs have been constructed at its upper reaches; two of them for power generation. The system provides excellent examples of collective action on the commons (Sengupta 1991: 121–51). When I visited the system one of its irrigation associations was celebrating its hundred years in style. The principle of large scale organizations that has been applied here has been termed nesting of enterprises (Ostrom 1990). The narrow view of CPRs has actually restricted development of useful theory, and meaningful development policies in certain areas.

"Many cases of resource management are neither small-scale nor large-scale but *cross-scale* in both space and time. As such, management problems have to be tackled simultaneously at several levels." From a survey of the literature Berkes (2000) identifies six different forms of institutions with potential for cross-scale linkages: (1) co-management, (2) multistakeholder bodies, (3) institutions oriented for development, empowerment and co-management, (4) institutions for linking local users with regional agencies, (5) research and management approaches that enable cross-scale linkages, and (6) institutions for "citizen science." Formal analysis should be aim to integrate all these forms in the theory of collective action.

Commons and markets

Another problem is the market compatibility issue. Starting from Jodha's (1985) seminal work, CPRs have been regarded as incompatible with markets. While grazing and fuel-wood collection have suffered from market expansion, traditional irrigation often gained by modernization and market advance. It is accepted that participatory management is possible in modern irrigation. Chopra et al. (1990) estimated the market value of the Sukhomajori forest, consequent to its participatory program. Still later, the *catechu* plantations at Sukhomajori have become more valuable. McKean (2000) listed the Chiclé latex extracted from the Maya biosphere reserve and used for chewing gum, birds' nests in Kalimantan for use in Chinese cooking, and gum acacia in Senegal, as items whose value as resources come almost entirely from their commercial demand abroad. But that demand itself has created the incentive for devising communal management institutions. If so, the development policies of traditional CPRs should focus on compatible modernization and market expansion.

How does commercial demand for resources taken from community-managed systems affect the dynamics of internal cooperation? McKean (2000) says that the evidence here is quite mixed, based again on anthropological studies. Many communally managed resources are managed for commercial extraction and are not worth extracting at all except for peculiar customers who pay cash. Yet at the same time, it appears that commercial demand accompanied by rapidly rising prices for the resources in question can exacerbate the temptation to harvest more now, to capture high prices, and solve problems of over-exploitation of resources later. We must not overlook the fact that CPR activities like fishery and certain kinds of forest product gathering have traditionally been based on market exchanges (Sengupta 1995: 196). The New Institutional Economic (NIE) literature, that admits hierarchies and organizations along with markets, has something to offer for CPR analysis.

Choosing a Model

The question about the tragedy of commons was settled long ago. Three decades have passed since then, enriching our knowledge about the field conditions of CPR. What additional theoretical insights may we get from the numerous field studies of CPR conducted in all these years? "The commons literature is full of examples of destructive state intervention . . . However, the literature also contains many examples in which the state has created enabling legislation or has otherwise facilitated the development of local-level institutions" (Berkes 2000). The question posed by the "tragedy of commons" debate was about conservation of natural resources. CPRs were suggested as an alternative strategy for conservation. But conservation is not an end in itself. An approach that necessitates communities to remain static for indefinitely long periods, rejecting the development aspirations of its members, puts its long-term sustainability in question. Unfortunately CPR policies are made for management by small communities, and that too primarily for "conservation" not "development." Increasing differentiation and market extension is viewed with suspicion. Game theory approaches are directed to find equilibrium. Once reached, that would require no further improvement. The design principles are based on a conjecture that institutions found in traditional irrigation systems, are long-enduring, lending strength to a static view. Instead, we need theories of collective action that would include development from small scale to large scale and be market compatible. Existing theoretical approaches fail to meet one or the other of these requirements. My effort in this article was to identify some of the areas where theoretical development is needed.

I have dealt primarily with formal theories of rationality based action. But I have shown how these theories benefited from exchanges with other disciplines. Essentially, it was an exchange, without diluting the methodological purity of the disciplines. What kind of interdisciplinary methods do we need? One approach is to borrow others' methodologies to enrich a theory. In my opinion, this is inappropriate because it homogenizes science against its rich disciplinary composition. Diversity is strength, not a liability. While other theories could use norms and conventions for explaining some phenomena, rational choice analysis added an approach for explaining the very occurrence of norms and conventions. Also, methodological individualism has succeeded in extending the possibilities of collective action beyond the feasible setting identified by cultural and moral economy approaches. Heterogeneity is not necessarily incompatible with collective action. Baland and Platteau (1999) find that in situations where agents freely interact without any intervention by a regulatory authority there is nothing like a one-to-one relationship between inequality and collective action. But in regulated settings, inequality tends to reduce the acceptability of available regulatory schemes making collective action more difficult. Dayton-Johnson and Bardhan (2002) argue that the relationship between inequality and economic efficiency in CPR is not linear but U-shaped. Gaps in theory that are noticed in interdisciplinary dialogues are certainly the weaknesses of each discipline. The task of interdisciplinary research is not one of borrowing and imitation. The task is a far more challenging one, that of developing specific disciplines for responding to the gaps. Human understanding will benefit more from studies of the same phenomena from different perspectives, by the use of all five fingers instead of one at a time.

References

Agrawal, A., 1995: "Dismantling the Divide between Indigenous and Scientific Knowledge," *Development and Change* 26: 413–39.

Aoki, Masahiko, 2001: *Towards a Comparative Institutional Analysis*, Cambridge, MA: MIT Press.

Baland, Jean-Marie and Jean-Philippe Platteau, 1996: *Halting Degradation of Natural Resources: Is There a Role for Rural Communities?*, New York: Oxford University Press.

Baland, J. M., and J. P. Platteau, 1999: "The Ambiguous Impact of Inequality on Local Resource Management," *World Development*, 27: 773–88.

Bardhan, Pranab, 1993: "Symposium on Management of Local Commons," *Journal of Economic Perspectives*, 7(4): 87–92.

——. 2000: "Irrigation and Cooperation: An Empirical Analysis of 48 Irrigation Communities in South India," *Economic Development and Cultural Change*, 48(4): 847–65.

Berkes, F., 2000: "Cross-scale Institutional Linkages: Perspectives from the Bottom Up," IASCP Conference, Indiana University, June.

Berkes, F., and C. Folke, eds, 1998: *Linking Social And Ecological Systems: Management Practices and Social Mechanisms for Building Resilience*, Cambridge: Cambridge University Press.

Brouwer, Jan, 1997: "The Goddess for Development: Indigenous Economic Concepts among South Indian Artisans," *Social Anthropology*, 5(1): 69–82.

Chopra, K., Gopal K. Kadekodi, and M. N. Murty, 1990: *Participatory Development: People and Common Property Resources*, New Delhi: Sage.

Dayton-Johnson, Jeff and Bardhan, Pranab, 2002: "Inequality and Conservation on the Local Commons: A Theoretical Exercise," *Economic Journal*, 112(481): 577–602.

Hunt, R., and Hunt, E., 1976: "Canal Irrigation and Local Social Organization," *Current Anthropology*, 17(3): 398–411.

Glick, T., 1970: *Irrigation and Society in Medieval Valencia*, Cambridge, MA: Harvard University Press.

Hardin, G., 1968: "The Tragedy of the Commons," *Science*, 162: 1243–8.

Jodha, N. S., 1985: "Market Forces and Erosion of Common Property Resources," in Agricultural Markets in the Semi-arid Tropics, Proceedings of an International Workshop, ICRISAT, Patancheru, India, 263–77 (unpublished).

Keohane, Robert O. and Elinor Ostrom (eds.), 1995: *Local Commons and Global Independence: Heterogeneity and Cooperation in Two Domains*, London: Sage.

Leach, E., 1961: *Pul Eliya, a Village in Ceylon: A Study of Land Tenure and Kinship*, Cambridge: Cambridge University Press.

McCay, B., and J. M. Acheson (ed.), 1987: *The Question of the Commons: The Culture and Ecology of Communal Resources*, Tucson, AZ: University of Arizona Press.

McKean, Margaret A., 2000: "Governance and Civil Society," paper presented at the Fifth Annual Colloquium on Environmental Law and Institutions, "Sustainable Governance," Durham, North Carolina, April 27–8 (unpublished).

Mitchell, W. P., 1973: "The Hydraulic Hypothesis: A Reappraisal," *Current Anthropology*, 14: 532–4.

Mosse, David, 2003: *The Rule of Water*, New Delhi: Oxford University Press.

Olson, Mancur, 1971: *The Logic of Collective Action*, Cambridge, MA: Harvard University Press.

Ostrom, Elinor, 1990: *Governing the Commons: The Evolution of Institutions for Collective Action*, New York: Cambridge University Press.

Ostrom, Elinor, Roy Gardner, and James Walker, 1994: *Rules, Games, and Common-pool Resources*, Ann Arbor, MI: University of Michigan Press.

Scott, J. C., 1976: *The Moral Economy of the Peasant: Subsistence and Rebellion in Southeast Asia*, New Haven, CT: Yale University Press.

Sengupta, Nirmal, 1980: "Indigenous Irrigation Organisation of South Bihar," *Indian Economic and Social History Review*, April: 158–97.

——. 1991: *Managing Common Property: Irrigation in India and Philippines*, New Delhi: Sage.

——. 1993: *User-friendly Irrigation Designs*, New Delhi: Sage.

——. 1995: "Common Property Institutions and Markets," *Indian Economic Review*, 30(2): 187–201.

——. 2001: *A New Institutional Theory of Production: An Application*, New Delhi: Sage.

Commentary 4: Disciplinary Perspectives and Policy Design for Common-pool Resources

Some Reflections

Kanchan Chopra

Introduction: Common Property, Common-pool Resources, and Disciplinary Perspectives

Environmental and natural resources provide a good focal point for the study of common property regimes. This is largely because these resources give rise to the need, in certain contexts both local and global, for management regimes that are based on community of ownership. The term we use in this chapter is "common-pool resources" (CPRs). This is because it captures better than "common property resources" both the physical characteristics that necessitate collective action (Stevenson 1991) and the presence of different degrees of access to resources. Typically, ownership is not "legal" but "historical." Whatever the source of authority, the local commons are not open to outsiders. A large literature has developed which describes the many ingenious rules and regulations societies have devised to manage their commons (Dasgupta and Maler 2004).[1] The term "common-pool resources," we feel, reflects these nuances.

The social and natural sciences are in agreement on the need for communitarian, nonmarket institutions for management of the commons, in particular of the local commons. However, the worldviews they bring to bear on the issue are different. Ecology, for instance, focuses on interconnectedness of living forms to focus on the need for a holistic management. Economics uses the concept of market failure, external effects and appropriate scale of management to stress the need for common property regimes. Social anthropologists draw attention to the communities' perceptions of the significance and content of common property. Legal analysts study the means by which rights of different kinds are formalized or otherwise recognized in societies. This methodological plurality needs to

---

[1] See for instance Wade (1988), Chopra et al. (1990), Feeny et al. (1990), Ostrom (1990), Baland and Platteau (1996).

find expression in the analysis of common property issues and in the framing of policy that impacts them.

A large part of the worldview of each discipline emanates from the role it perceives itself to play in the field of analysis and policy. The thinking of Development Economics, for example, is dominated by the need for policy intervention. The understanding with regard to the commons that emerges therefrom attempts to simplify and generalize for policy. In a somewhat parallel approach, policy interventions are far from the study objectives of social anthropologists. Their focus is on an understanding of reality. Hence their delving into complexity is but understandable. They are not looking for points at which policy interventions may be appropriate and useful.

Further, economists tend to think that significance depends on size of the commons and on being able to decipher trends that are common in different parts of the world in order to focus on broad policy directions. Sociologists analyze governance and social structures and the issues of norms and values, which enable the continued existence of common property. Legal experts study the legal and informal laws, which enable such institutions to continue. Each of these approaches results in differences of methodology and approach to issues of the commons. In this context, I shall in this brief commentary compare three components of a recent research project undertaken to understand the policy implications of common-pool resource knowledge.[2] It is argued here that the perceived differences between disciplines decrease and they move towards a common framework when they see policy design as the objective of their exercise. This is attempted by:

1   examining critically an approach followed by Chopra et al. (1990) in analyzing the role of common property resources in development in a region in Northern India;
2   reviewing three studies undertaken as part of a DFID project undertaken in 2001–3 to study the policy implications of common-pool resource knowledge in India, Tanzania, and Zimbabwe.

These two studies are interesting to compare. The first was undertaken by a team of economists coming into the common property field from a development perspective: the second was a study undertaken respectively by teams headed by a sociologist, an economist and a legal expert, in different cultural contexts, but with policy design as the focal point.

People and Common Property Resources: The Development Perspective

The first study we review (Chopra et al. 1990) is rooted in development economics and places socio-economic institutions linking resources, people and government at the center of its concerns. It begins in fact by saying "When conventional methods of development fail to yield any significant results, there is need for some rethinking about the

---

[2]   See UK Department for International Development Project on "Policy Implications of Common Pool Resource Knowledge in India, Tanzania and Zimbabwe" (2001–2).

socio-economic institutions that link resources, people and government." It is interesting to note that it first takes a national perspective and concludes therefrom that the magnitude and significance of common property resources in the country, in this case India. This predilection has both a policy reason and a methodological slant. Economists believe that significance of an issue emerges from its being empirically pervasive and applicable.

The major focus of the study is on the emergence of participatory institutions as a precondition for development for people living in a part of the lower Sivalik range of the Himalayas. The compelling evidence from the field points towards the significance of common property in development. The study establishes that this common resource base contributed to the better use of private property such as land and livestock and that this fact led to the people coming together in collective action. Further, the emergence of participation is attributed to the soil erosion problem faced by villagers, which affects the productivity (and magnitude) of privately held lands. This participation resulted in the creation of new institutions (such as societies for resource management) and new social norms (such as stall feeding of cattle), which impacted efficient use of the commons.

Finally, the study assesses the impact of participatory institutions in terms of methodologies which are rooted in the discipline of development economics: cost–benefit analysis of different investments, cluster analysis to look for patterns of dependence between common property, private property and incomes of different kinds. An attempt is also made to analyze the contractual arrangements in terms of emerging comparative static equilibrium. Policy implications are derived and some of them delve into the process aspects, which emerged from the field understanding. It is stated for instance "the existence of leadership is one of the first catalysts." Outside support by way of initial investments is recognized as significant. Other necessary conditions are identified as availability of labour and considerable effort in dispute resolution. We are told finally, "Taking into account the track record of alternative models in both poverty alleviation and environmental preservation, it seems well worth giving a chance to this new institution on a wider scale."

The study tells a consistent but incomplete story. An anthropologist may miss in it reference to the dominating role of the commons as an expression of the identity of villages and of the peoples' relationship with the commons "evolved over centuries of access and use based on customs and traditions."[3] Other social scientists may question the artificial "corporateness" foisted on rural communities. The thinking behind this indictment is best expressed as stated below:

> The benefits of community managed resources are propagated and perceived as short term material benefits rather than in terms of the basic right of the community to participate in the process of governance and decision-making at all levels – policy-making, planning execution and disposal of gains. *Short-term gains made as a result of benevolent acts are actually disemboweling.*[4]

---

[3]   See Saint (undated).
[4]   See Shivji (2002) for an elucidation of this viewpoint.

Disciplinary Approaches to Policy Design for the Commons

The disciplinary study we propose to examine next brings to the table conclusions with regard to the commons emanating from different country perspectives as well as different disciplinary perspectives. The shared focus was the design of policy and processes for policy-making with regard to common-pool resources.

Governance and property rights changes in the context of land dominated the perspective of the legal expert studying Tanzania.[5] For Shivji, the village as a site of governance comes prior to the village as a site for development. Such a standpoint has its roots in recent history of that country. Villagization as a movement in that country (the Ujaama movement of the 1970s) is seen to ignore traditional rights of common tenure and hence have disastrous effects on commons and ecology. Also development is associated with production for export after the Ujaama experiment had the effects mentioned above. So he focuses on village governance, implying elections to village councils. Participatory Democracy as against representative democracy is considered a prior condition for protection of the commons. The appropriation of common land is seen as being due to:

- the preference given to sedentary and agrarian interests over pastoral communities;[6]
- appropriation of common-pool resources of cultivating communities by the state;
- appropriation of land by private investors, both foreign and local.

Alienation of common land is the central issue: this alienation may be due to the government with foreign support to the private investors, intercommunity conflict over common resources. Therefore, if CPRs are to be protected, secured and developed in the interest of the rural poor, intervention has to be made at the level of devolution of power as opposed to simply decentralization of management. Such an approach sees the incorrectness of looking at the "use and benefits of CPR as problems of efficiency and management rather than those of ownership and governance." It also looks at the notion of ownership and property as "an organic whole wherein people, living, dead and yet to be born relate to each other not to a thing. Land is part of that organic relationship, not to be owned or managed."

Such an approach to ownership and property, while it may fit in with the approach of communities leaves the policy-maker without a starting point from where to initiate change. Land is a much-contested resource in developing countries with multiple uses. So one has to reckon with the fact that the commons and the ecosystems which they are a part of need to be used to advantage to contribute towards the different constituents and determinants of human well-being: cultural as much as material.[7] And policies need to provide directions for making choices in such situations.

---

[5] See Shivji (2002).

[6] "Among development writers and policy-makers, priority is given to sedentary communities and agrarian interests over pastoral communities, the latter being considered lower on the scale of development further rationalizing the alienation of pastoral lands" (Mwaikusa 1997; Mustafa 1986).

[7] For a succinct exposition of directions which the literature on human well-being is taking see *Millennium Ecosystem Assessment* (2003: ch. 3).

The study in Zimbabwe undertaken as part of the same project[8] accepts that policy on CPRs needs to address drivers of change as well as differences in cognition, interest and social location. As part of the drivers of change approach to the issue, the following are identified:

- demand increases due to population increases;
- tenure changes are affected by resettlement policies which may have both dangers and opportunities;
- national macro economic performance, in this case fostering an urban–rural drift due to negative economic trends;
- information and knowledge with likely positive results.

Following from an analysis of drivers of change and the role of CPRs in peoples' lives, key policy issues are identified as follows: a shift to a devolutionist stance, creating collective local regimes with strong legal entitlements. Newer collective models are analyzed. One case study[9] illustrates how a government initiated programme can motivate an approach to CPR commoditization which promotes equity at intra-community levels enhances motivation for the use of CPRs on a sustainable basis. However, the program had to be attenuated to limit devolution of power to district councils, rather than producer community levels. The second case study is around agricultural research and extension. Here, provincial and district level extension agents were able to create networks across conventional divides and explore "policy spaces" for influencing bureaucratic policy and policy stances. The approach in this case remained limited to matters of technical knowledge. Access and entitlement remained an unfinished agenda.

The Indian study[10] by its scope had to deal with CPRs of a larger magnitude spread over a larger geographical area with a more stable socio-economic context. A review of a macro-quantification effort which provides a perspective was combined with an in-depth study of policy initiatives to arrive at policy implications. The macro picture[11] suggested that the contribution of CPRs continues to be more in the context of a survival strategy for the rural poor. Certain complementarities in the production process continue between private and common property resources. Pockets of intensive complementarity with private property could be located in the larger picture of a continuing safety net role for common-pool resources in the larger economy.

More significantly, a review of two policy initiatives taken in the 1990s to move towards decentralized management of CPRs is attempted: joint forest management (JFM) and watershed development guidelines (WDG).[12] The study concludes: "In both cases, indifferent success has been reported."

---

[8]   See Murphree and Mazambani (2002).

[9]   The Communal Areas Management Program for Indigenous Resources (CAMPFIRE) has largely been a wildlife program and its sponsorship by a government department has been significant.

[10]   See Chopra and Dasgupta (2002).

[11]   Derived from data collected as part of NSSO.

[12]   Joint Forest Management introduced on a large scale in 1990 is a kind of "centralized decentralization" constituting a partnership between the forest department and the people through the setting up of committees for forest protection. The aim is poverty alleviation for local communities together with complementary conservation of forests. Watershed development guidelines aim at holistic development of land in a watershed, seen as a vehicle for rural development.

- The ground rules for the formation and operation of forest committees and water-shed development teams are often weighed heavily in favor of the respective line departments.
- Disputes over sharing of the produce have risen in JFM and in the absence of a legal enactment, promised share of output (to rural communities) in return for protection has not been implemented.
- In toto, JFM as implemented does not seem to have improved access of local people. Where pre-existing institutional structures have been ignored, it has even resulted in a deterioration of their status vis-a-vis the government departments.
- Such initiatives need to be complemented with a policy on land-use which prevents continued encroachments by industry and urbanization.
- With respect to watershed development guidelines as well, large variations exist across states, benefits have been negligible, by and large. It may have been a case of hastening social organization, which some commentators consider counter-productive.

Amongst the key policy implications of this study is the understanding that processes need to be designed which provide "level playing fields" for stakeholders with different endowments of information and power and interventions need to be designed which internalize the perception of different stakeholders in resource ownership and management and avoid "centralized decentralization."

Convergence around Policy Processes and Contexts

The three studies reviewed above started from different country contexts and different expert perspectives on the commons. They can be seen to be converging in the context of policy processes and policy dialogues considered appropriate.[13] Common ground that all studies move towards is that of devolution of power through provision of knowledge to all stakeholders and the significance of policy processes.

In this context, it is important to see that the knowledge that enables stakeholders to define problems of resource use is of three types:

- of the empirical context;
- of laws and institutions; and
- of beliefs, myths and ideas.

Policy often is based on a simplified view of the first two kinds of information and treats the third as irrelevant. This happens primarily because of the top-down perception of policy formulation and implementation. An in-depth understanding of the commons derived from different disciplinary perspectives enables an appreciation of the role of the three kinds of knowledge and its internalization into policy dialogue. Such policy dialogue can be characterized not as a one-time decision-making but as a cycle consisting of:

---

[13] See Adams, Brockington, Dyson, and Vira (2002) for one such attempt. Also see Jasanoff (2002) for a discussion of the need for a common rallying point for interdisciplinarity.

- problem definition, defined by the perception of knowledge of theory, knowledge of change and of earlier policy;
- a listing of response options;
- a determination of feasible options, feasible as per the political, social and economic domains;
- decision-making based on different decision criteria;
- implementation and experimentation;
- feedback from implementation to knowledge and to a redefinition of the problem in the next cycle.

It follows that design process is critical to the success of a policy. The legitimacy of decision-making processes may be as important as the regulations that result. Key stakeholders need to perceive a sense of ownership in the intervention being crafted. This is true at all levels of interaction, international, national and local.

Coming back to the context of common-pool resources, a macro-understanding of their nature helps in obtaining a more generalized picture of the empirical context, whereas ethnographic studies enable an understanding of the legal, and cultural context within which these empirical realities are constrained to change. An understanding of these interrelationships within the framework of a systems analysis approach can yield a set of variables that one could work with in framing policy without disrupting the resilience of the system in terms of the domains of the underlying physical and social parameters. Multiple perspectives enable us to learn about what leads a social system to maintain its property of resilience in the face of internal and external policy changes. It may also yield threshold values of critical variables which if crossed may lead to loss of resilience.

However, it is important to point out that political and social system constraints are fixed only in the medium run and change as a consequence of interaction with the empirical economic reality. This is the kind of methodological approach that this brief note seeks to highlight as a promising one for common-pool resource related studies in the future.

An Important Caveat and Future Directions

The legitimacy of the above decision-making process with respect to common-pool resources depends on the participation of all stakeholders on the basis of a level playing field. In a situation of differential input and market access, the emergence of innovative institutions is the essential condition for more equitable access to decision-making bodies, be they at local, national or international levels.

Such an understanding connects to the point that Sen (1999) makes in a wider context. He maintains that institutions and freedoms are central to the complex nexus of peoples' resource endowments, functionings, capabilities, and choice and their movement out of poverty. And institutions are by themselves created by individuals or groups. As people move from transforming their resources or endowments to functionings, their ability to do so is influenced by the freedoms available that in turn are determined by the institutions.

Complexity arises when some individuals or groups can influence the institutions in a manner that gives them an advantage in transforming their resources to functionings by excluding others from the process. Such influence creates differentiated levels of freedom and subsequently forces some individuals or groups to be disadvantaged vis-à-vis others who are able to capture rents by influencing the institutions underlying the provision of freedoms. This happens when freedoms are private goods that are available in differentiated measure to different persons in society.[14] This is true both:

- for the poor within a developing country context of access to the local commons;
- developing countries in the context of international institutions determining sharing of the global commons.

Such an understanding leads to the need for re-examining the links between development, power structures and the institutions governing their devolution. It is for this reason that this chapter argues for policy design as a focal point, which can compel disciplines to forge a common understanding of how common-pool resources contribute to the different constituents and determinants of human well-being. This understanding of policy design may be limited when a single disciplinary viewpoint is adopted. It is enriched considerably by the cumulative understanding brought in by different disciplinary perspectives as indicated in the critique of the selected studies reviewed in the chapter.

References

Adams, W. M., D. Brockington, J. Dyson, and B. Vira (2002) "Analytical Framework for Dialogue on Common Property Resource Management," Working Paper under UK DFID project on "Policy Implications of Common Pool Resource Knowledge in India, Tanzania and Zimbabwe," London: DFID.

Baland, J.-M. and J. P. Platteau (1996) *Halting Degradation of Natural Resources: Is There a Role for Rural Communities?*, Oxford: Oxford University Press.

Chopra, K. and A. Duraiappah (forthcoming) "Operationalising Capabilities in a Segmented Society: The Role of Institutions," in F. Comim (ed.), *Operationalising Capabilities*, Cambridge: Cambridge University Press.

Chopra, K. and D. Purnamita (2002) "Common Pool Resources in India: Evidence, Significance and New Management Initiatives," Working Paper under UK DFID project on "Policy Implications of Common Pool Resource Knowledge in India, Tanzania and Zimbabwe," London: DFID.

Chopra, K., G. Kadekodi, and M. N. Murty (1990) *Participatory Development: People and Common Property Resources*, New Delhi: Sage.

Dasgupta, P. and Maler, K.-G. (2004) "Environmental and Resource Economics: Some Recent Developments South Asian Network for Development and Environmental Economics (SANDEE)," Working Paper 7–04.

Department for International Development (2001–2) "Policy Implications of Common Pool Resource Knowledge in India, Tanzania and Zimbabwe," Working Paper under DFID project, London: DFID.

Feeny, D. F. Berkes, B. J. McCay, and J. M. Acheson (1990) "The Tragedy of the Commons: Twenty-two Years Later," *Human Ecology*, 18(1), 1–19.

Jasanoff, S. (2002) "Reading between the Lines: The Disciplines and the Environment," in S. Lélé, G. Kadekodi, and B. Agrawal (eds), *Interdisciplinarity in Environmental Research*, New Delhi: Indian Society for Ecological Economics, pp. 3–5.

---

[14]   See Chopra and Duraiappah (forthcoming) for the problems raised in situations where capabilities need to be operationalized in societies which are thus segmented.

Millennium Ecosystem Assessment (2003) *Ecosystems and Human Well-being, a Framework for Assessment: A Report of the Conceptual Framework Working Group of the Millennium Ecosystem* Assessment, Washington, DC: Island Press.

Murphree, M. W. and D. Mazambani (2002) "Policy Implications of Common Pool Resource Knowledge: A Background Paper on Zimbabwe," Working Paper under UK DFID project on "Policy Implications of Common Pool Resource Knowledge in India, Tanzania and Zimbabwe," London: DFID.

Mustafa, K. (1986) "Participatory Research and the Pastoralist Question in Tanzania: A Critique of the Jipemoyo Project in Bagamoyo District," Ph. D. dissertation, University of Dar-es-Salaam, Tanzania.

Mwaikusa, J. T. (1997) "The Policy Paper and its Implications on Pastoral Lands," in I. G. Shivji (ed.), *The Land Question: Democratising Land Tenure in Tanzania*, Dar-es-Salaam, Tanzania.

Ostrom, E. (1990) *Governing the Commons: The Evolution of Institutions for Collective Action*, Cambridge: Cambridge University Press.

Ostrom, E. (1992) *Crafting Institutions for Self-Governing Irrigation Systems*, San Francisco: ISC Press for Institute of Contemporary Studies.

Saint, K. (undated) *Community Management of Common Lands: Improving Land Management in Rajasthan Inter*, Jaipur: Cooperation Coordination Office.

Sen, Amartya (1999) *Development as Freedom*, New York: Knopf Press.

Shivji, I. (2002) "Village Governance and Common Pool Resources in Tanzania," Working Paper under UK DFID project on "Policy Implications of Common Pool Resource Knowledge in India, Tanzania and Zimbabwe," London: DFID.

Stevenson, G. G. (1991) *Common Property Economics: A General Theory and Land Use Applications*, Cambridge: Cambridge University Press.

Wade, R. (1988) *Village Republics, Economic Conditions for Collective Action in South India*, Cambridge: Cambridge University Press.

Commentary 5: Understanding Common Property Resources and Their Management

A Potential Bridge across Disciplinary Divides?

A. Vaidyanathan

Introduction

Back in the 1980s a group of social scientists met in Bangalore to promote a trans-disciplinary interaction on the methodology of social inquiry (see Bardhan 1989). The focus at that time was on the measurement of poverty. The choice of the subject reflected its topicality. It was, and still remains, a central issue in public discourse on development policy. Economists have devoted much effort to develop and conceptually refine the process, construct and estimate quantitative indices of poverty, and explore its characteristics. Their work occupies center stage in public discussions on this issue. But some economists (e.g., Jodha 1989) question the validity of inferences about poverty incidence based on data collected through typical sample surveys. Anthropologists offer even more fundamental objections to such measurements, which reflect their skepticism of generalizations based on structured surveys and, indeed, the very possibility of "objectivity" in studying social phenomena.

The divergent viewpoints on poverty measurement, however, exaggerate the divide across different social sciences. While cultural anthropologists typically contest the possibility of objective measurement and advocate participant observation at the micro-level, social anthropologists are interested in exploring both micro- and macro-levels. This derives from their interest in studying the organization of economic and social activities, the nature of social and economic stratification, and the influence of external linkages and the wider polity on these domains. These are also the areas of interest for sociologists, economists, and political scientists. Thus, commonality between anthropologists and other social sciences has emerged through shared topical interest, which has also led to methodological synthesis and overlap. The theme of the present volume, community management of Common Property Resources (CPRs), which shares the methodological difficulties and debates of poverty measurement, provides a good example of this trend. Access to and use of CPRs are not determined by private property rights or mediated by markets, but rather socially regulated. The institutional arrangements for this regulation have therefore attracted wide-spread attention across the social sciences.

The strong, shared interest in CPR management across social sciences, reflected in the composition of the participants and the discussions in the Goa conversations,[1] has facilitated an engagement in questions of methodology and research design. In Goa, the differences and compatibilities in methodology came into sharp focus. While the method-ological stances of anthropologists and economists represent two extreme positions, there are significant differences within these disciplines as well as commonalities between them that offer promising ground for collaboration. The purpose of this chapter is to spell these commonalities out in some detail. In doing so, I have drawn upon my impressions as a participant in the "Conversations II" workshop, as well as my knowledge of research on issues relating to macro aspects of water control and management and experience during field research in different parts of Tamil Nadu.

Theoretical Stances

Anthropologists are known for their skepticism of generalized theoretical schema. They, like sociologists and political scientists, use concepts like "shared norms," "symbolic value," "social capital" and "power" in studying social relations. The basic idea is that the chances of securing consensus in rule formulation and observance are greater when values and norms relating to rights and obligations in social relations are widely shared by members of a community. Persons/groups sharing a CPR in village communities are involved in multiple, interacting networks of kinship, caste, and other social relations. This "social capital" helps contain and resolve conflicts: Fear of disrupting or even destroying these wider and overlapping relational networks is often considered an important factor in preventing conflicts from becoming explosive. It also induces or facilitates conflict re-solution on the basis of compromises.

The effectiveness of this mechanism obviously depends on the strength and density of the relational networks. It will be less effective when these networks are weaker and thinner – as is likely to be the case in communities marked by stronger caste–class stratification, closer integration with the wider economic and political network and when conflicts/disputes transcend local communities. Moreover, "norms" and "values" are not universally and willingly shared, nor can "social capital" relating to inter-personal or inter-group relations ensure harmonious functioning of larger society. Stratification by class and caste being a ubiquitous feature of society, parties to conflicts are seldom evenly matched. Under such conditions the effectiveness of compromises depends crucially on the cohe-sion and strength of local power structures to make the rules and procedures by which such compromises are negotiated and enforced, hence the importance of "power."

It is important to note that concepts of "shared norms and values" and "dense networks of interpersonal relations" are far less, if indeed at all, useful for understanding CPR management beyond the confines of individual communities. Typically local CPRs are a part of a larger network covering numerous communities spread over a wide area and forming part of a complex and interconnected system. The management of the larger system

---

[1]   The author is referring to the "Conversations II" workshop held in Goa in August 2003.

necessarily calls for formal organizational structures manned by professional bureaucracies, with impersonal mechanisms for evolving, monitoring and enforcing of rules governing access to and use of the resource by constituent communities. The problem here is one of politics and governance.

Whether from the traditional Marxist view or the neoclassical presumption of rational, utility-maximizing entities functioning within a competitive market, economists and political scientists approach the study of socio-economic phenomena with a generalized theoretical framework often conflicting with anthropological perspectives. These perceptions are, however, undergoing major changes, some of which make these disciplines more compatible with anthropological starting points.

A significant new development in economics is the growing interest in institutions. This is reflected in attempts to extend the neoclassical framework to understand other social institutions like the firm, caste, marriage and family, philanthropy, and even government and politics. While still anchored in assumptions of the rational behavior of economic agents, this work draws on game, organizational and collective action theories to study a variety of institutions. The new institutional economics tends to focus on the conditions that provide incentives to sustained collective action in managing CPRs. Its framework and concepts (transactions costs, information asymmetry and game theory) are powerful tools for the study of CPR institutions. This framework has not only broadened and deepened economists' approach to the study of institutions, but also expanded the domain of interest shared by other social scientists.

Non-economists have widely criticized these theories' presumption that the attitudes and behavior of individuals are guided by the rationality of maximizing welfare. At least a section of economists, though, recognize the force of this criticism and the role of norms, social capital and power in shaping institutions. While many of them find these concepts too fuzzy for rigorous theorizing and quantitative analysis, some are trying to explore ways of incorporating them into institutional analysis. This trend is evident in much of the recent work on CPR management, including papers presented at the Goa conference. One idea that has been taken up is that "repeated games" can, under certain conditions, help create conditions conducive to collective action by increasing the predictability of responses and behavior under different contingencies. Repeated game theory is used in this way to study the evolution of institutions. Other approaches theorize and test the impact of caste homogeneity, inequality in land holdings and newly introduced technology on the propensity for collective action (see Bardhan 2001).[2]

The fact that the study of CPR institutions is becoming an area of shared interest across social sciences demonstrates the potential for interdisciplinary institutional analysis. Besides ongoing efforts in particular disciplines to refine their theoretical framework, concepts like shared norms, social capital, power and symbolic values can be sharpened through interdisciplinary collaboration. But this alone is not sufficient. Besides recognizing the fact that individual communities are part of and nested in a wider socio-political system, an adequately deep understanding of CPR management also needs to draw on the physical-natural sciences.

---

[2]   These aspects have been covered in comparative studies of selected tank irrigation systems in Tamil Nadu (Vaidyanathan et al. 2002).

The importance of viewing CPR institutions in such a wide perspective to comprehend their complexity can be illustrated by reference to water.[3] Irrigation helps increase the productivity of land in several ways. The magnitude of productivity gain, and hence the economic returns to irrigation, depends on the local climate; the nature, source and management of irrigation; and the state of agricultural technology. Irrigation potential is subject to limits set partly by climate, physical terrain and sub-surface geology and partly by the state of civil engineering and pumping technology. Further, realizing this technological potential requires financial capacity and choices on the distribution of costs and benefits. Community economic decisions along with the state's economic policies relating to water pricing involves "politics" in the broad sense of mediating and balancing competing claims and interests. Therefore the impact of technological investments depends not only on the quality of design and maintenance of irrigation systems, but also on the regulation of water allocations in time and space (which together determine the quality of irrigation for individual plots). Institutional arrangements are also themselves shaped and influenced in complex ways by the size and source of irrigation, socio-political configurations of users with other claimants to water and the framework and enforcement of state laws and policies.

The interrelated and variable factors that shape irrigation systems across space are prevalent for other CPRs as well. It is unrealistic to expect that these variables can be comprehended and explained in a unified theoretical framework. It would be more realistic to focus on improving theoretical frameworks and empirical verification of selected important technical and socio-economic facets and to progressively expand their scope to account for important linkages and interactions among them. A parallel approach would be to build comprehensive and integrated accounts of selected systems under diverse conditions, see whether they show any systematic patterns of association between different variables and then look for theoretically satisfactory explanations.

Sources and Methods of Collecting Information

Differences over the nature of information used and the sources and methods by which this information is collected and interpreted are major areas of contention between economists and anthropologists. Empirical studies by economists attach much importance to quantified measurement through structured surveys. They use methods designed to give a representative picture of a given community or a set of communities under study and to use statistical techniques of multivariate analysis to test hypotheses regarding underlying factors. On the other hand, some anthropologists are skeptical of researchers' claims of "objectivity" in their choice of issues, methodology and interpretation of findings.[4] They argue that the issues selected for research and the way they are posed are, consciously or unconsciously, shaped by and reflect preconceived, partial and biased notions of desirable outcomes. This extreme view is questionable. Research must not be judged by the questions posed, but rather on the systematicity and rigor of the practiced

---

[3]   For an extended discussion of this aspect and its implications for irrigation institutions and their dynamics see Vaidyanathan (1999: ch. 1).

[4]   Baviskar and to some extent Lélé (chs 6 and 11, both in this volume) take this position.

methods. This section looks for points of convergence between anthropological and economic methods.

Some economists assert that many, and perhaps most, qualitative characteristics can be quantified on the basis of information obtained through structured questionnaires. A wide range of sampling schema, questionnaire design and interviewing techniques are now available for the conduct of such structured surveys. These can be used – more in some cases than others – to collect quantitative or quantifiable information on qualitative aspects. For example, scoring systems have been devised to measure the nature and extent of participation of different stakeholders in management, differences in the quality of water supply to different users in an irrigation system, the observance of rules of maintenance and water allocation, and the nature and frequency of disputes/conflicts (see Sivasubramanian 1995; Vaidyanathan 2002).

However, the survey method, even when it is used carefully, is subject to several limitations: apart from considerations of cost, there are well known difficulties of ensuring that field workers understand the concepts and categories underlying survey questions and comply with their instructions. There are also problems arising from the willingness/ability of respondents to provide reliable information. Moreover, the survey categories and concepts are based on theoretical frameworks embodying a particular and often partial view of social phenomena. There is also considerable loss and even distortion of information in the (inevitable) use of standardized concepts and categories that permit quantitative analysis of diverse situations. These limitations get aggravated when survey design is standardized and canvassed across different linguistic and cultural regions. Nevertheless, so long as the concepts, design and fieldwork procedures and the data quality are open to independent assessment, users can evaluate how reliable and appropriate they are for the stated objectives.

Many cultural anthropologists argue that "participant observation" enables researchers to observe and record various aspects of societal functioning first hand without any preconceptions, in greater depth and with much greater sensitivity to nuances than quantitative methods. But, participant observation likewise has limitations and is a function of the informants' identity, knowledge, and representativeness. Therefore, social anthropologists combine participant observation with contemporary and historical secondary sources of both quantitative and qualitative information. Sociologists use survey data, archival material, focus group interviews and process documentation to determine how CPR decisions are made and implemented.

The truth is that no method can give complete, reliable or accurate information. All observational techniques are subject to error arising from the observer's position, her preoccupations/prejudices, the manner of eliciting information, communication between the observer and the observed, and informants' willingness and ability to give the required information fully, truthfully and accurately. Absolute accuracy is a mirage. One can only try to reduce the sources of error. However, this does not vitiate the usefulness of these methods: Even imperfect data collected systematically will give a picture of "reality."

The broader the perspective in which CPRs are viewed, the greater the necessity for a plurality in techniques of data collection and interpretation. Once this is accepted, the controversy over quantitative measurement, the use of sample surveys, quantified versus qualitative information, and the relative merits of rapid appraisal, participant observation and other techniques of getting information loses much of its edge. The challenge is to find ways to exploit the complementary role of different techniques to greater advantage.

Empirical Studies

A large number of micro-studies relating to different kinds of CPRs – water, village common lands, forests, and fisheries – are now available. By far the most numerous relate to different types of irrigation systems (small surface storages, large canal systems, groundwater and combinations thereof),[5] but studies also analyse managing institutions (see Coward 1980, Hunt and Hunt 1974), development project performance, agricultural productivity, rules/conventions governing CPR access and use,[6] impact on total and sectoral employment, and spatial and class-wise distributions of benefits. Most describe institutions primarily at the community level. A few relate to larger multi-community systems and the relationship between the system and individual communities, but comprehensive accounts of the structure and workings of these institutions *and their interactions* are relatively rare.

Micro-level studies of CPRs make extensive use of a variety of survey methods: purposive selection of sites and informants instead of representative samples, structured questionnaires to collect quantitative information, rapid appraisals, and open-ended interviews. Most are descriptive and tend to produce stand-alone studies in diverse locations. Because of the great variation in the scope, location, objectives and quality of these studies, it is impossible to piece them together to create a "representative" cross-sectional, not to mention longitudinal, picture. Few of these studies attempt to analyze the relationships between different aspects of CPR management and their effect on outcomes. Despite these limitations, the broader overviews of the CPR policies and strategies provided by macro-level studies are equally limited by their inability to account for regional specificities of CPRs. Region-specific, micro-level studies of different CPRs therefore remain essential.

Impact evaluations suffer from further limitations. The common practice is to compare the situation in intervention sites with that in "control" sites and, less commonly, the situation in a given location before and after interventions. In many cases interventions relate to particular physical or institutional aspects and therefore tend to be piecemeal. Impact studies of irrigation, watershed development and forests are often done too soon after projects are completed or institutional change is introduced. It often takes a long time – sometimes a decade or two – for the full impact of these changes to manifest. The magnitude and intensity of impact can only be properly assessed after several rounds of repeated surveys following the initial interventions. In the absence of such surveys, inferences about the relative merits and efficacy of different models of reform tend to be of dubious value.

Another major limitation of extant studies is that the best among them tend to view institutions per se without taking into account the physical environment, technological options, and economic and socio-political environment in which they function. Moreover, communities are not isolated units, but rather linked to and nested in a wider ecological, socio-economic, and political milieux. It is therefore important to place the study communities in a wider context covering all these factors along with government policies and the laws and institutional mechanisms that mediate conflicts and competing interests.

---

[5]   Several of these studies relating to different countries of Asia are listed and reviewed in Vaidyanathan (1999).
[6]   Singh (1994), Singh and Ballabh (1996), and Marothia (2002) give extensive bibliographies of studies on different CPRs relating to India.

Anthropologists were first to recognize this need and bring such a broad perspective to the study of institutions for managing CPRs. However, anthropology's chosen methods of "thick" description, besides being limited to selected communities, do not lend themselves to cross-sectional comparative studies or to generalized conclusions about patterns or factors shaping outcomes. This limitation applies equally to studies of the historical evolution of CPR use and management by Kelly (1980), Ludden (1979), Maass and Anderson (1978), and Mosse (2003).

Multi-location studies using comparable concepts and methods are essential for (1) better appreciation of the nature and extent of variations in the structure and functioning of CPR institutions and (2) exploring the role of differences in ecological, socio-political, and technological context. Jodha (1989), Wade (1994), and Sengupta (commentary 3, this volume) are among the notable attempts in this direction (see also Ostrom 1990, Bardhan 2001, Arya and Samra 2001, and Chopra et al. 1990). This approach has also been the basis of much of my and several of my colleagues' research at the MIDS on irrigation institutions during the last two decades.

The MIDS studies (Vaidyanathan and Janakarajan 1989, Sivasubramanian 1995, Rajagopal 1991, Vaidyanathan 2001, Neelakantan 2003) focus on different surface irrigation systems of Tamil Nadu. An eclectic combination of secondary and archival sources and primary surveys was used to get a composite picture of water use and productivity, institutions for maintenance and water management, rules of allocation and operation, the record of compliance and enforcement, major system changes, and conditions of water supply and use. An attempt was made to measure (or rather grade) the effectiveness of institutions and identify patterns of system variation. These studies also review, albeit in a sketchy way, the origins and evolution of the system and its organization; the demographic, social, political, and technological forces that led to their development; and the interactive impact of these forces on the functioning of institutions and system performance. Their main limitation is their heavy dependence on structured surveys ill-suited to gather reliable data on rule making and implementation and the nature and sources of conflicts and resolutions. They still fall in the category of "thick descriptions" (Geertz 1980), but are richer for being comprehensive, bringing out the interconnectedness of different system aspects, and enabling comparative analysis of variations. These studies open up promising avenues for analyzing and understanding institutions.

Future Directions

Current research on CPR management is exciting in several respects. There is a strong convergence of interest in the subject across a wide spectrum of social sciences. Innovative attempts are being made to break new ground by extending and even transcending conventional theoretical frameworks of different disciplines. Empirical research shows welcome signs of efforts to comprehend the many interrelated aspects of CPR management and place them in an historical perspective. There is also a growing interest and willingness among social scientists to incorporate insights from physical and natural sciences. Research on CPRs therefore offers a promising and creative opportunity for meaningful trans-disciplinary dialogue and collaboration.

How is this to be done? Basic ideas and knowledge about different technical and social aspects of CPRs and their interrelations can be gleaned from published literature and interaction with specialists. One does not have to be a civil engineer to grasp the essential concepts of the hydrological cycle. As noted earlier, recognition and understanding of biophysical aspects even at an elementary level has led to a broadening of theoretical and empirical perspectives in social science research on CPRs. While shared agendas and discourse across the social sciences has been built into CPR research, more work is needed in linking the social and the physical-natural sciences.

Combining information and knowledge from diverse disciplines to better understand CPRs is a daunting task. There are huge gaps in knowledge regarding practically every aspect of CPRs. Remedying these lacunae, therefore, calls for both more sustained and intensive research by different disciplines to improve specialized knowledge as well as willingness to transcend disciplinary confines to make use of other bodies of knowledge. By working in a collaborative manner, multi-disciplinary research can be a medium for purposive interaction between disciplines and provide multiple perspectives on common issues and locations under study.

A realistic and practical approach to build a more integrated picture is to use a systems analysis framework for exploring the individual and collective effects of multiple and interrelated technical, socio-political and economic factors on the functioning of CPR institutions. The value of a systems approach is that it provides a framework for focused interaction between different specialized disciplines. It does so by organizing the information and knowledge needed to get an integrated picture of the parts in relation to the whole, identifying key factors and gaps in knowledge, and organizing data gathering and further research to fill these gaps. It also encourages researchers to assess the quality of data used in estimation and system relationships. Interaction across disciplines in such a framework can stimulate innovative approaches to theoretical research. The payoff will however be limited unless accompanied by more empirical studies of CPRs in a variety of locations and contexts.

Such a strategy would provide a medium for a judicious and imaginative combination of quantitative surveys and qualitative inquiries and help exploit the potential complementarity and synergy of different approaches. Multiple perspectives are unlikely to provide an integrated picture, but will contribute to a richer understanding of the parts and their relation to the whole.

References

Arya, Swarn Lata and J. S. Samra. (2001). "Revisiting Watershed Management; Institutions in Haryana Shivaliks, India," Chandigarh: Central Soil and Water Conservation Research and Training Institute.

Bardhan, Pranab. (ed.) (1989). *Conversations between Economists and Anthropolgists*, Delhi: Oxford University Press.

Bardhan, Pranab. (2001). "Water Community: An Empirical Analysis of Cooperation on Irrigation in South India," in Y. Hayami and M. Aoki (eds), *Communities and Markets in Economic Development*, New Delhi: Oxford University Press.

Baviskar, Amita. (2007). "Culture and Power in the Commons Debate," ch. 6, this volume.

Coward, E. Walter. (ed.) (1980). *Irrigation and Agricultural Development in Asia*, Ithaca, NY: Cornell University Press.

Geertz, Clifford. (1967). "Organization of the Balinese Subak," *American Anthropologist*, 61.

Hunt, Eva and Robert C. Hunt. (1974). "Irrigation Conflict and Politics: A Mexico Case," in T. E. Downing and M. Gibson (eds), *Irrigation Impact of Society*, Tucson: University of Arizona Press.

Jodha, N. S. (1989). "Social Science Research on Rural change: Some Gaps," in P. Bardhan (ed.), *Conversations between Economists and Anthropolgists*, New Delhi: Oxford University Press.

Kelly, W. W. (1980). *Water Control in an Agrarian State: Irrigation Organisation in a Japanese River Basin*, Ann Arbor: University Microfilms.

Lélé, Sharachchandra. (2007). "Interdisciplinarity as a Three-way Conversation: Barriers and Possibilities," ch. 11, this volume.

Ludden, David. (1978). *Agrarian Organisation in Tinnvevelly District 800–1900*, Ann Arbor: University Microfilms.

Ludden, David. (1979). "Patronage and Irrigation in Tamil Nadu," *Indian Economic and Social History Review*, 16(3).

Maass, Arthur and Raymond L. Anderson. (1978). *". . . and the Desert Shall Rejopice: Conflict Growth and Justice in an Arid Environment,"* Cambridge, MA: MIT Press.

Marothia, D. K. (ed.) (2002). *Institutionalizing Common Pool Resources*, New Delhi: Concept Publishing Co.

Mosse, David. (2003). *The Rule of Water: Statecraft, Ecology and Collective Action*, New Delhi: Oxford University Press.

Neelakantan, S. (2003). *A Gossipmonger's Revisit to Chettipalayam: Water Conflict and Social Change in Amaravati basin*, Working Paper 182, Madras Institute of Development Studies, Chennai.

Ostrom, Elinor. (1990). *Governing the Commons: The Evolution of Institutions for Collective Action*, Cambridge: Cambridge University Press.

Rajagopal, A. (1991). "Water Management in Agriculture with Special Reference to Irrigation Institutions," Ph.D. thesis, Centre for Development Studies, Thiruvananthapuram.

Singh, Katar and Vishwa, Ballabh. (eds) (1996). *Cooperative Management of Natural Resources*, New Delhi and Thousand Oaks, CA: Sage.

Singh, Katar. (1994). *Managing Common Pool Resources: Principles and Case Studies*, New Delhi and New York: Oxford University Press.

Sivasubramanian, K. (1995). "Irrigation Institutions in Two Large Multi-village Tanks of Tamil Nadu," Ph.D. thesis, Madras Institute for Development Studies, Chennai.

Vaidyanathan, A. and S. Janakarajan. (1989). "Management of Irrigation and its Impact on Productivity under Different Environmental and Technical conditions; A study of Two Surface Irrigation Systems in Tamilnadu," mimeo, Madras Institute for Development Studies, Chennai.

Vaidyanathan, A. (1999). *Water Resource Management: Institutions and Irrigation Development in India*, New Delhi: Oxford University Press.

Vaidyanathan, A. (ed.) (2001). *Tanks of South India*, New Delhi: Centre for Science and Environment.

Vaidyanathan, A., Rajagopal, A., and Maria Susai. (2002). "Conditions and Characteristics of Well Irrigation in Palar Basin," MIDS Working Paper 179, Chennai.

Wade, Robert. (1994). *Village Republics: Economic Conditions for Collective Action in South India*, San Francisco: ICS Press.

Commentary 6: And Never the Twain Shall Meet?

An Exchange on the Strengths and Weaknesses of Anthropology and Economics in Analyzing the Commons

Ravi Kanbur and Annelise Riles

Background

This is our contribution to the project on conversations between anthropologists and economists, focusing on analysis of the commons. The short note is in the form of a "talk and response" exchange, coming as close to a conversation as it is possible to do on the printed page. This is worth trying because most conversations in print turn out to be separate papers from economists and anthropologists, brought together in a volume. We start by specifying what each of us believes the commons problem to be, and then, in perhaps a novel reversal, each of us specifies the weaknesses of our discipline and the strengths of the other in analyzing the problem as we have defined it. Finally, we discuss the way forward in light of the exchange. At every point in the exchange, each gets a chance to respond to the previous argument by the other. The exchanges are relatively short, because of the printed page space constraints that we face, and because (most) normal conversations are not of the form where 25 pages are followed by another 25 pages. We offer this exchange as an experiment in printed conversation between an economist and an anthropologist.

RK: What Is the Commons Problem?

I see the "commons problem" as consisting of two distinct components. First is a key characteristic such that one person's action impacts negatively another person's wellbeing (a negative externality, as economists call it). Examples of this can range from the concrete and tangible to the somewhat abstract and intangible: the effects of fishing on replenishment capacity and thus on future fish stocks for others; secondary smoke inhalation; the effects of reducing forest cover on general soil erosion and hence on the productivity of agriculture for everyone; the knock-on effects of "bad reputation" of one African country on the investment prospects for other neighboring countries, lack of religious observance on the part of some offending others of the same religion; etc.

Second, a socio-political-economic set of arrangements that organize activity and exchange in a setting with the above key characteristic. One arrangement is to have no arrangement at all. This is the case of "open access" discussed by Hardin in the tragedy of the commons. But, in fact, we see myriad arrangements in what the National Research Council (2002) has called "the drama of the commons" (see also Dietz et al. 2003). A canonical arrangement is that of "private property," where complete use and management rights on the resource (be it tangible or intangible) are accorded to individuals (perhaps one, in the case of monopoly). Another arrangement is government ownership and control, where the state, from outside the boundaries of the group in question, imposes and enforces use and management patterns. And then there is common property, where the group itself manages and allocates use and rights. There are, of course, many different arrangements that are possible, and that we see in practice. What is called "private property" itself depends upon a social consensus, or social imposition, to allow a particular pattern of use and management rights, and can be of many different types.

Each arrangement has associated with it a set of processes, perceptions, behaviors and responses which define it. Each arrangement also has associated with it outcomes in well-being (broadly defined) across individuals and groups. As features of the socio-political-economic background outside the system under study change, over time and across space, so do the arrangements, in their design and their outcomes.

An economist's definition of the "commons problem" might be the following: Identify the essential features of arrangements which lead to different patterns of well-being in outcomes, for given features of the background outside the arrangements being studied. Specifically, what essential features lead to higher well-being, and more equitable distribution of that well-being, in the population under study? While there will of course be different interpretations of the commons problem amongst economists, I feel confident that this formulation captures key features. (A standard graduate text that covers these issues for economists is by Cornes and Sandler 1996.)

AR: Response and What is the Commons Problem?

As an anthropologist of modernity, I understand the "commons problem" as a cultural artifact of a certain community – a small but elite community, defined by shared ways of thinking about political problems rather than by its physical locale. Its members are found inside the bureaucracies and academies of virtually every nation-state, no matter how small, and regardless of state policy on questions of globalization and market capitalism (Ferguson 1990; Dezalay and Garth 2002). The members of this community, whom I will call technocrats, have their internal hierarchies, their politics, their divisions, and their theoretical disagreements, but they also share a great deal – they share certain educational formations, certain disciplinary training, certain institutional affiliations, certain "ways of thinking," "ways of acting in the world." When they disagree, in other words, they do so in a particular vocabulary – with a particular set of models and metaphors – and one of these is the commons problem. Following the anthropological understanding that small-scale societies' most important resource is often their common intellectual property (Brown 2003), we might call these technocrats' shared norms, practices, and ideas, including, in this particular case, the models and arguments that make up the "commons problem," their common property.

Anthropologists who specialize in the character of knowledge have long been interested in how models represent "underlying realities" and motivate particular behavior for their users (Gudeman and Penn 1982; Geertz 1983; Morrison 1999; Morrison and Morgan 1999). More recently, some science and technology studies scholars have described models as "actants" – as agents of a kind that guide their human "users" reasoning in particular directions, foreclose certain paths, and even engage in theoretical struggles with their users over outcomes (Pickering 1997). An anthropological response to the commons problem therefore would need first to acknowledge the status of the Commons as a model, to think about the cultural resources this particular model draws upon, and then to consider its particular effects.

As the anthropologist of development Arturo Escobar has commented, economic models are grounded in particular late modern Euro-American cultural norms (Escobar 1995: 58–61). This does not make the commons problem "right" or "wrong"; it just makes it particular. The core of the metaphor itself, the "archetypal case" to which this analysis enables us to analogize phenomena as diverse as fisheries and the reputations of African nations, is an early English land-use practice, and its subsequent historical demise. The metaphor works in the following way: the economist locates something that can be *analogized* to an old English commons. The analysis draws upon particular cultural resources in order to make universal claims, in other words. But what is interesting from the point of view of the anthropology of technocracy is that such models and metaphors do not seem to come undone by virtue of their use by non-Euro-American technocrats (Riles 2000). Anthropologists surmise that that this is because the process of technical training in economics is at its core a process of acculturation – of learning to accept a set of (Euro-American) cultural norms, of learning to see through this lens and of learning to be skeptical of claims that are not easily reconciled with the Euro-American cultural assumptions embedded in these models. It is this shared normative framework, after all, that makes the technocrats a "community."[1]

Of course, you may say, the term "commons" is just a metaphor, an abstraction – economists are not really thinking about old English commons or about the lessons of English history when they analyze present problems in these terms. You are surely right about this. But one of the insights of anthropological work on images and metaphors is that the core of the metaphor, its baseline, what Roy Wagner calls its "ground" (Wagner 1981 [1975]) does a great deal of work. Moreover, it does this work precisely because those who use such metaphors (in this case, economists) are unaware that they are drawing on this image – because its power remains implicit, rather than explicit.

There are many possible anthropological responses to this phenomenon. A first would trace the intellectual, cultural, social and economic history of the specific Euro-American metaphors and norms underpinning the commons problem so that they can be better understood as the particular cultural products that they are. I want to highlight only two aspects of the specific historical location of this metaphor: its embeddedness in the historical emergence of Euro-American notions of personhood (autonomous individuality) and its embeddedness in the history of the emergence of modern capitalism.

---

[1]   Indeed, one could go further and surmise that the very distance between members of this community – the fact that the missionaries in the field must labor far away from the metropolis and surrounded by persons who do not share their models – may lead to even more dogged commitment to those models.

The particular social history of the enclosure of the English commons, of course, is also the particular history of the development of the modern rational individual (Foucault 1991). The two developments occurred together historically, and hence it is not surprising that one central Euro-American cultural norm at work in the commons problem is the assumption that the world is composed of autonomous individuals (Carrier 1997: 2). This is important for the following reason: economic discussions of the differing consequences of alternative institutional arrangements, such as common property or private property, assume the same kind of person as property owner in each situation, and this person is an autonomous individual. The question then becomes, how would this autonomous individual act differently under different institutional circumstances? Yet this line of questions fails to take into account that the character of personhood is integrally tied to the particular property regime at issue. As Marcel Mauss taught us long ago, autonomous rational individuality is the form of personhood that goes with private property ownership (Mauss 1990). It is no wonder, therefore, that if one assumes a rational and autonomous individual, private property seems like the best institutional arrangement.

Yet it has been a basic insight of anthropology since Mauss that other forms of ownership correlate with other forms of personhood. One of Sir Edmund Leach's lasting contributions was his insight, with respect to Sri Lankan kinship, that relations of property determined the character of kinship and hence that regimes of property could be analytically prior to regimes of personhood (Leach 1961). Likewise, Mauss pointed out that in exchange-based societies, the modern Euro-American opposition of persons and things, in which persons (individuals) are agents who own and act upon things, does not hold. First, things have agency too: the gift has a spirit, an agency, a force, Mauss argues, that compels action by persons as much as persons control things. Second, anthropologists have long argued that in many societies in which property is inalienable, persons and things are less easily distinguished from one another. Mauss gave the example of exchange objects that carry the "spirit" of the person with it as it is exchanged and hence transferred but not alienated. Lest this all sound overly exotic, recent Anglo-American case law concerning property in human embryos, human tissue, human DNA, debates surrounding ownership in human clones, and many more suggest that for modern Euro-Americans also, the boundary between persons and things is becoming increasingly difficult to draw (Strathern 1999).

From this point of view, anthropologists would want to point out that the distinction between common property and individual property at stake in the commons problem is overdrawn. One of the canonical insights of the early work of Bronislaw Malinowski was that in societies based on relations of exchange, property could not be understood as *either* individual or collective (Malinowski 1984 [1926]). Of course things were privately owned in those societies, he said, but they were also exchanged upon principles of reciprocity, such that an individual owner could be compelled to give up his property to others as return on a gift. Malinowski therefore proposed the concept of reciprocity as an alternative to either communal or individual property. In many other contexts, anthropologists have shown that lineage relations and affinal relations become the basis for resource sharing – but that because of the nature of the relations at issue, such property does not easily fit, analytically under either "individual" or "common" categories.

So much for personhood. Anthropologists would also want to point out that the particular social history of the enclosure of the English commons is also the particular social history of the development of modern capitalism. Economists of course would say that this is precisely the point: only with the enclosure of the commons can one have modern capitalism. But anthropologists would see the causation running in the other direction: putting aside old England, whose particularities provide the metaphorical template for all other histories in the commons problem, only with the spread of global capitalism do pressures build for enclosure and the transformation of non-private property into private property, anthropologists argue. Examples of privatization that are held to prove the model, anthropologists claim, often fail to take into account the effect of the wider introduction of a market economy on changes in attitudes toward property.

A nice example of this differing understanding, or talking at cross-purposes, concerns economic uses of anthropology in the commons debate. Harold Demsetz' famous article (Demsetz 1967) draws extensively on the work of anthropologist Eleanor Leacock concerning Native American ownership of beaver hunting grounds to make his point about the natural evolution of private property. Yet in order to use Leacock's data to make this point, Demsetz had to ignore Leacock's own central point: In the article Demsetz cites, Leacock had sought to demonstrate the (negative) effects on one indigenous community of its sudden introduction to the periphery of a global market. Leacock's point, then, was not that scarcity produced a need for private property, but that the intrusion of global capitalism produced scarcity (along with other harms). In a similar vein, anthropologists who work in societies undergoing transitions to private property often interpret these changes in a wider context of the introduction of the market economy into the community: the introduction of wage labor, the sale of land to absentee landlords and the resulting conversion of common owners into tenant farmers, the emergence of class differences within the community, the effects of differential treatment of particular regions by the state, resulting for example in differential access to infrastructure, the nature of the natural resources at issue, and whether these implicate the community in wider global forces (common property in farm land is very different from common property in a diamond mine in a war zone) (Spencer 1992).

For example, anthropologists working in the former Soviet bloc have sought to show the consequences of the particular form of market economy now emerging in those societies on the process of transformation from collective to private property ownership. Chris Hann has found that property rights are understood by the Hungarian villagers with whom he has worked as only one set of rights and obligations among others, such as rights to schooling, medical care, the right to respect from other segments of the society, a right to employment, and so on, and they are not overly eager to acquire property rights (Hann 1993: 313). Katherine Verdery provides a further explanation for this phenomenon based on her fieldwork in Transylvania: where property has little economic value, but brings with it a number of liabilities – new responsibilities for environmental pollution, the duty to pay taxes, and much more – people may be much happier to own property communally (Verdery 1999). These anthropologists report that because the emergence of property rights takes place not in a vacuum, but in the historical context of the confiscation of the property of some and then the granting of new property rights to others a generation later, the process of assigning individual ownership in practice often creates conflicting claims, and hence produces more uncertainty rather than less.

A second anthropological response to the commons problem would distinguish between ideology and practice in Euro-American societies: it would point out that even in Euro-American societies, property is far more commonly held than this tale of the fall from common property would suggest. The vast majority of American real-estate, for example, is held as common property by spouses or family members. And many new forms of property emerging as a result of advances in science – property in embryos, DNA, body parts, and so forth – are frequently treated by the courts as common property (for example, human embryos have been held to be the common property of the individuals whose DNA produced them). Ideas are common property, as are expressions, after a statutory period. Although economists will respond that ideas at least and perhaps expressions are suitably commonly owned because they are public goods – goods whose value does not decrease because they are shared – this is disputed, at least, by those who expend large sums of money lobbying Congress to extend copyright protection beyond the current statutory period.

Just to push the point, we might even experiment with understanding the notion of the commons problem itself as a kind of common property, the common property of technocrats: it is not "open access" property since access to the model is limited to those who share a particular kind of training. Once one has acceded to the priesthood, however, one gains a right to share in such ideas and debates. I would be interested in your views as to whether the model is really a pure "public good" – whether its value remains the same regardless of whether or not it is used (inappropriately) by outsiders like myself.

But what is interesting about the commons problem as a form of common property is that the proper use of the common property in this case is also the arbiter of who has a right to use the property: inappropriate invocation of the model is a sign that one is not a member of the priesthood and hence has no right to use the model. I have heard economists say that Albert Hirschman is not an economist, for example, although he was trained as an economist, because he does not use economic models in the proper way (and I should say that this would be absolutely true of anthropologists and their common property also!). I suspect that this fact that the kind of use determines the right to use is a much more general condition of many property ownership regimes than the commons problem would recognize. That model assumes that rights are more or less absolute: if one owns property, whether individually or communally, that means one has a right to exploit it at will. Yet the Anglo-American law of property certainly does not make this assumption. Property carries with it, as in Eastern Europe, many responsibilities, duties, and liabilities: one has a duty to pay taxes, to obey environmental regulations, zoning rules, to refrain from using one's land in a way that will inconvenience one's neighbors, even to allow others access when their rights to free speech so demand. The same is true of property ownership in Fiji, where I conducted fieldwork: who is a clansperson and hence a landowner (vanua) is defined by adherence to protocol, by one's ability to demonstrate proper behavior, rather than by some pre-ordained scheme of rights (Hocart 1915). The use of the commons becomes, in a sense, also the fence.

That is the cultural specificity of the model. What of its effects? A third anthropological response to the commons problem would focus ethnographically on the practice of economic knowledge-making in order to understand how metaphors from areas of social life outside of economics (such as the commons) come to play such an important role in economic arguments, but also in order to understand the subject position of the technocrat: how does he or she deploy, transpose, consume, and redirect such models? To what purpose? How does she imagine the world in which she must act, the pressures she labors under? How do metaphors and models such as the commons problem come to play into this self-understanding? This work is just beginning to be done in anthropology. I want to highlight only two here: its effects for agency, and its ability to cross domains.

Agency

Recently the sociologist Michel Callon has argued that the kind of rational thinking presumed by economic knowledge (and the commons problem would be one example), what Callon terms "calculating agency," is actually an *effect* of the proliferation of economic knowledge itself (Callon 1998). In what is essentially a restatement of the central assumption of the commons problem, Callon argues that values must be "calculable" in order for a market to come into existence, and hence most social institutions favored by economists such as private property rights are ways of making values calculable and of turning people into "calculating agents." The externalities to which you refer are, in Callon's vocabulary, instances of people failing to act as calculating agents.

So far, we have only a difference of vocabulary, I think. But the key insight of Callon's work concerns his treatment of economic knowledge itself, and not simply the institutions such as private property rights economists analyze, as ways of making values calculable and persons calculating. Contrary to the view of economic models as mere descriptions of the world, Callon has argued that these models shape actors' thinking, such that the models turn them into "calculating agents" for whom the assumptions of the commons problem hold. Where sociologists usually attack economists for thinking about the market in overly abstract terms, Callon argues that it is precisely this act of engaging in economic abstraction that fosters "calculability." Economic markets are embedded not just in culture or society (as economic sociologist has aimed to show), he has argued, therefore, but in economic knowledge itself. From this point of view, we can see the effects of the global spreading of models such as the commons problem – and not simply the private property regimes that the commons problem would seem to advocate – as a step in the global production of rational, calculating agents, agents suited for private property ownership, that is, agents less prone to producing "externalities."

Crossing domains

The second effect of this metaphor that interests me is nicely exemplified in your initial usage of it. In the passage above, you deploy the model to cross domains – to move from very "local" fishing practices to very "global" questions of geopolitics, and from agriculture, to economics, to international relations. That is its power. The anthropologist Roy Wagner has argued that this capacity for "spreading out" (Wagner 1986) is a fundamental feature of metaphor. Metaphor "works," Wagner argues, by moving from domain to domain, from one scale to another, without losing its form, and hence it "relates" domains as it crosses them. In other words, only because economics uses metaphors in this way is it able to cross so many domains, to come to have such global and general applicability.

RK: Response and the Weakness of Economics and the Strength of Anthropology

First of all, a technical answer to your specific question, "as to whether the model really is a "public good" – whether value remains the same regardless of whether or not it is used (inappropriately) by outsiders like myself." In economics the term "public good" is a technical term. A "pure" public good (by good is meant commodity) satisfies the twin requirements of "non-rivalry" (consumption by one does not reduce the amount) available for consumption by another) and "non-excludability" (within the relevant defined universe of discourse, no one can be excluded from consuming the good). The examples economist have range from an uncongested national park with free entry, to knowledge that is made universally available. I don't suppose they ever thought of the canonical economic model (or the specific commons model) as a public good in this sense. The technical answer to your question depends on how exactly you define the commodity in question. If the commodity in question is the use of the canonical model in the prescribed manner, then definitionally the question of "misuse" does not arise, since if it were to be misused it would not be the same commodity.

But enough of these economic technicalities. It is indeed an unusual turn – for an economist – to look at the commons problem, and at economists (actually, technocrats) themselves, as objects of anthropological inquiry. Anthropologists are well used to such reflexive exercises, economists are not. Discussions of method and methodology leave most economists queasy – among the younger bloods it is a common enough jibe that those who can, do; those who cannot, do methodology. Indeed, this lack of curiosity about the nature of their method is, in my view, the strength of economists as well as their weakness. It is a strength for all the reasons you lay out. The easy transference of the core metaphor across domains is at root the power of the economic method. But its consistent application, with variations to be sure, but always within the given overall frame, is built on a certain lack of self-criticism.

I want to illustrate the weakness of the economic method in addressing the commons problem, in economists' terms, by reference to what happened after Hardin's (1968) famous tragedy of the commons thesis gained ground. The basic analytics of Hardin's argument are easy for economists to grasp and model. Consider a resource such as a fishery, being exploited by identical individuals. Each individual over-exploits since no account is taken of the effect of each catch on restocking potential and hence on the future catch for all. One way to control the damage is to enforce catch limits on each individual (this may involve excluding some individuals from fishing altogether). Another is to give all the fishing rights to one individual. Yet another is to divide up the fishery into individual property rights – this should work in principle because now each individual bears the cost of his or her own overfishing. Following on from this generic and deductive argument, if it can further be argued that creating large number of individual fishing rights is not physically feasible (certainly the fish will not be respecters of any surface property rights drawn up), and if giving all the fishing rights to one person is not politically feasible, then the only solution left to the problem of overfishing is to enforce catch limits. Or timber-cutting limits in a forest. Or pollution limits for industry.

All economists will recognize the above as a classic economic line of thinking. What are the problems with it? Several. First, it does not take into account heterogeneity in the population – the issue of distribution of well-being is thus sidestepped, the focus is kept on "the size of the pie." Second, it sees private property and state intervention as "manna from heaven," an abstract entity that comes into being, unconnected to the social system actually existing. Third and most important, it sees no middle ground between private property and state intervention, where the community impacted by the resource or commons in question develops its own methods and techniques.

The first is a common charge levied at economists. Economists themselves differ on this. Some give a large weight to distributional issues, others do not. But there does seem to be a deep rooted desire not so much to ignore distribution but to separate out issues of distribution (how the pie is divided) from issues of efficiency (the size of the pie), despite mounting theory and evidence that it is not really possible to do this satisfactorily (see Kanbur 2002).

The second issue above is also a common critique of the economic mode of thinking. An inadequate account of private property, or of the state, can lead to erroneous analysis, predictions and prescriptions. Widespread nationalization of forests was carried out in the wake of Hardin's tragedy of the commons thesis. This is an interesting contrast to what one might have expected from the "private property regimes that the commons problem would seem to advocate" (as you characterize it). But no matter. The nationalization has now generally been recognized to be a disaster. The state was not an abstract disinterested entity, whose sole function was to "internalize the externality" as in the basic economic model. In fact, it turned out to be the agent of wealthy interest groups who proceeded to strip the forests and compounded overexploitation of forests.

Indeed, in bringing in the state, in exercising its rights of eminent domain, existing arrangements for managing forests were destroyed. They were there, despite the fact that economic analysis did not see them or found it too difficult to model them. This leads to the third issue. Modeling these arrangements in the framework of methodological individualism, where explanations of patterns are ultimately sought in the realm of individual behavior and responses, has led to a large game theoretic literature. But I think it would be fair to say that there is a deep dissatisfaction among economists about where we are. The initial euphoria after the insights of the 1980s, 1970s, or 1960s has now faded. It seems clear that a thoroughgoing rational actor approach cannot explain the complex patterns of norms, rules, sanctions, and behaviors we observe, in the commons or elsewhere. The best we can do is to come up with multiple equilibria, without a satisfactory theory of why some equilibria emerge at some times and not others.

I like to think that an anthropological perspective might have prevented some of the disasters of forest nationalization. The anthropological method would have looked for, and found, the myriad arrangements that exist between pure private property and state ownership. Indeed, the renaissance among economists in the study of common property resources in the 1980s and 1990s relies heavily for motivation and empirical grounding on case study materials developed by anthropological field study. Such recognition of ground-level complexities might have tempered the policy prescriptions of the 1970s.

An anthropological perspective might also have tempered a naïve belief in the benevolent state. Anthropologists seem to look instinctively for power relations in any social arrangement, and are always looking for the powerful to subvert arrangements to their end. Of course, the pendulum in policy economics has swung the other way from the 1970s. Some economists themselves reacted to the neutral role given to the state in policy analysis and argued that, since the state is indeed a battle ground for interest groups, the best strategy is to take the state out of production and to return as much as possible to private property rights. Economists are divided on this issue, but I believe anthropologists bring their nose for power relations again to this story – they are now warning that "private property" is only so because these rights are guaranteed by the state, and the power issues that were present in state ownership will not disappear simply with formal transference of ownership to private property.

AR: The Weakness of Anthropology and the Strength of Economics

First, in thinking about economists as "part of" the state, as you describe it in the previous section, I want to acknowledge the many ways that anthropology is also complicit in the processes we are discussing here. To begin with, economic anthropology has always taken the economic paradigm largely at face value. More recently, a few anthropologists, eager perhaps to have a voice in political and legal debates over property, have even begun to use the language of "the commons problem" as an analytical frame for their own work (Brown 2003). But even those anthropologists who persist in deploying economic models derived from Marxist theory think about their subject in ways that are far more similar to economic knowledge than they might wish to admit. Marxist models of economy share all of the aesthetic attributes of neo-classical economic models and certainly are just as hegemonic in their assumptions about the character of personhood, or in their unwillingness to recognize actual social practices that those models cannot easily anticipate.

More importantly, anthropology is complicit in another sense: Anthropology as a discipline also has its paradigmatic models – its well fenced common property – and these models share a great deal with "the commons problem" in the assumptions they make. I am thinking in particular of the key anthropological concepts of "society," and "culture." These concepts share a great deal aesthetically with economic models: they entertain a fundamental difference between theory and data, such that as "theory" models are assumed to be both universally applicable but locally variable.

Moreover, as Escobar has commented, these particular models articulate in important ways with economic models – they have long been imagined as another part of a whole:

> Anthropologists have been complicit with the rationalization of modern economics, to the extent that they have contributed to naturalizing the constructs of economy, politics, religion, kinship, and the like as the fundamental building blocks of all societies. The existence of these domains as presocial and universal must be rejected. Instead, we must ask what symbolic and social processes make these domains appear self-evident and perhaps even "natural" fields of activity in any society. (Escobar 1995: 61, quoting Yanagisako and Collier 1989)

And indeed, students of colonialism have pointed to the articulation between the models of economics and the models of anthropology as a crucial nexus of colonial knowledge and power. In other words, both anthropology and economics are products of a particular late modern Euro-American world view. As Marilyn Strathern puts it,

> part of the economist's job is that of description . . . Certainly Euro-Americans are constantly invited to understand the world of description against the "real world" it precipitates. The economists' position is thus part of – and central to – a more general Euro-American project: to describe the societies in which we live . . . [the economist's] description transforms its dimensions into calculable measurements. (Strathern 2002: 262–3)

But putting this issue aside, anthropology has a peculiar weakness. I am thinking here of anthropologists' disciplinary urge to "critique" economic models, to expose their contingency or cultural specificity, and to demonstrate again and again that "realities on the ground" are far more "complex" than such models would suggest. First, this urge can often become as reductive, as mechanical, as deaf to local conditions as any set of economic assumptions. But even more interesting to me is the quite obvious empirical fact that such critiques always seem to *fail*. We need further investigation of the conditions in which critiques can be heard and incorporated and the conditions in which they cannot. In this case, there seem to be multiple causes, some due to the particular character of economic knowledge, and some to the particular character of anthropological knowledge.

First, on the economic side, anthropologists' attempts to set the factual record straight continually bump up against the fact that the factual details are just not that important in the world of theoretical modeling. James Carrier notes that economists use models "in the technical sense of a simplification of a more complex whole that aids prediction and thus is not concerned with what Weber calls interpretive understanding." However, in public debate, he argues, "the model is assumed to have a clear interpretive element, as a strong link is asserted or assumed between the model and the real world of what motivates people and how they think about what they do" (Carrier 1997: 15). The result is that it is very difficult to critique the model with empirical data, since economists can always respond that it is only a tool to think with, and not a description of the world. And yet implicitly at other moments the model comes to be taken as a representation of the world and even a normative description of the way forward. At these moments, what does not fit the model gets relegated to the realm of the exception – these "distortions" or "complexities" do not challenge the validity of the model in the abstract.

Yet another cause is the character of anthropology and anthropologists. Chapman and Buckley, two anthropologically trained economists, sound an appropriately wry note of caution to anthropologists:

> One might readily conclude from all this, at least from within social anthropology, that transaction cost economics in the 1990s – scientific, rationalist, positivist, aspiring to determinate explanations, imposing observer categories, measuring and predicting, following an agenda written in the 1940s – was simply a hopelessly outmoded form of discourse, against which all the necessary argument had already been made. The great army of workers in the field, however . . . do not seem to have noticed that the rug has been pulled from under them. If anthropologists are kings of the castle, it is a castle most other people have never heard of. Perhaps you need to spend some time entirely outside social anthropology in order to be convinced of the truth of this. (Chapman and Buckley 1997)

AR: The Way Forward

It is appealing and even somewhat fashionable now to say that the solution is to democratize the field of knowledge producers – to include NGOs, villagers, farmers, anthropologists, and others in the process of economic model-making. But my fieldwork among NGO activists-turned-technocrats leads me have some doubts. Quite simply, what makes a technocrat a technocrat is the knowledge he or she uses. My fear is that to bring economics' "others" into the sphere of economic knowledge making is simply to turn these others into technocrats as well.

Would it be possible instead to seek other metaphors derived from non-Euro-American contexts around which to organize economic debate? For example what if instead of the commons problem, we had the reciprocity problem, or the kinship problem? How would the questions look different when inflected through non-Euro-American metaphors? This suggestion admittedly sounds quixotic, but perhaps no more so than the notion of democratizing economic debates did a generation ago.

We also need much more nuanced understandings of the actual uses of models like the commons problem in national academies, state bureaucracies, think tanks, corporations and social movements. Would it be possible for economists and anthropologists instead to have a more sustained, hopeful, and honest dialogue about the nature of technocratic knowledge – anthropological or economic (Riles 2004)? What I have in mind is a dialogue in which anthropologists would temper their naïve political critiques in order to understand economists and economic knowledge with the kind of seriousness and subtlety with which they would understand any other community on the one hand, while economists would also rethink their practices, in a more self-reflexive way, as a product of their own institutional cultures. Perhaps it is not too much to hope that such a project would yield new theoretical insights for economics and anthropology alike.

RK: The Way Forward

My worry is that debates at a very general level on method may not get very far. They will certainly not engage the economists. For this, I believe that starting specific will be the key to moving forward. One possibility is to start with a specific policy problem currently under discussion – low enrollment of girls in schools, high infant mortality rates, domestic violence, etc. – and have a dialogue on analysis of these issues, and especially on assessments of candidate policy interventions actively being discussed.

However, at the same time, as your contribution to this conversation has shown, focusing on specific and concrete issues, if it is too specific and too concrete, will lead to disagreements whose roots lie in more general perspectives and frameworks. Or rather, economists should not fear more general methodological concerns being raised in a dialogue on a specific issue. They will certainly need to be trained away from their knee jerk reaction to dismiss such general discussion as a distraction from the specific policy question.

Ultimately, I feel that "the commons problem" is too general, too emblematic, to advance dialogue. How about economists and anthropologists joining a debate on how to increase girls' school enrollment rates? Or is this also going to turn into a debate on the virtues or otherwise of economic theories of rational choice?

References

Brown, M. F. (2003). *Who owns native culture?* Cambridge, MA: Harvard University Press.

Callon, M. (1998). Introduction: the embeddedness of economic markets in economics, in M. Callan, *The laws of the markets*. Oxford: Blackwell Publishing, 1–57.

Carrier, J. G. (1997). Introduction, in J. G. Carrier (ed.), *Meanings of the market: the free market in western culture*. Oxford and New York: Berg, 1–67.

Chapman, M. and P. J. Buckley (1997). Markets, transaction costs, economists and social anthropologists, in J. G. Carrier (ed.), *Meanings of the market: the free market in western culture*. Oxford and New York: Berg, 225–50.

Cornes, Richard and Todd Sandler (1996). *The theory of externalities, public goods and club goods.* Cambridge: Cambridge University Press.

Demsetz, H. (1967). "Toward a theory of property rights." *American Economic Review*, 57: 347–59.

Dezalay, Y. and B. Garth (2002). *The Internationalization of Global Palace Wars: Lawyers, Economists, and the Contest to Transform Latin American States.* Chicago: University of Chicago Press.

Dietz, Thomas, Elinor Ostrom, and Paul C. Stern (2003). "The struggle to govern the commons." *Science*, 302(5652): 1907–12.

Escobar, A. (1995). *Encountering development: the making and unmaking of the third world.* Princeton, NJ: Princeton University Press.

Ferguson, J. (1990). *The anti-politics machine: "Development," depoliticization, and bureaucratic power in Lesotho.* Cambridge: Cambridge University Press.

Foucault, M. (1991). "Governmentality," in G. Burchell, C. Gordon, and P. Miller (eds), *The Foucault effect: studies in governmentality: with two lectures by and an interview with Michel Foucault.* London: Harvester Wheatsheaf, 87–104.

Geertz, C. (1983). *Local knowledge: further essays in interpretive anthropology.* New York: Basic Books.

Gudeman, S. and M. Penn (1982). "Models, meanings and reflexivity," in D. Parkin (ed.), *Semantic Anthropology.* New York, Academic Press: 89–106.

Hann, C. M. (1993). "From production to property: decollectivization and the family–land relationship in contemporary Hungary." *Man*, New Series, 28(2): 299–320.

Hardin, Garrett (1968). "The tragedy of the commons." *Science*, 162(3859): 1243–8.

Hocart, A. M. (1915). "Chieftainship and the sister's son in the Pacific." *American Anthropologist*, 17: 631–46.

Kanbur, Ravi (2002). "Economics, social science and development." *World Development*, 30(3): 477–86.

Leach, E. R. (1961). *Pul Eliya, a village in Ceylon: a study of land tenure and kinship.* Cambridge: Cambridge University Press.

Malinowski, B. (1984) [1926]. *Crime and custom in savage society.* Westport, CT: Greenwood Press.

Mauss, M. (1990). *The gift.* London: Routledge.

National Research Council (2002). *The drama of the commons.* Washington, DC: National Academy Press.

Morrison, M. (1999). Models as autonomous agents, in M. Morrison and M. S. Morgan (eds), *Models as mediators: perspectives on natural and social science.* Cambridge: Cambridge University Press, 38–65.

Morrison, M. and M. S. Morgan (1999). "Models as mediating instruments," in M. Morrison and M. S. Morgan (eds), *Models as mediators: perspectives on natural and social science.* Cambridge: Cambridge University Press, 10–37.

Pickering, A. (1997). "Concepts and the mangle of practice: constructing quaternions," in B. H. Smith and A. Plotnitsky (eds), *Mathematics, science, and postclassical theory.* Durham: Duke University Press, 40–82.

Riles, A. (2000). *The network inside out.* Ann Arbor: University of Michigan Press.

Riles, A. (2004). "Real time: unwinding technocratic and anthropological knowledge." *American Ethnologist*, 31(3): 1–14.

Spencer, P. (1992). "Re-enactment of the tragedy of the commons in Kenya." *Current Anthropology*, 33(4): 481–3.

Strathern, M. (1999). *Property, substance and effect: anthropological essays on persons and things.* London: Athlone Press.

Strathern, M. (2002). "Externalities in comparative guise." *Economy and Society*, 31(2): 250–67.

Verdery, K. (1999). "Fuzzy property: rights and power in Transylvania's decollectivization," in K. Verdery (ed.), *Uncertain transition: ethnographies of change in the post-socialist world.* Lanham: Rowman & Littlefield, 322.

Wagner, R. (1981). *The invention of culture.* Chicago: University of Chicago Press.

Wagner, R. (1986). *Symbols that stand for themselves.* Chicago: University of Chicago Press.

Index